RECONSIDERING UNTOUCHABILITY

A list of titles in this series appears at the back of the book.

Reconsidering Untouchability

Chamars and Dalit History in North India

RAMNARAYAN S. RAWAT

Indiana University Press
Bloomington and Indianapolis

This book is a publication of

Indiana University Press
601 North Morton Street
Bloomington, IN 47404-3797 USA

www.iupress.indiana.edu

Telephone orders   800-842-6796
Fax orders   812-855-7931
Orders by e-mail   iuporder@indiana.edu

Library of Congress Cataloging-in-Publication Data

Rawat, Ramnarayan S.
Reconsidering untouchability : Chamars and Dalit history in North India / Ramnarayan S. Rawat.
p. cm.—(Contemporary Indian studies)
Includes bibliographical references and index.
ISBN 978-0-253-35558-4 (cloth : alk. paper)—ISBN 978-0-253-22262-6 (pbk. : alk. paper)
1. Chamars—India, North—History. 2. Chamars—India, North—Ethnic identity. 3. Dalits—India, North—History. 4. Caste—India, North—History. 5. Leatherwork—Social aspects—India, North—History. 6. Agricultural laborers—India, North—Social conditions. 7.
Chamars—India, North—Politics and government. 8. Dalits—India, North—Politics and
government. 9. India, North—Ethnic relations. 10. India, North—Social conditions. I. Title.
DS432.C48R39 2010
305.5'688—dc22

2010031792

1 2 3 4 5 16 15 14 13 12 11

In loving memory of my mother, Kamla Rawat, 1945–1979,
and to my father Shiv Narayan Singh Rawat,
who raised three boys by himself and whose integrity and hard work
continue to be models for me.

Every Hindu in the [Indian] society is socially a conservative, but easily claims a radical position in politics [by taking an anti-imperialist stand]. Even Gandhiji is not an exception to this principle.

Nandlal Viyougi,
Ambedkar ki Awaz Arthat Achhutoin ka Federation

CONTENTS

ACKNOWLEDGMENTS

Since my high school days in Delhi Kannada School, New Delhi, in the early 1980s, I have found myself inspired by stories of democratic struggle in colonial and postcolonial India. The national movement's popular character, people's visions of a plural democratic society, and the history of struggles for social and economic justice motivated me and kindled in me a desire to study our history—and the motivations and dreams of the diverse peoples who constitute India. My teachers at Deshbandhu College introduced me to debates that enabled me to develop a more critical understanding of India's national movement, revealing its inclusive and exclusive dimensions and the roles played by class and caste. Many of these issues were discussed and debated even more critically in my MA classes in the History Department of Delhi University.

For creating remarkable conditions for debate and learning, and for their encouragement and deep engagement, I would like to thank my BA teachers at Deshbandhu College: Arup Banerjee, Rana Behl, Amiya Sen, Anil Sethi, and Savita Singh. In particular, Anil Sethi offered inspiring and committed teaching, an uncanny ability to nurture and engage students, and a willingness to give his students unlimited time. My college teachers and classmates introduced me to new categories of knowledge and to new ways of thinking about society and history, and it is to them that I owe my first intellectual debt.

A remarkable group of teachers and challenging new courses in the MA and M.Phil. programs in history at Delhi University played a crucial role in shaping my intellectual journey in the following years. Professors Shahid Amin, Aparna Basu, Rana Behl, Suhash Chakravarty, Partha Sarathi Gupta, Monica Juneja, Sunil Kumar, Gyan Pandey, Sumit Sarkar, and Nalini Taneja were generous with their time and teaching. I also want to thank my classmates in the first-year seminar courses of my M.Phil. program in 1992–93 for their intellectually stimulating discussions and camaraderie. A partial list includes Seema Arora, Avijit Chakarabarty, Mayank Kumar, Sanjay Kumar, Ruby Lal, Tarika Oberoi, Nilanjan Sarkar, Ruchika Saxena, Priyanka Sharma, and Shashank Sinha.

I gratefully acknowledge the support of the following institutions and funding organizations for sustaining this project and bringing it to fruition: the South-South Exchange Programme for Research on the History of Development (SEPHIS) fellowship program for a four-year doctoral fellowship, 1999–2003; the Harry Frank Guggenheim Foundation for a dissertation fellowship, 2003–2004; and the History Department at Bowdoin College for a one-year research associate position during the same year that provided me with an institutional space to finish my dissertation. A Rockefeller postdoctoral fellowship at the Simpson Center for the Humanities, University of Washington, 2004–2005; a visiting teaching position in the Department of History, University of Notre Dame, 2005–2006; and a three-year postdoctoral teaching fellowship funded by a Mellon grant at the University of Pennsylvania, 2006–2008 and 2009–2010, all supported the process of transforming my dissertation into a book. A senior research fellowship from the American Institute of Indian Studies during 2008–2009 to begin a new book project on the Dalit public sphere in North India also enabled me to collect the photos that appear in this book. In addition, I am grateful to the Warner Fund of the University Seminars at Columbia University for publication support.

Interviews and discussions with Dalit friends over the past sixteen years have had the most profound influence on my research and thinking. I participated in a series of conversations in the Valmiki Basti (colony) in Delhi in the winter of 1992–93 which first made me aware of the absence of Dalits as actors in mainstream Indian history and its historiography. Why is it, I was asked, that although history departments ignore Dalits, sociology and anthropology departments study the problem of untouchability in Dalit neighborhoods, when it is a problem created by caste Hindus? The Dalit activists of the colony recommended that university departments should not only send students to study caste Hindu localities in South Delhi, where the practices of untouchability are nurtured and perpetuated, but also rectify the teaching of Indian history by acknowledging and including the activities and contributions of Dalits. These very valid points have never left me, and have helped to shape the questions of this book. The Delhi-based columnist and intellectual Chandra Bhan Prasad, who combines acute sociological observations on Indian society with provocative writing, has been a sustaining source of inspiration. He has been a trusted friend and interlocutor since 1995, and in meetings at his house I have conversed and engaged with friends old and new who have helped to sustain this work. A number of Dalit and non-Dalit writers and activists whom I have met at these meetings have caused me to ask new questions.

During the course of my research I have also been fortunate enough to create new friendships in numerous cities and towns of North India, including Lucknow, Allahabad, Kanpur, Agra, Azamgarh, Etawah, Jhansi, Gwalior, and Chandigarh, and more recently in Hyderabad in South India. I want to take this opportunity to thank the BAMCEF group in Allahabad, who allowed me to participate in their discussions of various aspects of casteism and racism in Indian (Hindu) society and the struggle for a more democratic society. I spent several weeks in Agra meeting people, doing interviews, and collecting Chamar and Dalit histories, and I was inspired by the very committed and motivated individuals I met there. Hira Lal, Puttu Lal, and Daya Shankar were generous not only in sharing their libraries with me, but also in helping me gain a more detailed picture of Dalit histories and struggles in the Agra region. Radhey Shyam provided me with a home in Agra. Others to whom I'm grateful for their help in Agra include Mangat Ram, Khazan Singh, and Pratap Singh. I have been thankful for the friendship of Shant Swarup Baudh, Ish Gangania, and Dr. Tej Singh in Delhi, and Brijendra Kumar Gautam and Guru Prasad Madan in Allahabad. Mohan Singh Jatav and his family have offered kind support to this book and to my second project. He was very generous in giving me permission to publish most of the photos in this book. My intellectual debt to them and to others whom I met will be evident throughout this book.

I am deeply indebted to the archivists, librarians, and "bundle lifters" of various archives and libraries where most of the research for this project was conducted: in Lucknow, the Uttar Pradesh (UP) State Archives, the UP State Secretariat Archival Records Library, the Board of Revenue Library, and the Criminal Investigation Department archives; in Allahabad, the UP State Regional archives and the Kashi Nagri Pracharini Sabha Library; in Delhi, the National Archives of India, the Nehru Memorial Museum and Library, and the Central Secretariat Library; in England, the Oriental and India Office Collection in the British Library in London and the University of Sussex Library in Brighton; in the United States, the libraries of Columbia University, Bowdoin College, the University of Washington, the University of Notre Dame, and the University of Pennsylvania—my heartfelt thanks to all. In particular, I would like to thank the following individuals: research officers

Meera Devi, Sandhya Nagar, Amitab Pandey, Ajay Singh, and Shashi Upad-haya, and bundle lifters Jas Karan and Shiv Prasad, for their wonderful sup-port of my research during my many trips to the UP State Archives in Luck-now; sub-inspector Ajay Singh in the archives of the CID office in Lucknow; librarian Shashi Mishra of the Board of Revenue Library in Lucknow; Aavi-nash Kumar, Ajay Singh, and Ashish of the UP State Secretariat Archival Records Library; Dr. Johari, archivist, and bundle lifter Harish and his team, in the UP State Regional Archives in Allahabad; and librarian Mr. Sarkar of the NAI library in Delhi. I particularly want to put on record the important role played by the bundle lifters in Lucknow and Allahabad in my research. They possess immense knowledge of the archives, and also provided delight-ful distractions with their numerous stories about fellow scholars. My sincere thanks to Tim Thomas, reference manager, and Vince Harrison, issue desk manager, in the Oriental and India Office Collection of the British Library, for coming in on a Saturday (in the last week of August 2001, during my fieldwork in London) to look for uncatalogued records stored in the base-ment. Because of them I was able to consult the previously uncatalogued "UP Memoranda (non-official) to the Indian Statutory Commission" in the Q (constitutional) series (also known as ISC volumes), which included petitions and memoranda submitted to the commission by Dalit organizations.

My supervisor, Shahid Amin, has been my most ardent critic and sup-porter. I was fortunate that he took such interest in my project. He offered valuable suggestions at every stage of my work, and pointed me in the right directions in the archives.

The daunting task of transforming my research into a book turned out to be a pleasure because of the engagement and support of colleagues and staff in a number of institutions. I was very fortunate to start my academic career with a postdoctoral fellowship at the University of Washington, where a strong contingent of South Asianists engaged with my work and gave me ex-cellent advice as I began the process. K. Sivaramakrishnan, director of the South Asia Center; Anand Yang, director of the Jackson School of Interna-tional Studies; Tani Barlow and Madeline Yue Dong, directors of the Project for Critical Asian Studies; and Kathleen Woodward, director of the Simpson Center for the Humanities, all believed in my work and supported my efforts during the 2004–2005 academic year in Seattle. Kathy Woodward, together with Miriam Bartha, the associate director of the Simpson Center, and all the center's staff gave me the best possible space and encouragement while I wrote the book. The opportunity to share my work with colleagues was extremely beneficial, and I am indebted to the following at the University of Washington: my co-fellows at the Simpson Center for the Humanities, Boreth Ly, Katharyne Mitchell, and Fadjar Thufail; South Asianists Paul Brass, Frank Conlon, Priti Ramamurthy, Cabeiri Robinson, Michael Shapiro, K. Sivaramakrishnan, Keith Snodgrass, and Anand Yang; my colleagues in the History Department, including Tani Barlow, Madeline Yue Dong, Vicente Rafael, Illeana Rodriquez-Silva, Laurie Sears, Nikhil Singh, Quintard Taylor, and Adam Warren; in the Geography Department, Katharyne Mitchell and Matthew Sparke; Davinder Bhowmik in the Department of Asian Language and Literature; and Chandan Reddy in the English Department. I received unstinting support from the Department of History at the University of Notre Dame and I greatly appreciate the encouragement I received from the chair, John McGreevy, and from my colleagues Paul Cobb, Jon Coleman, Dan Graff, Lionel Jenson, Asher Kaufman, Margaret Meserve, Marc Rodriguez, and Julia Thomas. Anthropologists Susan Blum and Cynthia Mahmood were great mentors, and Cynthia read my manuscript and gave me great suggestions.

Three years at the University of Pennsylvania have proved most beneficial to my work. The Department of South Asia Studies, the Center for the Advanced Study of India, and the South Asia Center have provided me with outstanding support at every level. Devesh Kapur, the director of CASI and a man of great vision, raised $120,000 to help organize the first Dalit studies conference in the United States, December 3–5, 2008, opening new intellectual horizons. The Department of South Asian Studies and the South Asia Center also enabled me to organize the "Histories of the Present" conferences in 2007 and 2008. Colleagues at Penn were generous in supporting my work, and I am grateful for their friendship and intellectual companionship. Aditya Behl (1966–2009) brought me to Penn, and his untimely death was a great loss to all of us. Others at Penn to whom I'm grateful include Daud Ali, Sanjukta Banerjee, Jody Chavez, Jamal Elias, Surendra Gambhir, Vijay Gambhir, Kathleen Hall, Sunila Kale, Christian Novetzke, Deven Patel, and Rupa Viswanath; Cheikh Babou, Steve Hahn, Stephanie McCurry, and Barbara Savage in the Department of History; and Tukufu Zuberi in the Sociology Department. I gratefully acknowledge the support and enthusiasm of my colleagues at the University of Delaware.

My heartfelt gratitude goes to friends and colleagues who read the entire manuscript and offered comments and suggestions for improvement: Shahid Amin (University of Delhi), Christopher Bayly (Cambridge University), Neeladri Bhattacharya (Jawaharlal Nehru University), Sabyasachi Bhattacharya (Jawaharlal University), Ian Duncan (University of Sussex), David Gilmartin (University of North Carolina), Lori Ginzberg (Pennsylvania State University), Douglas Haynes (Dartmouth College), David Lelyveld (William Patterson University), David Ludden (New York University), Lisa Mitchell (University of Pennsylvania), Mridu Rai (Yale University), Mahesh Rangarajan (University of Delhi), Ajay Skaria (University of Minnesota), Romila Thapar (Jawaharlal University), Susan Wadley (Syracuse University), Anand Yang (University of Washington), and Eleanor Zelliot (Carleton College). Their remarks greatly helped in clarifying many of the arguments. If any errors remain, they are mine.

I must also acknowledge numerous scholars and individuals I met in India, the United States, and Europe while working on this project who made the process more enjoyable and offered opportunities for discussing my work in its various stages of completion. An incomplete list includes Cassie Adcock, Shyam Babu, Janaki Bakhle, Gautam Bhadra, Laura Brueck, David Campion, Catherine Candy, Dipesh Chakrabarty, Partha Chatterjee, Sean Chaubot, Jangam Chinnaiah, Lawrence Cohen, Kavita Datla, Rohan D'Souza, M. Gopinath, Charu Gupta, Gopal Guru, Nicolos Jaoul, Craig Jeffrey, Umesh Jha, Priya Joshi, Bodhisattva Kar, Suvir Kaul, Elizabeth Kolsky, Owen Lynch, Karuna Mantena, Abby McGowan, Sanal Mohan, Badri Narayan, Sikha Pathak, Indira Peterson, Sarah Pinto, Anupama Rao, Yasmin Saikia, Nilanjan Sarkar, K. Satyanarayana, Anil Sethi, William Siepmann, Sarah Tananbaum, Dipu Sharan, Arafaat Valiani, Roxanne Varzi, Amanda Weidman, and Vazira Zamindar.

Professor Ravinder Kumar (1933–2001) was a generous and unpretentious mentor, and I greatly regret that he did not live to read this book.

Portions of this book were presented at a number of institutions in India, the United States, and the Netherlands, and I am beholden to the organizers and audiences of those presentations for their comments and help in clarifying a number of my arguments. A partial list includes, in the United States, the Department of History, University of Delaware; Columbia University's Seminar on South Asia; the Dalit Studies Conference, University of Pennsylvania; the Caste in the Contemporary World Conference, University of Hawaii; the South Asia Colloquium, Syracuse University; the Department of History, Vanderbilt University; and the South Asia Conference and the Simpson Center for the Humanities, University of Washington; in India, the Department of History, University of Delhi; the Department of History and the Center for Political Science, Jawaharlal Nehru University, Delhi; the Department of Political Science, Punjab University, Chandigarh; the Govind Ballabh Pant Social Science Institute, Allahabad, Uttar Pradesh; the English and Foreign Language University, Hyderabad, Andhra Pradesh; the Anveshi Research Centre for Women's Studies, Hyderabad, Andhra Pradesh; the India Habitat Centre, organized by the Heinrich Boll Foundation and Zubaan Books, New Delhi; and the eighth Cultural Studies Workshop (2002), Shantiniketan, West Bengal, organized by the Centre for Studies in Social Sciences, Calcutta; and in the Netherlands, the Seminar Series of the Amsterdam School for Social Science Research (ASSR).

Over the years, Lucknow has become a second home to me, and I have made some lasting friendships in the city. My foremost debt is to Sufia Khala (Sufia Kidwai). During my frequent trips, she always made me feel welcome in her house in Hazratganj, and took a keen interest in my project. The other person I am deeply indebted to in Lucknow is Ram Advani, who, as a bookseller and as a person, is an institution. His bookshop always provided a welcome solace after a hard day's work in the archives. Another person who took keen interest in my work is Mr. A. K. Rastogi, former chairman of the Board of Revenue, whose generosity and support were truly outstanding. His personal assistant, Vivekanand Dobriyal, was always resourceful in helping me through all kinds of difficulties and ensuring that I received photocopies in time. Mrs. Sharma's guest house was more like a home, and I looked forward to her warmth and hospitality. Mr. Dhani Ram, his wife, and their children, Guddi, Pappi, Chandu (Dr. Chandra), and Neeraj, provided me with a second home in Lucknow and always offered a welcome distraction from work. Other remarkable individuals, now friends, whom I met during the course of my fieldwork in Lucknow have contributed immensely to my project: I thank S. R. Darapore for sharing his library and ideas with me; Chaman Lal, a senior police officer in the CID office, for his interest in my work; and Gama Ram, who deserves a special thanks for sharing his past and present with me. Vasudha Pandey and Ashish Banerjee let me stay in their house and offered support to my project while I was in Allahabad. Ashish's *chachaji* (Mr. Banerjee) welcomed me into his home in Allahabad with warmth and affection, told me stories of the 1940s, including of his trip to Africa, and made my stay a memorable one.

This book has been written in several places where friends have contributed in different ways to my work. Vidisha Apartments in Patparganj (Delhi), with its special community of friends, was the best place to start this work. My neighbors there, especially Bulbul, Joseph, and Revati, have been generous and sustaining friends over these many years; Geetanjali, Pankaj, Prabhat, Ravikant, Sanjeev, Saumya, Sharmishta, Sneha, Sudhir, and Vinita in Vidisha offered welcome breaks from my work. Also in Patparganj, I owe a special thanks to the house of Chanderbhan and Meera Prasad, their daughters Khushi and Drishti, and other part- and full-time members of the household, including Shyam Babu, Sheoraj Singh Bechhain, and H. L. Dosadh, who were my most engaged critics and a constant source of inspiration. A. S. Bhasin has been a wonderful friend and mentor. Shubha Parmar and Udyan Parmar helped obtain permission from the government of Uttar Pradesh to use the CID office in Lucknow. In Hyderabad, Lisa's friends became my good friends as they adopted me with unusual warmth. They include the family of Sunil Kumar Bernard, as well as Bhagya Lakshmi, Chaitanya, Ramana Murthy, and Suneetha. I also want to thank Nilanjan Sarkar for subletting his room to me in London and helping with my stay. William Siepmann has been a generous host and friend in London, and his Brunswick Centre apartment made for easy access to the British Library. A special thanks to Ian Duncan for inviting me to the University of Sussex and for numerous discussions of Uttar Pradesh. My greatest debt is to Rohan D'Souza for intellectual companionship and friendship over the last fifteen years, and for supporting this project. Finally, a block of Beaumont Avenue in Philadelphia is like an Indian *mohalla* (neighborhood); my heartfelt thanks to all our friends and neighbors who inhabit this wonderful *gulli* (street) in such a sustaining fashion, with communal happy hours on one porch or another, shared dinners, and stories.

I am grateful to Susan Wadley and the members of the American Institute of Indian Studies' Publication Committee for including this book in their Contemporary Indian Studies series. Sue's engagement with this book and her readiness to share her work on Karimpur (Mainpuri district), and that of the Wisers, have been much appreciated.

Rebecca Tolen, my editor at Indiana University Press, has been extremely patient and accommodating. She has deftly guided me through the publication process and taken an enthusiastic interest in this work. Thanks are also due to Dan Pyle and Peter Froehlich at Indiana University Press. Shoshanna Green, my copyeditor, has been the most marvelous editor, and her queries and suggestions have transformed this manuscript into a polished work.

I dedicate this book to my mother, Kamla Rawat (1945–79), in loving memory, and to my father Shiv Narayan Singh Rawat, who raised three sons singlehandedly. His commitment and integrity are a model and beyond compare. My brothers, Ved and Yogesh, have been a source of strength, as have my sisters-in-law, Seema and Pooja. My nephew, Akshay, and nieces, Gudiya and Muskaan, have brought delight and joy to our lives. My in-laws, Sara and Larry Mitchell, have been the most wonderful in-laws I could have imagined, and they have always been there for me. I am thankful to Clark and Jennifer Mitchell and the three Mitchell boys, Nick, Gavin, and Ethan, for their support. Our five-year-old daughter, Leela McElhinney Rawat, has been the greatest source of enchantment and happiness. Above all, I must thank Lisa Mitchell for reminding me, many times over, of the promise and pleasure that the archives hold. Her reading and discussion of my work have given this book a remarkable clarity and depth, and her presence in the other dimensions of my life continues to bring me much joy.

Philadelphia, Pennsylvania
September, 2010

RECONSIDERING UNTOUCHABILITY

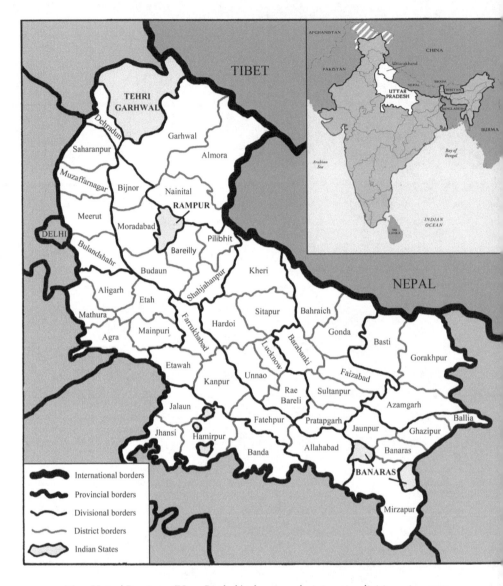

Map: United Provinces (Uttar Pradesh), showing administrative divisions circa 1920.
Inset: Contemporary map of India showing the location of UP. (Uttarakhand was carved
out of Uttar Pradesh in 2000.)

Untouchable Boundaries:
Chamars and the Politics of Identity and History

On October 15, 2002, in the town of Jhajjar in the North Indian state of Haryana, five men from the Chamar community (regarded as "untouchable" by Hindu society) were dragged, beaten, and stoned to death by a mob of caste Hindus while a magistrate and numerous police personnel looked on.[1] Although this incident made headlines in national and regional media for weeks, there was as much protest over the possibility that someone might be punished for this act as there was over the brutal killings themselves, with prominent politicians and officials coming to the defense of the attackers; ultimately, no one was arrested. The only action taken by the police to defuse the situation was to send the carcass of a cow for a postmortem to ascertain whether it had been poisoned. The five Chamar men who were killed in Jhajjar were involved in the leather trade, regularly collecting and skinning dead cattle. The leather industry in India depends primarily on these fallen cattle. Hides are sold for a nominal price to brokers, who in turn sell them to leather factories. In this particular incident, caste Hindus had accused the men of poisoning several cattle in order to claim the hides. Nearly two thousand people participated in the mob. Following the murders, the families of all five men converted—four to Buddhism, and one to Islam. While such tensions are not new—similar violence against Chamars and accusations relating to cattle poisoning were being made more than a century earlier—the immediate resort to conversion brings into relief the centrality of identity to such incidents of violence and domination, and to the resistance with which they are met.

Domination, social segregation, and violence are regular features of the daily lives of millions of Dalits—those who have been regarded as "untouchable" by orthodox Hindus.[2] The figures provided by the Indian government indicate the levels of violence involved; 98,349 cases of criminal atrocity were registered by Dalits between 1994 and 1996. Human Rights Watch reports that "1,660 were for murder, 2,814 for rape, and 13,671 for hurt," and 38,483 for other offenses listed under the Prevention of Atrocities Act.[3] These figures represent only the reported cases, a very small percentage of actual incidents. The majority of cases go unreported, both to the police and in the press.

Dalits constitute 166 million people, close to one-sixth of India's total population.[4] The following states have the largest number of Dalits: there are 35 million Dalits in the state of Uttar Pradesh; 18 million in West Bengal; 13 million in Bihar; 12 million in Andhra Pradesh; 11 million in Tamil Nadu; 9 million each in Maharashtra, Madhya Pradesh, and Rajasthan; 8 million in Karnataka; and 7 million in Punjab.[5] Still, their large numbers do not necessarily correlate with political power. Historically recognized centers of Dalit movements are the states of Maharashtra and Punjab. This is not to suggest that Dalit struggles have been absent in other states, such as Uttar Pradesh and Andhra Pradesh,[6] only that little research has been done on these areas.

The terms of self-reference used by Dalits have varied historically and regionally. In the first three decades of the twentieth century the terms widely used were "Adi-Hindu" in Uttar Pradesh, "Adi-Andhra" in Andhra Pradesh, and "Adi-Dharma" in Punjab, *adi* meaning "original inhabitants." It was replaced by the term "Scheduled Castes" from 1936 onward, coined by the colonial state to classify "untouchables" in a separate "schedule" to provide them with benefits in legislative assemblies, state employment, and education. Prior to 1936, "Untouchables" and "Depressed Classes" were the official categories used in the census and for other purposes. To this day the Indian government continues to use "Scheduled Castes" as its official term. The term acquired popularity among Dalits because of the Scheduled Castes Federation, the political party established by B. R. Ambedkar in 1942, which had gained support in prominent centers of Dalit activism. In Hindi books and newspapers, however, Dalit writers used the term *achhut,* "untouched," meaning "pure" as opposed to "untouchable." Since the 1970s, activists and intelligentsia have popularized the term "Dalit" to describe their community, both in the present context and historically. Throughout this book I will also use the term "Dalit." Beginning with the Dalit Panther movement in the 1970s, the term acquired a radical new meaning of self-identification and signified a new oppositional consciousness. (The term *harijan,* coined by Mahatma Gandhi, was unanimously rejected by Dalit activists and intelligentsia from the very moment of its coinage in 1932.)

The widespread practice of untouchability continues to deprive individuals and communities of access to resources, educational opportunities, employment, and other avenues of advancement. Many caste Hindus still do not allow members of Dalit communities to enter their homes, particularly the kitchen, and will not permit their children to marry into these communities. In most rural areas separate sources of drinking water are maintained, away from those used by caste Hindus, and Dalits are expected to reside in separate colonies at some distance from caste Hindu settlements. In many parts of South India, even today, teashops keep separate sets of cups to be used only by Dalits. The government of independent India abolished untouchability and caste-based discrimination in 1947, declaring them cognizable offenses (for which offenders could be arrested without a court warrant), and instituted an affirmative action program for federal and state employment. Nonetheless, practices of exclusion manifest themselves today more violently than ever before. Combining economic and social discrimination, untouchability has survived the constitutional changes made immediately after independence.

The factor that has contributed most to the continued subordination of Dalits has been the ghettoization of their communities into so-called "traditional" and "ritually impure" occupations. Chamars were deliberately encouraged to become laborers within the leather industries. Similarly, the Chamar women who had traditionally cut the umbilical cord of newborn babies in rural India were transformed into qualified *dais* or midwives by the medical establishment. Balmikis, because of their supposedly "traditional" work, are employed as sweepers by the municipalities of almost every city in North India. Government policies in both colonial and independent India have perpetuated the "untouchable" status of these communities and reinforced their domination by caste Hindu society, ensuring that individuals from "untouchable" communities remain in the margins, excluded from the privileges and opportunities of the twenty-first century. Today, this means that brutal beatings and murders are ignored by police, politicians, government officials, and a public that tacitly approves of the use of violence to maintain the status quo.

The long history of exclusion at the hands of caste Hindus has provided Dalits with a markedly different perspective on Indian history, society, and religion than that generally represented by the mass media, academia, and the government. It is therefore not surprising that Dalits have had an ambivalent relationship with both colonialism and Indian nationalism, one that has not always aligned with the views of dominant Hindus. In October 1999, Chandra Bhan Prasad, one of India's foremost Dalit thinkers and activists, concluded a long conversation with me on colonialism and its impact on Dalits in a rather dramatic fashion by claiming that the only thing wrong with British colonialism was that "the British came too late and left too early," an assertion quite shocking to a generation of postcolonial Indian nationalists who hold the British responsible for irreparable harm to the Indian nation and people.[7] Prasad went on to argue that the British had liberated the Dalit masses from the oppression of Hindu society by providing them with the most important tool of liberation, access to education. Over the years, during fieldwork in the cities of Lucknow, Kanpur, Allahabad, and Agra in the North Indian state of Uttar Pradesh, and in Delhi, it has become clear to me that many Dalits share Prasad's views. But even more significantly, as early as the 1920s, activists within the Dalit movement in North India had already articulated many of these same points. Indeed, Chandra Bhan Prasad can be seen as one in a long line of Dalit intellectuals and activists who have articulated similar ideological positions, but who have never been acknowledged in mainstream academic or historical writings. Both the leaders of the Adi-Hindu movement in the 1920s and 1930s and Chandrabhan Prasad at the end of the twentieth century bring home the point that Dalits have openly challenged the Indian National Congress's nationalist agenda, and have not universally shared the Indian nationalists' opposition to colonialism. Dalit perspectives on Indian history have little respect for the framework of colonialism versus nationalism mapped by Hindu-dominated mainstream Indian historiography.

Conversations with Dalit activists in Delhi's Valmiki Basti (colony) during the winter of 1992–93 first made me aware of the inadequacy of Indian historiography. One of these Dalit activists repeatedly emphasized the fact that there are no Dalits in Indian history. He pointed out that Dalits rarely appear as actors in Indian history and historiography. These activists also remarked that their neighborhoods had become laboratories for studies and research projects conducted by the sociology and anthropology departments of various universities. Caste Hindu localities of the city, however, were rarely the focus of such studies. Why is that caste Hindus are so often the primary actors within historical narratives, while Dalits appear only as objects of anthropological and sociological studies?

The focus of this study is the Chamars of the North Indian state of Uttar Pradesh, who from the beginning of the twentieth century have been the best educated, most politically articulate, and most prosperous Dalits in the state. The Chamar social background of a majority of Dalit activists and intellectuals underscores their prominence in politics. Four times since the early 1990s, Mayawati, a Dalit woman from the Chamar community and leader of the Bahujan Samaj Party (BSP), a Dalit political organization, has been elected chief minister of the state of Uttar Pradesh.[8] In May 2007, the BSP created an unexpected political upheaval by winning an absolute majority in the state legislative assembly. Mayawati was able to achieve such a historically unprecedented victory by creating a strong alliance between Dalits and Brahmans and other upper-caste groups. The idea that caste Hindus could ever be led by a Dalit political party was unprecedented in the long twentieth-century history of modern India. What is less well known is that in addition to their prominent ideological role, Chamars also make up the single largest social group among all communities and historically defined caste groups in the state. Dalits constitute 22 percent of the total population of Uttar Pradesh, and Chamars constitute almost two-thirds of the total Dalit population. The longstanding Chamar presence within agriculture, not just as landless laborers but also as tenants and owners of land in Uttar Pradesh, troubles the popular image of this group as primarily leatherworkers. This presence helps to explain how Chamars have been able to establish their own schools, avail themselves of educational opportunities, create their own political and social organizations, and, most recently, achieve electoral victory. Although these advances in social and political realms have been significant, Chamars, like other sections of Dalits, continue to confront social discrimination at numerous levels.

The occupational stereotypes of Dalit castes have provided justification for the continued exploitation, oppression, and abuse of Chamars and other untouchable castes. In the face of contradictory archival evidence, the salience of occupational stereotypes, not only for Chamars but also for other caste groups similarly regarded as "untouchable," is puzzling and needs to be explained. Without a historical understanding of how these assumptions and stereotypes have been created and, more importantly, sustained, they not only will continue to be used to exploit and oppress Dalit communities, but also will form an obstacle to adequately explaining phenomena like the dramatic electoral success of the Dalit-led Bahujan Samaj Party.

Dominant Narratives:
Questioning the Occupational Stereotype

The caste-based occupational stereotypes of Dalit groups like the Chamars perpetuated accusations of cattle poisoning against Chamars in Jhajjar in October 2002 and in the 1880s in eastern Uttar Pradesh. The persistence of the stereotype that Chamars are leatherworkers, which spans both colonial and postcolonial contexts, demonstrates the constitutive relationship between imagined occupation and the representation of Dalit identities. Every Dalit caste in India is defined solely in reference to a supposedly impure occupation that provides the basis for their untouchability.[9] In the case of Chamars, who constitute 14 percent of the total population of Uttar Pradesh, it is leatherwork. Anthropological and historical accounts of the "untouchables" of India have sustained this conceptual framework by equating untouchability with occupation, even in the face of radical changes in both disciplines in the last five decades. I will trace the intellectual genealogy of the conceptual framework central to the study of untouchability in India. Rather than helping us to better understand the history and society not only of Dalits but of Hinduism and India more generally, the perpetuation of an analytic framework that equates Dalit caste groups with hereditary occupations has actually worked to obscure and erase history. Writing a new history of untouchability must begin by questioning this theoretical framework.

Writing in 1920, the colonial official George W. Briggs summed up the dominant colonial assumption by arguing that "occupationally to-day the Chamar corresponds to the *charmamna* or *charmamla* and the *charmakara* [leatherworker] of the past."[10] This proposition was first formulated during the course of British colonial campaigns against cattle poisoning in the 1850s, led by George Campbell and recorded in his many reports, and it was further reinforced by colonial decennial censuses and ethnographic reports compiled in the 1870s and 1880s. In an 1854 report, Campbell invoked the traditional "system under which the Chamars become possessed of the bodies and skins of the dead animals" to explain the crime of cattle

"One of the Chamars is acknowledged as the best sower of sugarcane in the village."
Possibily the first photo of Chamar peasants cultivating the land.

"Occasionally one of them makes a basket for sale."
Both photos from William Wiser and Charlotte Wiser, *Behind Mud Walls* (New York, 1930). *Photos © Richard Smith, Inc., New York, and the Wiser family.*

poisoning, stating that "the latter perform certain services for the cultivators, and receive the bodies of all of the animals belonging to their own particular cultivators which die." Campbell concluded that after poisoning the cattle, Chamars "obtain possession of the body in virtue of a prescriptive right of the nature of a contract [that is] well established."[11] Surprisingly, this formulation of a traditional Indian village community has subsequently seen little change. The American anthropologists William and Charlotte Wiser, writing in the 1930s about various social groups in the village of Karimpur, Mainpuri district, in Uttar Pradesh, similarly define "the Chamars (leather-workers)" by associating them with what they describe as "their traditional trade."[12]

Three decades later, in his study of the politics of the Jatav Chamars of Agra (Uttar Pradesh), Owen Lynch devotes ten pages to explaining the Chamars' relationship with leatherwork in the past and in the present, and much of his exposition is drawn from the ethnographic works of Briggs and the late nineteenth-century colonial officer and ethnographer William Crooke. Indeed, he cites Briggs, writing that "the word Camar is derived from the Sanskrit *charmakara*, which means leather worker."[13] Bernard Cohn, one of the earliest scholars to substantially question the colonial construction of knowledge in India, begins his discussion of the Chamars of Madhopur and Senapur villages in the Jaunpur district of Uttar Pradesh with the same perspective, writing that the Chamars' "traditional occupation is skinning, tanning and working in leather."[14] Building on this heritage of knowledge production, the prominent postcolonial Indian anthropologist Kumar Suresh Singh, editor of the national series project *The People of India,* states in his volume on the scheduled castes, published in 1993, that leatherwork was the age-old work of Chamars, and therefore "their community name is derived from the Sanskrit word *Charmakara,* meaning leather worker."[15]

In all of these accounts—colonial and postcolonial—we are told that Chamars are "traditionally" leatherworkers and that their untouchable status stems from their impure occupation. This is the consistent explanation for why they occupy the lowest position in Hindu society. Indeed, this formulation has become foundational in Indian historical, anthropological, and sociological writings on Chamars, assuming a status of self-evident truth and providing the starting framework for subsequent studies, be they anthropological or historical. These views have been reinforced by an emphasis on Brahmanical texts as primary sources of authority and by colonial reconstructions of knowledge that privileged dominant Hindu social, political, and cultural groups as informants.[16] In this sense, then, the representations of the history and society of Chamars and other Dalit groups reflect the often unacknowledged agendas of caste and racial social privilege rather than the actual social experiences—both past and present—of those defined as "untouchables."

In this study I identify the colonial discursive practices through which occupational stereotypes were constituted and describe how they gained the status of established social fact assumed to represent the lived reality of a segment of North Indian society. Historicizing the process of knowledge formation, I examine the claims made for these representations in nineteenth- and twentieth-century Uttar Pradesh in order to explore the relationship between these dominant assumptions and the actual descriptions of Chamar lives during these two centuries.

Colonial, and later nationalist, formulations of Chamar occupational identities were questioned by Chamar organizations through their writings and political actions from the first two decades of the twentieth century onward. Indeed, Dalit writers, historians, and activists have consistently sought to confront colonial and postcolonial Hindu narratives by writing their own histories, defining their own political agendas, and deploying their own self-fashioned identities. A striking feature of Chamar struggles since the early decades of the twentieth century has been the contestation of dominant colonial and Hindu representations of the supposed impure origins of their communities, their occupations, and their identities. By tracing the efforts of Chamars to redefine their own identities over the course of the past century, I offer an alternative to existing historical models for writing Indian history by emphasizing the central relationship between domination and identity within the Chamars' ongoing struggles for liberation.

Robert Deliege tells us that prior to the 1960s "caste theories, in particular the earliest ones, [were] based largely on textual sources, often in Sanskrit."[17] Colonial anthropological writings focused on a separate Chamar religious world by identifying it as independent from Hinduism, and by contrasting the spirits, ghosts, local godlings, and magic present within Chamar beliefs with the pantheon of deities recognized within Hinduism. Thus, studies such as G. W. Briggs's 1920 work, *The Chamars,* and William Wiser and Charlotte Wiser's 1932 *Behind Mud Walls* characterize the religious and cultural world of Chamars as being constituted by animistic beliefs in contrast to what they portray as the more formal deity-centered belief system of Hinduism. Briggs's influential work on Chamars distinguishes between higher and lower religion and argues that Chamars belong to the latter category because of their animistic beliefs. According to him, the core of Chamars' religious and cultural rituals lay in their birth and marriage ceremonies and in the world of spirits and mysterious occurrences. Briggs concludes, "Not only is the moral standard of the Chamar low in respect of social purity, but also in matters of excessive use of narcotic drugs and intoxicating beverages."[18] This essentialist ethnography accepts a caste Hindu perspective of ritual "impurity" and further condemns them as possessing low social and moral standards.

From the 1960s onward, anthropologists conducted extensive fieldwork in an effort to move away from a text-dominated model. Deliege has identified two theoretical models of untouchability in postcolonial anthropology. The "models of separation" represents Dalit practices and beliefs as marginal and isolated, a distinct domain excluded from the dominant Hindu religious practices and beliefs.[19] In a 1958 article, Bernard Cohn writes that "in the past Chamars of Senapur [in Benares district, Uttar Pradesh] have centered their main religious activity in rituals to propitiate godlings of diseases such as Bhagauti, Sitala, and local ghosts and spirits." He concludes that their "other rituals include magical practices to revenge slights, cure diseases, and to recover stolen or lost property."[20] In contrast, "models of unity" for studying untouchability are "based on consensus, interdependence and continuity between untouchables and the rest of the population."[21] Michael Moffat's 1979 study of "untouchables" in South India argues that the Dalits live in conformity with Indian religious cultural practices and that they do not have a separate culture.[22] On the basis of his study of Tamil Dalits in South India, Deliege argues that they "do not see themselves as inherently polluted or impure."[23]

Prevailing assumptions about Chamars have played a powerful role in framing existing historiography on Chamar history and society as well. George Briggs, William and Charlotte Wiser, Owen Lynch, Mark Juergensmeyer, and, most recently, Tirthankar Roy, for example, discuss the presence of Chamars in the North Indian leather industries in the late nineteenth and twentieth centuries.[24] These writers argue that the modern leather industry contributed to the emergence of an educated and prosperous Chamar elite. The underlying assumption of these writers is that Chamars moved from traditional leatherworking occupations in rural areas to leather industries in urban centers like Agra and Kanpur. Because of the stereotype that leather-work has shaped the identities of Chamars, none of these scholars has ever thought to verify through archival research where Chamar workers in the leather industries of Agra and Kanpur actually came from. Drawing on colo-nial reports and a wide range of other archival sources, I demonstrate that rather than moving from "traditional" leatherwork in rural areas, the major-ity of Chamars employed in the new colonial leather factories actually came from agricultural peasant backgrounds. Unfortunately, the representation of a rural to urban transformation in the lives of Dalits has framed the question of Chamar liberation only in the context of their occupational stereotype, further reifying and even creating their identities as leatherworkers. Such ac-counts also represent Chamars only as the passive objects of others' actions— either as victims of domination or as recipients of others' reforms and innovations. Far from serving to liberate Dalits from the cultural stereotypes which have frozen them into positions of occupationally defined subordina-tion, the transitions identified by such works have merely repositioned the locus of their hierarchically defined occupational status from rural to urban contexts. Indeed, these studies further contribute to the circumscription of Dalit identities by failing to question the construction of cultural stereotypes grounded in occupational identities.

The first three chapters of this book investigate the colonial and na-tionalist discursive practices that transformed the caste Hindu textual un-derstanding of Chamars as leatherworkers into a social and administrative category in the nineteenth and twentieth centuries. The dominant discur-sive and administrative practices reinforced stereotypes concerning the po-sition and status of Chamars in North Indian society. The prevailing colo-nial assumption that defined Chamars as leatherworkers was worked out in the face of overwhelming evidence against it. This evidence, discussed in chapter 2, was produced by settlement reports during the last three decades of the nineteenth century. Chapter 1 examines dominant colonial and Hindu discourses that were united in accusing Chamars of cattle poison-ing, arguing that Chamars had an economic motive to poison cattle "for the sake of hides." The cow protection movement of 1892–93, led by lower-caste Ahir and Kurmi peasant groups, asserted a new Hindu identity in North India by establishing *gaurakshini sabhas* (cow protection societies) and accused not only Muslims but also Chamars of being murderers of the holy cow.[25] Chapter 3 describes how the notion that all Chamars were traditionally leatherworkers because of their caste became the basis upon which colonial and later nationalist policies and practices aimed at transforming them into trained workers of hides, skins, and leather products.

Shared Frameworks of Colonialism and Nationalism: There Are No Dalits in Indian History

The Dalit activist in Delhi who, in the winter of 1992, first pointed out to me the absence of Dalits as actors in Indian histories was not alone. The point was repeatedly made by Dalits in different parts of Uttar Pradesh during my field trips to Agra, Kanpur, Allahabad, and Lucknow. The paucity of historical attention to Dalits is one of the most remarkable features of Indian academia, even sixty years after independence, and it stands in sharp contrast to the considerable anthropological work that has been done. Until the 1990s, the sole significant academic history of Dalits was Eleanor Zelliot's 1969 study of Dr. Ambedkar and the Mahar movement in Maharashtra.

For almost a century, most mainstream academic historians have ignored or dismissed the writings of Dalit activists and intellectuals as polemical. One of the reasons that historians of India have been slow to recognize and address the role of Dalits in history may be that almost all of those whose writings have been accepted by the mainstream academy have come from caste Hindu or other non-Dalit backgrounds and have historical experiences that are radically different from those of Dalits. It is time that Dalit writings and the many active agendas their writings reflect were engaged with seriously. The colonial and nationalist discourses share a common perspective on Dalit society and history, a perspective that is perpetuated even today in Indian academia and that accounts for the absence of Dalits from Indian history. Because the ideas, struggles, and movements of Dalit writers and activists do not necessarily help to advance the historiography of colonialism versus nationalism, they have found little space for recognition.[26] When not completely ignored, Dalit perspectives have typically been rewritten to conform to nationalist agendas.

The significant participation by "untouchable" peasants, especially by those belonging to Chamar and Pasi communities, has never been acknowledged in histories of one of the most important peasant movements in Indian history, the Kisan Sabha (Peasant Association) struggle in the Awadh region of Uttar Pradesh from 1919 to 1922. From the 1936 work of the nationalist author Jawaharlal Nehru to a 1982 article by the historian Gyan Pandey in *Subaltern Studies* I, Dalits do not appear as important actors within the Kisan Sabha movement.[27] Two assumptions frame Pandey's understanding of the movement. First, like those who preceded him, he views the Kisan Sabha as a movement of the lower-caste peasantry, comprised primarily of Kurmi and Murao castes. Second, because of the existing occupational stereotypes that Chamars are traditionally leatherworkers and Pasis traditionally pig raisers, Pandey assumes that any Chamars or Pasis who may have appeared at events organized by the Kisan Sabha must have been landless laborers alienated from their "traditional occupation" who only joined the movement later on, rather than helping to initiate it. Pandey concludes that it was only during the high point of the movement, at the peak of violent confrontation between peasants and the police in the winter of 1920–21, that "the interests of the landless labourers [Chamars and Pasis] and the smaller, unprotected tenants of Awadh converged to a large extent." Chamar and Pasi participation is portrayed less as political engagement than as outright criminality, echoing colonial portrayals of an earlier period. Pandey writes that "[a]mong these crowds [in January 1921] were numbers of Pasis and members of other 'criminal' tribes . . . responsibility for the 'indiscriminate' looting of the village bazars." He goes on to distinguish between politically engaged peasants and "the rioters [who] were said to consist chiefly of Ahirs, Bhars, Lumias and the untouchable Pasis and Chamars."[28]

The absence of Chamars and Pasis in the study of peasant activism or their reduction to lawless or criminal forces is instructive in pointing to the role of the nationalist framework in obscuring Dalits from history. Historians have ignored Dalits' role in the radical struggles of the twentieth century chiefly because they assume that Chamars were only leatherworkers and never agricultural peasants, perpetuating preexisting colonial stereotypes. Indeed, historians don't tell us that in the famous police firing on Kisan Sabha activists in the Rae Bareli district in January 1921, the majority of the peasants killed were Dalits. The battle between protestors and the state took place at Fursatganj bazaar in the town of Rae Bareli and led to the deaths of twenty-four peasants. These twenty-four included sixteen Pasis and Chamars, suggesting that groups regarded as untouchable made up a large rather than marginal percentage of the participants.[29] In contrast to existing representations of Dalit participation in the Kisan Sabha movement, archival evidence demonstrates that Chamars and Pasis became active members of the Kisan Sabha and supported its activities precisely because they were agricultural peasants who, like the peasant caste groups of Kurmis, Muraos, and Ahirs, found their livelihoods threatened by the extreme rent demands of the landlords, which were backed up by the threat of *bedekhli* or eviction. Baba Ramchandra, the renowned peasant leader of the Kisan Sabha movement in Awadh, even specifically mentions the role of Chamar peasants in his accounts of the movement in his diaries. Ramchandra prominently notes the presence of Chamars and Pasis in the Kisan Sabha committee meetings in 1919 and 1920 at Rure village in Partabgarh. He lists the names of thirty-five participating castes, "Brahman, Thakur, Bania, Chauhan, Kurmi, Koeri, Teli, Pasi, Chamar, Barhi, Kahar, Ahir," suggesting that Chamars and Pasis were part of the movement from the very beginning, in 1919, and not just from 1921.[30] Further, this is not an arbitrary listing but reflects the important position that these two peasant groups occupy in the region; they are more numerous than the Ahirs. Baba Ramchandra's description of peasant groups is in sharp contrast to Pandey's description of the Kisan Sabha movement as a movement of Kurmis and Muraos. Furthermore, he gives us evidence of significant Chamar participation from 1925 to 1940 in the form of their membership in Kisan Sabha committees at the village level, their substantial financial contributions, and their supplying of provisions for activists.[31]

Baba Ramchandra highlights the role of Chamars and Pasis not because he sees them as landless laborers whose interests converged with those of peasants, but because he recognizes them as an important peasant group in the Awadh region. Thus, in Rae Bareli, the key theater of the Kisan Sabha movement, Chamars paid an annual rent of Rs 75,820 in 1898 for 19,005 *bighas* of land held under occupancy rights.[32] Similarly, members of the Dalit Pasi caste paid an annual rent of Rs 198,546 and cultivated 49,729 *bighas* of land. Compared with the Kurmis' 42,380 *bighas* and Muraos' 45,574 *bighas,* the area cultivated by the Chamars and Pasis is impressive and attests to their substantial position as cultivating peasants in the area rather than simply as landless laborers. These figures also indicate that many Dalit groups had very good reasons for joining the Kisan Sabha movement. Indeed, to exclude Pasis and Chamars from the Kisan Sabha movement on the grounds of occupational identities or on the assumption that they were landless laborers would amount to perpetuating colonial stereotypes about them. It is time that we rethink the widely shared assumption that the Kisan Sabha movement only addressed the concerns of lower castes, and recognize that Dalit caste groups joined it because it addressed their concern with *kisani kaam* (agricultural work) as well.

Even when the overarching historiographic framework is not a nationalist one, Dalit agendas are typically made to take a back seat. Vijay Prashad's sympathetic account of the Balmiki Sweepers' Union's labor strike in *Subaltern Studies* 10 is, for example, more centrally concerned with the socialist and anti-imperialist agendas of the left than with helping readers better understand the agendas and actions of this union. Prashad argues that the union's refusal to sustain an alliance with the Communist Party of India (CPI) destroyed a key opportunity for a radical transformation of its struggle. The union's first action was a hunger strike at which it also issued a charter of "eleven demands." Unfortunately, Prashad does not consider the Balmiki sweepers' "eleven demands" worthy of discussion, and he gives us no sense of what they contained. This is because the Balmiki agendas are not central to Prashad's main argument that Balmiki liberation was only possible under the socialist leadership of the CPI. In order to demonstrate this thesis, he devotes two-thirds of his article to proving the reactionary character of the Indian state by arguing that its promise of freedom to Dalits has remained elusive. Prashad identifies three possible strategies of liberation available to Dalits at the time of independence. The first focused on territorial independence by demanding a separate Achhutistan, or an independent nation-state. The second strategy sought a "cultural parity" with the Hindu community. The third and most viable strategy, according to Prashad, was the "socialist liberation" of the Balmiki struggle, which was led by the CPI.[33] In Prashad's essay we learn very little about the initiatives taken by the Balmikis themselves in the alliance set up by the CPI, or about the reasons behind their decision not to sustain a relationship with the CPI. The mere participation by the activists of the CPI in the Balmiki struggles does not in and of itself make it a movement of socialist liberation. It is evident in Prashad's discussion that the Balmikis' charter of eleven demands, their hunger and labor strikes, and their entire series of demonstrations were all organized independently of the CPI, but we are given no explanation into the nature of their engagement with the left. The most important conclusion that can be drawn from Prashad's discussion of the Balmiki protesters was that they made vigorous efforts to distinguish their struggle from the CPI's by dismissing a group of its activists from the Sweepers' Union. Reading Prashad's essay, it becomes obvious that the Balmiki strikers were acutely aware of the strength of their struggle and believed that they stood to gain more from the Indian state on their own than in an alliance with the left.

Dalitbahujan, a category that represents Dalits and lower-caste groups as a single interest group, is another formulation that similarly obscures the struggles of Dalits. In this formulation, Dalits again do not appear as the primary or initiating actors, nor have we generally been given a sense of what stakes they have in such an alliance. Instead, most representations of a Dalit and Bahujan alliance are offered by lower-caste leaders who frame their own agendas as though they represent the interests of both constituencies. In *Subaltern Studies* 9 (1996), Kancha Ilaiah defines Dalitbahujans as the "united whole of Scheduled Castes, Scheduled Tribes, and the Other Backward Classes [the lower-caste groups]," who socially and culturally have been excluded from the Hindu religion and who together can "challenge the Brahmanical historiography." Ilaiah contends that the struggle of Dalitbahujans is against Brahmanism and the efforts to Hinduize Dalits, tribals, and lower-caste groups.[34] Jotirao Phule led the first known Dalitbahujan struggle against Brahmans by establishing the Satya Shodak Samaj in 1873, later writing many books on the subject. Historian Rosalind O'Hanlon has argued that Phule, who belonged to the Mali caste (a lower caste), "posited conflict between Brahmans and the lower castes as a central feature of Maharashtrian culture."[35] Similarly, by establishing the Justice Party in 1917 and the Self-Respect Movement in 1925 in Madras, E. V. Ramaswamy Naicker attempted to unite lower-caste and Dalit groups into a non-Brahman Dravidian movement in Tamil Nadu to challenge Brahman domination of India and its institutions.[36] Likewise, in Uttar Pradesh Babu Ram Charana, a lower-caste leader, advocated a Dalit–lower caste alliance in the 1920s. All of these movements, though led by lower-caste leaders, have sought to mobilize Dalits and other groups who are assumed to have a natural opposition to the Hindu religion and its caste Hindu proponents.

But why has each of these writers assumed that there is a natural alliance between Dalits and lower-caste groups, and who has been the most instrumental in advocating this view? Considerable evidence suggests that lower-caste groups have historically asserted a visible Hindu identity by participating heavily in programs against Muslims and in violent reprisals against Dalits to teach them to remain "untouchable." In the cow protection movement in the 1880s and 1890s, for example, lower-caste groups like

Yadavs (Ahirs) and Kurmis targeted not only Muslims but also untouchables as *gau-hatyares* (cow killers) because some members of each of these groups were involved in the trade in hides and skins.[37] Dalit activists and intellectuals in North India have consistently challenged Dalitbahujan formulations on the grounds that Shudras, lower castes like Yadavs and Kurmis, are staunch defenders of Hindu religion and identity. Indeed, it is incorrectly assumed that Babu Ram Charana was a Dalit and a member of the Adi-Hindu Mahasabha.[38] In the 1920s and 1930s Dalit leaders like Swami Achhutanand actively opposed lower-caste leader Babu Ram Charana's calls for a Dalit-Shudra alliance.

Another area of obfuscation is mainstream Indian historiography's anxiety surrounding what Nandini Gooptu describes as "the efforts of Hindu reformist and revivalist groups to incorporate the untouchables into the caste hierarchy" of Hindu society.[39] A prominent theme within Indian historiography has been the efforts of Hindu reform groups like the Arya Samaj to reclaim "untouchables" within the fold of a newly imagined Hindu community that would be more inclusive.[40] In his chapter on the Balmikis of Punjab, Vijay Prashad argues that the Arya Samaj established *achhutuddhar* (uplift) organizations that asked Dalits to abandon "evil habits" like eating carrion and drinking alcoholic beverages, and instead follow Hindu practices.[41] In this type of narrative, Dalits do not appear as actors with their own agendas but rather as the objects of reforms. In contrast to this approach, chapter 4 reformulates the Arya Samaj's relationship with Hindu religion and society to claim that it responded to an agenda of reform outlined by the Chamars in western Uttar Pradesh. Evidence suggests that the Arya Samaj was reacting to Dalit initiatives in its Dalit-focused social reform efforts rather than the other way around. Through their agendas, Dalit activists have questioned the principle of inequality central to the Hindu religion. The first Chamar histories, written in Hindi and published in the 1910s and 1920s, worked out a set of arguments to claim a status equal to caste Hindus. For instance, the author of the Hindi-language *Shree Chanvar Purana* (A Puranic History of Chamars), published in Aligarh in the second decade of the twentieth century, stated that the Chamars were one of the great Kshatriya castes, who lost their status because one of their rulers showed disrespect for Vedic rituals. He further argued that this fact is attested to by the *Mahabharata,* which mentions the Chanvar dynasty.[42] Chamars were an agrarian group with a strong presence in the western part of the state, and their claim to equal status and Kshatriya lineage was part of a wider mobilization by lower-caste groups, including Jats and Ahirs, who were simultaneously making similar claims.

In short, the assumption that Chamars are and always have been leather-workers has been shared by colonial, nationalist, and postcolonial writers. This, in turn, has had important consequences for the study of Chamar society and history by creating two myths. The first is that modernization of the leather industry resulted in the creation of a prosperous Chamar elite in early twentieth-century Uttar Pradesh, reinforcing a natural association between caste and occupation even under conditions of modernity. The second myth is that because of both their occupational stereotype and their marginal role in Indian society, Chamars must have been natural supporters of the Congress-led nationalist mobilization in North India. As late as the 1990s, an absence of research on Dalits in Uttar Pradesh has been taken as evidence of the nonexistence of an independent Dalit movement. Finally, the fact that Dalits' own agendas do not tend to advance those of caste Hindus, Indian nationalists, or even the Marxist movements has meant that there has been little space within these other movements for the recognition of Dalit concerns. Dominant discourses have centered on elite and subaltern contributions to the nationalist movement, the agency of a radical peasantry belonging to lower-caste social groups, the possibilities of radical socialist transformation, and the agendas of Hindu social reform organizations. These dominant discursive formations have played a significant role in denying Dalits a place in Indian history as actors with their own agendas and initiatives.

Chamar Narratives: The Question of Sources

The last two chapters of this book introduce Chamar narratives that contest dominant interpretations of their occupations and identities and of Indian history more generally. Chamar activists in the first half of the twentieth century rarely directed their opposition against the colonial presence in India, nor were Chamars and other Dalits keen to show their loyalty to the struggle led by the Indian National Congress party against the British. The first Chamar activism in North India occurred in response to Hindu religious justifications of untouchability and hierarchical practices. Chamar activists and writers expressed their opposition by publishing Hindi-language books and pamphlets and by creating new organizations in the first three decades of the twentieth century. From the inception of the Adi-Hindu movement in the mid-1920s in North India, its social and political agenda was directed against the Congress because of the Congress's failure to address the issue of caste inequality. As a salient feature of its political strategy, the activists of the Adi-Hindu Mahasabha would stage vocal pro-British demonstrations at the same time that the Congress was staging its anti-British demonstrations.

A new Dalit history demands that scholars reassess available methodological tools and theories on two levels. First, we need to distinguish between the production of colonial knowledge for imperial projects like the census and the production of local knowledge in local districts by officers. These are two interrelated but distinct processes.[43] An overwhelming focus on the census and its modalities of representation of Indian society in the nineteenth century (e.g., tribe and caste surveys) has reduced the diversity of colonial archives to a single imperial monolith.[44] Only by recognizing the strength and diversity of the district and provincial repositories, in comparison with the imperial archives located in the metropolitan centers of Delhi and London, can we can break the impasse created by colonial knowledge. Records of local knowledge, like settlement reports, tenancy inquiries, and monographs on specific districts, contain accounts and narratives that are not concerned with meeting the objectives of census or other forms of classification. Operating within the domain of rent and revenue, the meticulously detailed settlement reports contain rich social and cultural histories of their districts. In his introduction to William Crooke's 1879 glossary of North Indian agricultural life, Shahid Amin writes, "The influence of caste, class and sect is largely absent from [Crooke's] compendium of agricultural and rural terms." Addressing the reason for issuing a new edition of the glossary in 1995, Amin claims that it "will aid a fuller understanding of rural north India, past and present," because it "contains a wealth of very useful information."[45] Repositories of local knowledge, like Crooke's glossary, were compiled for many reasons, and they created opportunities for district-level officers to contradict and challenge dominant frameworks and conventions that might not accurately represent their local society.

Chapter 2's argument that Chamars were much more likely to have been agricultural peasants than leatherworkers was made possible by paying close attention to details and to voices of dissent in settlement reports and land tenure inquiries. District-level settlement reports of the 1830s–40s, the 1880s–

90s, the 1910s–20s, and the 1940s provide a wealth of detailed information about Chamars, their occupational patterns, and their relationships with agriculture and cultivation. Settlement officers of Etawah, Saharanpur, Jhansi, and Moradabad districts show remarkable insight and awareness in their reports by challenging all-India census categories and ethnographic accounts that conflated and obfuscated the position of Chamars in the rural society of Uttar Pradesh. Various reports on and inquiries into the tenurial rights of peasants, which have been used extensively by historians of agrarian relations to understand colonial land tenure policies, need to be read again to understand the position of Dalit groups like Chamars and Pasis in North India.[46] These sources have opened up new possibilities for writing a social history of Chamars that emphasizes the nature of their relationships with land and agricultural life. Such sources provide more authoritative archival evidence about Chamars' agrarian practices and living conditions in nineteenth-century Uttar Pradesh than do caste Hindu religious texts, and serve to counter longstanding occupational stereotypes.

It is in the provincial archives—in the words of officials writing police reports and inquiries that were often ignored or sidelined—that we will find the small voices of dissent and confusion. Often such accounts were dismissed precisely because they did not fit with the dominant colonial stereotypes and categorizations made available in the census and ethnographic accounts, but instead raised problems with them. Such reports typically did not make it to the Indian Office archives in London or the National Archives of India in Delhi but remained in local provincial archives. For this reason, a reliance on archival research conducted only in metropolitan centers provides insights only into the dominant received formulations of Indian history and society. The multiple and often contradictory interpretations of data and the many expressions of dissent and confusion present within district-level reports disappeared by the time more "appropriate" and coherent reports were drawn up by the administrative officials in state capitals, to be dispatched to the viceroy's office in Delhi and the India Office in London. Chapter 1's analysis of the debates surrounding cattle poisoning was made possible by paying close attention to dissenting voices in official accounts. Examination of the annual provincial police proceedings makes it clear that the widespread colonial accusations that Chamars engaged in organized cattle poisoning were not accepted by all local colonial officials. Such points of view are absent from the widely cited "Papers Relating to the Crime of Cattle Poisoning," a report that is available in the metropolitan archives of Delhi and London but is not found in the Uttar Pradesh state archive.

Nonetheless, despite being ignored by mainstream historians, Dalit writers and activists have kept histories of their struggles alive by publishing their own versions of histories and by relying on their own presses, such as Bahujan Kalyan Prakashan in Lucknow, which began publishing in the 1930s. In this book's reconsideration of the place of Dalit history within larger narratives of Indian history, I have relied substantially on Chamar narratives present in Hindi-language sources produced throughout the twentieth century. Chapters 4 and 5 are based on Hindi-language Chamar histories collected during fieldwork in various parts of Uttar Pradesh. In conjunction with fieldwork interviews, claims made in these accounts were corroborated by the weekly reports of intelligence and police departments of the Uttar Pradesh government. I found these to be crucial sources for information on the activities of Chamar and Dalit organizations at the ground level. Indeed, weekly police records of the Criminal Investigation Department (CID) of the Uttar Pradesh government between 1922 and 1948 have proven to be a very useful and previously untapped set of sources. The police were keen to report on fissures within the Congress-led anti-colonial movement, and one of the ways they did this was by carefully documenting the activities of Chamar and Dalit organizations, activities that are conspicuously absent from the nationalist accounts of this same period. Police accounts of the Dalit and Chamar movements were further validated by reports in vernacular Hindi newspapers and magazines which occasionally took notice of Dalit struggles and commented upon the notable size and strength of their protests and activities. In the end it is the police reports that provide detailed reports, and not the nationalist sources. Indeed, given the immense value of these colonial government sources for writing Dalit histories, it is surprising that no one has yet tapped them for this purpose.

Instead of simply looking for elements of autonomy and resistance in Chamar narratives, I have sought to bring historical narratives documenting the many active Chamar agendas into conversation with mainstream Indian historiography. Chamar and Dalit histories published in the first five decades of the twentieth century are discussed extensively in chapters 4 and 5. These chapters use the widespread evidence of Chamar political struggle discovered in the archives to create a conversation with and challenge existing mainstream narratives of Indian history. Conversations and interviews with individual Dalits and with Dalit discussion groups in 1992–93 and from 1998 to 2002 in Delhi, Agra, Allahabad, Kanpur, and Lucknow helped me to form specific questions that I was able to take with me to the colonial archives. What was remarkable was how much the contemporary concerns of the Dalits I spoke with resonated with historical evidence of ongoing struggles and agendas dating back to the earliest decades of the twentieth century. As just one of many examples, the refrain of many I spoke with that they have always worked on the land helped me to examine more closely the relationship of Chamars with agriculture as it is recorded in the colonial archive. This yielded the quite startling results discussed in chapter 2. Indeed, the combination of ethnographic fieldwork and archival research was decisive in helping locate sources that had not previously been catalogued and that have therefore never been consulted by historians, such as the "UP Memoranda (non-official) to Indian Statutory Commission" in the Q series of the India office collection in the British Library. These unexamined sources were crucial in enabling me to understand the agenda of the Adi-Hindu Mahasabha and other Dalit organizations.

These strategies, focusing on provincial and district-level sources and engaging with the agendas outlined in Chamar and Dalit Hindi writings, have proven most useful in reassessing the social and cultural history of North India, as well as in helping us to recognize and understand Chamars' contestations of the dominant narratives that have produced accepted versions of Indian history. They have enabled me to rethink the history of Dalits outside of the dyad of colonialism versus nationalism that has shaped Indian historiography for the last century. Indeed, from the point of view of the Chamar accounts used in this book, colonial and nationalist discourses begin to appear as a single shared narrative.

* * *

Moving beyond the confines of identity or ethnicity politics, Dalit struggles have offered a resounding critique of social and cultural practices that have defined the shared frameworks of colonialism and nationalism. We can today speak of this critique as a movement, a perspective that has equipped us with tools and methods to question principles of hierarchy and discrimination. From its inception in the early decades of the twentieth century, the Dalit movement has interrogated hierarchical practices associated with Hinduism and nationalism, especially the persistent occupational stereotypes of Chamars and other Dalit groups. A Dalit critique of Indian historiography opens new debates about Indian history.

I have suggested that many nineteenth- and early twentieth-century attitudes and concerns resonate with present-day agendas and perspectives. The rest of this study builds the case that Chamar activists and ideologues have reenvisioned identity in an effort to question colonial and nationalist narratives that have described and circumscribed their origins, their pasts, their occupations, and their present-day identities and future possibilities. These efforts have been directed at eliminating the representations of the supposed impurity of their lives and have involved launching a series of struggles to achieve equal status for all Dalits on the basis of this new identity. The many documents I have been able to locate in the archives have contributed to the writing of this new counterhistory, but I would not have known to search for many of them in the first place had it not been for the many Dalits who were willing to share with me their alternative interpretations of their own pasts. Many sustained discussions with Dalit friends and acquaintances in Delhi and Uttar Pradesh and close readings of Chamars' own histories and writings have made me aware that Dalits' perspectives on their own histories are often dramatically different from the history taught in Indian universities and abroad. And it has been these perspectives which have motivated me to search for the possibility that a different story exists in the archives from the one that I had been taught during my formal education in school and university. I offer this book, then, as a way of thanking all those who took the time to share their perspectives with me, in the hope that the received wisdom of the dominant narratives can be changed by bringing Dalit perspectives and historical writings more centrally into the writing of Indian history, where they properly belong.

CHAPTER I

Making Chamars Criminal:
The Crime of Cattle Poisoning

*I have noticed with regret a development of crime which I had
never suspected, and which for its far-reaching effects may be
described as utterly diabolical. Chamars, we all know, will poison
cattle for the sake of their skins, but with each individual act the
mischief never ends. Here, however, we have the infected flesh
carried from place to place, and made the means of disseminating
the disease.*

—WILLIAM HOEY, August 26, 1899

*Dubey stumbled upon this discovery [of the cause of cattle deaths]
only accidentally. The condition of affected cows in the Sadan
initially made him suspect the neighbouring hide flayers [the
Chamars] of organised poisoning [of] the cattle.*

—*Times of India*, April 1, 2000

By the end of the nineteenth century, accusations of cattle poisoning
against Chamars had become the standard bureaucratic response to
large-scale cattle deaths. William Hoey's 1899 statement regarding the
criminality of Chamars was not an isolated accusation. The commissioner
of Gorakhpur was simply summing up the official view. He had, however,
discovered what he believed to be a new feature of Chamars' criminality.

Moreover, the association of Chamars with cattle poisoning did not disappear with the end of colonialism. A hundred years later, while conducting fieldwork in Lucknow, I read of the very same suspicions against Chamars in a national daily. The news story was trying to account for recent cattle deaths in Lucknow. The sudden increase in cattle mortality had made one officer, Ranjan Dubey of the Lucknow Municipal Corporation's *gaushala* (cattle shed), suspicious of the Chamars, leading him to accuse them of poisoning cattle for the sake of their hides. Only upon investigation did he confirm, as the local tanner had already told him, the presence of large numbers of polythene bags in the stomachs of dead cows.[1] In 1899 a white colonial officer accused Chamars of cattle poisoning, while a century later it was a Brahman Indian officer.

These accusations reflect the dominant view of Chamars as natural criminals because of what is assumed to be their traditional occupation. Both colonial and postcolonial officials have argued that Chamars had and continue to have an economic motive for poisoning cattle. Since tanning and shoemaking have been regarded as the hereditary occupations of those from the Chamar caste, their rights to fallen cattle have been considered payment for other forms of low-status labor performed within the village. The colonial state first put forward this view in 1854 by singling out the crime of cattle poisoning not just as an occasional occurrence, but explicitly as an "organised and professional crime." Later colonial accounts repeatedly claimed to have uncovered instances of this crime.[2] Before long the association of Chamars with cattle poisoning was extended to all crimes relating to cattle, including theft and the spread of cattle disease.

The colonial state did not merely rely on tradition. It also deployed "modern scientific" methods to corroborate its thesis. By conducting chemical tests to prove the use of arsenic in particular cattle poisoning incidents, the officers based their accusations of the criminality of Chamars on scientific evidence. Possession of arsenic by a Chamar (though not by others) became a mark of criminal intent and sufficient reason for arrest. Interestingly, this logic did not extend to non-Chamars engaged in the leather trade. Yet the colonial narrative of an "organised and professional crime," available in the metropolitan archives, could not withstand the scrutiny of all colonial officers. The colonial sources containing notes from local officers that are available only in the provincial archives offer us evidence to challenge the dominant narrative by establishing evidence of Chamars' involvement with the hide trade, with cattle, and with agriculture, suggesting that, far from being engaged in "organised and professional crime," individuals from the Chamar caste were involved in the export of raw hide as legitimate and enterprising entrepreneurs, no less professional than Muslims and others who were also engaged in the leather trade.

Like Ahirs and Jats, Chamars were not categorized as criminal castes under the Criminal Tribes Act of 1871, but were nevertheless described and pursued as criminal castes throughout the nineteenth century.[3] According to the 1881 census, the Chamar caste was the largest Hindu caste in Uttar Pradesh, comprising nearly 14.1 percent of the total Hindu population (appendix, table A).[4] The colonial state could not have categorized them as criminal, as the Chamars constituted one of the largest agrarian groups in the state, well settled in the craft of agricultural production. But this did not deter the British from characterizing Ahirs, Gujars, Jats, and Chamars settled in agricultural communities as castes with criminal tendencies.

Anand Yang has argued that the notion of hereditary criminals was "in conformity with prevailing criminological theories" of nineteenth-century Britain. The colonial state assumed that "not only were the dangerous castes readily identifiable, but their criminal tendencies were deeply anchored in the structure and functioning of Indian society," and this assumption was premised on a neat division of castes.[5] Groups with criminal traits, the dangerous castes belonged to Shudra and untouchable communities. In addition to "genetic traits," the colonial state recognized two other characteristic features of criminal castes and tribes: their "peripatetic lifestyle" and their position as the lowest in the Hindu ritual hierarchy.[6] Extending Yang's argument, Sanjay Nigam asserts that the colonial discourse, based on orientalist assumptions about Indian society, created stereotypes of criminal castes and tribes. Such a discursive production of criminality had little to do with "facts and figures" but alluded instead "to a mode of interpretation and argument which helped cast the record of these crimes into a pre-existing mould."[7] In her study of the Mev community in Rajasthan, Shail Mayaram explains that "the systematic construction of a mythology of criminality took place under the guise of 'scientific' modes of enquiry and description." The construction of Mev criminality "was founded not on case histories and police reports but originated from the premises of colonial intellectual practice."[8]

There is little doubt that the nineteenth-century ethnographic literature (which includes the census and accounts of castes and tribes) played an important role in constructing stereotypes of criminal castes and tribes, on the basis of nineteenth-century British ideas of criminality by birth. In the case of the Chamar caste, too, the colonial state created a stereotype by linking their caste occupation with cattle poisoning. Indeed, colonial historiography presents us with a dominant narrative which produces the community of Chamars of Uttar Pradesh as "natural" criminals. It is possible, however, to write an alternative history of Chamars by drawing from colonial archives located at the provincial and district levels. For instance, the police reports from the eastern districts of Uttar Pradesh that document cattle poisoning also offer us interesting insights into the Chamars' relationship with the leather trade and cattle. Such evidence serves to raise questions, reveal inconsistencies, and trouble dominant all-India narratives.[9]

The historiography of criminal castes, which considers the formulation of stereotypes by the colonial writers, has located their emergence firmly within the dominant colonial discourse. Blaming the colonial state for the stereotypical representation of Chamars as criminal begs the question of how this colonial formulation has come to be accepted by Hindu society. There is some merit to Andrew Major's claim that "the stereotype of the wandering hereditary criminal was not entirely constructed out of thin air."[10] Instead of viewing cattle poisoning as a caste crime by the Mahar "untouchables" of Maharashtra, Hiroyuki Kotani contends that it was a strategy by the hereditary inferior village officials, the Vatandar Mahars, in their struggle against the dominant peasant groups to maintain their control over the office of Vatandar.[11] Radhika Singha's nuanced study of colonial law and criminal communities is one exception to recent critiques of colonial discourse.[12] The elite caste Hindu attitudes to "the poor and low castes" were also based on "criminality by birth" arguments. Some sections of Hindu society were equally receptive to colonial formulations of Chamar criminality and that of other Dalit castes.

Constructing the Criminality of Chamars

Colonial officials relied upon the reports and conclusions of earlier officials in a chain of evidence that most often leads back to more such accounts. The correlation of caste and crime was worked out between the 1850s and 1870s, and historicizing it was crucial to the officials' argument. Norman Chevers, a medical official, noted in 1870 that cattle poisoning was not a new crime, claiming that in ancient times the Hindus were cautioned against cattle poisoning and that the *Manusmriti* mentions ways to dispose of the carcass of a cow to prevent it from coming into the hands of Chamars. Chevers went on to compare Chamars with the Gypsies of England (and Europe), who were "notorious for this practice" of cattle poisoning. Narrating various isolated incidents of cattle poisoning in different parts of India by Chamars, Chevers credited George Campbell, magistrate of Azamgarh, with discovering "a surprisingly extensive system of cattle poisoning" in 1854 which was linked to the trade in raw hides and arsenic. According to Chevers, the crime was first reported in 1831 by a British officer on the Grand Trunk route in Uttar Pradesh, before it had developed into an organized crime.[13] Chevers's account was extensively cited by the report of the Indian Cattle Plague Commission when it laid out a history of cattle poisoning in India. The Commission's report listed several instances of cattle poisoning: in Sholapur in the Bombay Presidency in 1846, in the Saran district of Bihar in 1851, in 1852–53 in Pubna and Jessore in Bengal, and multiple cases in the 1860s in the Madras Presidency and Punjab.[14] Nevertheless, the existence of an organized system of cattle poisoning was presented as unique to Uttar Pradesh. The Commission repeatedly singled out George Campbell's investigation in 1854 for making the "most important discovery of an organised system of cattle poisoning."[15] Campbell's report is foundational in emphasizing two constitutive features of the crime: first by insisting that the possession of arsenic by Chamars constituted evidence of their guilt, and second by advocating the procurement of a confession. These two features quickly became the key components in the persecution of Chamars and a reference point for all subsequent accounts of cattle poisoning.

George Campbell first reported the crime in October 1854 when he arrested fifty-four persons on the charge of poisoning cattle "for the sake of their hides." By the end of October he had convicted five hundred Chamars out of some fifteen hundred arrested. According to Campbell the crucial evidence for the prosecution of Chamars was the possession of arsenic, and all five charges by Campbell are framed this way: "conspiracy to poison cattle for the sake of skins," "individuals distributing arsenic with a view to poison cattle for the sake of their skins," "selling arsenic in large quantities . . . for most unlawful purpose," "secretly selling arsenic under the strong presumption that the same will be used for illegal purposes," and finally "poisoning certain cattle of certain individuals for the sake of hides."[16]

During their investigations Campbell and his assistants obtained numerous confessions from Chamars admitting to the use of arsenic. He also notes, interestingly, that this admission of guilt was an expression of public spirit hitherto unknown in India. Convinced that arsenic was being extensively used in cattle poisoning, Campbell believed that "a large portion of the population has been familiarized with the use of a most fearful instrument of destruction."[17] He successfully created an image of Chamars as violent and dangerous criminals, portraying the crime in eastern districts of Uttar Pradesh as something of an epidemic. He urged the government to enact laws to deal with this peculiar crime and to regulate the sale of arsenic.

Another significant feature of Campbell's method of investigation was his emphasis on the economic motive for the crime. He identified the distribution network of arsenic, consisting of the leather merchants and traders who loaned money to village Chamars for its purchase and distribution, as the font "from which the whole system [of cattle poisoning] flowed."[18] Two trading towns of eastern Uttar Pradesh, Kopagunj in Azamgarh district and Bahadurgunj in Gorakhpur district, were identified as the main centers of crime. Campbell's investigation into Kopagunj provides us with information concerning the so-called network. The traders of Patna imported large quantities of arsenic from Calcutta and passed it to merchants in Kopagunj, who dispersed it to the leather merchants and Chamars in eastern Uttar Pradesh. The suppliers of arsenic bought hides from the Chamars, taking a third of them in return for the arsenic and paying for the rest. In cash transactions, a fixed price was put on the arsenic and deducted from the price of the skins. The *dalals* or brokers collected their commissions by charging a percentage of the price of the arsenic and hides. The leather merchants collected a substantial quantity of hides at very low prices, while the traders gained through their premium prices for illegal arsenic and also through their high sales of the poison. According to Campbell, traders "sworn to secrecy" roamed the countryside, distributing poison "to subordinate agents along with advances for leather, and the latter distributed it to the village Chamars."[19] There is no doubt in Campbell's report that a conspiracy was operating at various levels.

By the end of the nineteenth century the colonial discourse had already established a context where the relationship between caste and occupation was considered hereditary. Campbell's report of 1854 emphasized that Chamars' caste and occupation allowed them rights over dead cattle. In it, he referred to the "system under which the Chamars become possessed of the bodies and the skins of the dead animals." According to Campbell, under this system the Chamars "perform certain services for the cultivators, and receive the bodies of all the animals belonging to their own particular cultivators which die." Campbell concluded that "chamars, when they poison a particular animal, obtain possession of the body in virtue of a prescriptive right of the nature of a contract, and well established."[20] In his report on female infanticide among the Rajputs of Azamgarh, Campbell had similarly attributed a high percentage of cases to their caste.[21] The relationship between caste and crime was far more strongly argued by the colonial Thuggee department in its campaigns in the 1830s. W. H. Sleeman, the founder of campaigns against Thuggees in India, consistently argued that crime in India was organized along caste lines.[22] In the context of the Thuggee Act of 1836 and 1843, Radhika Singha has argued that it was easier to prosecute a collective criminal community than to establish individual responsibility.[23] Almost half a century later, in 1899, William Hoey considered the association of Chamars with cattle poisoning natural and unremarkable.[24]

In 1869 the government conducted an inquiry to document the extent of cattle diseases, an investigation which was extended by the British government to other provinces as well. The colonial concern for cattle deaths had a more immediate cause in Uttar Pradesh—the "discovery" of an extremely high cattle mortality. In 1869 the government received a report of unusually frequent cattle deaths in the districts of Hardoi and Banda. In Banda in June, 2461 cattle had died out of an estimated 5035.[25] This unusual death rate, a blemish on the colonial government's claim of efficient administration, needed some explanation. The popular explanation for cattle mortality at the time attributed the deaths to a disease called *puschima,* or "Western," a disease known in Europe as rinderpest (a form of cattle plague or foot-and-mouth disease). Popular opinion held government cattle responsible for its spread. The cattle in military cantonments, which were imported for draught purposes, for consumption, and for crossbreeding, were held particularly responsible for the cattle plague because they were known to be imported from England. H. Farrell, a veterinary surgeon of the Bengal government, was eager to demonstrate that rinderpest (under the "various names given to it") had a local history and was not of "recent importation."[26] With the rebellion of 1857 still fresh in their minds, the British were acutely aware of the potential role of rumor in undermining their authority. The 1869 inquiry was a response to widespread popular accusation against the colonial state, and its conclusions similarly sought to deflect blame away from the colonial authority.

Farrell's investigation in the Bengal Presidency informs us that cattle disease had an annual character in India and tended to assume epidemic proportions at regular intervals.[27] He refuted the existence of rinderpest by arguing that the annual loss of cattle was relatively small when compared with the high mortality usually associated with rinderpest. His refusal to accept the existence of rinderpest was also meant as a rejection of the theory that cattle imported from the West were the cause of cattle deaths. A substantive statement to this effect was put forward in the report of the Indian Cattle Plague Commission in 1871. Further, the commission accused the Chamars of taking advantage of the cattle plague to poison the cattle, because the symptoms of poison and of cattle plague were often very similar, making it difficult to differentiate between the two. In its report the commission came to the remarkable conclusion that the high rate of cattle mortality was primarily due to poisoning by the Chamars, who "work[ed] under the cloak of *murrain*" (rinderpest).[28]

Cattle poisoning was rarely reported between 1857 and 1870, until R. D. Spedding's reports from Gorakhpur in 1873 and 1878, which located the crime, once again, in the eastern districts of Uttar Pradesh. In the aftermath of the 1857 rebellion and the transition from Company to crown rule in India, a new set of concerns had acquired importance for the officials, one of which was to reestablish the British administration in North India. Before Spedding's report, the 1869 "Report on Cattle Diseases" and the 1871 report of the Indian Cattle Plague Commission mentioned systematic cattle poisoning by Chamars. Spedding's 1873 and 1878 reports built on the earlier accounts in holding Chamars responsible for the "organised crime of cattle poisoning."[29] In addition, Campbell's and Spedding's investigations shared a remarkable feature: in both cases the crime of cattle poisoning was never identified or reported by the people. The two district magistrates, Campbell and Spedding, had initiated the police investigations on their own initiative. Cattle poisoning was not yet a cognizable crime and therefore its investigation required prior permission from the district magistrate.

The most distinctive feature of Spedding's 1873 and 1878 reports is that they for the first time assumed a natural connection between Chamars' traditional occupation and cattle poisoning. These reports no longer felt it necessary to advance an economic motive for the crime. Spedding launched police investigations against Chamars merely on suspicion rather than on any hard evidence, arresting Chamars found possessing arsenic. He also focused on the role of arsenic and the supposed "organized" character of cattle poisoning. In his view the role of Muslim hide dealers was limited to giving advances for hides.[30] Making a clear distinction between Muslim and Chamar hide dealers, Spedding was keen to demonstrate the role of Chamars, both as poisoners and as distributors of arsenic, by showing an arsenic distribution network that connected Gorakhpur to Lower Bengal. In particular he highlighted the role of Boolakee Chamar of Dinapur (Bengal) as a key supplier of arsenic in eastern Uttar Pradesh to Toofanee Chamar of Azamgarh and Kutwaroo, Ramgati, Chitani, Jatan, and Bhajan Chamars of Gorakhpur.[31] Spedding's report was part of a wider effort to document and report organized cattle poisoning. Like Campbell, Spedding concluded that the crime could only be prevented by banning the sale of arsenic.

By the 1880s police reports began to identify new facets of Chamar criminality. Chamars were increasingly accused of a whole clutch of crimes against cattle, not just poisoning. It was argued that, as a consequence of stringent police action against cattle poisoners, Chamars had shifted to the crime of cattle theft. This development was first noted in the 1883 police reports of Barabanki in the Awadh region.[32] But soon such crime was noted in other districts of eastern Uttar Pradesh, like Mirzapur and Ghazipur.[33] Noting another aspect of this "shift," the 1894 police reports claimed that Chamars "have added the still more brutal practice of flaying cattle alive," adding that "this practice was discovered in Benares and Jaunpur Districts and something somewhat similar was reported from Ballia."[34] From Jaunpur and Benares districts, this crime spread to Gorakhpur in 1894. The 1894 and 1895 reports claimed that the practice of flaying live cattle had spread to all the districts of eastern Uttar Pradesh: Azamgarh, Benares, Ballia, Mirzapur, Gorakhpur, Ghazipur and Jaunpur.[35]

In August 1899, the commissioner of Gorakhpur division, William Hoey, accused Chamars of systematically spreading cattle plague from village to village in Azamgarh district. Hoey had discovered what he believed was a novel aspect of Chamars' criminality. The Chamars, according to him, carried the infected flesh from place to place to disseminate the disease, a safer method for killing cattle than using poison. He pointed to a complaint made by Har Narain Singh from a village in Sarda which claimed that Chamar women were spreading the disease by carrying the infected flesh from village to village in the guise of performing *puja*.[36] Hoey's accusations, similar to those of the Indian Cattle Plague Commission report of 1871, coincided with a virulent cattle plague in Azamgarh that led to a large number of cattle deaths. By accusing Chamars, Hoey was absolving the administration from any responsibility.

Hoey provided a scientific rationale to support his stand in the form of a report by L. Rogers, a government bacteriologist. Rogers agreed with Hoey that it was possible to spread the infection "by means of the blood or the intestinal contents being carried from one village to another."[37] He recommended that the most effective way of preventing the spread of plague would be to bury all cattle that died of rinderpest, advising that this be required by law. He also added, drawing from his experience of the Himalayan region, that there was a widespread belief that Chamars spread the disease. W. H. Moreland, director of the Land Records and Agriculture Department, approved these suggestions and forwarded them to the Uttar Pradesh government for adoption as a general policy targeting Chamars.[38] On December 7, 1899, the Uttar Pradesh government issued a general order to all commissioners of Uttar Pradesh adopting Moreland's suggestion. The new policy first argued that Chamars artificially spread the cattle plague, and therefore cases of cattle death by disease should be investigated. Second, it proclaimed that cultivators should be "advised to destroy the hides of cattle dying of disease and never to give them to the Chamars."[39] Hoey's accusation against the Chamars was not an exception. By 1899 his view reflected a substantial body of literature that had already elaborated the linkages between Chamars and cattle plague. From Spedding in 1873 to Hoey in 1899, colonial officials repeatedly relied on assertions made by earlier officials in order to claim a "natural" link between Chamars and cattle deaths through poisoning, disease, and plague.

The Role of Arsenic: First Doubts

The dominant narrative of an organized crime of cattle poisoning was worked out by the colonial state in the second half of the nineteenth century. But colonial sources not explicitly concerned with generalizing about cultural communities and their typical practices suggest an alternative history of cattle poisoning. The role of arsenic was central to the colonial un-

derstanding of the crime, and banning it was the key demand of the officials. But the trade in arsenic was neither banned nor regulated. Representing
voices of dissent, some officers and local officials recognized in their reports
that arsenic was an important chemical used for medical and commercial
purposes, including as a preservative of hides.

Despite the lack of evidence, Campbell insisted that arsenic was used to
poison cattle, because he was convinced that Chamars did so. In an 1854 report on the arsenic trade, Campbell argued that arsenic was imported primarily to poison cattle and "that this traffic has enormously increased within
the last two or three years, and especially the last year."[40] He claimed that a
massive increase in the importation of arsenic from 1853 onward contributed
to the decline in its price, by making it plentiful. The Bengal Presidency questioned Campbell's claim and argued that "from the statement of the importation of white arsenic during the last four years furnished to us by the Collector of Customs it would seem that there has been no increase of importation,
as had been supposed by Mr. G. Campbell, but on the contrary a decrease."[41]

Yet Spedding's investigation in the 1870s renewed the focus on arsenic
and prompted a new round of inquiries into its usage. These inquiries and
debates among the officials reveal that arsenic had multiple medicinal and
domestic uses. The Calcutta police commissioner admitted in 1872 that police inquiries had "ascertained that white arsenic is very extensively used
throughout India for medicinal purposes, especially with Native practitio-
ners, who hold that it ranks next to quinine, and has the advantage of being
cheaper."[42] A. C. Mangles, the collector of Patna, argued in the same year that
white arsenic (*sunkeah*) was procured and used in small quantities for medical
purposes by native druggists, used in the manufacture of fireworks, and
mixed with paint to prevent the destruction of wooden beams by white ants.
Since arsenic was effective as a preserving agent, large quantities were needed
by the Medical College hospital for injection into bodies intended for dissec-
tion. Mangles also pointed to the large purchases by the military.[43] In his 1873
report, Dr J. C. Brown mentioned that Indian druggists used arsenic extensively, providing it to patients for consumption in very small quantities.[44]

H. B. Buckle, surgeon general in the Bengal government, acknowledged in his own report that arsenic was extensively used by native Indian
druggists for medicinal purposes, being commonly prescribed for fevers,
rheumatism, skin diseases, leprosy, neuralgia, chronic diarrhea, snakebite,
impotence, and various other illnesses.[45] According to the pharmacists of

the East India Company, imported arsenic was "purchased by up-country dealers" to preserve timber and to be mixed with paint to protect "the bottoms of ships."[46] The observation made by Kanny Lall Dey, a teacher of chemistry and medical jurisprudence, that arsenic was used for curing hides gave another reason why those who handled hides might have been in legitimate possession of arsenic.[47] Indeed, it is appropriate to end this discussion with J. D. E. Holmes's conclusion. Holmes was a veterinary doctor, and in a 1912 article he concluded that "the value of arsenic in veterinary practice, as a general tonic, is well known and it is occasionally given to improve the coat and condition of horses," as well as being used widely to improve the condition of emaciated animals.[48]

What also comes across is the absence of precise knowledge about the use of arsenic as poison. The *Encyclopaedia Britannica* mentions that a dose of 0.12 gram of arsenic has caused death, though larger quantities have been taken without fatal result.[49] Likewise, individual susceptibility to arsenic poisoning varies widely, with some persons known to have developed a tolerance of doses that would kill others.[50] Nowhere in the colonial accounts is there a mention of the exact dosage required to a kill a cow. Indeed, this aspect of the matter was the least debated or discussed. Nevertheless, the absence of such data appears to have had little effect on the conviction of Chamars, because their guilt was largely decided on the basis of their confession or their possession of arsenic. The Indian Cattle Plague Commission's report acknowledged that the Chamars were convicted on the basis of confession, but not on the evidence of "the discovery of the poison in the body of the animal."[51]

Despite the absence of a clear official understanding of arsenic's poisonous characteristics, the widely shared perception was that arsenic was a potent and deadly poison in the hands of Chamars. This perception generated a debate in the colonial bureaucracy over the best method for controlling their perceived menace. The debate encompassed two strategies: to regulate or ban the sale of arsenic or to make cattle poisoning a punishable crime under the Indian Penal Code. Campbell, in pre-Mutiny days, had recourse to Muslim law, which vested considerable authority in his hands. Following George Campbell's campaign against cattle poisoning in 1854–56, the government passed Act IV of 1856, which declared the crime of cattle poisoning an offense cognizable by police, laying down severe fines and punishment. We don't have much information about the implementation of this act.[52]

The Indian Cattle Plague Commission recommended that trade in arsenic be restricted and regulated, because only by monitoring arsenic could the hide trade be scrutinized. Only the Bombay Presidency acted on the commission's recommendation, by passing the Bombay Act VIII of 1866 to restrict the sale of arsenic. This act regulated the sale of poison through licenses issued by the collector or commissioner and made registration of sales mandatory.[53] Other provincial governments did not follow the Bombay Presidency's lead. The commission's recommendation received fresh backing when cattle poisoning was reported extensively from Jaunpur district in 1869, and again after 1873 when Spedding claimed to have discovered organized poisoning in eastern Uttar Pradesh.[54] Spedding became the chief advocate for regulating the sale of arsenic and proposed elaborate networks of bureaucratic controls, and the Uttar Pradesh government made a formal request to the government of India to implement the recommendations of the commission.[55]

Act XI of 1874 declared cattle poisoning a crime cognizable by the police under the Indian Penal Code.[56] The act, however, made no effort to regulate or even hinder the trade in arsenic or in hides. It was merely a half-hearted attempt to satisfy the bureaucracy. The government of India, led by the governor-general, was opposed to any move that could harm the trade in hides. It opposed and overruled subordinate officials not because it disbelieved them, but because it also represented the commercial interests of the British East India Company and the empire. It was concerned about the possible implications of interference with the trade in hides, which made up almost 5 percent of India's total export trade.[57] From the point of view of the Indian government, regulations on the trade in hides and in arsenic were a bad business proposition. In 1880 the secretary to the Bengal government had no qualms about putting on paper the significance of arsenic for the leather industry, arguing that it was "one of the cheapest and most effective" methods of preserving the skins. This is relevant because the Bengal government was also in charge of all-India affairs. To substantiate his point, the secretary quoted Dr. Alexander Pedler, professor of chemistry in the Presidency College (Calcutta), reporting that a mixture of arsenic and lime was used to remove the hair and as a preservative for transport.[58] The 1892 police report acknowledged that arsenic was used extensively by "hide contractors" "in the preparation of hides for the export market" to pack "their hides for export to Europe."[59] In fact, not only Indian traders but also European firms supplied arsenic to their agents in Dinapur for distribution to the tanners and flayers.

The Indian government passed a resolution in February 1880 advising provincial governments not to impose any ban on the arsenic trade. It also opposed any proposal to raise the tax on the trade, because doing so would raise the price of arsenic. It even argued that the Bombay government's 1866 act to regulate the arsenic trade had proved to be ineffectual.[60] Because of this the Bombay act was not implemented elsewhere. Taken together, such debates suggest that the actual role of arsenic was secondary to the colonial prosecution of cattle poisoning as an organized crime. The conviction of the Chamars for the crime of cattle poisoning was based on their caste identity and not on the use of arsenic. Yet Muslims and other non-Chamars involved in the leather trade were never convicted or even suspected of engaging in cattle poisoning, either in individual incidents or as part of an organized criminal network. The privilege of this recognition, even in the face of little or no evidence, was saved for Chamars alone.

Making "A Scapegoat of the Village Chamar": Interrogating the Crime

The procedures by which Chamars were implicated in the crime of cattle poisoning suggest that evidence was irrelevant to their conviction. Therefore it is important to investigate the representation of the crime by investigating the investigators, the colonial officials and police personnel, and the methods adopted by them. Conviction was based entirely on the confessions extracted by the police constables. As long as the accused was a Chamar, the evidence did not matter.

The flaws in investigating the crime of cattle poisoning became evident during Campbell's investigation itself. Two *thanedars* (chiefs of police stations) of Azamgarh district, Syed Roshun Ali and Sheikh Mohamud Ali, along with their subordinates, were convicted of culpable homicide.[61] They were accused of killing two Chamars in separate incidents while forcibly extracting confessions. The Nizamut Adawlut (the superior criminal court) at the Azamgarh bench also passed strictures against Campbell for misusing the laws. These two cases, to quote the court, "represent[ed] cruelties practised by Police Officers in two different localities of the same district with the same object on the same day—29 October [1854]."[62] In the first case, the chief of police, Roshun Ally of Belurigunj, and his three *burkundauzes* (native policemen), Boodhoo

Khan, Ally Buksh, and Runjeet Khan, were accused of the killing of Ramdehul Chamar. He was arrested in connection with cattle poisoning on October
27, 1854, on the suspicion of trading in arsenic. Ramdehul Chamar denied the
charge and a search of his house also failed to produce any evidence.

The observation by M. Smith, one of the judges, is telling. Roshun Ally,
"arriving at a village during night time, seizing the inhabitants of the Chamars'
quarter (men and women), searching their houses, and finally, with a view of
extracting poison from one Ramdehul Chamar," tortured him to death. But
the *thanedar* declared that Ramdehul Chamar died after consuming arsenic, a
case of suicide. In the second case, the *thanedar* Sheikh Mahmud Ally and his
burkundauzes Ashruf Ally, Byjnath Sing, and Deen Bahadoor were also convicted of "culpable homicide." The judge, M. Smith, observed that "though he
[Mahmud Ally] had made one previous search and found nothing, [he] pro-
ceeded again to institute an enquiry regarding alleged poison in the possession
of Kodge Chamar," forcing a confession through torture resulting in his death.
The *thanedar* and his subordinates were accused not only of the culpable homicide of Kodge Chamar, but also of fabricating evidence and abusing their
official position. In this case an official witness took the police to the house of
the accused. In his memorandum the judge remarked that the two police officers should have been charged with murder and not with culpable homicide.
He argued that Campbell gave extraordinary power to subordinate native police officers and cited the October 12 communication to native policemen that
empowered them to act with or without complaint. Smith concluded that the
crime of cattle poisoning should have been considered a misdemeanor. The
crime did not require the extra-constitutional methods adopted by the magistrate, which Judge Smith described as "quite illegal."[63]

The registrar to the Nizamut Adawlut of the province, H. W. Dashwood,
endorsed Judge Smith's memorandum. The correspondence among the judicial officers and Campbell's explanation provide information about the enormous scale of these investigations. Campbell's October 12 order mobilized
the *thanedars* at the village level, who, "on hearing of cases of poisoning cattle,
whether *with or without complaint,* [proceeded] to institute enquiries, and as
far as possible discover the facts and apprehend the guilty parties."[64] Judge
Dashwood declared that Campbell's order gave local policemen a "dangerous latitude of action" that was bound to be abused. He made a particularly
telling comment concerning the lack of evidence and reliance instead upon
the caste identities of the accused to achieve conviction, observing that "it

would be likewise material to know whether, in the generality or in how many of the cases in which conviction had ensued, distinct proof was obtained of the death of the animals having been caused by *actual poison* duly traced and detected in the carcasses."[65] The sessions court judge acquitted all forty-five Chamars that Campbell had committed to the sessions court, on account of "various and serious irregularities" by Campbell.[66] As district magistrate, Campbell had arrested 765 Chamars, of whom 619 were convicted of the crime without actual evidence.

In effect, the judges accused Campbell of abusing power at the cost of the law of the land. They questioned his judgment in addressing the crime under Muslim law when the English law provided adequate guards.[67] Indeed, William Muir, the secretary of the Uttar Pradesh government, had approved Campbell's special request to launch criminal and judicial proceedings against the Chamars. Because cattle poisoning was a non-cognizable crime, he needed prior approval from judicial and administrative officers, including an arrest warrant, to launch his campaign. Yet Campbell relied more on Muslim law. He was accused of having had recourse to a provision of Muslim law called *tazeer* (or *tazir*), which allowed discretionary powers to a *qazi* (Muslim judge).[68] Campbell had invoked Muslim law precisely to acquire the special discretionary power it allowed him. Under Muslim law confession was considered the best method for securing a conviction, especially in the absence of evidence.[69] The two Chamars were killed by the *thanedars* while being forced to confess the crime. During the period of the East India Company's rule (1757–1858), police often extracted forced confessions, having already selected individuals as "guilty" or as "eyewitnesses."[70]

Islamic law was the basis for much of the criminal law in India until 1858, when the British government acquired control over India. The Criminal Procedure Code was implemented in 1861. Under Company rule the decision taken by English judges required approval by "the *fatwa* [legal decree] of its own Muslim law officers, [and] their decision was naturally guided in the ultimate analysis by the principle of the Muhammadan law itself."[71] By combining executive and judicial offices, the *fatwa* equipped Campbell with enormous discretionary powers to unilaterally make decisions and hand down sentences. As William Muir, secretary to the Uttar Pradesh government, put it, in "offences liable to a futwa of tazeer the Regulations leave it open to the Magistrate to exercise his discretion, either to award the penalties within the limit of his powers or to commit the case to the Sessions Court."[72] George Campbell and his superior police officer of the Benares division, H. C. Tucker, blamed the native policemen for damaging the reputation of European officers by "running amuck" to get awards and promotions.[73] Campbell wanted to avoid a judicial inquiry into the case and advocated a departmental inquiry as a method of diverting blame to his own subordinate police personnel.[74]

There is no doubt that Campbell abused the law and launched a campaign against Chamars. By raising doubts about the procedures he adopted in his investigations into cattle poisoning and his arrests of Chamars, and by releasing forty-five arrestees for lack of evidence and "serious irregularities" committed by his subordinates, the judges of the sessions court provide us a rare insight into the method of Campbell's investigation.[75] We don't know how the other 750 Chamars were arrested and convicted, but we do know that these forty-five were arrested on the basis of confessions extracted through torture and fabricated evidence, and that two of them died. Prior to Campbell's investigations in 1854, there was no mention of cattle poisoning in Azamgarh district or the eastern districts of Uttar Pradesh in general. From 1849 to 1853 the police reports from the eastern districts do not mention even one case. And after 1854 there was never again a mention of an "organised system of cattle poisoning."[76]

Two decades later, at the height of the second round of accusations of cattle poisoning, Captain C. A. Dodd and Officer William Walker refuted the theory of "organised professional crime" by accusing the police constables of fabricating the crime. In 1869 Captain Dodd, in a stinging report, refuted the dominant view that the organized crime of cattle poisoning existed in eastern Uttar Pradesh. He investigated two issues, first the "popular belief in the prevalence of the crime" and second "the unusual cattle mortality in 1868–69." Dodd was certain that most cases against Chamars were false. He wrote,

> In many cases substances sent for chemical examination were manifestly made up; . . . in some the amount of arsenic said to have been placed before a bullock with intent to kill was not sufficient to poison a mouse; . . . in others, chalk or marble or articles of similar appearance were substituted; and . . . in frequent instances not only no arsenic and deleterious drugs, but positively nothing at all was found mixed with the animal's food.[77]

In addition to starvation and exposure, Dodd identified cattle diseases as a major cause of high cattle mortality in 1868–69. In the absence of knowledge about such diseases, people would always suspect foul play. Yet, significantly, Dodd's report was criticized and rejected by his superiors, including the commissioner of Allahabad division, F. O. Mayne.[78]

The chemical examiner of the Uttar Pradesh government, W. Walker, also refuted the case for cattle poisoning. Walker concluded that in general police personnel were not aware of what arsenic actually was or looked like. His report offers an insight into the campaign that the police had launched against the Chamars. His exasperation is clear in his criticisms of the methods for achieving convictions:

> The circumstances of the cases were almost invariably the same. A chamar is charged with having placed some stuff before a bullock or cow in a surreptitious manner, and the stuff is sent to me for analysis; or a chamar is suspected of being concerned in cattle poisoning; his person and his house are searched, and certain suspicious substances said to have been found are sent for examination.

He stated that many of the cases seemed to have "been very clumsily trumped up," with no arsenic at all having been produced. In some cases the quantity produced was so small that it could not have killed a cow or bullock. In three cases a simple piece of cloth was said to have caused poisoning, and in another a fourteen-inch bamboo. It was too easy, Walker felt, for people to "accuse some social pariah of the crime of poisoning the village cattle." He compared the accusations against Chamars to "the burning of decrepit old women, under similar circumstances, in our own country two hundred years ago."[79]

Walker also pointed to a more important point when he identified the absence of adequate means to medically test cases of suspected arsenic poisoning. In fact, he laid out a plan for medical and scientific examination which would enable testing for "the existence of this presumed cattle poisoning." He suggested that when frequent cattle deaths were reported, an immediate postmortem of sample cows should be undertaken. A doctor should take liver and kidney samples from dead cattle and keep them in a clean bottle filled with strong country spirit to protect them. In this way, Walker argued, deaths from disease could be distinguished from deaths by poisoning.[80]

How do we then explain the sudden increase in reports of cattle poisoning from 1869 onward? Both Walker and Dodd point to the official circular issued by the inspector general of police, Uttar Pradesh, in March 1869 "calling upon District Superintendents to make close enquiries into the subject of cattle poisoning."[81] Dodd argued that "an order for enquiry into the existence of a particular crime is apt to be regarded by subordinate natives as an order to substantiate its prevalence."[82] Walker demonstrates Dodd's point by illustrating the impact of the inspector general's order. In 1867 he received only one case of cattle poisoning, in 1868 five, and in 1869 the figure jumped up to 117, roughly 42.2 percent of all the cases referred to him. In almost all the cases that he examined, the quantity of arsenic was very small and not enough to kill a cow.[83] Murray Thomson, Walker's successor, came to similar conclusions in 1876 on the cases sent to him for investigation.[84]

The March 1869 circular introduced a system of rewards, in the form of promotions and financial remunerations, to induce the police to act. Reports of cattle poisoning, cattle theft, and other crimes against cattle operated under special rules. All district magistrates were directed to pay special attention to crimes against cattle and file annual reports on them. A fairly large amount was distributed by way of awards to policemen and *chaukidars* (village watchmen) every year for reporting cases of cattle poisoning. For instance, in 1889 a total of Rs 2,454 was given as rewards "to deserving men of the District Police."[85] Generally *chaukidars* received a large amount, and the constables also collected a tidy sum. In 1895 *chaukidars* received Rs 3,837 and policemen Rs 1,061, for a total amount of Rs 4,898; the inspector general of police expressed his satisfaction at the increase from the previous year's Rs 3,102.[86] The maximum award for an individual *chaukidar* was Rs 4–5, and for a policeman Rs 8–10.[87] The disbursal of cash rewards became a marker of administrative efficiency and of police alertness in tackling crimes of cattle poisoning.

The annual police report of 1883 complained that "the value of rewards as an incentive to *chaukidars* does not appear to be sufficiently appreciated" by the district magistrates.[88] In 1892 F. W. Porter, inspector general of police, complained "of sparing grant of rewards in certain districts." He was particularly critical of the fact that "some District Superintendents of Police continue to undervalue the effect of giving prompt and substantial rewards for good service." He was confident that good work done by police in reporting cases of cattle poisoning in the district of Gorakhpur was directly connected to a liberal distribution of cash rewards, whereas rewards were scarce in Azamgarh, where the police failed to report such cases.[89] A decline in the number of reported crimes was ascribed to the magistrate's failure to offer monetary rewards. For instance, in one of the many cases, the inspector general of police admonished the district magistrates of Mirzapur and Benares for their lackluster disbursal of cash awards to increase police efficiency.[90] The system of cash rewards for pursuing cases of cattle poisoning suggests that the district authorities in eastern Uttar Pradesh were under severe pressure to report the crime.

Walker and Dodd argued that the system of rewards instituted by the colonial state encouraged false reports and the fabrication of evidence. Stray reports from annual police proceedings and from the district magistrates help us question the existence of any "organised crime of cattle poisoning." The magistrate of Ghazipur was clearly worried about the fact that circumstantial evidence was being used to decide a large number of cases. The local *thanedars* and their subordinates were keen to earn rewards, and were willing to file false cases to do so.[91] The district magistrate of Gorakhpur warned that a dangerous situation had arisen as a result of the large number of false cases being reported by the police.[92] The 1892 report of the Ghazipur magistrate further elaborated on the 1889 report of his predecessor regarding earlier large scale arrests of Chamars. His doubts concerning the making of a Chamar criminal are instructive:

> The evidence in these cases is remarkably similar, and it is to me incredible that there should happen so often to have been eye-witness to a crime, the commission of which by stealth is so easy. I have little doubt that when an animal dies with symptoms suggestive of poison, the owner and the police make a scapegoat of the village Chamar or some member of his family, who would in the ordinary course have obtained the animal's skin.[93]

Captain Dodd's 1869 report was the first to connect massive cattle deaths in 1868–69, due to disease and famine, with the export of an unusually large number of hides from the eastern districts of Uttar Pradesh. The hides were transported to Calcutta for export.[94] We have evidence, in the form of trade reports and livestock censuses (begun only in the 1880s), to further substantiate Dodd's conclusion. The police reports noted that cattle poisoning was very extensive in the years from 1894 to 1896 in the districts of Benares, Ghazipur, Azamgarh, Gorakhpur, Ballia, and Jaunpur.[95] Yet the 1897 annual trade report ascribed the rise in exports to cattle disease: "in 1895–96 cattle disease prevailed during the greater part of the year in the Allahabad Division and the exports in that year were abnormally high."[96] This was the same year in which the police reports mentioned extensive cattle mortality because of the "organised crime of cattle poisoning." According to the annual trade reports, the export of hides and skins from Uttar Pradesh almost doubled, increasing from 248,819 *maunds* in 1893–94 to 462,509 *maunds* in 1894–95 (appendix, table K).

Similarly, William Hoey attributed high cattle death rates in Azamgarh and eastern districts of Uttar Pradesh in 1899 to extensive poisoning by Chamars, but the official statistics on livestock and trade reports contradict his claims.[97] The cattle censuses for the years 1896 to 1900 indicate that the numbers of cattle in the eastern districts of Uttar Pradesh, including Azamgarh, fluctuated between 1890 and 1896 and increased steadily from 1897 onward (appendix, table B). Between 1894 and 1895 the numbers of cattle declined markedly as a result of disease, famine, and floods, but not of poisoning by Chamars.

By identifying at least half a dozen cattle diseases, the colonial state realized that cattle deaths were a significant feature of the agrarian rhythm in the rural society of Uttar Pradesh. A desire to understand and monitor cattle diseases spurred the 1869 "Report on Cattle Diseases" and the 1871 Indian Cattle Plague Commission, which provided further evidence that diseases were responsible for cattle mortality. Reports from different parts of Uttar Pradesh noted that cattle diseases usually occurred in the summer months of June through August or during and after the monsoon rains. The most common disease was cattle plague or rinderpest. In 1869, the district magistrate of Muzaffarnagar sent a detailed note describing rinderpest: "the symptoms are lethargy, want of appetite, watery discharge from nostrils and eyes and looseness of the bowels; at first the animal passes very liquid matter of a yellow and greenish hue, which is afterwards followed by blood." The other disease described was *rorha* or murrain, a disease which usually occurred after the rainy season.[98] The 1869 report of the district magistrate of Kumaon mentioned another disease that appeared regularly, *maan*, considered particularly contagious and deadly if it appeared after a lapse of three years. Cattle that recovered from the disease were considered immune; known as *murtwar*, they were particularly valuable.[99] In his 1869 memorandum to the Cattle Plague Commission, the district magistrate of Benares identified two principal diseases. The first, *khorah,* a foot-and-mouth disease, was known to the majority of Indian cattle owners in the Benares district. The second disease was known as *seetla, mata,* or *chechuk,* which were local names for cattle smallpox.[100]

The colonial state did not associate the crime of cattle theft, or *languri,* with a particular caste. It was the most widely reported crime investigated by the Uttar Pradesh police in the 1880s and 1890s, and was considered the most organized and widespread agricultural crime because cows were regarded as the most valuable animal in Indian society. They played a crucial role in agrarian prosperity in rural communities. Caste returns for the 1892 annual report are particularly revealing about convictions for cattle theft: "621 Ahirs, 325 Chamars, 248 Thakurs, 180 Kurmis, 150 Gujars, and 144 Muhammadans." The report noted that the Thakurs, Ahirs, Brahmans, and Chamars were convicted "in almost every district in the provinces," but only in the case of Chamars was their guilt associated with their caste occupation.[101] If Ahirs and Kurmis had motives to steal cattle, they also had other motives for poisoning cattle. In fact, the poisoning of a cow is a crucial element of Premchand's 1936 novel *Godaan* (Gift of a Cow). Premchand is widely regarded as the Hindi language's most eminent author for bringing realism into Hindi literature, and *Godaan* is one of his most celebrated novels. It is set in a small village somewhere in Awadh in the 1920s. The main character, Hori Mahto, is a member of the lower-caste Kurmi peasant community; his brother Hira poisons his prize cow out of jealousy and a desire for revenge. This incident of cattle poisoning is central to the plot and even involves the use of arsenic, but Chamars, though present within the narrative, are never suspected of the crime.

The stray voices of dissent within the colonial archive allow us to question many assumptions about the crime of cattle poisoning, especially the occupational stereotype.[102] Dissenting explanations for cattle mortality relied more on diseases, famine, and floods than on cattle poisoning. But because of their caste, and because of occupational stereotypes based on Hindu religious texts, Chamars were frequently arrested and tortured to make them confess the crime. They became the easy scapegoats for a crime they rarely committed.

Chamars' Relationship with Hindu Society

The colonial archival material, especially the writings of William Crooke, suggests that the Chamar community played an important role in the rites

and rituals necessary to prevent cattle and human diseases, one that was recognized by caste Hindu society. On the basis of his folkloric knowledge of
North India, William Crooke described the goddess Chamariya as one of the
seven sisters of Sitala, the goddess responsible for pustular diseases. Chamariya, who appeared in the form of a Chamar woman leatherworker who had
died an untimely death, represented all kinds of pustular diseases, including
the worst form of smallpox. The Neem tree was considered her abode and
patients were treated with the leaves of the tree, but she could only be propiti-
ated by offering a pig through a Chamar or other low-caste priest. Another
Chamar goddess or demon, Nona Chamarin, was responsible for cattle diseases. Offering gifts to Chamars was a way of appealing to Nona Chamarin
to leave the village. The shrines of these goddesses clustered around the special shrine of Sitala, located west of the village. Rice and other articles of food
were placed in front of her shrine, and later distributed to Chamars.[103]

The district magistrate of Benares identified three important remedies for
cattle diseases. Two involved medicines, and the third required that Chamars
conduct *puja*. It was *puja* "performed by Chamars, in return for money" that
the local population considered the most effective remedy.[104] William Hoey
also noted Chamars' role in containing and controlling cattle diseases.[105]

The goddess Chamariya, the demon Nona Chamarin, and other folkloric associations between Chamars, cattle diseases, and their prevention reflect at the cultural level the fundamental connection of the Chamar community to all aspects of agricultural life. Chamar life was closely associated
with cattle not because of leather or hides but through a wide range of agricultural activities. Some Chamars may have had rights to the hides of fallen
cattle in exchange for their labor in removing the carcasses, but it is clear
from archival evidence that these hides were rarely their primary livelihood.
Instead, cultivation of crops was central, with the working of hides into useful agricultural implements such as bags and buckets, ropes, and covers for
carts, boxes, and boats making up only a minor part. As one villager acknowledged in his evidence to the Indian Cattle Plague Commission, the
Chamars in his village not only made shoes but also produced various agricultural equipment.[106] The district settlement reports of Uttar Pradesh in the
1880s make one point repeatedly, namely that Chamars were one of the most
important peasant castes, cultivating a range of crops, including commercial
crops like sugarcane, indigo, wheat, and rice. I explore Chamars' central role
in all aspects of agriculture (not just leatherwork) in more detail in chapter 2;

here I merely wish to draw attention to the fact that Chamars had as much stake in protecting the population of healthy cattle as any other agricultural caste, like the Kurmis, Ahirs, and Jats.

Dominant colonial and nationalist discursive practices, consisting of campaigns against cattle poisoning, urban-based nationalist newspapers, and Hindu religious movements, used Hindu religious texts to define Chamar identity exclusively through leatherwork. Chamars' diverse occupational activities and identities were erased in these dominant discourses. This was largely because social and cultural movements in nineteenth-century Hindu society were extremely receptive to the colonial argument that cattle poisoning was motivated by the economic interests of Chamars. Two examples will make this clear.

One of the most well known and widely documented movements for cow protection occurred in 1892–93 in the eastern region of Uttar Pradesh, which was the center of cattle poisoning accusations.[107] *Gaurakshini sabhas,* cow protection associations, staged a violent struggle by successfully mobilizing a large section of the Hindu community to promote a new, aggressive Hindu identity. The cow protection movement was directed against the Muslims, protesting the sacrifice of cows (*qurbani*) during the festival of Eid. What has not been documented in previous study of this movement is that it was also directed against the Chamars. Archival evidence suggests that the Chamars in the eastern region of Uttar Pradesh, as well as the Muslims, were identified as enemies of cows and of the Hindu community. The presence of Chamars in the hide trade was seen as evidence not just of their involvement in cattle poisoning but also more generally of their crimes against the "holy cow."[108] In a cow protection meeting in 1892, held at Kajha, near Mau in Azamgarh district, a resolution was passed opposing any sale of bullocks or cows to Chamars and Muslims, and this was not an isolated instance. During the movement's peak, Chamars' lives were at risk, especially if they were seen with a cow. People stopped selling cows to Chamars and even took away cows that they had legally purchased.[109] Police reports from Azamgarh in 1894 noted that the cow protectionists also raised the issue of cattle poisoning.[110]

The emerging Hindu middle class in the urban centers of Uttar Pradesh readily shared the anxieties of the cow protection movement and its suspicion of the Chamars. This is apparent especially in the regular accusations against Chamars made in the Hindi- and Urdu-language newspapers, which repeatedly held Chamars responsible for poisoning cattle. Newspaper reports on cattle poisoning became frequent after the advent of the cow protection movement of 1892–93. These news reports combined popular stereotypes with official accounts taken from annual police reports and inquiries.[111] In November 1894 the *Hindustan,* published in Hindi in Kalakankar, in Partabgarh district in Awadh region (central Uttar Pradesh), criticized the *gaurakshini sabhas* for not targeting the Chamars. It claimed that "the *Gaurakshini* Sabhas, which are so ready to quarrel with Musalmans in order to rescue a small number of Kine from their hands, are quite indifferent to the large destruction of cattle by disease, poisoning by Chamars and wild animals," calling upon the *sabhas* "to take steps for the protection of cattle from Chamars and wild beasts."[112] A similar report was also published in the *Almora Akhbar,* published in Hindi from Almora (Kumaon). Both papers paid attention to such reports in the decade of the 1890s. The *Hindustan* reproduced verbatim William Hoey's report accusing Chamars of spreading cattle plague, and told Hindus that the only way to save cattle from poisoning and disease was to expel Chamars from the villages.[113]

Accusations against Chamars received new support from within Hindu society, with many *gaurakshini sabhas* passing explicit resolutions not only against Muslims but also against Chamars. In 1894, at the height of the cow protection movement, a Chamar from a village in Mau, in the district of Azamgarh, lodged a complaint with the district superintendent of police against a Koeri (low-caste peasant). "A Chamar came up and said he had bought a bullock from a Koeri for ploughing, but the Koeri now wanted him to return it, as there had just been a meeting in Kajha, and it had been ordered that no bullocks or cows were to be sold to Chamars or Muhammadans, so the Chamar asked if all their cultivation was to be stopped."[114] He had bought the bullock not to kill and skin it, but to cultivate his fields and those of Hindu proprietors. What is significant is that the cow protection movement willingly shared the colonial state's belief that Chamars, because of their caste, would poison cattle. This belief is with us even today, as is evident in the 2000 Lucknow and 2002 Jhajjar incidents.

The relationship between the "mother cow," the Hindu community, and the Chamars was put in perspective by one Hindu commentator a few decades later. "Go-raksha aur Achhut Jatiyan" (Cow Protection and Untouchable Castes): the title of Baldev Chaube's article alerts readers to his tone and argument. Chaube held Chamars responsible for *go-hatya* (killing cows) and argued that it was part of their "culture and tradition" to eat all kinds of animals, including beef. He argued that there was a large gulf between the values of *dwijas* (caste Hindus) and Chamars, and that the latter had "not yet developed the consciousness of respect toward the 'mother cow' that is found among the Hindus." Such an attitude toward and assessment of Chamars was made possible by the values ingrained within Hindu religion and culture, which regarded Chamars as impure by birth, fitted not for equal treatment from the Hindus but only for *begari* (unpaid labor). Chaube characterized the attitude of Hindus toward the Chamars as *ghrna, ghin,* and *nafrat,* disgust and hatred, expressing values that were culturally ingrained as well as created through their experiences.[115]

William Crooke noted that for the Hindus, "Chamrauti" was a "synonym for a place abounding in all kinds of abominable filth."[116] Indeed, the proximity of Chamar *mohallas* (neighborhoods) to Hindu ones in the new urban areas added to the feeling of unease among the Hindus. In rural areas, "untouchable" or Dalit communities had been separate from Hindu settlements, lying to their south because of the eastern and western winds. But the Hindus could not regulate the Dalit communities in urban areas. This was particularly true in cities like Kanpur, Allahabad, and Agra, where Hindu discomfort was expressed not just against Chamars but also against other "untouchable'" communities like those of sweepers. Hindu opposition to the presence of Chamar *mohallas* was articulated on the grounds that their trades polluted the air with bad smells and filth and caused the spread of diseases.[117] If these complaints were not enough, other objections were raised. Trade had increased not only in rawhide but also in related items like bones and hair, which, one newspaper reported, had "created great suspicions in the native public mind." The paper explained that the Chamars benefited from the increased trade in bones, which were used in manufacturing.[118] The Hindu middle classes similarly protested against sharing railway carriages with Chamars and sweepers and wanted their own separate carriages, like those maintained for Europeans.[119] Another newspaper report objected to the employment of a Chamar in a municipal waterworks plant in Agra.[120] These reports represent wider concerns among the emerging Hindu middle class, a community which was marking its identity in opposition to Chamar and Dalit communities.

The cow protection movement and other examples make it evident that in both rural and urban areas a united Hindu community was being constituted in opposition to Muslims and to Chamars and other Dalit groups. Chamars' diverse relationship with the Hindu community through a range of occupations, especially the agricultural, was ignored in favor of an occupational stereotype. Yet such a reading of the relationship of Chamars to the cow protection movement goes against other, more elitist and nationalist understandings of the significance of the cow protection movement. Gyanendra Pandey, for example, has argued that the cow protection movement's attacks on Chamars were aimed at integrating them into the Hindu community. He says that they

> represent the demand of an increasingly aggressive and determined move-
> ment that all erring Hindus ("betrayers") must fall into line . . . (like the
> Chamars) who sometimes responded to the degraded position assigned to
> them in Hindu society as cow-herds, lifters of carcasses and curers of animal-
> skins by turning to cattle poisoning and the sale of cattle skins.[121]

The middle-class Hindus in urban centers and the organizers of the cow protection movement did not consider Chamars and Dalits as part of an imagined Hindu community. Rather, they saw them as committing acts similar to those of Muslims. The Hindus singled out Chamars not because they represented "erring Hindus" and therefore needed to be made better Hindus, as Gyan Pandey has argued, but because they were not considered part of the Hindu community, at least not in the 1890s.

Chamars as Leather Traders

Despite Chamars' engagement with agricultural practices, a small number of them were involved in some kind of leatherwork. According to the 1881 census only 4 percent of Chamars did full-time leatherwork, while poor or landless Chamar laborers and tenants were involved in the leather trade to varying degrees. They would only occasionally skin dead cattle and sell the hides in the *hat* (periodical market) or to a dealer, while tanners and *mochis* (shoemakers), who were mostly located in *qasbas* or market towns, were more fully involved in the hide trade. Most were traders, not criminals, although they were characterized as criminals by the colonial state because of their caste. Stray references in police reports on cattle poisoning offer insights into Chamars' participation in the leather trade and provide rich evidence of their robust engagement with it.

In the last four decades of the nineteenth century Chamars were increasingly forced to purchase cattle from peasants who at one time might have abandoned their old cattle to them. The inspector general's 1892 report distinguished between valuable and worthless "stray" cattle by arguing that the owners of the latter did not care about their loss.[122] Cattle of greater value were well guarded and rarely stolen, but when they were stolen, the rewards to the thieves were greater. The district magistrates of Azamgarh and Benares observed that Chamars had begun to buy old and sick cattle for their hides.[123] Often they would poison the animals, because they had no stake in keeping them alive. The sellers of these cattle were not initially bothered by this, as they stood to gain a few rupees. Increasingly the district magistrates began to distinguish between valuable and ordinary cattle by arguing that only "old and comparatively useless animals would be subjected to this treatment."[124] The district magistrate of Ghazipur stressed that the cattle sold at state pounds were "bought by Chamars" because they were "animals of small value, barren cows or worthless bullocks abandoned by their owners."[125] They were disposed of "for a rupee or so to a chamar who wants the skin . . . and the demand for bones for export (which I am told fetch Rs 2 per *maund* at Ghazipur) adds to the value of the animals."[126] These reports indicate that a new trade had emerged in which valueless cattle, either old, sick, or dying, were sold to the Chamars rather than being simply abandoned. Large numbers of cattle deaths due to floods in the eastern districts of Uttar Pradesh in 1890 made many more than usual available to Chamars.[127]

The report of the Indian Cattle Commission noted the emergence of an organized leather trade, providing new opportunities to Chamars as contractors and tanners. The report argued that "it is the independent hide contractor or merchant, who does a large business and frees himself from village restraint and traditional obligations, who is the object of suspicion or dread, and his myrmidons sometimes made poisoning forages into foreign district [*sic*] or villages."[128] In fact, so lucrative had the leather trade become by the 1890s that zamindars were only too willing to sell the Chamar contractors the right to collect hides in their areas, and Chamar contractors were similarly willing to pay increasingly large sums for the privilege. They were a visible feature of the cattle trade in the eastern districts of Uttar Pradesh, especially Benares, Azamgarh, Ghazipur, and Ballia from the late 1880s.[129] The district magistrate of Ballia reported that zamindars would auction off the right to collect hides in the villages to the Chamars.[130] The Chamars also began to buy cattle from government-owned cattle pounds at a very cheap rate of less then Rs 2 each. In Ghazipur in 1899, for instance, "Rs. 131 was obtained for 70 head of cattle."[131] Most of the cattle brought into the pounds were old and sick animals that owners had let loose. The inspector general of police noted that there was no doubt that the leather trade in eastern Uttar Pradesh was linked to the export of hides and skins to Europe through the agency houses in Calcutta.[132]

In central Uttar Pradesh and the Awadh region, zamindars began to take advantage of the rapidly expanding leather trade in the 1890s by selling the *theka* or contract for fallen cattle to Chamar contractors. In a 1922 report entitled "Cesses in Oudh," D. M. Stewart mentioned practices that had recently emerged in response to the growth of the hide trade in the Awadh region. Stewart was referring to the emergence of the *thekadari* (contractorship) system that emerged in the 1890s in the districts of Bahraich, Fyzabad, and Partabgarh, among others, under which the zamindars auctioned off to Chamar *thekadars* (contractors) the right to collect hides in their *zamindari*. The price of the *theka* depended on the size of the village, grazing facilities, and the strength of the hide trade. More generally in Awadh the zamindars began to demand cash payments from Chamar, Bhangi, and Pasi tanners rather than the agricultural implements, like water buckets or shoes made from the hides of fallen cattle, which they earlier expected and received.[133]

The town of Ghazipur in eastern Uttar Pradesh had become a major center of the leather trade by the 1890s. The district magistrate of Ghazipur district noted in 1895 that the six major hide merchants of Ghazipur town had direct connections with the shippers and exporters in Calcutta.[134] The district magistrate of Azamgarh also noted that Ghazipur had become a major hub of the leather trade in the Benares division and attracted hides from eastern and central districts of the province.[135] Azamgarh boasted twelve hide markets, in which Muslims controlled the trade by collecting the hides through Chamar contractors.[136] Police reports acknowledged that these contractors used the much maligned arsenic to prepare hides for transport to Calcutta and Europe. The treated hides were better preserved and therefore fetched higher prices. Since arsenic was expensive, Chamar contractors received advances from the Ghazipur merchants or directly from Calcutta. Such practices suited both parties; the Chamar contractor did not have to pay for the arsenic, as the cost was deducted from the price of the hides, and the merchants in Calcutta received a regular supply of hides and skins in return.[137]

It is possible that Chamars may have poisoned individual old or sick cattle which had been abandoned by Hindus and left to fend for themselves. Yet many genuine cases of cattle poisoning by arsenic which were part of their professional activities, not unlike the work of a butcher, became marked as a crime. To characterize the poisoning of abandoned or purchased cattle over which Chamars had rights as an organized crime is to criminalize legitimate professional activities, purely on the basis of caste identity. Chamars began to purchase cattle from Hindu peasants and zamindars as soon as the latter recognized that there was money to be made from cattle hides. In fact, by the latter half of the nineteenth century, zamindars had begun to demand their own share of the hide trade, which had grown significantly. Selling Chamar contractors the right to "collect the skins of dead animals" became a way for zamindars to add to their income.[138] Three decades later Baldev Chaube, in his article "Go-raksha aur Achhut Jatiyan," attested to this while lamenting the loss of the "mother cow." He noted that such practices had become common in every village of the state; the Kisans or peasants sold their old or sick cattle to Chamars for a few rupees.[139]

* * *

As Uttar Pradesh's director of land records and agriculture, William H. Moreland was responsible for compiling the district's annual trade reports. In his introduction to the report for the year 1905–1906, he commented that the "scarcity of fodder in the districts affected by drought led to a considerable loss of cattle; hence the exports of hides and skins increased by" 17 percent, most of which was "drawn from the Allahabad block" and in general from the eastern districts of Uttar Pradesh.[140] But only a few years earlier, in 1899, Moreland had approved a new official policy on the basis of suggestions by William Hoey, commissioner of Gorakhpur division, according to which cultivators should be "advised to destroy the hides of cattle dying of disease and never to give them to the Chamars," because Chamars spread the diseases.[141] Explaining the rise and decline of various trade articles in 1906, he failed to notice the contradiction in his logic. Chamars were entrepreneurs and not criminals.

CHAPTER 2

Investigating the Stereotype:
Chamar Peasants and Agricultural Laborers

We have had jotes [land] here for years; our fathers and
grandfathers were assamees [tenants] here; our fields have not been
changed and we have paid [rent] at one rate, but we claim
nothing; the talookdar is the proprietor of the soil, and he could
have raised our rents or ousted [us] on refusal to pay.

—Luchha, Kesra, and Purtab Chamars, interviewed by E. O. Bradford,
settlement officer of Hardoi district, Uttar Pradesh, 1867

The fact is that the chamar, just because he is considered to be
qualified by caste to do the flaying of animals, does not necessarily
become a primary producer of hides. The chamar is largely an
agriculturist like others[,] holding land ranging between 2 and 9
bighas[,]paying Rs 9 to Rs 51 rental, and having as assets the grain
he raises and the proceeds he obtains from sale thereof.

—"Notes and Orders," J. C. Donaldson, director of industries,
Uttar Pradesh, February 18, 1931

How do we understand Luchha, Kesra, and Purtab Chamars' unusual claim that they had traditionally been peasants and had plowed the land for generations? While acknowledging zamindars' proprietary rights over their land, Chamars were unwilling to accept that they had no legal rights over the land they cultivated. They asserted such rights on the grounds that they had cultivated it for generations and that they paid rent to the zamindars. During a colonial inquiry into peasants' land rights held in 1867, Chamars made similar assertions throughout the Awadh region. Six decades later, in 1931, J. C. Donaldson acknowledged these claims when he described Chamars as primarily peasants. According to the Uttar Pradesh census of 1911, only 130,233 Chamar workers out of 3,467,317 (4 percent) were engaged in their "traditional" occupation of leatherwork, while 1,373,184 (40 percent) were identified as cultivators, including both *maurusi* (occupancy) and *ghair-maurusi* (non-occupancy) tenants. Another 1,355,387 (40 percent) were identified as agricultural laborers, 331,244 (9 percent) as unspecified laborers, 142,786 (4 percent) as industrial workers, and 107,922 (3 percent) as livestock owners and milkmen.[1] In 1961 cultivators had increased to 50 percent of the total Chamar work force (1,788,134 workers), and the percentage of leatherworkers had declined to 0.6 (appendix, table C).[2] Not only do these statements and statistics identify Chamars as primarily peasants, they also force us to question the assumption that their traditional occupation was leatherwork.

How do we reconcile these statistics with the widely shared assumption that Chamars were primarily leatherworkers and landless laborers? How did colonial and postcolonial historians, sociologists, and other scholars come to assume that leatherwork was the exclusive identity and occupation of Chamars? William Crooke, in his 1896 survey of castes and tribes, described Chamars as "the caste of curriers, tanners, and day-labourers found throughout Upper India." He said that Chamars were involved in a variety of occupations, but their primary business was curing skins and making shoes.[3] A hundred years later, in his 1993 People of India project, K. S. Singh defined the Chamars in similar terms: "being traditionally landless, they are engaged in skin and hide work and agricultural labour."[4] This understanding of the Chamars' occupation has continued to influence postcolonial anthropologists' and historians' understanding of the Chamars' role in Hindu society.

The belief that leatherwork was the traditional and primary occupation of Chamars was developed in nineteenth-century Uttar Pradesh through debates surrounding the census, the caste and tribe surveys, and the gazetteers, the typical all-India sources housed in Delhi and London. In contrast, the district-level settlement reports and inquiries, housed in provincial archives, detail information on Chamars that offers a radically different picture. Despite Chamars' "untouchable" status, they were primarily a peasant caste in nineteenth- and twentieth-century North Indian society and had far closer connections to agriculture and land than have generally been recognized. A key objective of this chapter is to investigate Chamars' relationship with the land and agriculture by examining their diverse roles in the nineteenth-century rural society of Uttar Pradesh.

The first section discusses the colonial "discovery" of the Chamar population of Uttar Pradesh in order to scrutinize contemporary explanations of their large numbers, their presence within agriculture, and their apparent lack of "fit" with their supposedly "traditional" occupation. Colonial ethnography transformed "Chamar" from an abstract textual category (or identity) to an administrative and social category. The second, third, and fourth sections investigate their lack of "fit" by exploring their position within agrarian society. Although the colonial state classified them as non-proprietary tenants and non-agriculturists,[5] the presence of Chamar peasants as *maurusi* and *ghair-maurusi* tenants remains an outstanding feature of the nineteenth-century agrarian history of Uttar Pradesh. The fifth section considers Chamars' remarkable social, spatial, and especially occupational mobility within the rural society of Uttar Pradesh. Building on the previous sections, the sixth and final section surveys Chamars' social and cultural practices which indicate a close connection with agriculture, including their participation in one of North India's most well known peasant movements.

The British Discovery of Chamars

In the latter half of the nineteenth century, with the beginning of the decennial census, the British discovered the large number of Chamars in Uttar Pradesh. Indeed, Chamars were the most numerous Hindu caste. And by the time of the 1911 census it was clear that as many as 80 percent of Chamars were primarily cultivators and agriculturists. According to the 1881 Uttar Pradesh census, Chamars constituted 14 percent of the total Hindu population, followed by Brahmans with 12 percent and Ahirs with 9 percent (appendix, table A).[6] Briggs described this as a most "striking fact," since it was clear leatherwork, supposedly their traditional profession, could not possibly have supported such a large number.[7] Their numbers came as a total surprise to colonial administrators, forcing them to reexamine their ideas about Chamars. The colonial state was forced to come to terms with the fact that Chamars were an integral part of an agricultural community. Such a discovery had two implications. First, it undermined the long-held view of Chamars as a small community of leatherworkers. Second, it required colonial ethnography to resolve the contradiction between existing understandings of the Chamars and their numerical strength in the population of Uttar Pradesh.

Prior to the start of the decennial census in 1871, the dominant colonial perception of the Chamars was as leatherworkers and servants of zamindars, and it was therefore assumed that, because of their work, they had to constitute an insignificant portion of the population. Reverend William Tennant, an Anglican clergyman and traveler, described them in 1804 as a small group of "the lowest and most despised order of tradesmen in India" who primarily produced leather articles like shoes, ropes, and harnesses.[8] Uttar Pradesh settlement reports of the 1830s concur. E. A. Reade's comment in the Gorakhpur settlement report of 1837 captures this early colonial perception of the Chamars:

> The Moossulman inhabitants are singularly few in number; the strength of the population is in Rajpoot, Brahmins and Aheers, but almost every caste is to be found, and generally in the same village, there being without reference to extent or prosperity, in most instances, one or more families of Chumars, Buhrs, Bunneeahs, Kamkurs, Quoeries, and Koormees.[9]

The impression conveyed is that each village in Gorakhpur had only a few Chamar families, constituting a negligible part of the total population, particularly in relation to Rajputs and Brahmans (with whom, incidentally, colonial officials had far more direct contact).

Thomason's well-known 1837 settlement report for Azamgarh similarly portrayed Chamars as the personal slaves of zamindars, settled on the latter's estates and wholly dependent on them. He never mentions Chamars as part of the cultivating community.[10] In the 1839 Saharanpur settlement report, Edward Thornton represented Chamars as slaves of zamindars, who settled them on lands according to their convenience.[11] In his 1842 settlement report for Hamirpur, C. Allen identified "Brahmins, Rajputs, Lodhees, [even] Bunyahs, Aheers, Koormees, Kachees and Khungas" as major castes of the district but did not even mention the Chamars.[12] In general Chamars were not mentioned in the settlement reports of the 1830s, and Reade's statement in the Gorakhpur settlement report of 1837 sums up the pre-census colonial image of the

Chamars. This image was so widely accepted that the author of the 1866 census report from Chhattisgarh in central India could claim that the Satnami Chamars "in no way resemble the Chamars who are leather workers and dwellers of Northern India," because the Satnami Chamars owned land.[13]

In sharp contrast to Reade's 1837 Gorakhpur settlement report, Cruickshank's 1891 report described Chamars as the second largest "Hindu" caste, and fourth largest community of cultivators, in the district, putting their total population at 210,108.[14] The decennial censuses and most settlement reports in the 1880s commented on the surprisingly large population of Chamars. Faced with these numbers, in the latter half of the nineteenth century colonial ethnographers set out to resolve the contradiction between their conceptual framework and the actual conditions of Chamars. They attempted to offer explanations for the large numbers of Chamars and the fact that leatherworking was clearly not their only occupation.

Following the first two decennial censuses, in 1871 and 1881, J. S. Nesfield solved the problem by claiming that the untouchable castes, like the Doms, Kanjars, and Cherus, might have recently added to the numbers of the Chamar community.[15] Briggs agreed with Nesfield that the Chamar community received additions to their numbers from other castes below them, including Doms, Kanjars, Kols, and Jaiswaras, and from other tribal groups. He extended Nesfield's point by arguing that the heterogeneous character of the Chamar caste pointed to "definite geographical origins." The geographical names of some of the subcastes, he said, suggested that the Chamar caste might have been expanded by the addition of groups from specific regions over centuries of conquest, as conquered tribes lost their prestige and status and became subjugated to the victorious tribe. He listed some thirteen *jatis* (subcastes) of Chamars whose names suggest geographical or local origins, including the Azamgarhiya, Aharwar, Gangapar, Purabiya, and Jhusiya.[16]

Terming conquest and the resulting loss of prestige and status a distinctive feature of Indian civilization, Briggs argued that the "fixed status of an occupational group may go hand in hand with the repeated recruitment of the group by those who have been degraded from better positions." Therefore, he concluded that "some clans lost their identity and prestige with the changing order, and consequently they have sunk to lower levels." The Jatiya Chamars of western Uttar Pradesh were a good example of this because of their "light complexion" and "higher physical type." He claimed that "some occupational demand drew Jats into this lower form of work;

or, more likely, that some pressure or penalty resulted in their degrada-
tion." Briggs sought to account for Chamars' numbers through every possible means, and even argued that the existence of fair Chamars was due to
illicit relations between Chamar women and high-caste men.[17]

Most conceptually important was accounting for the presence of Chamars
in a variety of occupations outside of what was viewed as their traditional
work. Late nineteenth-century colonial ethnography most commonly explained the transition from traditional to non-traditional occupations like ma-
sonry, carpentry, factory work, and agriculture as a recent development.[18] This
explanation prevails to this day. C. G. Chenevix-Trench, in his 1904 monograph on tanning in the Central Provinces, believed that with the establishment of the modern leather industry "the numbers of Chamars returned as
field and casual labourers" would rise.[19] The Chamars' control of land under
maurusi and *ghair-maurusi* right, agreed Briggs, was a recent development and
a departure from traditional practices.[20] Several decades later the 1931 census
commissioner, A. C. Turner, added to these explanations by arguing that the
Jatavs, Jatav-Rajputs, and Kurils might be Chamars who had adopted "a new
name, which is considered more suitable to their new social position and new
occupation" of agriculture.[21] Sixty years later, in 1992, Kumar Suresh Singh
reiterated this point by arguing that "many of them [the Chamars] have, in
recent times, taken to cultivation," thereby reaffirming the assumption that
they had not traditionally been cultivators.[22]

In 1911, E. A. H. Blunt identified four reasons for the lack of "fit" between
the Chamars' supposedly traditional occupation and their present condition.[23]
He explained that if the traditional work of a caste was insufficient for the size
of the community, then some members would move to other avenues. Second,
he suggested that other occupations might prove more attractive than the traditional ones. Third, some traditional occupations had been lost to modern-
izing influences like the development of industry. Finally, he suggested that
the element of pollution in Chamars' "traditional" occupation might have
contributed to its unpopularity. He cited the "abandonment of a degrading
occupation" by the Chamar-Julahas of Moradabad, who were Jatiya Chamars
but who took up weaving in an attempt to improve their social status. It is
significant that he characterizes all of these as recent developments, departures
from what he accepts as Chamars' traditional occupation of leatherwork.

Colonial ethnographers clearly made heroic efforts to come to terms
with the "lack of fit" between their conceptual assumptions and social real-

ity, but at the same time they also sought to fit Chamars back into a relationship with leather and their untouchable origins. As part of their effort to standardize the category of "Chamar" in the census and the caste system, colonial ethnographers in 1867 looked first at the etymological origins of the caste names in order to connect them with occupations. They concluded that "the Chamars, like some of the other lower castes, take their names from the trades to which they are given" and therefore looked for myths, both textual and popular, to legitimize their argument.[24] An argument can be made that the discovery of the etymology of "Chamar" in the Brahmanical texts was purely coincidental, especially since the names of most Dalit castes should also have had roots in Brahmanical texts, which is not the case. We do not hear of similar origins of the names of other lower and "untouchable" castes.

Although the colonial ethnographers had little difficulty explaining the past of Chamars, their present posed a much greater challenge. Indeed, the present continued to rupture the "fit" that colonial discourse sought to establish between theory and practice. The ruptures became increasingly evident toward the end of the nineteenth century, as settlement reports and government inquiries began to reckon with this fundamental contradiction. The authors of the 1875 settlement report for Etawah concluded,

> I do not know on what principle this classification [of agricultural and non-agricultural castes] is based, and the figures may be perfectly correct. But, speaking from my knowledge of the district, I am sure that if by non-agricultural is meant persons who are in no way dependent on farming or field labour for their subsistence, but are employed on trades or other work, the classification must be erroneous; most probably all the numerous caste of Chamars have been reckoned as non-agricultural. A great many Chamars, however, live entirely by farming, while numbers of those who habitually labour for hire have a few bighas of land as well.[25]

The settlement officers of Aligarh, Shahjahanpur, Kanpur, Bahraich, Azamgarh, and Basti also expressed their unease with a classification that created confusion about the position of Chamars. J. Hooper, the settlement officer of Basti district, could not hide his surprise at finding that "many of the Chamars are genuine cultivators, that is to say, they earn their subsistence entirely by farming on their own account, but a great many are ploughmen or labourers depending chiefly for their living on wages."[26] Yet another example of the puzzle with which late nineteenth-century administrators were confronted comes from one of the most well known reports of the period, the report of what was popularly known as the Dufferin Inquiry. This inquiry into the living conditions of the lower classes in the 1880s offers us a rare glimpse into the Chamar world of nineteenth-century Uttar Pradesh. It divided the lower classes into four groups: a) cultivators with rights of occupancy in land or holding more than five acres (*maurusi* peasants); b) those who had no such rights or held less than five acres (*ghair-maurusi* peasants); c) agricultural day laborers; and d) artisans.[27] At the outset the report classified Chamars as agricultural day laborers, yet this did not stop it from mentioning them in the three other categories: as peasants with *maurusi* and *ghair-maurusi* rights, agricultural laborers, and artisans. The report discussed 31 Chamar families, out of which 11 were identified as *maurusi* peasants, 11 as *ghair-maurusi* peasants, 5 as weavers, and only 4 as agricultural laborers and part-time leatherworkers.

Chamars and the Regime of Proprietary Tenures

In 1909 the Chamar peasants of Moradabad district paid an annual rent of Rs 324,571. Out of total rent payments of Rs 3,021,394, the Chamars' share was the largest of any caste's in the district. In that same year the Jat tenants paid a rent of Rs 281,268, while the Sheikhs paid Rs 313,733, the Thakurs Rs 164,419, and the Brahmans Rs 142,597 (appendix, table D).[28] Given that Chamars cultivated 107, 525 acres of land, they paid the third most rent of any peasant caste, after Jats and Sheikhs. These statistics do not represent an isolated example; rather, Chamars paid among the greatest rents in many districts of Uttar Pradesh (appendix, tables D–J). These examples also point to the contradiction between the existence of Chamars as a peasant caste and their classification as leatherworkers and non-agriculturists in nineteenth-century land-revenue settlement reports and tenancy legislation.

The relationship of Chamars with land and agriculture was shaped by the revenue policies of the colonial state which specifically altered the position of non-proprietary tenants. In Uttar Pradesh, separate revenue settlements were implemented in the North-Western Provinces and in Awadh. The North-Western Provinces, divided into eastern districts, with Benares as the center, and western districts, with Agra as the center, were settled between 1790 and 1820, whereas the princely state of Awadh was settled after its annexation in 1858, when it became the central region of the province, with its capital at Lucknow (see map). In the eastern districts the land tenure system was called *zamindari* because proprietary rights were held by a family or group of landlords, the zamindars. In the western districts the land tenure system was called *bhaiyachara* because proprietary rights were held by dominant peasant communities with strong kinship ties, like the Jats, Gujars, or Sheikhs. And in Awadh the land tenure system was known as *taluqdari* because the proprietary rights were held by the *taluqdars* of the region. The *taluqdars* belonged to an elite landed aristocracy that was much more powerful than the zamindars because they had greater control over land and because of their genealogical ties to the precolonial rulers in Awadh region. The major difference for Chamars between the revenue settlements in Awadh and in the rest of Uttar Pradesh was that the *maurusi* or occupancy rights of the non-proprietary tenants like the lower and "untouchable" castes were not recognized in the Awadh settlement in 1866–67, whereas in the eastern and western regions of Uttar Pradesh the rights of non-proprietary tenants were not only recognized but also protected through tenancy legislation.[29]

Historians generally agree that Thomason's 1837 settlement report for Azamgarh became a crucial reference point in delineating the rights of the non-proprietary cultivators by distinguishing them into Ashraf and Arzal peasant castes, basing their inclusion in one category or the other almost solely on their caste. He further divided Ashraf cultivators into two kinds, those who possessed "hereditary and transferable right to hold their land at a fixed [rent] rate" and those who possessed "right of occupancy at a fixed rate, either for [a] certain period or during their own lives." Thomason identified two distinctive features of the Ashraf cultivators. First, the rent they paid was generally less than that paid by "the lower classes, or *Urzal* [Arzal]." Second, Ashraf cultivators were "generally connected by ties of religion, family connexion, or friendship, and hence are somewhat favoured" by the zamindars.[30]

The Arzal were the third class of cultivators, consisting of the "Bhurs, Chumars and low caste persons, who are generally located on the estate at some expense of capital, and are liable at any time to be left entirely dependent on the zamindars, who must either support them during a season of scarcity, or see their estates depopulated and their future source of profit destroyed." The relationship between zamindars and Arzal peasants was based on personal exchange or what Thomason called "pecuniary obligation," but not on rent.[31] Under this system, the zamindar provided Arzal tenants with houses, food, seed, grain, and implements (at a high interest rate) and expected services such as land cultivation in return. The colonial land tenure policies regarding Arzal peasants were based on this assumption, and therefore they lost any claim to hereditary rights over cultivated land. This is because, explains Bernard Cohn, an Arzal cultivator "was not entered in the *jamabandi* [record of rights to land] as being responsible for payment of the Government revenue and . . . by custom and law was not considered to be a member of a corporate proprietary body," and therefore had no hereditary rights.[32]

Thomason's model of three classes of non-proprietary cultivators represents a theoretical abstraction of the ties between the cultivators and the land, especially those of the Arzal cultivators. As he acknowledged, the "non-proprietary cultivators of this third class [the Arzal] by long prescription would rise to the second class [of occupancy tenants] and acquire the right of holding their land at fixed rates."[33] Thomason accepted that Chamars could and did hold land under *maurusi* as well as *ghair-maurusi* tenure because there was a good deal of mobility among social groups. Henry Elliot's 1869 report on Meerut district underlined the fact that Arzal peasants acquired *maurusi* or occupancy rights, even hereditary and transferable rights, by continuously working land.[34] Indeed, the 1869 Uttar Pradesh government report on tenant-right recognized that peasants from Arzal castes had rights over land as long as they paid rent. The report acknowledged that the zamindars had the right to oust a peasant, but this right was rarely exercised, because it constituted "simply an appeal to a custom."[35] In precolonial Mughal India, according to B. R. Grover, cultivators who rented lands from landlords and other cultivators but still possessed hereditary title to the land and enjoyed equal rights as cultivators as long as they paid the rent were known as *muzarian*.[36]

The colonial state did not recognize the hereditary rights of Arzal cultivators but protected them from summary eviction in Act X of 1859. This act protected the *maurusi* rights of cultivators in the *zamindari-* and *bhaiyachara*-administered districts of eastern and western Uttar Pradesh who had regularly cultivated the same land for twelve years. Arzal or non-proprietary tenants were provided with fixed rights of occupancy, and both their tenure and their land were secured.[37] The colonial state's claim that the act gave tenants from the menial and inferior castes, like the Chamars, *maurusi* rights and a legal title to their land for the first time is to a large extent true.[38] Arzal tenants generally benefited from colonial land tenure policy's efforts to identify and "fix by law" the "total area that could be demarcated as *sir* [land for personal cultivation]" of Ashraf or dominant landlords and peasant communities.[39]

Similar legal protection was not provided to Arzal peasants in the *taluqdari*-administered districts of the central or Awadh region of Uttar Pradesh because of the specifics of revenue policy. In Awadh, *maurusi* rights were denied to the non-proprietary low-caste cultivators like Kurmis and Chamars.[40] In 1865 C. Currie, the settlement commissioner of Awadh, outlined two reasons for this. First, protecting such tenants would hinder "the working of the natural laws of supply and demand, and, by holding out an extra inducement to the cultivating classes to cling to the land which their forefathers occupied[,] would keep back labour from entering the most advantageous market," thereby preventing the creation of a laboring class. Second, by pointing to "the difficulty of defining the conditions by which the class" of non-proprietary tenants could be recognized with *maurusi* rights, Currie made it clear that doing so was not an option.[41]

Currie was an advocate of the *taluqdars* of Awadh and favored a revenue policy that would strengthen their rights, particularly their right to raise rents. Despite the two Oudh (Awadh) Rent Acts of 1868 and 1886, only 1 percent of the vast number of tenants held rights of occupancy, while the rest were provided with "security" of tenure only for a period of seven years.[42] In the wake of the peasant movement in Awadh in 1920–21, V. N. Mehta, in his 1920 report, argued that the tenants of Awadh had lost "fixity of tenure" on their land through the Oudh Act of 1886, which "allowed the justifiable and unjustifiable ejectment through the seven year rule." Mehta pointed to the stark conditions of the peasantry in Awadh, in contrast to those in the neighboring districts of Uttar Pradesh, giving as an example Jaunpur, "where even a Chamar is a fixed rate tenant," or "Allahabad where the number of secured tenant[s] is large."[43]

The 1867 inquiry into the rights of the non-proprietary tenants of Awadh also indicates how the Chamars responded to the land tenure policies.[44] The report of this inquiry documents Chamar claims to have rights over the land they cultivated. Chamars asserted the right to cultivate their land and contested the right of anyone else to dispossess them from their holdings. Mohna Chamar, for instance, asserted to G. B. Maconochie, settlement officer of Unao, that as long as he paid the rent nobody could evict him from the eleven *bighas* of land that his forefathers had cultivated for generations. Likewise,

Lullowa Chamar claimed that his family had cultivated two *bighas* and eighteen *biswas* for generations, in addition to many *bighas* of his zamindar's *sir* as *ghair-maurusi* tenants.[45] Mungray Chamar cultivated twenty-four *bighas* and held another under privilege tenure for his services as a laborer.[46] E. O. Bradford, settlement officer for Hardoi district, summed up such claims by Chamars from all over Awadh by suggesting that the Chamars "have a right to hold [land] at fixed rates" and argued that "if these tenants are classed with those at the will of the landlord, injustice will be done, and harm will come of it . . . however inconvenient and complicated the system of tenures is in Oude [Awadh], whatever is should be maintained."[47]

Despite the extensive evidence that Chamars were *maurusi* and *ghair-maurusi* tenants, they were barred from buying and owning agricultural land by a number of laws and acts. The Bundelkhand Alienation of Land Act (No. II of 1903), for example, barred all non-agricultural castes from owning land.[48] Vijay Prashad has argued that the Punjab Alienation of Land Act of 1901 similarly barred Dalits from "access to land ownership," even though the act was ostensibly "designed to protect the cultivators from the avariciousness of the financiers."[49] Yet despite land tenure polices and legislation, Chamars and Pasis, the two largest Dalit groups in Uttar Pradesh continued to possess land and in some districts expanded their holdings.

Revenue Settlements and the Position of Chamar Peasants

Despite being categorized by the colonial state as non-agriculturists, Chamar *maurusi* and *ghair-maurusi* peasants have been prominent participants in the agriculture of Uttar Pradesh, especially of its western districts, for the last 150 years. The most important influence on the relationships between different castes in a village and on the relationship of Chamar tenants with land was the nature and character of proprietary tenures. The conditions of Chamar peasants, I suggest, were dramatically different under the *bhaiyachara* and *zamindari* tenures, and they were always better off under the former. There were three important features of *bhaiyachara* tenure: the members of the proprietary body directly cultivated their own shares of land, the cultivator's share of revenue was linked to the land cultivated, and the rent charged to tenants was not fixed. Instead, the share of each of the members of the proprietary body changed every year. For instance, in Bundelkhand, the southwest region of Uttar Pradesh, the shortage of skilled cultivators played a crucial role in setting the share of rent.[50] Since cultivators were in short supply, the proprietary peasant groups, who were engaged in cultivation themselves, readily granted, encouraged, and accepted Chamars' *maurusi* rights and in some cases made them co-sharers of revenue payment.[51]

This trend was most evident in the western districts of Uttar Pradesh that were predominantly settled under *bhaiyachara* tenure. The settlement officer of Jhansi district, in Bundelkhand region, noted in 1893 that because of the shortage of cultivators the Chamar peasants were the co-sharers most sought by the proprietary cultivating body.[52] By 1921, the Chamars in Saharanpur district had gained more land under *bhaiyachara* tenure but also a bit of proprietary share, because the proprietors considered them good tenants.[53] In Agra district, too, *bhaiyachara* tenure enabled Chamars to acquire *maurusi* rights, because the proprietary bodies "are always slower to move, and have not sufficient unanimity to carry out any sustained measures for preventing the acquisition of occupancy rights."[54] The settlement officer of Muzaffarnagar district succinctly observed in 1896 that Chamar peasants gained proprietary rights living alongside the dominant cultivating castes, which included Jats and other groups.[55]

In the *zamindari* areas of western Uttar Pradesh, like Bareilly district, Chamars acquired *maurusi* rights because most of the estates in the district were owned by absentee landlords who lived off their income in the towns.[56] In most of eastern Uttar Pradesh, by contrast, zamindars were powerful magnates who made it impossible for the non-proprietary tenants to acquire *maurusi* rights.[57] The settlement reports of Farrukhabad and Aligarh districts underlined this point by noting that in the *zamindari* areas marked by absentee landlordism the percentage of *maurusi* tenants was higher, and even Chamar peasants acquired such rights.[58] As one sociologist observed, the Chamars of western Uttar Pradesh, because of their larger holdings, maintained a better quality of cattle than did those of eastern and central Uttar Pradesh.[59] The Azamgarh settlement report of 1903 noted that because low-caste tenants were "submissive," their acquisition of *maurusi* rights did not bother zamindars.[60] A few decades later, in 1947, Mohinder Singh concluded that in many parts of the province the peasants had cultivated landlords' private land (*khudkasht*) for forty or fifty years, but such land was "entered in the government records as *khudkasht* of the landlord."[61] Because of their ignorance and servitude to zamindars, the peasants didn't make legal claims to these lands under the tenancy laws, especially in central (Awadh) and eastern Uttar Pradesh, where the large majority of them were Chamars and Dalits.

Even though the colonial state did not recognize the proprietary land rights of non-proprietary Arzal castes like Chamars, it accepted the possibility that they possessed rights over land under *maurusi* and *ghair-maurusi* tenures. Yet the proprietary tenures introduced by the British played an influential role in shaping the position of Chamars in the three tenure zones of Uttar Pradesh. In the following pages I will illustrate this point through a discussion of Chamar land-holding patterns in western (*bhaiyachara*), and eastern (*zamindari*) regions of Uttar Pradesh.

In the Bundelkhand region, the distinction between rent (paid to the zamindars) and revenue (paid to the government) had never been an important one, as the Marathas had collected revenue from individual peasants through a village head, which meant that all peasants were independent proprietors. The crucial point, as the settlement officer acknowledged in 1893, was that the colonial tenure categories of proprietary and non-proprietary peasants did not exist, because dominant peasant groups like Bundelas and lower-caste peasants like Chamars both paid revenue to the Maratha rulers. However, as he put it, "one class had some foundation for claim to proprietary right because their connections had been recognised as proprietors, while the others had not."[62] Therefore peasants from the inferior or ritually impure castes, including Chamars, were recorded as *maurusi* tenants but not as proprietors in the second settlement of the 1890s, though not in the first settlement of the 1830s.

The Jhansi settlement reports provide fascinating data on the condition of Chamars in the Bundelkhand region. In Jhansi district Chamars were one of the more important *maurusi* and *ghair-maurusi* peasant castes, the favored plowmen and tenant co-sharers. Their reputation enabled them to get advances for seed and cattle, because it was recognized that the money would be invested back into agriculture.[63] Indeed, they occupied "a very much larger area of land" than is mentioned in the records. In 1893 Chamar peasants in Jhansi cultivated 23 acres as proprietors, 17,291 acres as *maurusi* tenants, and 5,952 acres as *khatas* or shared proprietary holdings (see appendix, table G, for a comparison with other castes).[64] According to Atkinson's 1874 gazetteer (volume 1) on Bundelkhand, a peasant needed an average of nine acres to support a family, and Chamar peasants were doing well.[65] Their best holdings, according to the 1943 rent rate report, were in Mau *tahsil* (subdivision), with an average holding there of 8.2 acres, most under *maurusi* tenure; next was Garotha *tahsil,* where an average holding was 8.1 acres.[66] By the 1940s Chamars had expanded the land under cultivation to nearly 67,206 acres, allowing the proprietors to increase their rent and fulfill revenue obligations.[67]

In Agra district land was controlled by proprietary castes through *bhaiyachara* tenure, but Chamars held most of their land under *maurusi* rights, which were not contested by the proprietors.[68] In the 1880s the Chamars of Agra district held 60,286 acres of land, amounting to 7.1 percent of the total land under cultivation. By the 1930s Chamars had managed to increase their land to 65,000 acres, out of which 40,000 was held under *maurusi* rights and the rest (25,000) under *ghair-maurusi* rights and other tenures (appendix, table E). Their gain of 5,000 acres was the highest among all the castes.[69] In Etamadpur *pargana* (subdivision) they held 42 percent of the total cultivated land, indicating that there could be substantial variation in their position even within districts.[70] They were also in the forefront of the extension of agriculture in Bah *tahsil.*[71]

In Bareilly district Chamars were recognized as one of the most efficient cultivating castes because all members of the family, including the women, worked in the field. Chamar peasants with smaller holdings usually had additional jobs, like weeding, hoeing, reaping, threshing, winnowing, and serving as watchmen, to supplement their income. Their best holding was in Aonlah *tahsil,* where they held 14.0 percent of the total land, more than any other group except the Thakurs; Aonlah was followed by Furidpur *tahsil,* where they held 9.2 percent. Their average holding in each of the *parganas* of the district was more than 5 percent of the total, which was better than the average holdings of the Brahmans, Thakurs, and Ahirs.[72] By the beginning of the twentieth century, Chamars held 7 percent of the land in Bareilly, 49,506 acres, and they paid an annual rent of Rs 209,905 (appendix, table H).[73] Their holdings had not changed much in the 1940s.[74]

In Saharanpur district Chamars were noted for the cultivation of wheat, basmati rice, and sugarcane. In 1921 they were the sixth largest community of *maurusi* tenants, and their annual rent of Rs 263,260 put them in fourth position, after Gujars, Garas, and Malis or Sainis, but ahead of well-known peasant groups like Jats, Ahirs, and Rajputs. They controlled a good percentage of land both as tenants and as proprietors. As proprietors, Chamars held 15,209 acres in 1921, an increase from the 13,332 acres recorded in the 1890 settlement report. As *maurusi* tenants they held 41,465 acres of land, of which 31,457 acres were rented for cash (appendix, table J).[75] In many cases high-caste proprietors like Rajputs preferred Chamars as co-sharers of their *sir* land to other lower-caste groups because they were considered fine peasants.[76] According to Drake-Brockman, Saharanpur in 1921 was considered "the granary of the Empire," and if this was the case then it was a tribute to the skills of Chamar peasants.[77]

In his 1891 report on Bulandshahr, B. T. Stoker noted that Chamar peasants in the district not only held a large percentage of land but sometimes possessed proprietary rights. This smaller group of Chamars held 133 acres of land under proprietary tenure, although this figure had declined from 258 acres in the settlement of the 1840s, while the number of sharers had increased from 27 to 34. The real strength of the Chamar peasant community in Bulandshahr lay in their position as tenants, holding 81,179 acres and owning some 7,722 plows. Most Chamar cultivators also owned a pair of bullocks.[78] But by the 1920s their holdings had declined to 65,000 acres, primarily because the zamindars and proprietors were increasing their *sir* land by evicting Chamar and lower-caste Lodha tenants. It is not surprising, therefore, that Chamar *ghair-maurusi* tenants paid a rent of Rs 11 per acre, almost double what a *maurusi* tenant paid.[79]

Gorakhpur district exemplifies the eastern region of Uttar Pradesh, offering a sharp contrast to the western. Gorakhpur was marked by non-cultivating *zamindari* proprietors who exercised enormous power over non-proprietary peasants. In 1881 Edward Atkinson observed that the cultivators "had no rights of occupancy, and were almost all of the lowest castes," including Dalits.[80] A. W. Cruickshank, in his 1891 settlement report for Gorakhpur, mentioned that Chamars held 6 percent of the total cultivated area. A total of 72,857 Chamar peasants cultivated 117,501 acres at an annual rent of Rs 387,753 (appendix, table I). Chamars held more land in Padrauna and Maharganj *tahsils* than they did in others, 29,000 acres in each, with an average holding of 3.47 acres (better than the district average of 2 acres).[81] In the latter half of the nineteenth century peasants had good bargaining power, because the population was low relative to the land available. Chamar peasants had played an important role in extending cultivation to the north of Gorakhpur.[82]

Untouchability, *Begari,* and Agrarian Labor

Given the overwhelming data suggesting that nearly 97 percent of Chamars were not leatherworkers, why has the myth persisted that those who were not leatherworkers must have been landless laborers? As we know from the census reports, 40 percent of all Chamars in 1911 and 50 percent in 1961 were peasants. The answer, I believe, lies in the disparity between the size of the Chamar population in Uttar Pradesh and the amount of land they could cultivate. H. F. Evans, in his 1880 settlement report for Agra, captured this contradiction when he wrote, "The difference between them [Chamars] and the castes mentioned above [Jats, Thakurs, and Brahmans] lies in this, that though they form 16 percent of the population, they cultivate only seven percent of the land, the reverse of the position of the Thakurs and Jats."[83] Settlement reports from other parts of Uttar Pradesh also commented on such a divergence.

What is meant by the statement that Chamars were landless or agricultural laborers? In order to answer this question, we have to recognize that Chamars were situated in a unique socioeconomic position within rural society. Despite being stigmatized as "untouchables," they worked in a range of trades, as plowmen, cultivators, laborers, and artisans. Varying economic conditions meant that even Chamars who cultivated their own land as *maurusi* or *ghair-maurusi* tenants would have labored for or assisted other cultivators as well. In a seminal essay Neeladri Bhattacharya has summed up a new position on this issue: "most scholars on the subject now tend to doubt whether there was at all any significant transformation of peasants into agricultural labourers." On the basis of his study of rural society in Punjab, Bhattacharya shows that "landlessness was not a necessary characteristic of agricultural labourers."[84] Such observations make us aware that we should not assume that laborers did not own land.

E. Rose, the collector of Ghazipur, writing in 1880, distinguished between small cultivators of land, on the one hand, and laborers, servants, and artisans on the other. However, Rose argued that the distinction between a tenant and a laborer was hazy, because "the divisions of classes . . . made by me is not an entirely definite one." He acknowledged that "in a large proportion of instances it will be found that the day-labourer, Chamar . . . or whatever his caste may be, and whether he is a servant or not, has also his one or two *bighas* of land, held not in lieu of wages, but in most cases at privileged rates." It is worth underlining Rose's observation that a Chamar plowman would have land as a *ghair-maurusi* tenant, in addition to his work as a laborer or a servant. According to Rose, Chamars were considered fine *halwahas* (plowmen) and as such were crucial to the zamindars: "the competition is as a rule amongst the zamindars for ploughmen, and not amongst the ploughmen for zamindars," and therefore the Chamar's "family are upon the whole well clothed and fed." In eastern Uttar Pradesh, caste Hindu zamindars with both large and small holdings employed Chamar plowmen because of the cultural strictures that barred them from plowing with their own hands.[85]

Halwaha (plowman) was widely recognized as a skilled occupation in eastern and central regions of Uttar Pradesh. According to the Gorakhpur-Basti settlement report of 1871, a Chamar plowman and his family earned Rs 59 annually, of which Rs 18 was paid for his services as plowman and the rest for agricultural labor. His expenses would average around Rs 49, giving him a profit of Rs 10 in a year, most of which would typically go to the *mahajan* (moneylender) as debt payment.[86] Girwar Saksena, in his ethnographic survey of a village in Lucknow district in 1929, described Chamars as low-caste tenants "who supplement the income of small farms by menial service, and work as labourers on the fields of others."[87]

Hari Har Dayal's 1929 sociological study of agricultural laborers in Unao district, Awadh region, observed that Chamars and Lodhs were regarded as "unsurpassed cultivators." Sought after as plowmen, they were offered better wages and other remuneration than those belonging to more privileged social groups, like Kachhis, Kurmis, and Ahirs. Dayal provides us with a thick description of a Chamar *halwaha*'s arduous but rewarding life over the course of the year. During the *kharif* season, stretching from the month of Sawan (July–August) to Aghan (November–December), he would harvest the chief crop of the season, rice, as well as cotton, maize, *juar,* and lentils. At the same he would get the fields ready for the major *rabi* crop of wheat. In the *rabi* season, from Poos (December–January) to Baisakh (April–May), he would harvest potatoes and sugarcane and prepare *gur* or jaggery, mustard, barley, and wheat. The wheat crop required the most work throughout the season, from regular watering to harvesting, winnowing, and husking.[88] According to Saksena, Chamar women also played an important role in the annual agricultural cycle, being employed for *bowai* (sowing), *nikai* (weeding), reaping and picking, threshing, winnowing, loading, and removing grass.[89] Highlighting a Chamar *halwaha*'s expertise in agricultural production, Dayal claimed that in a year with good monsoon he might earn more then a small tenant, like a Lodh, with six *bighas* of land.[90] Premchand, that astute observer of Indian society, attested in his chilling 1930 short story "Poos ki Raat" to the superior position of *halwahas* and laborers compared to that of small peasants in the Awadh region. Halku and Munni, the story's two protagonists, are petty peasants, and they are relieved at the loss of their field because they can now become laborers and earn more.[91]

Begari has traditionally been defined as unpaid labor performed for caste Hindus. According to Crooke, *begari* referred to a system involving a group of people

> known collectively as the begar of the village, or persons who are liable to perform certain compulsory duties for the landlord and other residents. The Chamar, in consideration of repairing the well water-bag, providing leather straps and whips, and helping in cleaning the grain, similarly gets 20 seers at each harvest per plough. The light grain and sweepings of the threshing-floor are the Chamar's privilege in consideration of the help he gives in threshing and winnowing. The meat of dead cattle also falls to him; but he does not get the skin. If an animal dies, the hide goes to the owner, and the Chamar expects 10 or 15 seers of course as the rangan, or fee for curing it. In some cases he is expected to mend shoes for nothing.[92]

Crooke's 1888 description indicates the range of work done as *begari,* including both leatherwork and agricultural work. *Begari* was constitutive of the Chamars' subservience to the dominant Hindu proprietary castes and zamindars. Regardless of whether they were prosperous *maurusi* tenants, *ghair-maurusi* tenants, or laborers, they were all expected to do *begari.* Kamle Chamar of Jait village in Mathura district owned sixteen *bighas* of land, of which he held twelve under *maurusi* rights, but he nevertheless provided *begari* not only to caste Hindus but also at the army station.[93]

The nature and character of *begari* had changed by the beginning of the twentieth century. *Begari* should not merely be considered "unpaid forced labor," a timeless feature of North Indian society. Rather, it acquired new meaning for Chamars, as well as for the lower-caste peasants, as it became more brutal. As rents became more fixed under the British, benefiting the Dalit and lower-caste peasants, zamindars and other dominant proprietary castes expanded the scope and meaning of *begari.* By the late nineteenth century *begari, hari* (plowing), and *nazrana* (tribute) had become the most visible forms of rent enhancement, means by which the zamindars tried to circumvent the tenancy legislation of 1886 that had fixed rents for seven years in the Awadh region. As V. N. Mehta has noted, *hari* and *begari* were no longer the "old time-honoured system of requiring ploughing in Asarh and ploughing in Kartik [one day in each of these months], helping in transplantation of rice and working at the basket lift for *rabi* irrigation," for which Chamars were paid two *seers* of grain for a whole day's work or parched grain for a half day's work. And *nazrana* was a land rent imposed on and extracted from Dalit and Shudra peasants under the threat of eviction.[94]

The zamindars had enormously increased their *sir* land to counter the *maurusi* rights provided by the tenancy legislation, and were therefore increasingly dependent on *begari* for the cultivation of those lands.[95] *Hari* and *begari* were forms of rent extracted from Chamar peasants to reduce the zamindars' costs by ensuring plowing services at crucial times in the season. The loss of time for plowing their own land on those days directly affected the yield of the Chamars' crops and made them more dependent on zamindars and *banias* (traders). In places where Chamar tenants with small or meager holdings paid very little rent, they were often expected to contribute more fully to the zamindars by way of *begari, hari,* and *nazrana*.[96] Under the new conditions of *begari,* a Chamar peasant was expected to work one day in each week on the zamindar's land throughout the agricultural season, for which he either received no payment at all or was paid arbitrarily. One Chamar complained to V. N. Mehta that he had to give *begari* one day in every ten, for which he received no payment, plus paid *nazrana* of Rs 15 on his land and various cesses of Rs 1.[97]

In the literature on colonial India, the term *chamrai* is generally assumed to refer to a tax on leatherwork. But it was also a form of *begari* in which tenants plowed the zamindar's land, and in some cases it was a cash payment. Stoker lists a range of *chamrai* or agricultural cesses that Chamars were expected to pay in Khurja *tahsil* of Bulandshahr district, on their plows, land, irrigation, and crops, to zamindars and officials.[98] Chamars objected to cesses that they were forced to pay during Dussehra and Holi in addition to the usual *nazrana* paid to the zamindar, the local revenue officer, and his subordinates like the clerk and the peon.[99] Lest we assume that these services were exacted only in Awadh, there is enough evidence that Chamars paid them in other parts of Uttar Pradesh as well. Touring government officials, along with their entourage, expected *begari* from local Chamars. This practice was believed to be "sanctioned by immemorial custom," and the British officials believed that they were "entitled to a reasonable amount of perquisites of the landlord," who also considers "it an honour to entertain at his own cost." The 1920 report on *rasad* (payments of provisions) and *begari* protest concluded that "the laboring classes . . . by custom give a certain amount of free service to their landlords in return for house room rent-free in the homestead, and protection." One officer claimed that *begars* received land at privileged rates from zamindars, and therefore Chamars were adequately compensated for their labor. The report declared that *begari* was customary between zamindars and the *begars* of the village.[100]

Chamar peasants, like other lower-caste peasants, were liable for a wide range of *raqam siwai* (payments) to zamindars on social and economic aspects of rural life, including equipment (such as plows), crops, hay, sugarcane juice, cooking oil, ghee, and festivals like Holi and Dussehra. These payments were made either in kind or in cash, at twice the market rate. At the same time zamindars demanded *rasad* and services from Chamars at rates which were normally half the market rate. In 1920, five Chamars objected to the zamindars' "new" practice of demanding *bhusa* (hay) from their fields. Kalu Chamar alleged that he was coerced to supply Rs 5 worth of ghee twice a year at half the market rate.[101] In most villages of Azamgarh Chamars supplied fowl to the caste Hindus and zamindars. If the zamindars were Muslim, as they were in Musta'abad in Azamgarh, then the Chamars supplied fowl at festivals like Eid and Baqr-id. They might also provide irrigation buckets and other agricultural equipment. For marriages and other celebrations in a zamindar's family, Chamars were expected to provide *rasad* and *begari*. In Bidyamanpur village of Azamgarh district, they gave a goat, while in Reora village, they gave a goat, five *seers* of uncooked food, half a *seer* of ghee, and fowl to the zamindar's family.[102]

It is clear that Chamars occupied a range of vocations. This fact should makes us rethink the meanings of the ritual notions of purity and pollution that have so centrally defined the abstract relationship of "untouchables" with "touchables." The ritual impurity of Chamars, which constituted their "untouchable" status, was derived from the Hindu texts but did not necessarily map to the social world. Buchanan-Hamilton pointed to the privileged position of Chamars in North India in comparison to South India. In his 1813 account of Gorakhpur and Shahabad districts, he compared the conditions of Chamars in Malabar and South India, "where they [were] slaves," to their condition in the "Gangetic belt," where they had "direct access to higher castes" and even to the landlord.[103] In the latter part of the nineteenth century, Kamle Chamar, mentioned earlier, was a peasant and a laborer, but he also sold ghee in the *hat* market. Similarly Gobinda Chamar, a peasant from *mauza* (village) Pahloi in Etah, sold milk and ghee, and his wife wove cotton and also helped him with agricultural work. Munni Chamar, from *mauza* Manderiya, sold *gur* in addition to cultivating sugarcane.[104] Crooke, in his account of Etah district in 1888, mentioned that Chamar peasants, along with members of other lower castes, would sell ghee, milk, curd, and hand-spun cotton cloth. Some Chamars were full-time weavers, who made a country (coarse) cloth called *gazi* or *gafi*.[105] In Mirzapur they were known for "domestication and breeding of the silkworm."[106] Chamar women would often grind corn, grain, and lentils (*dal*) at the houses of caste Hindus or in their own homes.[107] Chamars and Pasis were involved in *dal* splitting in the Mundera bazaar adjacent to Chauri Chaura, where "hundreds of men, women and children worked all day long."[108]

One of the most striking features of the Chamars' lifestyle was their quickness to take advantage of new opportunities created by the colonial state. Chamars were very much involved in the construction business in North India, both as laborers and as contractors. Many Indian sociologists believe that the Chamar elite that emerged in Agra acquired their wealth from leather, but this is inaccurate.[109] The Jatav elites that emerged in the first two decades of 1900 in Agra were largely contractors who acquired wealth by supplying labor to construction sites, especially in Calcutta and Delhi. Indeed, even in the 1940s they had significant influence over this industry, especially in the mining of red stones from Rajasthan. The man who founded the Jatav Mahasabha in 1917 was a textile entrepreneur and owner of a printing press.[110] The Jatavs took particular pride in having played an important role in the building of Delhi, the new capital, during the first decade of the twentieth century. In the words of one, "We supplied [the British] with labor and stones."[111] Jatavs were also employed in railway and canal projects, not just as an alternative to work in villages, but as a way of moving out of the confines of the villages.[112]

In the late nineteenth century Indian indentured laborers began to emigrate to the plantation colonies of Fiji and the West Indies. This emigration was a new feature of colonial political economy. Most of the indentured laborers came from the lower castes of rural North India. By examining the landing tickets of indentured laborers, Brij Lal has determined that the largest number (13.4 percent of all emigrants) came from eastern Uttar Pradesh and belonged to the Chamar caste.[113] High levels of emigration from the districts of Basti, Gorakhpur, Gonda, Bahraich, and Azamgarh had a negative impact on the agricultural income of the proprietary castes. In 1900 the zamindars in Basti district were complaining that their best plowmen had emigrated, and the wages of agricultural laborers had risen as a result.[114] Family emigration was also more common among Chamars than caste Hindus, among whom generally only a male would emigrate. Families of "untouchables" like Chamars were able to negotiate the new society of the colonies better than caste Hindus. A major indication of this is that suicide rates were lowest among them and highest among caste Hindus. The folk songs of Chamar and lower-caste emigrants began to represent their journey to the colonies as escape from Hindu religious oppression. The position of Chamars and other Dalit castes in the Indian social hierarchy played a more important role in their decision to emigrate then their poor economic condition: the colonies offered a new place for them, beyond the pale of India's caste system.[115] In the face of criticism of the indentured labor policy from the Hindu middle-class intelligentsia, the colonial officers claimed that emigration to colonies offered social groups like the Chamars an escape from their servile conditions.[116]

The World of Chamar Peasants and Agricultural Laborers

What did the world of Chamar peasants and agricultural laborers look like in the nineteenth century? Was leatherwork a significant or core part of their daily life? In order to answer these questions, this study draws on the two-thousand-page Dufferin Report of 1888, which provides a rare glimpse of the nineteenth-century world of the Indian rural lower classes. In 1887 the viceroy, Lord Dufferin, had ordered an inquiry into "the actual condition of the lower classes" of agriculturists in different parts of India.[117] The Dufferin Report also offers evidence of the colonial drive to classify groups of people according to their castes and occupations, especially the lower castes and Dalits, even if the descriptive part of the report contradicts such a classificatory regime. In its descriptions of the "actual conditions" of Chamar families, there are few accounts of them as leatherworkers and landless laborers. The report discusses 31 Chamar families, out of which 22 are described as tenants, 4 as agricultural laborers, and 5 as weavers. Indeed, the very report that classified Chamars as leatherworkers and agricultural laborers provides us with fascinating material about their lives as *maurusi* and *ghair-maurusi* tenants, the crops they cultivated, and their annual income from agriculture. In cases where leatherwork is mentioned, it forms an insignificant part of their income.

The report identifies three categories of Chamar tenants: *maurusi* and *ghair-maurusi* tenants, agricultural laborers, and weavers. In the first category was the family of Kamle Chamar, of Jait village in Muthra district, who owned sixteen *bighas* of land, twelve as a *maurusi* tenant and four as a *ghair-maurusi*. He cultivated a wide range of crops, including *juar, urad, arhar,* oilseed, cotton, millet, mung beans, indigo, and hemp. In addition to family labor, Kamle Chamar employed eight workers in the sowing and reaping seasons. He was a proud owner of two cows and one bullock, and borrowed another bullock to plow. Despite his reasonable status, he was expected to provide *begari* to government officers during their tours. His annual earnings in 1878–79 were Rs 91 while his expenditure was Rs 104, resulting in a deficit of Rs 13 and a debt of Rs 80. The *kharif* and *rabi* seasons kept the family employed for seven months of the year; the rest of the time they worked as laborers to earn extra income, including by selling ghee made from the milk of their two cows. They lived comfortably, eating two meals a day and consuming luxury items like oil, salt, tobacco, and milk.[118] We have similar descriptions of other Chamar tenant families. Hari Singh Chamar of *mauza* Jorsimi in Etah district, for instance, was a hereditary cultivator of ten acres of land, for which he paid an annual rent of Rs 61, and also cultivated another three acres as a subtenant for a rent of Rs 32. Although they were prosperous, his family also worked as laborers.[119]

The Dufferin Report also describes the family of Gobinda Chamar of Pahloi village in Etah. They were primarily cultivators, but also sold milk, ghee, and cotton thread, and they occasionally skinned cattle. Gobinda owned ten acres of land under various tenures. The annual family income from the farm was Rs 154, plus additional income of Rs 6 from hides, Rs 16 from home-manufactured ghee, and Rs 5 from cotton yarn, for a total of Rs 181; they had expenses of Rs 171. Similarly, Munni Chamar of Manderiya village in Pilibhit district cultivated thirty-one *bighas,* growing sugarcane, rice, *kodon,* wheat, barley, linseed, and mustard and earning Rs 40 a year. Although he was a cultivator, he augmented his income by working on other people's land, constructing embankments, skinning dead cattle, and sewing shoes and water bags, for which he earned Rs 20 a year. He paid rent worth Rs 16.[120]

F. N. Wright, in his 1877 report on agriculture in Kanpur district, claimed that the Chamars, Kurmis, and Kachhis were the most important non-proprietary cultivator castes. According to him, a Chamar family with three children in Kanpur district would hold an average of twelve *bighas* of land and a pair of bullocks. In the *kharif* season the family would sow corn, cotton, barley, and maize, and in the *rabi* they would sow wheat, *arhar,* and mustard. They would hire between seven and twenty men and women to sow and reap the crops, especially cotton, in addition to the family labor. In the *kharif* season the family would spend Rs 6 to produce crops worth Rs 39, and in the *rabi* season they would spend Rs 9 to produce crops worth Rs 55. They would also pay Rs 28 in rent and another Rs 4 to make and repair agricultural equipment. Their total annual income would thus be Rs 94-8-0 and their expenses Rs 48-8-3, for a profit of Rs 45. There is no mention of leatherwork.[121]

The Dufferin Report's second category of Chamar cultivators and agricultural laborers comprised those who had less than five *bighas* of land and were dependent on other occupations for their livelihood. William Crooke, in his report to the inquiry, described a small tenant as one who owned on an average five *bighas* of land and a single plow, or perhaps ten *bighas,* harvesting half in *rabi* and half in *kharif.* Or he might own a couple of plows and four oxen and earn income from other sources.[122] A Chamar in *mauza* Dhaurahra in Rae Bareli was described as a cultivator, weaver, and tanner who owned three bullocks and a plow. His family owned seven *bighas* and produced crops, including opium, worth Rs 87, with an additional income of Rs 22 from weaving. Their annual expenditure was Rs 38, for a profit of Rs 70.[123] We have considerable detail about the family of Sumera Chamar, a laborer from *mauza* Mohauli Khurd in Etah district. He and his wife worked as agricultural laborers on others' land eleven months of the year and received a regular income: Rs 28 for him, and Rs 6 for her. They earned most in the harvest season, when, besides their wages, they were also entitled to fallen grain.[124]

The family of Dhanna Chamar from *mauza* Chakeri in Etah district best matches the colonial stereotype of the typical Chamar family. They worked as agricultural workers during the season and otherwise as masons, building mud walls and thatching roofs; they were unemployed during the two months of monsoon. Their wages were mostly paid in grain, and their annual income for ten months of work was Rs 58. The income of such Chamar families varied greatly, depending on their occupational acumen and skills. Another Chamar family, in *mauza* Mustafabad in Rae Bareli, did agricultural work for six months of the year, earning two and a half *seers* of grain per day. The husband also worked as a litter-bearer and earned Rs 36 annually by carrying people from the village to the town of Rae Bareli (a distance of twenty-four miles). The work was casual and varied from month to month, as did the payment. According to the Dufferin Report, "poor people pay . . . 50 percent more than the rich," because the rich were more "regular customers." He also skinned cattle, with the help of another Chamar laborer, and earned Rs 3 annually from this. His wife was a midwife, and like him charged different rates for rich and poor. The rich paid her Rs 2 and food and grain for one month of work, whereas the poor paid Rs 1 and food and grain for six days of work. The annual income of the family was Rs 52.[125]

In the final category were the Chamar weavers belonging to the Koli subcaste. One, identified in the colonial records as Nanha, could not sell his cloth in 1879 because of a famine. He was therefore forced to work as a laborer, while his wife and son gathered *saag* (mustard) from the fields to live on, along with the grain of his daily wage. But he was able to move from one occupation to another not merely in times of famine but also during lean seasons: whenever he needed to augment his income. He earned fourteen *annas* (slightly less than a rupee) by weaving *dohra* (cotton cloth), and his wife and son alternated between helping him and working in the fields. In good years, they may have eaten twice a day. They were among the poorest in the weavers' community.[126]

Crooke's examples from Erah district offer a different picture of Chamar weavers. In *mauza* Mohanpur the family of Asa Koli, comprising two men, two women, and one girl, wove the country cloth called *gazi*. They wove cloth for wages at clients' houses or produced cotton yarn for the local market. Their annual income was Rs 48, though their living expenses were a rupee more. Hanuman Koli, from *mauza* Manotar, was another weaver, and his wife spun thread. They also worked for wages to produce cloth for others, being paid in grain and occasionally in cash. Their annual income was Rs 68.[127]

Many passages in the Dufferin Report tell us in detail about the "actual living conditions" of Chamar families, and on their basis we can draw some reasonably firm conclusions. Leatherwork is not mentioned as the primary occupation of any family, and families described as agricultural laborers are not always landless. The poorer Chamar families still earned their livelihood primarily by cultivating land, growing a wide variety of *kharif* and *rabi* crops, and supplemented their income with other work, including leatherwork as well as plowing, other labor, and selling milk and ghee.

The Agrarian Context of Chamars' Social and Cultural Lives

In a petition to Baba Ramchandra dated January 1931, Chamar representatives of fifteen villages of Partabgarh district claimed that they had been doing *kisani kaam* (agricultural work) for years, but recently Thakur zamindars had ejected them from their lands, even though they had regularly paid rent.[128] Because the Thakurs did not give rent receipts, Chamar peasants started a movement to demand them so that they could assert their legal claims to the land and fight eviction. The Thakurs responded by depriving Chamars of their land. The Chamar representatives, declaring themselves to have neither the knowledge necessary to raise such issues nor the money for a lawyer, sought Baba Ramchandra's help because of his reputation as a defender of peasants. They also demanded that the government provide them land so that they could have their own villages.

This is neither the first nor the only evidence of communication between Chamar peasants and Baba Ramchandra. Chamars had also participated in the famous Kisan Sabha movement in Awadh in 1921–22. Chamars joined the Kisan agitation because of eviction from their land and the threat to their agricultural occupation. According to Baba Ramchandra, many Chamars became members of Kisan Sabha committees and played an active role in meetings and agitation. Chamar peasants figure prominently as members in the pledge letters written to establish Kisan Sabha in villages. Chamars also provided *rasad* in the Kisan Sabha meetings and contributed financially to the organization.[129] But despite overwhelming evidence of their participation in the Kisan Sabha movement, it has been viewed primarily as a movement of lower-caste tenants like Ahirs, Kurmis, and Koeris. Chamar involvement in the movement is assessed in the historiography in terms of "looting" and "riots," as I have discussed in the introduction to this book. Yet evidence suggests that Chamars and other Dalits had much in common with other agricultural peasants. Chamars and Pasis were almost half of the peasants injured or killed in the police shootings in the town of Rae Bareli in January 1921. In the Fursatganj bazaar shooting, sixteen of the twenty-four casualties were Chamars and Pasis.[130] Baba Ramchandra also noted the active participation of Chamars in his diary.[131]

They were ready to die because their *kisani kaam,* their livelihood and dignity, had been severely threatened by the zamindars' eviction policies.

There is no other explanation for their active participation in these events except that their lives were fundamentally defined by their agricultural work. The peasants of Malhera and "ten neighbouring villages" participated in the *aika* (unity) movement of 1922, which was largely confined to Hardoi district in Awadh.[132] A student of Radhakamal Mukherjee, Krishna Asthana, in his survey of Malhera village in Hardoi district in 1929, tells us that forty-two of the seventy-eight families in Malhera were Chamars.[133] The Chamars hardly fit the profile of "leatherworkers" or "landless laborers" that both colonial and nationalist historiography have imposed upon them.

Despite the radicalism of the Kisan Sabha, celebrated by historians, Baba Ramchandra's understanding of rural society was very much located within a caste Hindu framework. In his long note on the moral improvement of the people of Oudh, written in 1921, the Baba warned the *dwijas* or caste Hindus of social evils that had led to the decline of their social and moral standards. He accused them of freely interacting and "developing friendship with Chamars and prostitutes," whose morals were very low and whose living conditions were impure. His agenda of *samaj sudhar and jati sudhar* (social and caste reform) clearly envisioned that caste Hindus should maintain a distance from the degrading influences of Chamars and Muslims. They should not use the Muslim greeting *salaam,* and women should stop visiting and worshipping at the Mazar of Ghazi Miyan, a Muslim saint.[134] The Kisan Sabha enforced caste rules and sought to work within the caste system to create a peasant alliance that could engage in radical social struggle.[135] In this hierarchical framework, Chamars and Pasis were always mentioned last in lists of contributors of *rasad* to the Kisan Sabha, reflecting their "true" place in the Hindu social world.[136] It is only appropriate that Baba Ramchandra makes barely a passing reference in his memoirs, a mere three lines, to his wife, a Chamar woman in Fiji whom he left there when he returned to India.[137]

The fact that Chamars were involved in peasant activism against *bedekhli* (eviction) from "their land" is evidence that land and agriculture were central features of their existence. The Dufferin Report, settlement reports, and other colonial sources all suggest that the religious and cultural processes of the Chamar world were crucially linked to agricultural production. But both colonial and postcolonial anthropological literature on Chamars and other Dalit castes have been dominated by a model of ritual purity and impurity drawn from Hindu religious texts.[138] The underlying methodology of this literature, evident in Briggs's 1920 work and in Cohn's 1958 essay, is to study the ritual practices through which Chamars are excluded from dominant Hindu religion and contrast them to the Chamars' own religious world, comprising spirits, ghosts, godlings, and magic.[139] Yet there is considerable evidence for an alternative characterization of the religious and cultural world of the Chamars, one that sees it as grounded in the fertility of Mother Earth and centered on the production of agricultural wealth.

Chamars had an elaborate set of agricultural ceremonies focusing on the fertility of the soil and covering plowing, sowing, and reaping. Worship of the plow, an important ceremony, preceded the planting of wheat, rice, sugarcane, and cotton. For instance in Bareilly, where Chamars formed a particularly a strong non-proprietary peasant group (appendix, table H), they would begin the *kharif* and *rabi* seasons only after identifying an auspicious day (*mauhoorut*), usually with the help of the pandit. The Chamar peasant would inaugurate the agricultural season at dawn of that day by scratching his field five times in different places with his plow, ensuring each time that he was facing east or north, with the moon at his right or front. After performing this ritual, he would return home, wishing good luck to people on his way and avoiding bad omens. On his return, his wife would offer him curd to mark the auspicious occasion. Not all peasants consulted the pandit. Some would choose an appropriate day themselves, and at dawn go to their field, make a few scratches with their plow, and return home to celebrate the new agricultural season by eating *poories* (thin flour cakes, deep fried) and *mithais* (sweets).[140]

Buchanan-Hamilton noted that Chamars were *bhagats* (priests) of village deities that protected the village from evil and disease and whose blessings were sought before the beginning and end of each crop season. Described by Brahmans as ghosts but popularly known as *dihuyars* or *gramdevatas*, these deities were worshipped not only by Chamars but by members of all communities. *Dihuyars* or *gramdevatas* (village gods) were worshipped in the consecrated places in the villages known as the *sthans*, usually elevated mounds or a spot under a large tree. The *dihuyar* had no image, being represented usually only by a lump of clay placed on a platform. Chamars would offer swine and liquor during harvests and festivals, with the cost shared by the entire village.[141] During threshing and the measuring of the grain, a *puja* was performed to protect the grain, and after winnowing one handful was given to the Brahman priest and another handful to the *dihuyar*.[142] Although these gods were not part of the mainstream pantheon of Hinduism, local Brahman priests accepted the popularity of *dihuyars*.[143] The *dihuyars* played a crucial role in the annual agricultural cycle in Gorakhpur and much of eastern Uttar Pradesh because peasants performed regular *pujas* to protect their crops.[144] After every harvest, both the village deity and the Chamars received a small offering.[145] In Mirzapur, Chamar cultivators offered local gods *chappatis* (unleavened bread) and liquor on the first day of sowing and harvest, in hopes that their fields would be protected and their harvests good. The ceremony took place in the field at noon.[146]

The agricultural ceremonies were specific to each crop, further indicating the agrarian character of the Chamar community.[147] For instance, before sowing sugarcane, the Chamars would rub a piece of *gur* on the plow. That piece was then offered to the *dihuyar* and the rest was distributed among the cultivators. The first day of plowing was celebrated with a formal dinner at which *kheer* (sweet rice pudding) was served. Special care was taken to ensure that the rice, sugar, and other ingredients blended well, a good omen for a generous and sweet crop of sugarcane. Outside the door auspicious designs were made with cow dung to pray for an abundant harvest. And the harvest itself was also preceded by rituals and ceremonies. Before it began, a bunch of cane stems were tied together at the top and kept in a pot filled with water, as a prayer for a rich crop. They were not separated until the harvesting was complete. A fire sacrifice was also performed, in which women worshipped the *gramdevata* or *dihuyar*. The person who made *gur* cut the first cane, from which *gur* was made, and this was shared by the cultivators. A fire sacrifice of the first canes was also performed, to ensure the purity of the crop. In the evening a special dinner was cooked with rice and *urad dal,* followed by festivities.

Similar *pujas* were performed for other crops. In the case of wheat, at the start of the sowing season handfuls of grain were placed in small earthen pots and buried under the soil, a handful was thrown across the field in the direction of the Ganges, and five handfuls were buried in different parts of the field. The completion of sowing was followed by a fire sacrifice to honor the plow. It was also believed that the owner of the field must not be hungry at the time of sowing. At the wheat harvest, like the sugarcane harvest, first offerings were made to the *dihuyar*. Similar rituals were performed during various stages of the cotton crop. Before harvesting the crop, a ritual of fire worship was performed in the field, and the women who picked the cotton sat around and ate rice. There were also specific ceremonies to pray for good rain and to protect new crops from damage by hailstorms in autumn and winter. Blessings for a good monsoon were sought in various ways, like hanging a small plow in a well or placing an earthen pot filled with water and *chappatis* in the field. During the construction of a well for agricultural purposes little bowls of water were set out around the proposed site on a Saturday night. The one which dried up last marked the exact spot where the well should be dug.

Briggs described these Chamar agricultural ceremonies as "mysterious," suggesting that they differed from upper-caste religious rituals and had no relationship to the Chamars' social and economic lives. But these rituals and ceremonies represent efforts to negotiate the uncertainties of peasant life. They were not exclusive to Chamars but shared by peasants of all castes, especially the lower castes involved in cultivation. Yet Briggs, and the authors of many settlement reports for Uttar Pradesh, specifically mentioned Chamars in discussing religious ceremonies associated with agriculture.

*   *   *

In his interview with the historian Shahid Amin, Sita Ahir, a low-caste cultivator in Gorakhpur district, declared that "the Chamars did not hold any land, they only ploughed" for the caste Hindus. Amin tells us that "the small holdings of the Chamars, in distant and unfertile corners of the village, had probably receded beyond the pale of Sita's memory, or perhaps the forty years after 1885, marked by price rise and rising rents, had seen the Chamars of Dumri dispossessed by their Sikh landlords."[148] There is a striking parallel between Sita Ahir's memory and the dominant Indian historiography that has failed to recognize Chamars' important relationships with land and agriculture. Chamars constituted an important and skilled cultivating caste that was very much valued by the agrarian society of North India. Despite untouchability, Chamars have continued to maintain a significant presence as cultivators. Leatherwork was not their exclusive occupation and identity; they were involved in a wide range of occupations.

CHAPTER 3

Is the Leather Industry a Chamar Enterprise?
The Making of Leatherworkers

The leather industry in this country is, as is well known, in the hands of men who hold one of the lowest places in the social and religious scale of the Hindus, viz., the Chamars and the Muchis. It is very likely that Chamars and Muchis were originally mere subdivisions of one main caste, whose occupation was rearing leather and working in it. They have, however, been two distinct castes since a long time.

—ROWLAND N. L. CHANDRA, 1904

B. Jitulal, pointing out that there were about 1,15,00,000 Charmkars in the whole of India, said that it appeared that the discussions related only to the Charmkars working in factories, and that the agenda dealt with very few problems which really needed attention and were vital for the uplift of the Charmkars. According to him only 10 to 15 percent of the Charmkars were working in the factories while the bulk of them were working inside their own huts in the villages. It would be wrong to assume that by improving the conditions of the factory workers alone, the conditions of those working outside the factories would also be improved.

—*Summary of Proceedings of the Industrial Committee on Tanneries and Leather Goods Manufactories, 1949*

The Chamars came to be so strongly linked with the leather trade and leather industry that policies concerning the leather industry were assumed to be policies concerning the Chamar community. The two epigraphs, representing colonial and nationalist positions, share a common perception of the role and status of Chamars in Indian society. If the British considered Chamars to have naturally been leatherworkers since the ancient past, so did the nationalists. And this image of them was acquiring new meaning through the force of legal and administrative polices. B. Jitulal, a Dalit member of the Indian parliament, argued that independent India's leather policy should take into account the entire Chamar community. Chamars, he said, produced leather goods not only in the factories but also, throughout India, in their homes. This assumed connection between the fortunes of Chamars and those of the leather industry requires further investigation.

How do we understand and explain the Chamars' relationship with the leather industry? How have the two come to be seen as so intertwined and to be spoken of as virtually one and the same? This stereotype sits somewhere between a popular notion and an academic understanding. For example, historian Chitra Joshi wrote in 2003 that "Chamars, traditionally associated with leather work, were dominant in tanneries and leather factories." Their dominance arose, she said, because "managers preferred Chamars because of their 'traditional' skills in the occupation, and middle- and higher-caste workers shared a prejudice against leather as 'unclean.'"[1]

The presence of Chamars in the leather industry has always been explained with reference to tradition. These references were first put forward, and systematically sustained, by colonial ethnography. The first section of this chapter evaluates the claims put forward by colonial ethnographers (such as Rowland Chandra) of a relationship between Chamars and the emergence of the leather industry. In his important survey of the leatherworkers of India in 1946, Ahmad Mukhtar argued that it was natural for Chamar workers to "predominate in the tanneries."[2] A decade later, Arthur Niehoff viewed Chamars' work in the leather factories of Kanpur as merely an extension of their traditional occupation from rural areas into urban industry.[3] In the context of Agra, Owen Lynch has explained the dominance of Jatavs (Chamars) in the shoe industry by saying that this is the "occupational status traditionally assigned to the Jatavs," and Peter Knorringa adds that they do "not suffer much competition from other castes, from whom such an occupation was precluded."[4]

The future of Chamars was increasingly identified with the opportunities created by the leather factories, not merely in their economic promise but also in their potential for social changes. A 1999 study by Tirthankar Roy on artisan communities like Dalits is premised on the assumption that the development of a modern leather industry promised economic and social liberation for the Chamars; "for some of the most numerous and exploited castes, the process involved a social transition as the market opened up avenues of mobility which the society had previously denied them."[5] Indeed, this assumption has a long history. In his evidence to the Hides Cess Enquiry Committee in 1929, A. C. Inskip, of Cooper Allen and Co. in Kanpur, justified the expansion of the leather industries by arguing that they had "opened up new avenues of employment to different classes of people[,] from the illiterate Chamar to the university science graduate."[6] S. K. Sharma's study of Chamar artisans takes the same view: "Since shoe making has been an exclusive occupation of Chamars for centuries together, development of shoe industries and creation of demand for skills in shoe making in the market will definitely open up new avenues for the traditionally skilled leather artisans who continue with their traditionally endowed occupations."[7] It is worth noting that the opportunities for social and economic mobility celebrated by Roy and Sharma exist only within caste-defined limits. Despite bearing the patina of a revisionist economic history, Roy's work merely repeats the colonial argument that the leather industry would liberate Chamars from centuries of oppression and exploitation at the hands of caste Hindus in the rural areas by encouraging them to migrate to the towns and cities.

Tirthankar Roy proposes that the leather trade grew out of "quasi-services that became commercialized during the colonial period."[8] A significant assumption underlies Roy's formulation, and I discuss it at length in this chapter. It is that there was no organized leather trade in India prior to the 1870s, except in the form of the rural *jajmani* system, in which each caste owes specific duties or "quasi-services" to others in the village. In the middle sections of this chapter, I pose two questions in response to Roy's assumption: what were the broad contours of the leather trade in the early nineteenth century, and who were the producers of leather goods?

It is certainly true that Chamars constituted the largest social group of those working within the leather industry. By the 1940s they made up 64 percent of the total work force of the leather industry, followed by Muslims, who made up 32 percent.[9] Chamars were 14 percent of the total working population in the city of Kanpur, the center of the leather industry, the second largest community of workers after Muslims.[10] Their overwhelming presence within the industry reinforced the stereotype that leatherworking was their traditional identity. What were the specific conditions under co-lonialism that promoted and entrenched this stereotype? The colonial state's efforts, through policies and prescriptions, to "make a fit" between Chamars and the leather industry are discussed in the fourth and final sec-tion of this chapter. I examine these efforts and their impact through a discussion of the industrial schools established by the government of Uttar Pradesh in different parts of the state, whose explicit mission was to train Chamars for employment within the leather industry.

Under conditions of colonial domination, industrialization and the formation of the working class follow a trajectory that is significantly dif-ferent from the Western experience. Dipesh Chakrabarty's study of jute workers in Bengal qualifies the earlier assumption that modern industries break premodern ties, arguing that in fact the colonial entrepreneur in-creasingly relies on such ties to promote a continuous supply of labor.[11] Cheap labor was key to the profits of the Bengali jute industry, and for this reason it focused on the "areas of origin" of the workers.[12] The solution to the industry's problems lay in the *sirdars* (jobbers), who were crucial both as suppliers and as supervisors of laborers. The geographical background of the *sirdar* determined the social composition of the work force, for he was the employer, provider, and master. In the Indian leather industry the dominant colonial concern shifted from the workers' geographical origin to their caste identity: they had to be Chamars.

In a 1976 article, Ranjit Das Gupta alerted us to the significance of the caste identity of the worker by arguing, on the basis of the 1911 and 1921 censuses, that the working class in the Bengali jute industry was drawn predominantly from Dalit, tribal, and lower-caste groups within the Hindu community. "The bottom of the industrial hierarchy was formed, in the main, by those at the lowest rung of the traditional [Hindu] social order." Gupta also pointed out that the Chamars constituted 17 percent of unskilled laborers and 5 percent of the skilled work force of the jute industry, more than any other "Hindu" caste.[13] Herein lies the para-dox. The Chamars were not only the largest caste in the leather industry but also the largest in the jute industry; they were also the largest group of emigrants from India to the plantation colonies.[14] Chamars and Koris, the two "untouchable" castes, were also the largest in the Kanpur textile in-dustry in 1906, constituting 32.4 percent of the work force, followed by Muslims at 29.8 percent.[15]

The Chamarization of the Leather Industry

The leather industry that emerged in the second half of the nineteenth century was imagined by the colonial state as a Chamar enterprise. This image was sustained and shaped by ethnographic accounts and official policies that defined an intrinsic relationship between Chamars and the leather trade. The relationship was bolstered by a theory of caste that "Chamarized" the leather industry and by the fact that the industry's work force largely came from the Chamar caste. The caste identity of the working class became a specific concern of the leather industry, and was an important factor in the choice of the city of Kanpur for its establishment. The choice of Kanpur was rather odd. In nineteenth-century colonial India, most industries were being established in the coastal cities of Calcutta, Bombay, and Surat, not in the hinterland of North India. The presence of a military cantonment, which created a demand for leather goods, and the availability of cheap raw material are the usual reasons cited for the choice of Kanpur.[16] However, no historian has recognized that the presence of a large population of Chamars, which the British viewed as a ready source of cheap labor, was one of the most important factors.[17]

The large population of Chamars was central to the selection of the site of the Government Harness and Saddlery Factory, the first modern leather factory in India. The factory's location was chosen after considering its distance from the Chamar neighborhood in Kanpur city. The site that was initially selected was "3 miles from the city, and five or more from the suburbs inhabited by the Chumars, who would be employed in large numbers." It would be expensive, the planners noted, to construct worker housing closer to the factory. It was also feared that the project might take a few years, which would discourage Chamar laborers. The site that was therefore finally chosen for the factory was well within the city, in a disused military harness depot locally known as the Kila (fort) factory. The most important point in favor of the Kila factory was that it was very close to the Chamar settlement.[18] Chamars were certainly an important presence within the Kanpur cantonment, having with their own *mohalla* (neighborhood), which was surrounded by the *mohallas* of artisans and sweepers. Yet these urban Chamars worked in the factories, on the railways, or as domestic servants outside the cantonment.[19]

John Stewart played an important role in setting up the Government Harness and Saddlery Factory. He went to England to learn the latest techniques of leather production and to compare Indian leather with English leather. He convinced the Indian government that with its financial backing he could establish a leather industry to produce top-quality leather products. The backbone of such an investment, Stewart later claimed, was the Chamars' presence in Kanpur and his excellent relationship with the Chamar community. According to Zoe Yalland, Stewart was convinced that "if he could revive the old skills of the local Chamar and introduce European methods of tanning and currying leather, it should be possible in time to produce leather articles as good as any imported from Europe." Yalland highlights Stewart's personal relationship with members of the Chamar community in Kanpur. The Chamars called him "Burra Mochie" (the great English sahib or shoemaker) and installed a statue of him in the Bhagwatdas temple outside the factory gate as a mark of their love for him.[20]

In promoting the selection of Kanpur as the site of the leather industry, the theory that workers' caste identity was crucial had acquired a concrete shape. As well as being supported by ethnographic work, the theory gained enormously from economic factors operating in the latter half of the nineteenth century, to which the colonial state paid particular attention. By the end of the nineteenth century Indian raw hides and skins had become a major export, constituting nearly 10 percent of total exports from the port of Calcutta. Kanpur and Calcutta had become major centers of the production of raw hides and skins. Export of finished leather products promised even higher returns to the colonial state. In order to understand the existing state of the leather industry, including its manufacturing techniques and the workers engaged in it, the colonial state commissioned a survey of the Central Provinces in the first decade of the twentieth century. The objective of these investigations was "to state the condition of the leather industries of the Provinces from the commercial point of view," since that condition was "a fact of some importance to those who may contemplate founding tanneries and leather factories in the Central Provinces."[21] This survey, published in 1904, examined the economics of the trade by focusing on the role of Chamars as workers. The theory that leatherworkers naturally originated in the Chamar caste directed attention to six topics: the transition from artisanal to modern industry, the inefficiency of Chamar methods of tanning, Chamar social and economic uplift, the modern leather industry as a new opportunity for the Chamars, the revival of rural tanning as a handicraft, and the long tradition of Chamar leatherworking.

The survey framed the Chamars' future as the inevitable result of the transition from artisanal to modern industry in which they could be reemployed as workers. Chenevix Trench, its author, predicted the fate of the vast majority of Chamars: "although the leather-working in the district *mufussil* [interior] must always be carried on by the hide and skin castes, the number of these castes actually engaged in trades must be soon reduced to a minimum and the vast majority sink, irretrievably, to the ranks of casual labour."[22] He was convinced that a laboring class would emerge from their ruination to work in the modern factories. But Chamars wouldn't need to "abandon their own profession," because they could be provided with jobs in tanning factories.[23] Briggs agreed that the Chamars should be trained for jobs in the new industries, enabling them to take advantage of new opportunities to offset their displacement from their "traditional" forms of labor. He was convinced that the Chamar flayers and tanners would lose out to the tanning industries in urban areas because of their relative lack of technology and financial support. He believed that the growth of a modern tanning industry in Kanpur had usurped the role of rural tanners by creating new patterns of demand and outflow. For example, raw hides were increasingly sent to Kanpur because they fetched better prices there, making it costlier for the rural tanner to obtain them.[24]

The increased demand for Indian hides and skins was put forward as a major reason to industrialize the leather industry, making it possible to produce tanned hides for both export and the domestic market. By the early twentieth century there appeared to be general agreement that the tanned leather produced by Chamars would lose out to factory-produced leather, which was cheaper and of better quality. Walton observed in his 1903 report that the Chamar tanner produced an "inferior grade of raw materials [from] the skins of animals dying of disease or from starvation."[25] A 1918 report by the Industrial Commission appeared to be stating the inevitable when it remarked that the leather factories would replace the Chamar village tanners because of the inefficiency of the Chamar methods of tanning. The report described the Chamar tanner as "making a good hide into bad leather; and there seems little hope that his industry can or will ever deserve to be saved."[26] In these circumstances it was only natural that Chamars would migrate to cities like Kanpur to work in the leather industries.[27] The Industrial Commission report summed up its position by suggesting that Chamars "who were originally village tanners" constituted a ready work force for the leather industry.

Authorities were concerned with the caste identity of the workers not only because they wanted to create an urban Chamar working class, but also because they desired the Chamars' social and economic uplift.[28] Walton was confident that the good wages offered by the leather factories would persuade the "hand-to-mouth Chamar or Chikwa to retire from his own business and enter the service in one of the large tanneries."[29] Robert Ewbank, registrar of co-operative societies in the Bombay Presidency, told the Industrial Commission in 1917 that the leather industry provided many opportunities for Chamars to improve their social and economic standards. He claimed that "the conditions under which these Chamars live are so degrading that they had better go into the factories at once."[30] In his evidence to the Hides Cess Enquiry on November 6, 1929, A. C. Inskip of Cooper Allen & Co. maintained that the recent expansion of the leather industry represented a great opportunity for "the illiterate Chamars" of the province to improve their conditions.[31] Ewbank and Inskip summed up the widely shared colonial belief that the urban leather industry would liberate Chamars from centuries of oppression by Hindu society. Recently Tirthankar Roy has asserted that "the process [of industrialization of leather production] involved a social transition" and offered the Chamars "avenues of mobility which the society had previously denied to" them, another instance of striking continuities between colonial and postcolonial opinions on Chamars.[32]

Chenevix Trench, writing in 1904, argued that the tanning industry had redefined the traditional role of Chamars in rural areas by providing them a new opportunity from which they stood to benefit. Instead of tanning hide to make shoes, they could buy factory-tanned hide, which was both cheaper and of better quality. Despite his concerns, Briggs too reiterated that "Chamars' traditional occupation offers increasing opportunities" in the context of the modern leather industries. He felt that although in rural areas their numbers as tanners might decline, they would find alternative employment as shoemakers (*mochis*), buying cheaper chrome-tanned leather.[33] In Briggs's view the rural Chamars also stood to benefit from the increasing demand for shoes in the countryside. He suggested that European-style shoes had become popular in urban areas and demand for them would only increase, so Chamars would do well to learn the new techniques needed to manufacture them. Indeed, he said, the number of *mochis* had increased by 33.2 percent, according to the 1911 census.[34] Rowland Chandra emphasized that, if necessary, Chamars could be "acquainted with up-to-date methods of leather manufacture, [which would] prepare the way to the establishment of regular tanneries." The "few industrial institutions in the country," Chandra argued, could provide technical training to Chamars as a step toward their economic uplift.[35]

By the 1920s the UP government was preoccupied with "reviving" native industry by equipping rural Chamars with the necessary "modern" skills of tanning and shoemaking.[36] In order to do so, it organized poor Chamar tanners into cooperatives. Chandra, for instance, cautioned that "any prospect of an expansion of their business or its improvement is most remote" if it were left to individual entrepreneurs, but that cooperatives could better both their conditions and that of the industry.[37] Another officer of the government added that cooperatives would also give Chamar tanners access to cheap credit from government agencies and banks, as well as letting them buy materials more cheaply. By increasing Chamars' earnings, cooperatives would encourage them to tan more hides rather than selling them raw.[38] Several surveys suggested that demonstration parties could be organized for cooperatives to teach modern tanning methods, since the "local ways of tanning by Chamars" were "very crude."[39] Alternatively, "material improvement in their time honoured methods of work" could be effected by making them "conversant with modern methods of work" in modern tanneries or in the newly established leatherworking schools at Kanpur or Meerut. The government believed that by providing technical training to Chamars in the "few industrial institutions in the country," both their conditions and the conditions of the industry could be improved.[40]

All the monographs on the leather industry were eager to argue that the caste identity of leatherworkers dated to ancient India. Walton argued that Chamars were leatherworkers of non-Aryan origin who had continued in this trade even after the Aryans settled in India. He, like Crooke and Briggs, believed that the presence of the word *charmakaram* (worker of leather) in Brahmanical literature attested to the "undoubted antiquity" of this industry and the role of Chamars in sustaining it.[41] The emergence "of the native leather industry in India," Walton said, coincided with "the establishment of Muhammadan rulers in India" and marked a major departure in the history of Indian leatherworking.[42] A variety of leather articles began to be produced, including the army equipment and luxury items that are associated with the pomp of the medieval period. Many colonial accounts reported that the trade in hides and skins began during this period, with evidence suggesting that the trade was primarily in *halali,* hides of slaughtered cattle, rather than *murdari,* hides of cattle that had died naturally.[43]

The theory that the Chamar working class had originated in the context of the leather industry, evident in the six points discussed above, played an influential role in the ethnographic literature. Colonial ethnographers consistently claimed that there was one Chamar caste throughout India. Even though they might call themselves by different names in different regions, they were the same caste because they all shared the occupation of leatherwork, despite their diverse regional backgrounds and identities. William Crooke, for example, identifies sixteen "sub-castes" of the Chamar caste, and the 1891 census mentions 1,156.[44] The 1943 *Report on the Marketing of Hides* declared that Chamars "are known by different names in the various tracts but their functions are generally common throughout" India. Their "principal occupation," according to the report, was "to recover hides from dead animals, occasionally tan them, and prepare cheap and crude leather goods. Dheds in western parts of India, Dhore in the Central Provinces, Madiga and Vettian in the Madras Presidency, Khalpa and Mahar in the Bombay Presidency—all these are identified as alternative names for Chamars."[45]

But a definition of the Chamar caste that relied solely upon leatherworking as the basis of their identity also had its moments of crisis. The colonial ethnographers had to explain the significant presence of Muslim leatherworkers. Conversion of Hindu Chamars to Islam was offered as the most likely explanation. J. S. Nesfield first proposed in 1882 that "a considerable proportion of the Mochi caste has become Muhammadan."[46] Even Walton claimed that the Muslim leatherworkers in the towns and cities of Uttar Pradesh were Chamar converts from Hinduism.[47] The fact that they could suggest such an explanation gives us insight into the way such categories were created and acquired meaning, and into the ethnographers' desire for consistency in their system of classification. Conversion was an explanation that made sense, given the Chamars' oppression under Hinduism. But it also served another important purpose: it allowed their theory of the caste identity of the working class to better fit the economics of the leather trade. Such an explanation grew out of colonial perceptions of the *jajmani* system. The next section explores these colonial perceptions in more detail.

The Leather Trade in Nineteenth-Century Uttar Pradesh

Two assumptions have informed much of our understanding of the emergence of the leather trade in India. They are evident in Tirthankar Roy's proposition that the leather trade was "probably the most important of the quasi-services that became commercialized during the colonial period." The first assumption is that leather is, in Roy's words, "the most important example of outright market creation" and became "a major tradeable in the late nineteenth century," eventually becoming one of South Asia's leading exports. Roy locates the creation of this market to the period after 1875, when the British government abolished the 3 percent export duty on hides. The second assumption is that, before that date, leather was a "quasi-service," "a rural craft" performed by a Chamar who as "an individual was primarily a labourer for the village, invariably an agricultural labourer, and occasionally a crude artisan on the side." Roy suggests that the leatherwork was "unfree for the artisans in a number of senses," because they "were unfree to specialise, to choose customers, or to set prices," and these statements are typical of colonial understandings of the *jajmani* system.[48] Yet there is considerable evidence to suggest that there was a great deal of domestic trade in the early decades of the nineteenth century, including a remarkable diversity of trade in leather goods, and it was policies of the East India Company that prevented the emergence of an export trade in hides and skins. Moreover, it was not the villages but the *qasbas* (market towns) that were the centers of leather production and trade, and the industry was predominantly controlled by Muslim merchants, who were involved at various stages of leather manufacturing.

Prior to 1875 the East India Company did not promote the export of hides and skins, even though contemporary commentators noted the potential for sales to England and Europe. Drawing upon his observations of domestic trade in hides in Bengal, H. T. Colebrooke in 1804 commented on the great potential of such a trade between India and England.[49] In the same year, William Tennant shared Colebrooke's optimism about the hide trade and its potential benefit to England.[50] George Prinsep pointed out in 1823 that the most important export item in the catch-all category of "sundries" was hides, which were exported not just to Britain but also to other countries, including the U.S.[51] Prinsep noted that there was great potential for the trade to increase, if it were freed from the control of the Company or the export duty lowered. He explained that the East India Company earned massive profits by regulating the export and import of goods between India and Britain. With a complete monopoly over the trade route, it determined which items could be shipped and had tremendous power to set prices, control quantities, and generate demand, by controlling shipping rates and the number of ships making the voyage. Merchants in England and India had almost no voice. "It is sufficiently probable," Colebrooke wrote, "that, at the freight of six pounds for a ton, hides might be exported with advantage and afford a profit of twenty per centum; but the rate of fifteen pounds sterling for the ton is prohibitory."[52] The high cost of shipping inhibited the trade in commodities like hides.[53]

K. N. Chaudhuri has argued that the Company's economic policies in the latter half of the eighteenth and first half of the nineteenth centuries "caused serious distortions" in the internal and external trade between Britain and India.[54] The first half of the nineteenth century, however, saw a series of official interventions that divested the Company of its exclusive monopoly on Indian trade in 1813, barring it from trading altogether in 1833. John Crawfurd, in his 1837 criticism of the Company's policies, argued that the abolition of the Company's monopoly allowed the export trade from India to expand, as Europeans invested heavily in various Indian industries, especially the tanneries in Calcutta.[55] The Company acknowledged a significant growth in the hide trade, marked by the fact that in 1829 it removed the trade in hides from the miscellaneous category of "sundries" to give it a separate heading in the Company's log book. In that year, exports totaled 357,610 pieces of hides and skins, with a weight of 178,805 *maunds*.[56] This figure is much less than the annual figures of 600,000–700,000 *maunds* in the 1880s (appendix, table K), but we must take into account the Company's trade barriers, which were still in place.

Contrary to Roy's claim, an export trade in hides did exist prior to the 1875, but it was regulated by the Company. There was also a substantial domestic trade in hides and leather products in Uttar Pradesh in the 1810s and 1820s. A few examples well illustrate this point. In Allahabad a total of 60,000 *maunds* of leather passed through the custom house in 1816, and 75,000 *maunds* in 1817.[57] These figures, from just one town of Uttar Pradesh in the early decades of the nineteenth century, compare well with the province's total export to Calcutta in 1880 (145,404 *maunds*) and 1881 (136,883 *maunds*). Trade in hides was a significant component of the leather trade, as was trade in "superior" and "country" shoes, to borrow the language used in the ledgers of nineteenth-century custom houses, and Allahabad also saw considerable export and import of manufactured shoes and boots. The 1816 report of its custom house noted that "the amount of duties collected on leather have also been nearly doubled owing to the abundant supplies of raw hides which have during the past year been sent from Goruckpore to Jounpore to the westward."[58] Campbell's 1854 report on cattle poisoning had noted the significant role of Azamgarh and Gorakhpur in the North Indian hide trade; they were key centers for trade to Calcutta.[59] In 1831 and 1832 a total of 93,674 *maunds* of hides passed through the Farrukhabad custom house, an impressive figure considering that the total export of hides from Uttar Pradesh was around 200,000 *maunds* a year in the 1880s (appendix, table K).[60] Farrukhabad was regarded as the most "prominent commercial and financial city of the Doab," and the royal mint was based there until its closure in 1832.[61]

According to C. A. Bayly, the volume of India's internal trade was considerable in the eighteenth century, and "the vast trade of the Indian interior continued to dwarf its external trade."[62] Leather was a small but significant part of this trade, and Patna in particular was an important center for it.[63] Francis Buchanan-Hamilton mentioned a great deal of trade in shoes and leather goods from Patna, Danapur, and Bengal, and between Lucknow and Patna. Patna and Danapur were prominent manufacturing centers for leather goods and were known for the quality of their shoes. A major trading center, Patna imported raw hides from Shahabad, Saran, Tirhut, Azamgarh, and Gorakhpur, imported shoes and leather goods from Lucknow, and exported shoes to Bengal.[64] In the nineteenth century Lucknow was an established center of the shoe trade, exporting to Agra, Meerut, Bareilly, Rampur, Moradabad, Kanpur, Fatehpur, Benares, and Patna.[65] A considerable number of leather bags and hides were exported from Bihar to eastern and western Uttar Pradesh. Hameeda Naqvi mentions the export of shoes from Benares to Calcutta in the latter half of the eighteenth century.[66] All of this is in sharp contrast to Roy's proposition that "tanning in the early nineteenth century was almost wholly a rural industry."[67] Robert Montgomery calculated that in the 1840s the annual import of raw hides into Kanpur city from different parts of Uttar Pradesh was worth Rs 100,000 annually, and the local production was worth Rs 75,000. Kanpur also exported Rs 25,000 worth of leather goods to other parts of Uttar Pradesh.[68]

Other indications of the diversity of the trade in leather products come from the Kanpur *Book of Rates* of 1829 and from the Agra *Book of Rates* of

1815.[69] These books of rates provided detailed price lists for various types of articles, including three kinds of buffalo hides, "best, middling, inferior, buffalo large tanned hide, [and] two kinds of small tanned and untanned hides." Similarly, three kinds each of tanned and untanned bullock and cow hides were listed, each with a specific rate. Skins of sheep, goats, and deer were classified along similar lines. These books also listed the rates for boots, shoes, and slippers, of both "native and European kinds," that were being manufactured in Calcutta, Kanpur, and Patna. As Prinsep has shown, the printed books of rates were used to set duties in various custom houses, and for this reason they give us a fair idea of the articles traded.[70]

The vibrant character of trade in leather products suggested by the books of rates indicates the diversity of the artisans based in the towns. Buchanan-Hamilton, in his list of artisans in the city of Patna, included ten professions connected with the leather trade.[71] John Crawfurd's 1820 survey of Bareilly town identified seventy professions, out of which fifteen dealt with leather: "curriers, shoemakers, saddlers, makers of leather bags and bottles, bow and arrow makers, furriers, horse-clot makers, rope makers, leather dealers, tent makers, brush makers, goat dressers, whip makers, butchers and dyers." He argued that most of the towns of North India had a similar range of occupations, and he listed hides as one of North India's great "objects of inland trade."[72]

Historians have seen the diversity in trade and manufactures in Mughal India (1500–1800) as one of the period's characteristic features. Manufacturing was based primarily in *qasba* towns, but urban centers also produced luxury goods. Raychaudhuri has argued that "the traditional consumption pattern of the affluent created a demand for a wide range of comfort goods," including leather-related products.[73] Cooking and drinking water for Emperor Akbar was supplied in leather bags from the Chenab River and the Ganges, and water was also drunk from leather bags. Indeed, all kinds of liquid items were transported in leather bags. Ghee was transported to Delhi in leather bags or bottles known as *kuppis*. We have one fragment of evidence that some 1,300 carts loaded with leather bottles of ghee were looted on their way to Delhi in the year 1730. The imperial *karkhanas* (factories) manufactured a range of leather articles, like harnesses, saddles, and shoes, and paid their workers regular wages. Hameeda Naqvi mentions massive trade between Delhi, Lahore, and Agra, especially in saddles and shoes. Leather goods from Sind were famous all over India and were exported regularly to all the major cities and towns of North India.[74]

Delhi's Qarol (Karol) Bagh neighborhood, which was inhabited by *mochis,* was well known for its shoe and leather manufacturers, and its Kuppe Wala *mohalla* was inhabited by Muslim workers manufacturing leather jars and bags. Lahore and Multan were renowned for shoes, boots, harnesses, and saddles.[75] Leather goods, particularly raw hides and tanned leather, were important taxable commodities in the reign of Akbar.[76] Ray-chaudhuri writes, "Despite the dominance of subsistence-oriented production, in rural manufactures as in agriculture, exchange had made deep inroads: both the peasant-manufacturer and the artisan bound to the village community responded to the development of the market."[77] There was a great deal of commodity exchange between *qasbas* and *katras* (market towns) in rural regions. Each *qasba* had its share of artisanal and occupational classes like shoemakers. Stray pieces of evidence from disparate sources all suggest a robust trade in leather commodities and a range of artisanal crafts in the seventeenth and eighteenth centuries. *Qasbas* were the centers of leather production and trade in North India, and leatherworkers and shoemakers were important fixtures of these towns.[78]

The role of *qasbas* was also highlighted by the district industrial survey conducted by the government of Uttar Pradesh between 1920 and 1922, which provides a wealth of information about various aspects of the leather trade and industry. The leather trade of the time was summed up by the report on the Rae Bareli district: "Specialisation and large scale production at central places and not the principle of self-sufficient economy for every village is the order of the day."[79] Such district industrial surveys make clear that *qasbas* were the leather manufacturing centers, producing raw hides and skins, shoes, *kuppis,* saddles, and bags, not the villages enmeshed in the *jajmani* system as suggested by Tirthankar Roy.

On the basis of these surveys I distinguish between two kinds of tanning centers. The first kind produced raw and tanned hides and finished leather products, exporting only a few raw hides to Kanpur, Agra, and Calcutta. Despite the emergence of a tanning industry, the *qasbas* continued to produce hides and finished leather products, and the traditional centers of production (Jhansi, Saharanpur, Lucknow, Jaunpur, Ghazipur, and Rae Bareli) maintained their importance. It was not a simple case of hides being shipped from the countryside to production centers in Kanpur or Calcutta and manufactured goods being sent back to the rural areas. Rather, trade patterns varied in different regions of Uttar Pradesh. In 1890, the annual trade report of Uttar Pradesh noted that the district of Saharanpur was renowned for its products "made of *sambar* [deer] leather" and also had a "pretty large business in articles made of common leather."[80] The district survey report of 1923 mentioned that Saharanpur produced around 15,900 *maunds* of hides annually, out of which half were consumed locally and the remainder exported to Kanpur. It was famous for its shoes and sandals, which were exported to eastern districts of Uttar Pradesh and to Calcutta, and for leather "gun covers, cartridge cases, cartridge belts, bedding straps, bottle cases, tumbler cases, harnesses etc."[81] In the 1920s, *mochis* and Chamar tanners were based in the four prominent *qasbas* of leather production in Muzaffarnagar district: Budhana, Lisadh, Gafoorgarh, and Shoron. They tanned and consumed nearly 12,000 *maunds* of hides and skin annually. In Hardoi district each *tahsil* had *qasbas* of tanning and leather production: Shahabad, Pihani, and Pali *qasbas* in Shahabad *tahsil,* Sandi and Mallawan *qasbas* in Bilgram *tahsil,* and Hardoi and Gopamau *qasbas* in Hardoi *tahsil.* Locally tanned leather was used to manufacture the soles of shoes, and imported leather from Kanpur was used to make the uppers. From Hardoi five thousand pairs of shoes were shipped to Bihar and Bombay.[82]

Jhansi was well known for its leather products and maintained its position into the early part of the twentieth century. In 1923 it produced about 28,514 *maunds* of hides (including 8,514 *maunds* imported from the native state of Tikamgarh), out of which 21,440 *maunds* were consumed locally and 7,000 were exported to Kanpur, Agra, and Delhi. It also imported tanned leather worth Rs 129,600 annually from Kanpur, Delhi, Agra, and Calcutta. This impressive trade was based in the *qasbas* of Moth, Jhansi, Lalitpur, Chirgaon, and Mau, controlled by Muslim merchants and artisans and Chamar tanners.[83] Aligarh district was a major center of shoe production in Uttar Pradesh, producing 250,000 pairs of "native shoes" (worth nearly Rs 200,000) and 37,500 pairs of English-style shoes (worth Rs 84,375) in that year. Out of 28,000 pieces of hides and skin produced, 70 percent were consumed locally by the shoe industry.[84]

Rae Bareli was known for its *salim shahi* shoes, which were very light and much in demand among the landed gentry. Regular shoes were exported in large numbers to Bihar, Calcutta, and Bombay, apparently for the "up-country labourers" of North India, but most of the hide and skin produced in Rae

Bareli was consumed locally.[85] Lalganj, Maharganj, and Bachhrawan were major centers of tanning and manufacturing, employing regularly paid *mochis*. Lucknow was another center of leather production, famous for its shoes, sandals, and boots, and its tanning and manufacturing were still organized around the city's *karkhanas*. Most of these were located in the neighborhoods of Molviganj, Yahiaganj, and Raneeganj, and some hides were also tanned in the *qasbas* around the city and in neighboring Malihabad *tahsils*.[86] Lucknow and the surrounding areas produced 54,000 pieces of hide and skin, much of which was locally tanned and consumed. Shoes, however, were exported from Lucknow to all parts of India and even to Mesopotamia and Egypt, with an annual export of 10,000 pairs.[87]

The second kind of tanning centers were those primarily engaged in the production of raw hides and skins for export to Kanpur, Agra, Calcutta, and Delhi. Adjacent to Kanpur, Fatehpur played an important role as an ancillary center for the distribution of raw and tanned hides and skins to Kanpur for reexport to Calcutta or Madras.[88] Hariharganj, Baqarganj, and Jahanabad were the major markets, receiving a weekly supply of 5,000 *maunds* of hides and skins and with an annual turnover of 80,000 *maunds* in 1923. Their weekly business in 1907–1908 was nearly 7,000 pieces of hides and skins. Azamgarh and Gorakhpur districts in eastern Uttar Pradesh were major exporters of raw hides and skins, with the latter exporting 34,150 *maunds* of hides and skin in 1922.[89] Mau, Mubarakpur, and Kopagunj in Azamgarh were major centers of hide export, though Azamgarh's export of 4,000 *maunds* in 1922 was very low, considering its importance to the hide trade.[90] Hamirpur district produced an annual surplus of 12,000 *maunds* of hides and skins in 1923, out of which 9,000 *maunds* were exported to Kanpur and Agra. Its prominent *qasbas* of tanning production were based in the *tahsils* of Kulpahar, Mahoba, Maudaha, Hamirpur, and Rath. For example, the *qasbas* of Supa, Panwari, Jaitpur, Ajnar, Mahwabandh, and Kulpahar were centers of leather production in Kulpahar *tahsil*.[91] In most such districts 80 to 90 percent of the raw hides and skins produced were exported to Kanpur, Calcutta, and Agra.

The district industrial surveys made a crucial distinction between full-time and part-time workers, locating the difference in the production process, not the workers' caste. Full-time Chamar tanners were usually based in the *qasbas*, where there was regular work and a supply of hides and skins, and were most likely known as *mochis*. B. R. Bhatta noted in 1924 that "country

Chamars do ordinary tanning in a small way and are to be found in almost all large towns and *qasbas* like Bisalpur, Puranpur, Dharmapur, Mohammadpur, Piparia, Tanda, Nawadia, Naogawan, Kalinagar, and etc."[92] B. K. Ghoshal, in the 1923 survey of the Kheri, wrote that "the *mochis* are generally agriculturists, except the *mochis* of Kheir and Mhaumdi [*tahsils*] where there is regular demand."[93] The production of tanned hides and leather goods was seasonal, and thus attracted Chamar cultivators from the neighboring villages who were eager to earn extra income. In Hamirpur district the seasonal or "part-time" work force constituted 40 percent of the work force in 1923.[94] The Jhansi district survey gives us a gender breakdown, with 959 male and 289 female full-time tanners, out of which 227 males and 47 females were agriculturists.[95] These examples show that the *qasbas* were strong centers of production with full-time workforces.

More significantly, the 1923–24 district industrial surveys underscore the diverse social composition of the work force in the *qasbas,* compared to the "modern" leather industry. It was not just Muslims or Chamars but also other "untouchable" castes like Khatiks, Bhangis, and Pasis who lived in the *qasbas* and worked as *mochis* and as full-time leatherworkers.[96] In Fyzabad and Bahraich it was the Bhangis who were involved in the leather trade.[97] In the Bhopa bazaar Chamars constituted nearly 50 percent of residents, working for Muslim traders not just as tanners but also on odd jobs connected with other kinds of trading activities.[98] Full-time jobs and the presence of a regular market attracted these diverse groups to *qasbas.*

The dealers in the *qasbas* formed the axis of the trading network by collecting hides from the *hat* (periodical market) in the countryside. The weekly market was the major venue for trade in the rural countryside. The best description of the trading network, from the *hat* to the tanneries in Kanpur, is given by J. S. Vatal in his survey of the adjoining Fatehpur district:

> People from the neighbouring villages of this [Fatehpur] and the Banda district bring raw hides and skins to the bazaars. These are sold to beoparis [traders] personally visiting the markets or are purchased by local dealers. The latter in their turn treat them with salt and send them to their Cawnpore agents in carts paying Rs. 1-4-0 for every 20 hides as cart hire. The agents sell them to the exporters charging a commission from Rs 2 to Rs 2-8-0 per 20 hides. Commission on sale of skins is Rs 2-8-0 per 100. The seller has to pay to the proprietors of the markets a royalty at the rate of 1 to 4 pice per hide and Re 0-4-0 per 100 skins.[99]

R. Saran, in his survey of the Moradabad district, mentions that Chuchaila town in Hasanpur *tahsil* was the largest market for hides and skins in the district and attracted hides from neighboring districts like Bijnor: "about 500 pieces are brought for sale on the market days [every Saturday]."[100] The weekly market also produced good tanned hides and skins which were bought by the merchants "for export to mofussil [interior] towns."[101] Railway stations also became centers of trade; for example, Chauri Chaura became a prominent center of hide export to Kanpur.[102] Bhopa bazaar, "located at a distance from Chaura because of its peculiar leather trade," was a major center of the hide trade, and lightly cured hides were exported from the Chaura railway station to Kanpur and Calcutta. Once a week "about 300–400 persons came together to do business" at Bhopa from neighboring villages, and among them were Muslim and Chamar cultivators who would bring hides to sell.[103]

The Relationship of Muslims to Leather Production and Trade

It is clear that Muslims played important roles at many levels of the *qasba*-centered leather industry and trade. By investigating these roles, we can also identify the position of Chamars in this trade. First, I contend that the Muslims not only controlled the domestic and overseas leather trade but were also involved in leather manufacturing in the *qasbas* and worked as retailers in towns and cities. Chamars were predominantly workers. Second, in the late nineteenth century colonial officers came to understand Chamars' association with the leather trade purely in terms of the *jajmani* system, and postcolonial ethnographers inherited this understanding. Such a disjunct understanding of Muslims' and Chamars' role in the leather trade prevented the colonial state from considering the possibility that the Chamars had entered the trade within the last two centuries.

The most significant feature of the leather trade was its domination by Muslim artisans and traders. Chamars appeared mostly as tanners or producers of low-end native shoes. Francis Buchanan, in his 1813 survey of North India, mentioned only Muslims as wage-earning workers and traders in leather products in the city of Patna. In Gorakhpur, Muslim *mochis* like Siraj and Sawarwala were artisans producing exquisite shoes and saddles from the skins of goats, sheep, deer, and buffaloes, while Chamars worked for wages as tanners and shoemakers. Buchanan explains their involvement in leather as related to agriculture, not as deriving from any "traditional" occupation. Chamars would mostly make low-end agricultural products like leather bags for use in irrigation and ropes for drawing plows, along with musical instruments like drumheads and occasionally shoes.[104] In his 1880 monograph on trade and manufactures in North India, William Hoey explained that the term *chirmfarosh* was "used to cover all classes of leather dealers," who were Muslims.[105] *Chirma,* a word perhaps related to "Chamar," was used to describe a profession dominated by Muslims, not Chamars.

Shahid Amin's discussion of the Bhopa bazaar in the town of Chauri Chaura in eastern Uttar Pradesh is instructive because the Muslim traders controlled it, both socially and economically.[106] The bazaar can be taken as representative of leather trading centers in Uttar Pradesh as a whole. Not only there but throughout the province Muslim traders, dealers, and agents controlled the hide trade and the leather manufacturing business, a point on which the district industrial surveys are unanimous. As local traders and dealers in hide in the *qasbas* and towns, they employed Chamar tanners and exported leather to Kanpur and Calcutta. In most of the cities and towns of Uttar Pradesh, Muslims had a significant presence in the shoe and boot business because they produced English-style shoes for the burgeoning urban population.[107] By the 1920s, the Agra shoe industry had become the most important business in Uttar Pradesh, employing some 25,000 persons, of whom 95 percent were Muslim.[108] Muslims also controlled much of the retail trade in the city. In Kanpur city they controlled the entire boot and shoe business and much of the trade in hides.[109] A notable feature of the retail trade in the 1920s was that Muslims produced English-style shoes and the Chamars produced native shoes.[110] Muslims also controlled the urban butchering and meat selling business, in which they were typically known as *chikwas* if they slaughtered goats or sheep and as *qassabs* if they slaughtered cattle.[111] The establishment of municipal slaughterhouses from the 1860s onward opened new opportunities for Muslim butchers.[112] As meat sellers in cities and towns they controlled the trade in skins and hides, a point made in all the district industrial surveys.[113]

Who were the primary producers of hides in India: Chamars or Muslims? This question was part of the debate surrounding the additional "cess" or tax that was imposed on the export of raw hides during the First World War. The cess continued after the war, despite opposition by hide producers, and in 1929 the Hides Cess Enquiry Committee was set up to determine whether it should continue unchanged, or be imposed on some other item related to leather, or be abolished. Chaudhari Sahab-ud-din, MLA from Punjab, claimed in his deposition before the Committee that the hide and skin industry was the only business that Muslims controlled in India.[114] He appealed to the British government to abolish the cess, otherwise the Muslim community would lose control over it. Sahab-ud-din explained that the cess had affected the Muslims in three ways. First, it led to a significant decline in the export of raw and tanned hides during and after the war. Second, the depressed export market led to a decline in the number of cattle slaughtered and an increase in the price of raw hides and skin on the domestic market. Third, the decline in slaughtered cattle raised the price of meat, both beef and mutton, which were primarily eaten by Muslims. As an elected representative, Sahab-ud-din was trying to protect the interests of the Muslim merchants and traders in Punjab who controlled the export and domestic trade in hides and leather goods. By claiming that the leather industry was a "Muslim industry," Sahab-ud-din was appealing to British notions of governmentality, which were particularly receptive to appeals in the name of a community. Yet he was also genuinely concerned that if the cess continued it would cause a minority community to lose its occupation and industry, with disastrous effects.

E. L. Price, a member of the Hides Cess Enquiry Committee, disagreed with its report and wrote a "minute of dissent." He was the most vocal advocate of abolishing the cess on the export of raw hides, claiming that its continuation would affect Chamars more than Muslims. He succinctly framed the debate as a "struggle between primary producers [the Chamars], who demand untrammelled access to world markets," and Indian tanners, who demand a "preserved market" in which to buy their raw material." According to him, the Chamars were primary producers because it was their "traditional occupation." Without an "alternative career," the Chamars would suffer most if prices continued to decline, because they would continue to sell hides. There was no one "poorer than the Chamar," whose "poverty is so extreme [he] has the greatest claim on our consideration," and he needed access to "free and untrammelled markets." He argued that the tanning and leather industry was in favor of the cess because it wanted to preserve its control over the domestic market by making export prohibitively expensive and keeping domestic prices low.[115]

The question we should ask is why Price was so concerned with the fate and conditions of Chamars. His arguments sound as though he represented

Chamars before the Hides Cess Enquiry Committee, but he did not. Price represented the Karachi Shippers and Merchants of Hides. The members of the Karachi Shippers and Merchants were primarily Muslim exporters of raw hides. The cess had already increased their costs. By raising the question of the Chamars' condition Price was cleverly making the cess a moral issue, one that would appeal to reform-minded sections of Indian society. His statements were shaped by the immediate political context. By 1929 Dalit politics had become a very contentious issue in the eyes of many sections of Hindu society. Both Gandhi and Ambedkar had raised the issue centrally in their movements. The liberation of Dalits (including Chamars) was an issue that concerned both the nationalists and the British. Making an appeal in the name of impoverished Chamars was a convenient way for Price to justify his position.

J. C. Donaldson, director of industries in Uttar Pradesh in 1930, refuted Price's argument that the cess weighed heavily on the Chamars. First, he argued that the cess provided a necessary "protection and encouragement to Indian Tanners," shielding them from foreign competition. Second, Donaldson did not agree that the Chamars were the primary producers of hides in India. He argued that in India "it is a butcher or a hide merchant or both" who should be regarded as a primary producer, because in India cattle were not raised "for meat or skins."[116] Donaldson maintained that a Chamar did "not necessarily become a primary producer of hides" merely because of his caste, insisting instead that "the Chamar is largely an agriculturist like others holding land ranging between 2 to 9 *bighas* paying Rs 9 to 51 rental, and having as assets the grain he raises and the proceeds he obtains from sale thereof." He was keen to emphasize that the Chamars were primarily cultivators, and questioned the way that the category of "Chamar" had become a metaphor for the leather trade.[117] Chamars had no stake in this debate but appeared in it nonetheless, although the export trade and the domestic leather industry were both largely dominated by sections of the Muslim community.

Despite the Muslim domination of the leather trade and industry, it was Chamars who became almost exclusively linked to it. One good reason for such a linkage to emerge was that colonial ethnographers explained Chamars' relationship with the leather trade as part of the *jajmani* system. George Campbell first highlighted the role of the *jajmani* system, through "which the chamars became possessed of the bodies and skins of the dead animals," in his 1854 investigations into cattle poisoning:

The cultivators of each village are parcelled out among certain families of chamars. The latter perform certain services for the cultivators, and receive the bodies of all the animals belonging to their own particular cultivators which die. Hence individual chamars, when they poison a particular animal, obtain possession of the body in virtue of a prescriptive right of the nature of a contract, and well established.[118]

This explanation became an important reference point for subsequent investigations into the crime Campbell had identified. The 1871 report of the Indian Cattle Plague Commission also claimed that Chamars "assert a right by tradition . . . to the hides of all animals dying in the village to which they are attached (and one or more families of these people is attached to every village in India)." Stating that the "rights" of Chamars had regional variations, it listed eight different ones, including a prescriptive right to hides, payment for the hides, and a nominal rent of land in return for skinning the cattle.[119] William Crooke, in the introduction to his celebrated ethnographic account of the castes of Uttar Pradesh, reiterated the · role of the *jajmani* system in determining Chamars' role in village society. He claimed that "as a rule, he [the Chamar] has a circle of constituents (jajman) whose dead cattle he receives, and to whom he gives leather and a certain number of shoes in return."[120] William Hoey's classic study called Chamars' involvement in the leather trade a "well known" fact, claiming that "chamars having a jajmani of dead animals resort to poisoning to procure death of animals that they may have the skins."[121] The official investigation into cattle poisoning framed the role of Chamars in the leather trade as a product of the *jajmani* system.

In a revisionist study of the *jajmani* system Peter Mayer has argued that menial castes like the Bhangis and the Chamars were transformed into the possessors of *jajmani* ties in the late nineteenth century. Mayer contests that the *jajmani* system, "as it exists in the anthropological literature, is largely a special kind of invented tradition" and not a timeless, ancient one.[122] Similarly, in his extensive study of land rights and records in colonial Punjab, Richard Smith has concluded that the *wajib-ul-arz* or "record of classes of rights" was transformed into an idea of "customary" rights and duties of all classes of a village. Smith has argued that the *wajib-ul-arz* transformed the village community into a community of castes by assigning each caste a set of practices and duties. The ability of each person to independently determine his own share of rights and duties was "undermined when the shares were written down, classified, given legal substance and filed away in the records room."[123]

In Uttar Pradesh, too, the association of Chamars with leatherwork was recorded in the land settlement surveys that were cited by inquiries and ethnographers as evidence of the Chamars' rights and duties. In the process, Chamar shares in a village community were transformed into what Smith has called "preordained legal categories," protected and guaranteed by the courts and the government. D. M. Stewart, in his 1922 inquiry into the cesses of Awadh, made clear the transformations that such classifications had achieved. He concluded that the *wajib-ul-arz,* "from the circumstances in which it was prepared, . . . has, as a rule, been regarded as very strong evidence of the facts stated in it and an entry in the *wajib-ul-arz* has usually been reckoned as almost sufficient proof of the existence of a custom."[124] The *wajib-ul-arz* were transformed from a "record of classes of right" into customary rights and duties. The Chamars' relationship with leatherwork, with fallen cattle, and with the hide and leather trade came to be considered part of the customary *jajmani* system that was guaranteed by Hindu religious beliefs and customs.

Indeed, even when persons identified as members of the Chamar caste showed initiative in participating in the leather trade, this was interpreted as their hereditary caste duty prescribed under the *jajmani* system. Evidence in the police reports shows that by the late 1880s Chamars had begun to buy and sell old or sick cattle that had been disowned by the Hindu peasantry, rather than relying on a notion of customary rights.[125] By the 1890s a new breed of entrepreneurs had appeared in the form of Chamar contractors who bought the right to collect hides from the local zamindars. This became a particular feature of the trade in the eastern districts of Benares, Azamgarh, Ghazipur, and Ballia.[126] In the Awadh region the practice was known as *thekadari* or contractorship, and D. M. Stewart, in his report of 1922, described it as "of recent origin." In districts like Bahraich, Fyzabad, and Partabgarh, among others, the zamindars auctioned the right to collect hides in their *zamindari* to Chamar contractors or *thekadars.* The cost of the *theka,* or contract, depended on the size of the village's grazing facilities and the scale of the hide trade. Across Awadh the zamindars began to demand cash payment from Chamars.[127] It is apparent that the colonial economy, ethnography, and legal system enabled Chamars to carve out a role in the leather trade.

It was not because of any traditional role, but because they took advantage of the opportunities available to them, that Chamars became important in the Kanpur leather industry. In his biographical account of the "rise and progress" of Kanpur, Gavin Jones claimed that "the humble Chamars, the chief labouring population of Cawnpore, were the first to benefit by the British occupation; being of low caste and exceedingly poor, they served as menials in the British camp." He went on to argue that they took advantage of the situation in Kanpur to fulfill the immediate needs of sepoys and camp followers by repairing their leather accoutrements, especially their shoes.[128] British and European firms like Bathgate & Campbell controlled the leather trade in Kanpur.[129] Chamars were "able to make passable leather" and products that they had never made before, but which over a period of time acquired a good reputation.[130] Baboo Ram, a Chamar saddle and harness maker, was among the first of the Indians to advertise in the *Pioneer* in the 1860s, demonstrating the entrepreneurial spirit found among many of those Chamars who took advantage of the new opportunities.[131] By 1849 Kanpur had become the most renowned center of leather production in India, exporting leather products like carriage harnesses and saddlery to other parts of the country.[132]

Producing Chamar Workers for the Leather Industry

S. H. Freemantle, in his 1906 survey of the industrial workers of Uttar Pradesh, underlined the importance of caste to employment in leather industries. He claimed that Chamars were recruited for work relating to tanning, curing, and saddlery, work that involved touching raw leather, while the stitching and finishing were done largely by Muslim workers.[133] The 1930 report by the Royal Commission on Labour acknowledged that caste played an important role in the recruitment of labor to the various industries. The commission claimed that each occupation had a traditional and hereditary relationship to a caste that forbade occupational mobility.[134] The policies of the colonial state also drew on this assumption in order to ensure Chamar participation in the leather industry, making Chamars into leatherworkers even when they had not previously been such. The colonial discourse created a particular and time-honored image of Chamars in the leather industries by establishing leather training schools.

The Uttar Pradesh government focused on Chamars and the leather trade for economic reasons. By the end of the nineteenth century the leather trade was the East India Company's eighth most profitable export business.[135] The export of hides and skins brought in almost 5 percent of India's total export earnings between 1880 and 1930.[136] Eighty-five percent of India's total hides and skins were exported from Calcutta, and Uttar Pradesh's share of these was fairly significant; in the 1880s its annual contribution was around 20 percent of the total export, and this fraction increased to around 25 percent in the 1890s (appendix, table K).[137] Between 75 and 80 percent of the hides and skins produced in India during this period came from "fallen" cattle, and the rest from slaughtered cattle.[138] Export was particularly brisk during times of drought and famine, when cattle mortality was high.[139] Three kinds of raw hides—dry-salted, wet-salted, and arsenic-dried—were exported, chiefly from Calcutta, to England and other parts of Europe and America.

A. C. Chatterjee was appointed by the Uttar Pradesh government in 1907 to "enquire into the condition of the local industries and the possibilities of their development." He recommended "a judicious encouragement of the tanning and leather industries that would afford employment to a very large number of Chamars and poorer Musalmans, without the absolute necessity of removing them from villages to congested areas in towns." Introducing new techniques would make leatherwork more profitable in the rural areas and encourage Chamars to remain there. To achieve this objective he suggested the creation of two kinds of schools. First, tanning schools should be established to demonstrate the new methods and techniques. These schools should be opened in districts with large Chamar and Muslim populations, like the Lucknow, Gorakhpur, and Saharanpur districts in Uttar Pradesh. Second, special schools should be opened for those Chamars skilled at producing finished leather products. These schools, he felt, could teach Chamar *mochis* new techniques in "boot and shoe-making, saddlery and harness with modern tools and appliances." He proposed that these schools not be located in areas like Kanpur, Benares, Agra, or Meerut, which already had trained laborers.[140] The 1924 district industrial survey reports, especially those on Fatehpur, Kheri, Rae Bareli, Sultanpur, Muzaffarnagar, and Meerut, placed a similar emphasis on improving Chamars' flaying and tanning techniques.[141]

In the inaugural address of the industrial conference held at Nainital in 1907, the lieutenant governor adopted most of the measures Chatterjee outlined in his report. He agreed that the government "should start small tanning demonstration schools" to encourage the industry. The conference adopted a resolution requesting the government to open a chrome-tanning school for "teaching boot and shoe-making with improved tools being attached to it."[142] Indeed, in 1908 the government opened schools in Lucknow at an annual cost of Rs 15,000 to train Chamar boys and men "who have already some knowledge of leather working." The governor was hopeful that "a good deal of Government work might be done at the school."[143]

The first boot- and shoemaking school was established in Lucknow in 1908, and admission was restricted to students from Chamar castes.[144] In other words, no non-Chamars were to be given this opportunity to learn new leatherworking techniques. In 1915 a tanning school was established at Kanpur and a proposal was approved for a third school at Meerut. E. A. H. Blunt, secretary to the provincial government, believed that the Meerut school would provide technical know-how to the local leather industry. It would "work on the lines of the leather-working school at Cawnpore and it is believed that passed students will find no difficulty in getting employment at Delhi and other places in the vicinity."[145] The government approved the Meerut school on January 9, 1919, and it opened in 1921.[146] These locations were chosen because leather industries and a Chamar work force already existed there.

In 1925 the government decided to open a tanning school in Agra, on the principle that the schools in Kanpur, Lucknow, and Meerut had served the industry well and a school in Agra would do the same. The Industries Department wanted this school to be closely associated with the "immediate need of the leather industry." It argued that "Agra is one of the chief centres of the footwear industry and it is just possible that the need for such a school there may be greater than elsewhere," and therefore the school should focus on developing and teaching footwear manufacture.[147] The government started another tanning school in the neighboring district of Fatehpur in 1927 to train students "in modern methods of curing, tanning (both bark and chrome) and finishing." It promoted Chamar candidates by reserving five stipends out of ten for "students with hereditary connexion with the industry."[148]

Chatterjee had also suggested that the government should utilize the caste networks in promoting leatherworking schools, because "caste influence is very strong among these communities."[149] The government decided to ask the help of an important Chamar leader, Babu Khem Chand, who was also invited to the Round Table Conferences in London. It believed that such schools would "improve the conditions of the depressed classes from which Babu Khem Chand comes," and his presence would "help us [the government] in getting the necessary recruits."[150] By ensuring his involvement, the British were sending a message to the Chamar community that the initiative was for their benefit. The focus on skilled Chamars who were already employed in factories or self-employed in small-scale leatherwork was intended to strengthen leather production. A particular feature of the schools in Agra, Kanpur, and Meerut was that they provided "evening classes for helping *mistris* [carpenters] and *mochis* in the trade to improve their general outlook." In addition, they were "taught a little reading and writing, a short history of their trade, also drawing, so that they may be able to copy out an illustration in solid or reduce a solid three dimensional article to a figure on paper."[151]

The leather schools of Kanpur, Meerut, and Agra adopted curricula that were perceived to suit the local system of production. The schools in Kanpur and Meerut taught "hand-sewn" systems, "in which one man makes a whole shoe, that is, he completes all the various parts and prepares a complete pair of shoes himself."[152] Under this system, production was organized in small factories which were controlled and owned by a skilled worker and produced only limited numbers of shoes. A different system of shoe production prevailed in the bigger factories, such as the Government Harness and Saddlery, where different sections produced different parts of shoes, forty to fifty pairs a day. The school in Agra taught this system, followed by a six-month apprenticeship.

Besides leatherworking schools, the government also organized classes and demonstrations to establish direct contact with Chamars in rural areas. The industrial surveys of Fatehpur, Rae Bareli, Sultanpur, and several other districts suggested such projects, in the hope that they would equip Chamars with modern techniques.[153] In villages that had a large population of Chamar tanners, a short series of classes would be organized to educate the Chamars "in correct methods of flaying and curing by actual demonstration." In an undated report, L. N. Srivastava claimed that by the middle of the 1930s some four thousand Chamars and butchers had been trained in modern techniques of flaying, and twenty-six classes had been held in different parts of the state.[154]

But the attempt to Chamarize the leather industry by opening training schools in Uttar Pradesh failed to realize its objective. Officials had presumed that these schools would attract students from the Chamar caste, but they did not. The few available statistics on students' social background show a stark incongruity between official beliefs and social reality: Chamars were conspicuously absent. In 1919 the school in Kanpur had 45 students, out of whom 38 were Muslim, 3 Christian, 2 Brahman, 1 Eurasian, and 1 Parsi.[155] In the school at Meerut, out of 25 students, 22 were Muslim, 2 were identified as Hindus, and 1 was identified as Chamar. In the Kanpur school in 1921, out of 41 students, 34 were Muslim, 3 Christian, 2 Brahman, and 2 Kayastha.[156] Muslims overwhelmingly dominated these schools, constituting nearly 90 percent of the students. This is not all that surprising, for Muslims controlled the leather trade. But the Muslim community's relationship with leather, unlike that of the Chamars, was never conceptualized as traditional or hereditary. In 1928 the government recognized that the schools were training individuals "who have no hereditary connexion with the industry." The director of industries emphasized that it was Chamars who needed training and education in the latest techniques of tanning.[157]

As the chief entrepreneurs in the leather industry, Muslims immediately saw the benefit the leather training schools brought to their business. The promise of improvements to their skills and to the trade in general inspired a private initiative for a leatherworking school from the Muslim community. Noor-ul-Uloom, the first such private school, was established in Bahraich in January 1937, with the assistance of an annual grant-in-aid of Rs 600 given by the Department of Industries. The school was part of the Masudia Noor-ul-Uloom, which had been providing religious and secular education in both Persian and Arabic for the last seven years. Government support was sought in order to create "a good field of employment for the youths of our community which is specially shy and backward in joining vocations of trade."[158] In its first year fourteen students registered in the madrasa to study at the leatherworking school.. The director of industries and commerce, H. N. Sapru, opposed a request for additional funding for the school by arguing that Chamar students didn't attend it; it was a Muslim initiative on behalf of Muslim youth. "The school will serve no useful purpose either to the industry or unemployed youths."[159]

The government-run Saddlery and Harness Company relied on the Chamarization theory by focusing on the caste identity of its workers. It utilized the caste networks of its employees to recruit new workers. Ahmad Mukhtar wrote that if there was a "shortage of trained labour," the company would "send some of the employees or agents to their native places to bring in new recruits"; it also employed the "sons and relatives of retiring or old employees."[160] The superintendent of the Saddlery and Harness Company at Kanpur, in his deposition to the Royal Commission on Labour, acknowledged that the company preferred to employ Chamars. He stated that "our labourers comprise low caste Hindus employed in the tannery, curriery and saddlery departments and mixed castes of Hindus and Muhammadans, employed in the metal fitting, smithy, carpentry and tailoring sections." The government company also adopted the policy, recommended by the state government, of starting schools to train the children of employees as "boy artisans." Some sixty such children regularly attended the factory schools in the 1930s.[161] Such policies aimed at producing Chamar workers. Yet Ahmad Mukhtar concluded that workers "from the professional chamars" background were recruited because of their skills and experience, and were paid better wages than workers from other castes.[162] This conclusion is still widely accepted by scholars, as is evident in Chitra Joshi's 2003 book.

Ahmad Mukhtar, along with the vast majority of Indian nationalists, shared the colonialists' belief in the potential of the leather industry to liberate Chamars from poverty and oppression. The nationalists, like the colonial administrators before them, also emphasized that children of *harijans* or "untouchables" should be trained in their "parental occupation." The Indian National Congress established a Harijan Udyougshala or workshop at Kingsway Camp in Delhi in 1936. Out of twenty-five boys, nineteen were Chamars, who were taught shoemaking. The rest—one Brahman, two Khatris, one Jat, and two Bhangis—were taught carpentry. By training students to use modern techniques in their parental occupation, the Congress hoped to equip them to achieve "a higher standard of life than their parents." By establishing the school, the Congress sought to engage the "sympathy of all those interested in the well-being of Harijans," i.e., reform-minded upper-caste Hindus. It also brought to the notice of caste Hindus that "most of the boys being Chamars have taken up the parental occupation without being squeamish about leather work."[163] The nationalists were equally desirous to reinforce caste hierarchies, and caste Hindus were especially receptive to actions which would further fix the Chamars in rigidly defined roles. However, this was hardly a reflection of tradition. Like the schools run by the colonial government, the schools established by the nationalists could not have been more modern.

The 1937 Report on Congress Ministries readily adopted the agenda of training the "poor and depressed classes" by improving the village tanning industry, which could "provide work for thousands of people living in villages." The report claimed, "If we export leather instead of hides and skins we can place more than a crore [i.e., ten million rupees] in the pockets of the poor."[164] According to Gopinath Srivastava, a Congress member and parliamentary secretary in the Congress ministry, the Uttar Pradesh government had started "a scheme for the development of raw hide industry . . . for the economic uplift of the [Chamars]." The Congress government introduced tanning classes in all the urban industrial schools, and in the rural centers it provided "tuitional classes in tanning" given by an "expert instructor known as *ustad* [master] who gave demonstrations in the use of improved tools and appliances." The classes focused on "flaying, preservation and curing of hides and tanning by improved methods."[165]

By ignoring the absence of Chamars in leatherworking schools and ignoring the industry's recruitment strategies, the nationalists, like the colonial administrators before them, redefined "tradition" by turning Chamars into full-time professional leatherworkers. At a meeting to discuss the tanning and leather industries, two members of the Indian parliament, B. Jitulal and Ram Prasad Soni, argued that the leather industry should be declared a cottage industry, as it would provide jobs to millions of Chamars in the villages.[166]

*   *   *

A. Carnegie, a leather manufacturer from Kanpur, made an observation in his evidence before the Indian Industrial Commission in 1916 that nicely summarizes the argument of this chapter. Carnegie wrote, "Chamars as a rule do not take up leather working as their life-work. Most of them are cultivators and only leave their villages for the leather factories when they wish to earn a little money."[167] Chamars sought work in leather factories not because of any tradition, but because this was one of the few employment opportunities available to them. Another example is even more instructive. Writing about Seth Surajdin Kori, a patron of radical Dalits in Allahabad in the 1920s, the Dalit author Nandlal Viyougi tells us that Surajdin came from a poor agricultural family who took advantage of the business opportunities provided by the shoe business and the leather trade.[168] The "natural" association of Chamars with leatherwork was created during colonial times. Dominant representations of the leather industry, the opening of leatherworking schools specifically for Chamars, and the colonial association of Chamars with the "centuries-old *jajmani* system" all helped to ensure that leatherwork became their sole occupation and identity in the eyes of others. And this happened regardless of whether particular Chamars had ever actually been involved in full-time leatherwork. In the end these practices created a myth of the caste identity of the leather work force. Analysis of the leather trade in the nineteenth and early twentieth centuries also shows that Chamar leatherworkers, like Muslim ones, were based not in the villages but in the *qasbas,* the archetypical artisanal centers of production in precolonial times. It was not the Indian (Hindu) nationalists but Chamar ideologues and activists who protested against the association of leather with their identity. Their resistance to such formulations forms the subject of the next chapter.

Swami Achhutanand and members of the Adi-Hindu Mahasabha with Sir William M. Hailey, governor of Uttar Pradesh from 1928 to 1930 (undated photo). *Photo courtesy of Mangal Singh Jatav (used by permission).*

ओ३म्

✳ यादव जीवन ✳

(प्रथम-द्वितीय भाग)

—◦:०:◦—

लेखक

पं॰ सुन्दरलाल सगर

संस्थापक

श्री जाटव महासभा व जाटव प्रचारक महामण्डल
(आगरा)

—✳—

हम कौन थे क्या होगये, अब तो तुम्हें कुछ ध्यान हो ।
वहु-काल बीता गुप्त रहते भूलो न यदु-सन्तान हो ॥

—❊—

प्रकाशक

श्री जाटव महासभा (आगरा)

संवत् १९८६ वि॰ सन् १९२९ ई॰
विजयदशमी

सर्वाधिकार सुरक्षित

द्वितीय संस्करण } { दोनों भागों का मूल्य
१००० } { ॥)

Title page of Pandit Sunderlal Sagar's *Yadav Jivan* (Agra, 1929), first published
in 1924 as *Jatav Jivan*.

नोट :— जो दुराचारी थे वे सब निकाल दिए गए हैं ।

सूर्य-वंश
क्षत्रिय जैसवार सभा
लाहौर
प्रथम भाग

जिसको—

प्रधान लाला बुद्धरामजी ने बनाया
और
मन्त्री लाला लाहौरीमलजी ने

मनेजर रामचन्द्र लखनपाल के प्रबन्ध से बाम्बे मशीन प्रेस लाहौर में छपवा कर

प्रकाशित किया ।

पौष वदि १९८२ विक्रमी तदनुसार जनवरी ११२६ ईस्वी.

'प्रथमवार १०००] [मूल्य -)

Title page of a booklet on Chanvar Purana published by the Suryavansh Kshatriya Jaiswar Sabha (Lahore, 1926).

CHAPTER 4

Struggle for Identities:
Chamar Histories and Politics

There are millions of people in India today who call themselves Chamars and [others] who also call them that. However, it is fully established by the Chanvar Purana that this word is "Chanvar" and refers to the suryavanshi or royal lineage, who belonged to an influential family of rulers at the dawn of civilization.

—U. B. S. Raghuvanshi, *Shree Chanvar Purana,* n.d.

Hence it is not incorrect to imagine that by erasing the glorious literature and history of their opponents, the daityas-danavas-asurs, and etc., by characterizing them as black and irrational people in their epics, they [the Aryans] had covered their tracks well. It is difficult to accept what the Brahman-pandits have said with regard to 80 percent of the population [of India], that they are descendants of the natural-unnatural succession of an illegitimate or mixed varna.

—Chandrika Prasad Jigyasu, *Bharat ke Adi Nivasiyon ki Sabhyata,* 1937

Chamar activists and intellectuals wrote the first histories of "untouchables" in the early decades of the twentieth century, in response to those histories written by colonial and Hindu historians. These histories took the form of the decennial censuses, caste and tribe surveys, and various ethnohistorical and folkloric accounts which worked out a narrative of Chamars' "untouchable" origins. Indian histories written by the Hindu middle-class literati from the late nineteenth century onward were concerned with celebrating the glorious Hindu past. Bharatendu Harishchandra and Raja Siva Prasad Simh were among a host of such writers in North India in the late nineteenth century whose histories of India were histories of caste Hindus.[1] In these histories there were no Chamars or Dalits, because they were not yet considered part of the Hindu community, nor were these writers concerned with "untouchables" and their histories. In the context of Bengal, Partha Chatterjee has shown that there was no discussion of Dalits in the "histories of [Indian] nations" published by the Hindu and Muslim middle-class intelligentsia.[2] Such writers offered little or no discussion of untouchability and caste inequalities and paid no attention to Dalit writers and activists. Hindus and Dalits inhabited two different worlds with separate agendas.

One example both captures the meaning of the Chamars' struggle of the 1920s–30s and brings into relief their overwhelming concern with the issue of untouchability and identity. Ramnarayan Yadvendu, an important member of the Jatav Mahasabha and founder of the All-India Jatav Youth league, wrote a history of Jatav Chamars. In it he highlighted a victory that is virtually absent from the pages of Indian historiography. The All-India Jatav Youth League, in its seventh session (at Ghaziabad in December 1937), celebrated the Uttar Pradesh government's decision to allow the use of "Jatav" as a surname. This meant that Jatav students filling out official forms would "no longer be required to use the other term [Chamar] along with their name, which was the case earlier."[3] Struggle against the word "Chamar," the supposed "untouchability" of Jatav origins and occupations, and the daily humiliation that Jatavs were subject to has remained a central concern of Jatav historical writings and politics. Reading the wide range of Chamar and Dalit histories written in the first half of the twentieth century makes clear that the writers were not primarily concerned with questions of economic equality, land distribution, economic injustices, or the anti-colonial struggles. Instead, they sought to reclaim the dignity of their community by questioning dominant Brahmanical theories of their origins. This subject was central to Chamar histories but of little or no importance in the histories written by caste Hindus.

The first step in the Dalit political struggle centered on the question of identity and the strategies of liberation that might overcome the "untouchable" status assigned to them by the caste Hindus. How do we write about such struggles, and what meanings do they hold for historians? Genera-

tions of caste Hindu historians have been accustomed to writing about social and economic contradictions, anti-colonial and class struggles, but
have never encountered the humiliation of being addressed as a Chamar.[4]
During my fieldwork in Lucknow, Allahabad, Agra, and Delhi I was often
bluntly asked about my caste identity. Many Dalits questioned my ability
to write their history. I was asked how I could understand what it means to
be an "untouchable" in Hindu India. Many times I was told by Dalits that
their struggle is against the Hindu interpretation of Dalit history. "How
can we have an 'untouchable' past? How can you write a history that attri-
butes untouchable origins to millions of people?" I was asked.

The epigraphs that open this chapter capture two significant moments
in Chamar history. The first marks a beginning, and the second a qualitative shift. The first is representative of the Chamar histories that borrowed
from the Hindu Puranic tradition to redeem and reclaim their past by
claiming "pure" Kshatriya status equal to that of the dominant Hindu
castes. Such a claim was made not only by the Chamar histories discussed
in the first section of this chapter, but also by the nature and character of
Chamar politics in the 1920s, which negotiated their position within Hindu
religion, especially within the form of religion propagated by the Arya
Samaj. In their efforts to claim an equal status, discussed in the second section, Chamars questioned markers of their "untouchability," especially *begari* (unpaid labor) in the forms of agricultural work, leatherwork, and personal services to zamindars and government officials.

In the third section I reexamine the relationship between Chamar assertions of identity and the role of the Arya Samaj in creating new Hindu
rituals and idioms to address Chamar concerns. Two assumptions have
characterized Indian historiography on the Dalit movements of the first
two decades of the twentieth century. First, almost all liberal and radical
historians assume that Dalit histories must begin by critiquing Hindu religion and claiming the status of original inhabitants.[5] Second, these writers
also assume that Hindu organizations like the Arya Samaj wanted to Hinduize Dalits in order to make them part of the Hindu community. Both of
these assumptions ignore actual Chamar writings and fail to take seriously
the agendas laid out by Chamars in their own histories and politics.

Those politics underwent a qualitative shift in 1928. Their second phase
was marked by a new generation of histories that began to articulate an inclusive history of all Dalits: Chamars, Bhangis, Pasis, Dusadhs, and others. By

the 1930s Chamar activists had raised a new set of issues and constituted an effective Dalit political force. This shift, discussed in the fourth and final section, first became evident in the mid-1920s with the emergence of the Adi-Hindu movement, which claimed that the Dalits were the original inhabitants of India. Rather than being included from the first phase of the Dalit struggle, this claim represents a second stage in the development of the Dalit movement. Only in the 1930s did Dalit histories take it up. The earliest Chamar and Dalit histories, far from critiquing Hindu religion (as many scholars have assumed), sought to establish high-caste origins for the Dalits.

The First Phase: Making Claims of Kshatriya Status

A series of Chamar histories were written and published in Uttar Pradesh during the first half of the twentieth century. The four that I take up for discussion are U. B. S. Raghuvanshi's *Shree Chanvar Purana* (between 1910 and 1916), the Jaiswar Mahasabha's *Suryavansh Kshatriya Jaiswar Sabha* (1926), Pandit Sunderlal Sagar's *Yadav Jivan* (1929), and Ramnarayan Yadvendu's *Yaduvansh ka Aitihas* (1942). Sagar and Yadvendu, who were Jatiyas, claimed a Jatav-Kshatriya status by associating their lineage to the Yadav tribe of Lord Krishna. Jatiya Chamars were predominantly located in western Uttar Pradesh, with a large presence in the Meerut, Agra, Moradabad, and Badaun districts. Jaiswara Chamars were dominant in eastern Uttar Pradesh, where they asserted a Kshatriya status by claiming descent from the Chanvar dynasty. Jatiyas and Jaiswaras are the two major Chamar *jatis,* and together they constituted two-fifths of the Chamar population of Uttar Pradesh.[6]

Raghuvanshi's seventy-nine-page *Chanvar Purana* was published in Kanpur. The author was a lawyer in Aligarh, a prominent center of Dalit politics in Uttar Pradesh, and by choosing the surname of Raghuvanshi, he sought to underscore his learned status. The Jaiswar Mahasabha of Lahore's *Suryavansh Kshatriya,* a ten-page chapbook that had a print run of a thousand, is a simplified retelling of the *Chanvar Purana* story. Written in a very accessible style, it addresses the Chamars directly, urging them to liberate themselves by reclaiming their true Kshatriya identity. The publication of these two texts, in Kanpur in Uttar Pradesh and Lahore in Punjab, is also an indication that the story of *Chanvar Purana* had become popular in North India, and it is thus worth discussing Raghuvanshi's themes and claims at some length.

My discussion of these overlooked Chamar narratives is intended to bring them into conversation with the colonial and Hindu histories of Chamar pasts. Without taking them seriously, we cannot even begin to appreciate and understand the focus of Chamar histories and critiques. Chamar histories were not produced in isolation, but were rather a part of the larger corpus of caste histories, or *vamsavalis,* written around this time. The themes and methodology of Chamar histories have much in common with those of the histories produced by the caste Hindu literati like Bhartendu Harishchandra from the late nineteenth century onward. Both Chamar and caste Hindu writers claiming Kshatriya status were borrowing from an already existing tradition which relied upon *itihasa-puranic* sources (using Puranas as historical texts). Even the colonial authors drew from these sources to account for the "untouchability" of Chamar and other "untouchable" castes. We cannot understand Chamar histories unless we recognize that these Chamar writers were responding to colonial and Hindu representations of their caste, what Ranajit Guha has described as "a question of power."[7]

Raghuvanshi claimed that the *Chanvar Purana* was discovered by a *rishi* (sage) who lived in a cave in the high reaches of the Himalayas in Tibet, where he translated it, with great effort, from Sanskrit into Hindi for publication.[8] The *Chanvar Purana* testifies that the original name of the Chamars was "Chanvar." It tells us that in the *dwija kula* (pure or pious age) the present-day Chamars were powerful rulers belonging to the *suryavanshi* (royal Kshatriya) Chanvar dynasty. Raghuvanshi is aware that the sweeping claims being made in the *Chanvar Purana* may create doubts about the authenticity of the text. He therefore offers a reward to anyone "who can prove that *Chanvar Purana* is false." To him the text's legitimacy derives from the Puranic tradition in India. He draws the attention of Hindu society by writing, "It is commendable that our Hindu brethren have such faith in the Puranas, and it is our humble request that they will show similar devotion to the *Chanvar Purana,*" which is backed by the same evidence as the *Gurada Purana,* considering that Shri Narad Bhagwan, Lord Narada, is the narrator of both the texts.[9] He also adds that the *anushasan parva* (section) of the *Mahabharata* mentions the Chanvar dynasty as a Kshatriya caste that lost its status because of its members' failure to respect "Brahmanical knowledge."[10] Lord Narada recounts the story in the *deva lok* (abode of the gods), giving an account of the dynasty's glorious past and the reasons for its decline, and explaining how it acquired the name "Chamar." The *Chanvar Purana* predicts that Saint Raidas's birth in the Chamar community will mark the recovery of its lost status.

Both the *Chanvar Purana* and *Suryavansh Kshatriya* claim that the *Bhaktamala* (Bhakti literature) includes many stories of the greatness of Raidas in fifteenth-century Hindu society and his popularity among the ruling families.[11] According to these two texts, the truth about the Chamars and the Chanvar dynasty was revealed in the court of Lord Vishnu when Saint Raidas arrived in the *deva lok*. Upon his arrival "the *deva lok* began to reverberate with the words 'Chamar, Chamar' and the frightened *devatas* [gods] began to fall at the feet of Lord Vishnu. . . Oh Lord! What a terrible tragedy, a Chamar in the *deva lok?*"[12] At the request of Lord Vishnu, Narada tells the story to the terrified *devatas* and the world. In the *satyug* age the Chanvars were the most powerful dynasty of India and of the world. They ruled the earth for many centuries and played a crucial role in spreading the Vedic religion. He describes in great detail the glorious lineage of this dynasty and the people who lived a charmed life under their rule.[13]

The greatest Chanvar king was Chamunda Rai, who was also the last king of the dynasty and was responsible for the eclipse and disappearance of the Chanvar *vansh* (lineage). A *rishi* had told his father the danger that Chamunda Rai posed, and after considerable anguish the king decided to sacrifice his son to save the *vansh*, but the *rani* (queen) tricked him into killing the son of her maid Shramkala instead. Shramkala helped the *rani* by not only suggesting the solution but also willingly offering her son. The king, thinking he had killed his own child, died of grief and remorse.[14] Following his death, the *rani* announced that the prince was still alive. The news was welcomed by all and Chamunda Rai was declared the new ruler.

Chamunda Rai followed the rules of *varnasharam dharm* (education, marriage, family), eventually retiring from social life to become an ascetic. His vigorous penance and devotion to Lord Vishnu earned him general praise and the respect of Vishnu. The *devatas* felt threatened by Chamunda Rai's growing reputation, and they conspired to destroy his standing by interrupting his prayer and ruining his dedication to Lord Vishnu. They connived with one of his enemies to avenge his humiliating defeat at Chamunda Rai's hands. Appearing in the guise of Shiva, Chamunda Rai's enemy questioned his devoutness and loyalty to Vishnu by pointing out that he had no statue of the god, and succeeded in convincing him to worship the god as *sagun* (having form) rather than *nigun* (formless).[15]

The *sagun* form of devotion is against the tenets of the Vedic religion. Chamunda Rai's adoption of it offended Lord Vishnu, who decided to visit him in the guise of a Shudra (low-caste person) to test his dedication. The *Chanvar Purana* describes this encounter in great detail. Disturbing Chamunda Rai's worship, the Shudra questioned his devotion to Vishnu, on the grounds that he had adopted the *sagun* form of worship, and recited *shlokas* (verses) from the Vedas to assert his position. An already annoyed Chamunda Rai was furious at seeing a Shudra reciting the Vedas and admonished him, reminding him that his caste had no right to do so. Hearing this, Lord Vishnu appeared in his true form and "replied that in this world a Shudra is one whose actions (karma) make the person a Shudra." "A man is not a Shudra merely because he is born in such a family."[16] Readers are reminded of the oft-quoted Vedic saying that status is defined by actions and not by birth. Realizing his mistake, Chamunda Rai begged for forgiveness, but an enraged Lord Vishnu cursed him and his descendants out of Kshatriya status to a position even lower than Shudras, as Chamars and untouchables. Hence, the Chanvar *vansh* and its history disappeared from the Earth.

After appeals from various gods, including the sun god, who had been hiding in a cave, Lord Vishnu relented. The Chanvar dynasty would be revived in the age of *kalayuga* (the present dark age), when a *rishi* (Saint Raidas) would be born, who would bring Vedic knowledge back to the Earth and remove all ignorance. His appearance would allow this caste to rise up from their position as "untouchables" and return to their original position as a Kshatriya caste.[17] The *Suryavansh Kshatriya* concluded by exhorting its readers, "Dear friends! Please think, who are we and what's our worth? First we were Suryavanshi Kshatriyas and now we are called Chamars. Dear readers! Put your mind, soul, wealth, and knowledge to help our community which has forgotten its past; our welfare lies in its reawakening."[18]

The Jatiya Chamars of western Uttar Pradesh also asserted a Kshatriya identity, as Jatavs or Yadavs, by claiming lineage from the Yadu tribe, whose most famous member was Lord Krishna. These claims were made in *Jatav Jivan*, first published in 1924, with a second (108-page) edition published in 1929 with the new title *Yadav Jivan*. Sunderlal Sagar, the writer of the book, was a prominent activist and member of the Jatav Mahasabha of Agra, the organization that financed and published the book's two editions. Part 1 of the book looks at various aspects of the Jatiya Chamars' claim to Yadav status. Part 2 is a commentary on the "clean" social and cultural practices that Sagar recommended to the Jatavs. Sagar also laid out a program for the development of the Jatav caste and gave information about the aims and objectives of the Jatav Mahasabha. In 1946, Ramnarayan Yadvendu published an even longer book, entitled *Yaduvansh ka Aitihas.* Yadvendu rehearsed many of the arguments made in *Jatav Jivan,* and also provided an exhaustive history of various Jatav organizations and personal sketches of the members of the Jatav Mahasabha.

Sunderlal Sagar believed that "we learn about each nation, country, lineage, and caste through its history," and he wrote the history of his caste because he wanted to enlighten his community about its glorious but forgotten past. The book is written in a question-and-answer format, with the author instructing an ignorant Jatav. It is the absence of history, the lack of knowledge of the community and its past, that has resulted in the degraded and impure status of the pure *yaduvansh* clan, claims Sagar. "It is a matter of great sorrow that our fellow Jatav brothers are not able to give an appropriate answer to questions of their identity from the arrogant casteist."[19]

Innovatively using evidence from contemporary sources, Sagar strengthens his case for Jatavs' Kshatriya status by borrowing from the Puranas and folklore. His first piece of evidence is taken from his personal experience and is part of what compelled him to revise the book. He claims that two Hindu lawyers opposed his attempt to record his surname as Yadav in the list of voters. He contested their decision in the court, and the commissioner of Agra, R. L. H. Clarke, accepted his claim of the Jatavs' social status. Sagar proudly quotes Clarke: "Sunder Lal Yadav has written a book (*Jatav Jiwan*) which has been produced expressly to show that as a matter of fact all Jatwas are really Yadavas."[20]

Sagar refers to Swami Atma Ram's *Gyansamundra,* written in 1888, which mentions the Kshatriya status of the Jatavs and their origins in the *Shiv gotra* (lineage of Lord Shiva). He cites J. S. Nesfield's *Brief View of the Caste System of the North-Western Provinces and Oudh* (1882), which states that Jatavs "may be an occupational off-shoot from the Yadu tribe from which Krishna came"; volume 4 of Edwin T. Atkinson's *Gazetteer* (1881), which mentions the superior status of the Jatavs in relation to the Aharwariyas; and Chohte Lal Kshatriya's *Brahman Decisions,* which refers to Jatavs as Kshatriyas.[21] Moving to Puranic and folkloric sources, Sagar narrates the story of Parashuram and his pledge to wipe out all the Kshatriyas. According to him, the Jatavs' ancestors fought against Parashuram. But the Kshatriyas were defeated, and to escape persecution the Jatavs disappeared from the Earth by hiding in the forests, becoming artisans to hide their Kshatriya identity and in the process losing their "pure" status. Hindu discrimination against Jatavs began at that time.[22] Sagar tells his readers that "Jatav" is an *apabhramsa* or corrupt form of "Yadav." On the authority of the *Mahabharata* and *Manusmriti,* he traces the Jatav lineage to the Raja Yadu and Krishna. He argues that Jatav surnames, like Sagar, Pipal, Kardam, Maurya, Son, Neem, Karnik, and Harit, were all linked to the lineages of Yaduvansh.[23]

The methodology of these histories was derived from the Hindu *itihasa-purana* traditions of history-writing. In a thoughtful discussion, Romila Thapar has described the *itihasa-puranic* tradition as "embedded histories." Non-Kshatriya dynasties claimed a Kshatriya status that was "embodied in the *itihasa-puranic* tradition," and on those grounds declared their social and political legitimacy. Thapar has suggested that from the middle of the first millennium AD new ruling dynasties "often observed the formality of claiming Ksatriya status" by using the *itihasa-puranic* tradition to claim genealogical ties with the royal families mentioned in the *Ramayana* and *Mahabharata.*[24] Such royal genealogies were a powerful source of social and cultural legitimacy and a unique feature of precolonial Indian polity.

In the latter half of the nineteenth century, the urban middle-class Hindu literati in North India borrowed from the *itihasa-puranic* tradition to question colonial interpretations of the Hindu past. Vasudha Dalmia has argued that they utilized diverse sources from the Puranas and folklore to refute "the authority of the Orientalists." Dalmia mentions Bharatendu Harischandra, "who as litterateur and amateur historian tried his hand at writing manifold histories in Hindi," and this example illustrates the point that borrowing from Puranic sources was an integral part of writing history in Hindi.[25] A comparison of Harischandra's "Khatriyon ki Utpatti" (Origin of the Khatris) and the Chamars' histories reveals striking parallels in their methodology. Harischandra wrote this pamphlet in support of efforts by the Khatri community of Punjab, hitherto classified as Shudras, to claim a Kshatriya status for themselves.

Harischandra, inspired by the "the new ethnologising trend," borrowed from popular folklore, Puranic sources, and Orientalist accounts to claim that even though the Punjabi Khatris were not occupationally Kshatriyas, they were nevertheless still Kshatriyas.[26] Borrowing from colonial accounts, Harischandra argued that Punjab was the original home of the Aryas in India, and the Khatris were their descendants because it was also their home. But because Punjabis cannot pronounce "ksa," the word "Kshatriya" came to be spoken and written as "Khatri." Harischandra recounted many popular stories to strengthen his claim. When Parashuram launched the war to eliminate the Kshatriyas, the Punjabi Kshatriyas went underground to preserve their lives, taking the name Khatri and following the customs and occupations of Vaishyas and Shudras. Harischandra quoted extensively from the ancient *Sarasangraha Purana* to support this origin story. He also argued that by adopting Shudra practices they escaped persecution at the hands of Emperor Chandragupta, who was of Shudra origin.[27] In addition to "Khatriyon ki Utpatti," Harischandra also wrote a history of his caste entitled "Aggarwalon ki Utpatti" (Origin of the Aggarwal Caste) in which he used a similar methodology to claim that the Aggarwals lost their Kshatriya status by giving up the Vedic religion.

There are striking parallels between Harischandra's histories of the Khatris and Aggarwals and the histories written by Chamar advocates three decades later. Raghuvanshi used the discovery of a new *Chanvar Purana* to claim a *suryavanshi* past by creating a story from the familiar tropes of the *Mahabharata*. The key tropes are the birth of a genius son, who is predicted to be both a blessing and a disaster to the royal lineage; a maid's sacrifice of her own son to protect the son of the *rani;* Chamunda Rai's remorse; the curse of Lord Vishnu, that explains the lineage's present status; and signs of the reclamation of their Kshatriya status in the *kala-yuga*. The Chamar stories utilize such familiar tropes, which are repeated in numerous stories in Hindi religious and secular literature. Both the Jatavs and the Jaiswaras claimed in their accounts that they had lost their true Kshatriya status because of persecution or punishment. The Jatiyas or Jatav Chamars of western Uttar Pradesh told the Parashuram story to explain their present "impure" status.[28] Like Harischandra, Sagar focused on the *apabhramsa* or corrupt form. Not only Harischandra but a whole generation of writers and advocates were writing in the context of Puranic texts and folklore. In their efforts to question dominant colonial and Hindu narratives of their past, Chamars used the same Puranic accounts to offer an alternative interpretation, with the immediate political objective of convincing the colonial state of their Kshatriya status.

The Puranic sources acquired a new authority in the colonial period that added to their importance in Indian society. The colonial officers and ethnographers relied on Puranic sources to explain the untouchability of the Dalits and the Shudra status of the lower castes in order to classify them as such in decennial censuses. The Uttar Pradesh census of 1865 for the first time systematically documented accounts of the origins of the Chamar caste, gathered from a variety of districts. In Moradabad, Farrukhabad, and Bareilly the caste was explained as deriving from "an Aheer father and Koorme mother," both ostracized from their communities—the latter turned out for theft and the former for killing a cow. One colonial account explained that "they took to the trade of skinning dead cattle and selling them, which is the occupation still followed by their descendants." In Muthra it was claimed on the authority of the *Varaha Purana* that Chamars were the offspring of a Mallah (boatman) and a Chandala (outcaste) woman. Three explanations were offered from Agra: Chamars were "descendent from a Mullah by a Chundal woman," descended "from a Soodr father and Nishad mother," or "the offspring of a Bhungee woman and a Brahmin."[29] Henry Elliot also noted that Chamars "are said, on the authority of the *Varaha Purana,* to be descended from a Mallah, or Boatman and a Chandal woman."[30] By citing many Hindu texts, such origin stories gained legitimacy in the eyes of colonial administrators. Colonial ethnographers—officers like Henry Elliot, Herbert Risely, M. A. Sherring, and William Crooke—subsequently quoted them as authoritative explanations of Chamars' history. Briggs argued that the origins of the term "Chamar" lay in the *Rig Veda* and that the term had been mentioned in all the main Brahmanical texts.[31] Given this historical methodology, it is little wonder that Chamar and other Dalit historians adopted many of the same conventions, tropes, and strategies to present their histories in a different light.

The real strength of colonial ethnography lay in its power as a form of objective sociological knowledge. Let me quote a celebrated Indian anthropologist who in the 1990s compiled a series of volumes as part of the *People of India* project. In his introduction to the Chamars, Kumar Singh has this to say about their history:

> Their community name is derived from the Sanskrit word *charmakara,* meaning leather worker. Risley (1891) writes that, according to the Puranas, the Chamars descended from the union of a boatman and a Chandal woman.

But scholars identify them with the Karewara or leather worker mentioned in the tenth chapter of Manu's *Dharmashastra*. The father of the caste was a Nishada (the offspring of a Brahman father and a Sudra mother) and the mother a Vaideha (offspring of a Vaisya father and Brahman mother).[32]

The persistence of a framework that seeks to explain the Chamars' past in terms of their impure and mixed origin is striking. Rather than offering any new historical evidence, postcolonial narratives of Chamar history produced by dominant (and usually caste Hindu) historians simply cite the very same narratives offered by their British colonial forebears.

Popular Mobilization: Claiming Kshatriya Status

The themes outlined in the Chamar histories of the 1920s had a wider social base among the Chamars of Uttar Pradesh. Weekly police reports give evidence of Chamar protests and meetings between 1922 and 1928.[33] Unfortunately, no such evidence exists for the period prior to 1922. Chamar protests, described in great detail in the weekly police reports, were not noted in the nationalist press. Hindi-language newspapers in Uttar Pradesh like *Pratap, Abhyudaya,* and *Aaj* began to report on them when Hindu reform organizations started their campaigns among Dalits. The Chamar movement is an indication of the first phase in the twentieth-century Dalit struggle in North India. A distinguishing feature of this phase is the adoption by Chamars of pure Hindu rites and practices, such as vegetarianism, and the abandonment of impure practices like eating beef and doing leatherwork, as part of their claim to Kshatriya status. In 1929 Sunderlal Sagar referred to the ongoing struggles among Chamars in western Uttar Pradesh, which he hoped would succeed in changing their status.[34]

Although Chamar protests were evident in many parts of the state, police reports indicate that the most organized and sustained agitation took place in western Uttar Pradesh. These protests were first noticed in 1922 in the districts of Meerut, Moradabad, Bulandshahr, Badaun, Bijnor, Bareilly, Pilibhit, Agra, and Aligarh. By 1923–24, evidence of Chamar protests had also appeared in the districts of Saharanpur, Etah, Etawah, Mainpuri, Muthra, Dehradun, Lucknow, Unnao, Kheri Sultanpur, and Partabgarh in central Uttar Pradesh and in eastern Uttar Pradesh in Benares, Jaunpur, Basti, and

Gorakhpur.[35] But the police reports described the meetings and activities in western Uttar Pradesh as a "movement." In Moradabad we hear of "a general revolt of Chamars," in Bulandshahr we are told that "there is scarcely a large village not having trouble with the Chamars," and in Meerut it was noted that "the Chamar movement continues to cause trouble."[36] A notable feature of the movement in this region was the collection of donations during meetings to fund various reform activities, particularly schools for Chamar children. In 1922 and 1923 the money collected in these meetings varied from Rs 200 to Rs 1,000 in Moradabad and was as much as Rs 1,500 in Rampur.[37] The meetings appear to have been fairly well attended, with an average attendance of five or six hundred and often as many as one or two thousand. In one case seven thousand Chamars met in Bijnor in 1924.[38] Chamar *sabhas* (organizations) and *panchayats* (councils) organized such gatherings in both eastern and western Uttar Pradesh.[39] In Moradabad, Bulandshahr, Meerut, Bijnor, Saharanpur, Jaunpur, and Basti such meetings provided a context to establish Chamar *sabhas*.[40] Yadvendu says that Jatav Mahasabha branches were set up in Etah, Bareilly, Muthra, Mainpuri, Etawah, and Agra.[41]

Chamars were keen to demonstrate their loyalty to the British government, a fact reflected in the resolutions passed at these meetings. They distanced their activities from the ongoing non-cooperation movement (1920–22) launched by the Congress. At Lalkati *tahsil* in Meerut a meeting of a thousand Chamars passed a resolution against the non-cooperation movement and pledged loyalty to the British government. Similar resolutions were passed in meetings in other places in Meerut.[42] In the Didauli *tahsil* of Moradabad, Chamars refused to allow members of the Congress and Khilafatists to speak and passed a resolution against the Congress.[43] In its annual conference held in April 1922, presided over by Babu Khem Chand, the Jatav Mahasabha passed a resolution pledging its support for the British.[44] In Bijnor a meeting of seven thousand Chamars criticized the Congress's demand for *swaraj* or independence.[45] Similar resolutions were passed in Badaun, Bulandshahr, Dehradun, and Kumaon.[46] Open hostility to the Congress forced the Uttar Pradesh Congress Committee to ask its district committees to build an egalitarian relationship with Chamars.[47] But in the eastern Uttar Pradesh district of Gorakhpur, the Congress's activists played an important role in communicating "the message of nationalism to the lower castes [which] served to widen the influence and role of their *panchayats*." A Congress activist named Babu Guru Prasad organized a *panchayat* at a gathering of "500 Chamars of *tahsil* Bansgaon of Gorakh-pur district" in February 1921 to undertake various reform activities.[48]

In their protests and meetings, the Chamars sought to claim Kshatriya status and emphasize their "pure" and "clean" ritual. By embracing many of the caste Hindus' practices they were trying to remove their "untouchable" stigma. The Chamar *sabhas* were the most vocal advocates of abstaining from meat and alcohol. In his novel *Karmabhoomi,* Premchand identified three factors that defined Chamar untouchability: *daru-sharab, murda-mans,* and *aur chamra* (drinking alcohol, eating beef, and doing leatherwork). One of the main characters, Amarkant, a caste Hindu and Congress activist who settles down in a Raidassi village somewhere in Haridwar, convinces the Chamars to give up the first two as a way of attaining a pure status like Hin-dus.[49] In eastern Uttar Pradesh, Dalit caste *panchayats* of Chamars, Dhobis, and Bhangis did pass resolutions "not only to abstain from liquor and *ganja* but also meat and fish." Shahid Amin described the adoption of such novel dietary taboos "as an extension of the Gandhian idea of self-purification."[50] Yet in other parts of Uttar Pradesh, especially in the western region, Chamar *sabhas* accepted the agenda of reform and the aspiration to Kshatriya status without outside intervention. Extensive debates over these issues at meetings in the districts of Moradabad and Meerut were regularly reported. In the *tahsils* of Chandausi, Sambhal, Rehra, Dilara, and Gujrala in Moradabad, the Chamars asserted a status similar to that of Jats, claiming to be vegetarian caste Hindus.[51] The Meerut district was particularly noted for the strength of this movement.[52] At a meeting of four thousand Chamars gathered from dif-ferent parts of the district at Mowane *qasba* in November 1922, a series of resolutions were passed claiming Kshatriya status and committing to a puri-fied lifestyle.[53] In Mainpuri a Chamar *sabha* was formed in May 1924 explic-itly to claim Kshatriya status for Chamars.[54]

Chamars' vegetarianism and the purity of their living conditions were repeatedly mentioned in resolutions passed at meetings held throughout the twenty-four districts of the state. Some *sabhas* instituted fines to en-force their new rules of purity.[55] Baba Ramchandra participated in the meetings of Chamar *sabhas* at Partabgarh and in surrounding districts.[56] In eastern Uttar Pradesh Gorakhpur was a major center of reform and protest, particularly in Hata and Padrauna *tahsils.*[57] In July 1926 Chamars passed resolutions in different areas of Benares to abandon the impure and defil-ing occupation of leatherwork and the practices of removing carcasses, skinning, and tanning.[58] Interesting details include the refusal of Chamars in Moradabad to repair and stitch shoes, the refusal to skin dead animals in the Siana *qasba* of Bulandshahr, and desertion of the occupation of *mochi* in the Rajpura *qasba* of Badaun. In Saharanpur town the Chamars sold their annual contract for hides to the Bhangis.[59]

Access to education, the opening of municipal schools for their children and the founding of their own independent private schools, was a very important part of the Chamar reform agenda. When Amarkant, the protagonist of Premchand's novel *Karmabhoomi,* decides to settle down in a Raidassi village, the Chamars ask him to open a school for their children and teach English.[60] Similar demands were made early on by Chamars in meetings at Meerut and Moradabad.[61] In Dehradun in October 1923 a Chamar meeting of two thousand people insisted on the right of Chamar boys to attend the municipal schools.[62] In Mainpuri Chamars decided in May 1924 that reform of their caste was not possible without the education of their children.[63] In Etawah, Chamars decided to start a school for their children instead of wasting their money on Hindu festivals.[64] Both Sunderlal Sagar and Ramnarayan Yadvendu emphasized that education for Chamar children was the best way to improve the position of their community.[65] Yadvendu even wrote a letter to the Hindi monthly *Chand* in September 1933 seeking money to help two Jatav students to enroll in higher education and asking Indian nationalists to take the initiative in such measures if they were genuinely interested in *achhutuddhar* (uplift of untouchables).[66]

Central to these issues of reform was the question of individual dignity. One way of reclaiming dignity was to mount a challenge against the humiliating practice of *begari*. Chamars protested against its numerous forms and the illegal cesses that they were required to pay to zamindars. *Begari* determined their collective identity in the eyes of Hindu society; all Chamars were expected to provide services on demand without expectation of payment, regardless of their economic position, whether they were prosperous *maurusi* or *ghair-maurusi* peasants or poor agricultural laborers. By the early decades of the twentieth century *begari* included cesses, *hari* (agricultural services like plowing), and *nazrana* (tribute), all of which were used by the zamindars to illegally increase rent.[67] In addition to zamindars, touring officials of the state also requisitioned *begari* services, including the provision of grass, firewood, straw, fowl, eggs, meat, and milk, as well as various kinds of manual services, from pitching tents to cooking.[68] Premchand's 1922 novel *Premashram* captures the meaning of *begari* in the lives of Chamars by providing us a graphic description of how Chamars from neighboring villages were forcibly rounded up and confined by the zamindar's servants in the collector's camp to work for long hours without food or pay.[69]

In the 1920s protests against *begari* and other extortions was a central feature of the Chamar and Dalit struggles. Chamars in the Awadh region participated in the Kisan Sabha agitation of 1921–22 which fought against *bedekhli* (eviction) and *begari*. Protests against *begari* continued even after the movement ended. They were noted in many districts of western Uttar Pradesh, including Meerut, Moradabad, Bulandshahr, Aligarh, Saharanpur, Agra, Bijnour, Muthra, Aligarh, Bareilly, Etah, Kanpur, and Etawah—all districts where a significant number of Chamars possessed *maurusi* and *ghair-maurusi* tenure rights. Police reports from Meerut, Moradabad, and Bulandshahr compared the Chamar movement to the *aika* (unity) movement in Awadh, since both raised the issues of *begari* and illegal cesses.[70] A report by the Hindi weekly *Pratap* in April 1928 commented on the two-day conference organized by the Raidass Sabha of Kanpur to demand the abolition of *begari* and similar practices.[71] In this region *begari* included police demands to remove dead bodies and other such menial tasks.[72] In the eastern districts of Uttar Pradesh, like Azamgarh, Jaunpur, Allahabad, Benares, Ghazipur, and Gorakhpur, however, protest against *begari* was less evident than the promotion of vegetarianism and purity.[73] This difference is an indication of the strength of the zamindars in eastern Uttar Pradesh, who favored reform movements.

As in other lower-caste reform movements, women were an important subject of reform. But the Chamar movement was not unanimous on the topic. In western Uttar Pradesh Chamars repeatedly asserted that their women should be confined to their houses and put in purdah. Indeed, such resolutions were passed in rural and urban areas of Moradabad, Meerut, Bulandshahr, Muthra, Saharanpur, Agra, Dehradun, and Bijnor.[74] In Dehradun and Saharanpur it was recommended that "women should wear dhotis [saris] at home and stay at home and not go out to sell grass in bazaars."[75] By removing women from production processes and eliminating their contributions to the family income, Chamar men were domesticating them, removing them from public spaces and asserting a new form of patriarchy modeled on caste Hindu norms. These resolutions were in sharp contrast to the position laid out by Chamars in eastern Uttar Pradesh, who strengthened women's roles by demanding better payment for their work as *dais* and agricultural laborers.

For example, in the Rudhali area of Basti district in the eastern Uttar Pradesh, Chamars demanded wages for their women's work as *dais*.[76] These demands were an important dimension of the protest against *begari*.

The east-west divide was also evident in another reform that was popular among Chamars of western Uttar Pradesh but not in the east. Many Chamar groups in the west were redefining their relationship with Muslims as part of their efforts to claim a socially superior and clean status in Hindu society. They did not want to end all social interactions with Muslims, but ceased to take food (cooked or uncooked) from Muslims and refused to dine with them, adopting caste Hindu practices. These restrictions on social interaction with Muslims were an important element of Chamar reforms in western Uttar Pradesh from very early on. Such resolutions were made in meetings and conferences held between 1922 and 1926 in the western Uttar Pradesh districts of Bulandshahr, Moradabad, Dehradun, Saharanpur, Meerut, and Muthra.[77]

A notable feature of Chamar protests in this period is that discussions and debates were held before any decision was made. A disagreement was aired at a meeting of the Jatiya Chamar Sabha in June 1923 in Meerut city. Chamar representatives from Meerut city agreed with most of the reforms on the agenda, but opposed abandoning the tanning and shoe trades, an indication that they had found prosperity in these trades in the cities. These urban Chamars threatened to break marital ties with Chamars in the countryside and send back recently married brides.[78] The Chamars of Lucknow also opposed the decision of the Kanpur Chamars to excommunicate members of the community who continued to "skin and tan the animals."[79] In a 1923 meeting attended by nine thousand Chamars at Rampur *tahsil* in Saharanpur district, in which the Arya Samaj played a leading role, a total of Rs 1,500 was collected for the cause of Chamar reform. One faction of the meeting, led by the Aryas, wanted to build a temple, while another was equally keen on using the money to build a school. This latter group had little interest in converting Chamars to Hinduism. As a mark of protest against the ultimate decision to build a temple, many of them walked out of the meeting.[80]

The Response of the Arya Samaj: A Reassessment

William Pinch has argued that the *jati* reformers of the twentieth century claimed a Vaishnava religiosity by advocating a pure lifestyle, which meant abstaining from beef and liquor, confining women to the home, and abandoning practices like gambling and polygamy, which were increasingly considered social evils. A crucial feature of such a religiosity was establishing "genealogical ties to either Ram or Krishna, the well-known avatars of Vishnu." Reform on the basis of Kshatriya identity was adopted not just by "the major peasant *jatis*" of Shudra castes like the Kurmis and Ahirs but also by "communities that often combined traditional occupations with agriculture," like Kalwars, Tambulis, Kahars, Tantis, and Malis.[81] We may also add Chamars to this list. But the Hindus and the British accepted the Shudra castes' claim of Kshatriya status while refusing that of the "untouchable" Chamar caste. The Mahar advocates of Maharashtra, in an 1890 petition to the British, made a similar claim to Kshatriya status in order to qualify for recruitment into the army. Shivram Janba Kamble, the most prominent Mahar leader prior to Ambedkar, founded and edited a Mahar newspaper entitled *Somwanshiya Mitra,* which also argued for Mahars' Kshatriya origins.[82]

The Arya Samaj responded to the Chamar claims in the 1920s by addressing two inequalities in Hindu society that were criticized by Chamars: access to temples and to public wells.[83] The Hindu Mahasabha also addressed this issue at a 1923 Benares conference by offering "untouchables" access to schools, temples, and public wells, but opposed their *shuddhi* or purification. Jordens has argued that the Arya Samaj forced a compromise on the Hindu Mahasabha by demanding the *shuddhi* of Chamars, promoting the adoption of Vedic rituals among Chamars, and encouraging closer social interaction with the caste Hindus through interdining. Despite the Hindu Mahasabha's official opposition to the *shuddhi* of Dalits, it allowed its local branches and other Hindu bodies to make their own decisions, and in Uttar Pradesh the Hindu Mahasabha fashioned its approach to the matter in response to competition from the Arya Samaj.[84] Chamars were very receptive to the Arya Samaj's agenda, and the relationship between them was further cemented by opposition from orthodox Hindus who saw the Arya Samaj as just as radical as Chamar reformers. From its small beginning in 1923 in the Arya Samaj, the *shuddhi* movement peaked in 1925, after which it petered out, largely because of the rise of the Adi-Hindu movement. Mainstream Hindi nationalist newspapers like *Pratap* and *Abhyudaya* in Uttar Pradesh began to report the Arya Samaj's *shuddhi*-related activities in March 1924, as did the weekly police reports.[85] A vocal advocate of "untouchables" in the Hindu Mahasabha, Swami Shraddhananda launched *shuddhi* activities among them in 1924.[86] The activities of these organizations were primarily confined to western Uttar Pradesh, where they targeted well-off Chamar cultivators, and a few locations in the east, in Gorakhpur and Benares districts.[87] The Arya Samaj had established a fair number of Raidass *sabhas* and *achhutuddhar sabhas* in different parts of western Uttar Pradesh.[88]

By adopting measures designed to support their claim of clean status and questioning the practice of *begari,* the Chamars were asserting a status equal to that of caste Hindus. Nandini Gooptu describes the Jatav protest in the 1920s in Agra and surrounding rural areas as an effort to claim "higher status and respectability through 'sanskritisation.'"[89] But Chamar protest against the existing structures of domination can be better understood as a demand for equal status. In recent years scholars have reminded us of the inadequacy of M. N. Srinvas's model of sanskritization by subjecting it to a range of criticisms. David Hardiman has offered an insightful suggestion by arguing that protest by *adivasis* or tribal people in Gujarat sought to deprive the dominant Hindu classes "of their power of domination" by appropriating their value systems. He suggests that "one great strength to such programmes of assimilation to dominant values—as opposed to programmes of outright rejection of such values—was that they provided a meeting point between the adivasis and certain progressive members of the dominant classes."[90] In Uttar Pradesh the Arya Samaj facilitated the creation of such a "meeting point" with the Chamar protesters. From the Chamars' point of view the Arya Samaj certainly played a crucial role, because it criticized Hindu practices like untouchability and organized efforts to open temples and wells to them.

Pratap and *Chand,* two journals with a liberal and social reform agenda, welcomed the Arya Samaj's decision to challenge Hindu orthodoxy on the issue of untouchability. Published in Hindi from Kanpur and Allahabad in Uttar Pradesh in the first half of the twentieth century, *Pratap* and *Chand* were extremely influential in North India. North Indian Hindi literati and journals appreciated the *shuddhi* and *sangathan* efforts of the Arya Samaj and the Hindu Mahasabha because they believed these two organizations could change the orthodox values of Hinduism and Hindu society.[91] The Hindi literati in North India believed that Chamars and other Dalit castes were Hindus who had to be protected from Muslims, Christians, and the British by securing their rightful place in Hindu society. In 1925 Ganesh Shankar Vidyarthi praised the Calcutta session of the Hindu Mahasabha for raising the question of *achhut* and criticized the *sanatanists* (fundamentalists) who opposed such an agenda: "Hindu Mahasabha had the courage to put Dalit Hindus into the category of humans." In a long editorial entitled "The Short-Sightedness of the Hindus," Vidyarthi criticized the Marwari Samaj, among others, for creating obstacles in the name of *sanatani* religion— obstacles which impeded the service that the Hindu Mahasabha was performing for the Hindu community. He reminded readers that "every week 2,000 [Dalit] Hindus are becoming Christians" and that they were also "rapidly multiplying as Muslims."[92] His description of them as "Dalit Hindus" shows that Vidyarthi had no doubts about the religious identity of all "untouchables"; they could only be Hindus. *Chand* also shared this concern, and an editorial in its special *achhut* issue argued that Muslims and Christians were converting Chamars en masse, while the practice of untouchability was bringing Hindu society into crisis.[93] In another editorial *Chand* claimed that "in north India our battle is with Muslims, and in the south it is with Christians."[94]

In another editorial, Vidyarthi discussed the decision of some five thousand Chamars in Badaun to convert to Islam as a protest against the practices of *begari* and untouchability. He described this move as making a "business out of religion" and quoted a Chamar as saying that "many Chamars agree that the Hindu religion is better than Islam, but we will decide which is more profitable to us."[95] By portraying Chamars' concerns as a petty game of profit and loss, Vidyarthi was urging reform-minded Hindus to join in his struggle against the *sanatanists* who were bent on destroying the Hindu community. Supporting Chamar struggles was for him a means to another end rather than an end in itself. *Chand* claimed that the position of Chamars was an ethical and economic issue that could be solved only by enlightening all sections of Hindu society.[96] Vidyarthi congratulated the Hindu Mahasabha for passing a resolution at its 1926 Delhi conference to begin *achhutuddhar*. Although he remarked that the efforts were not sufficient, he praised the fact that they had at least begun, despite opposition from the *sanatanis*.[97]

Such positions in the editorials of two recognized liberal journals, *Pratap* and *Chand*, stand in sharp contrast to a general consensus in Indian historiography on the relationship between the Arya Samaj and Chamars.[98] It is widely believed that the Arya Samaj entered the villages and colonies of Dalits to "communalize" and "Hinduize" them. In his 2000 study, Vijay Prashad asserts that the Congress did not formulate a reform agenda for the Dalits, but rather formulated an agenda "in favour of the Hindu militants from 1917 to 1993" which emphasized *shuddhi* and *sangathan*. Located in an elitist framework, Prashad's discussion does not acknowledge Dalit autonomy or ability to negotiate with and respond to the Arya Samaj.[99] Gooptu's 2001 study suggests that by the beginning of the twentieth century the "untouchable" leaders and "the mass of the untouchables . . . had increasingly become the targets of caste uplift initiatives" by the Arya Samaj. She maintains that the Arya Samaj was primarily concerned with bringing "untouchables" within a "pan-Hindu community" through *shuddhi* and social uplift. This is how she explains Swami Achhutanand and Babu Ram Charana's rejection of the Arya Samaj in the early 1920s.[100] From this elitist perspective, Chamars are mostly the "targets" of the Arya Samaj, in which Chamars and other Dalit castes had no say or role. Gooptu never discusses what had initially prompted the two luminaries and leaders of Chamar activism to join the Arya Samaj. Rather than assuming that Dalits played only a passive role in Arya Samaj initiatives, understanding the Dalit agenda in the 1920s and 1930s and the reasons for shifts within this agenda helps to reframe the question by asking what encouraged Dalits to enter into a relationship with the Arya Samaj in the first place. Instead of assuming that Dalits played a passive role as targets of Arya Samaj reform, we can see the Arya Samaj as playing a significant role, for a time, within Dalits' own agendas.

The logic of the Chamar claim of clean, Kshatriya status provided what Hardiman has called a "meeting point" between Chamar agendas and reformist Hindu organizations like the Arya Samaj. It was not just Swami Achhutanand and Babu Ram Charana but a whole generation of Dalit ideologues and activists who were members of Arya Samaj in the first two decades of the twentieth century. In the urban centers of Uttar Pradesh, such as Agra, there was a good deal of interaction between the Jatav Mahasabha and the Arya Samaj.[101] The first and second generations of activists belonging to the Jatav community were educated in schools run by the Arya Samaj. The early Chamar advocates Pandit Sunderlal Sagar and Ramnarayan Yadvendu were both educated in Arya Samaj schools, and both of their families were members of the Arya Samaj.[102] The first Jatav organization, the Nagar Jatav Committee, was established in 1888 in Agra city by leading Jatavs, and it advocated the Arya Samaj lifestyle of vegetarianism and Vedic teachings. A Jatav Mahasabha was established in 1917, also in Agra city, and by 1924 branches had been established in Etah, Bareilly, Muthra, Etawah, and smaller towns surrounding Agra.[103] In Aligarh city Paras Ram established a Jatav Mahasabha with support from the leaders of the Agra Jatav Mahasabha.[104] Swami Achhutanand, who was educated in an army school, joined the Arya Samaj in 1905 and worked with it until 1918. He established and taught in an Arya Samaj school in Manipuri district and was an active member of its *shuddhi* program.[105] According to Lajpat Rai, the Arya Samaj had opened schools throughout the western districts of Uttar Pradesh that were open to Chamars.[106] In March 1925 *Pratap* reported that it had opened some thirty-seven schools in different parts of Uttar Pradesh, among which the Kumar Ashram in Meerut, established by Algu Rai Shastri, was the most famous.[107] The ideals of the Arya Samaj had a particular appeal to Chamars because they strengthened their claim to superior status.[108]

In Punjab the Arya Samaj "provided an organizational model" and a "maternal context in which [the Ad Dharm] movement was conceived, and from which it grew." Many members of the Ad Dharm movement in Punjab had a "certain sympathy for the Samaj" because "it had done much to bring enlightenment and egalitarian beliefs to" the Dalit neighborhoods.[109] Indeed, because of its activities among Dalits in Punjab, members of the community were always attracted to the Arya Samaj.[110] By opening schools and establishing Dalit organizations in the first two decades of the twentieth century, the Arya Samaj gained popularity in Punjab. For instance, Dalit members of the Arya Samaj established the Dayanand Dalit Udhar in Hoshiarpur, Achhut Udhar, and the Jat Path Torak Mandal in Lahore. The first generation of Dalit leaders was educated at Arya Samaj educational institutions with economic support from the institutions.[111] The Arya Samaj raised similar issues and founded similar initiatives among Chamars and Dalits in western Uttar Pradesh. And in the 1920s the Mahars led by Ambedkar in Maharashtra were waging similar struggles for the rights of "untouchables" to use public wells and to enter Hindu temples.[112]

The Arya Samaj and the Hindu Mahasabha used *shuddhi* extensively to provide Chamars with access to public wells while at the same time taking into account Hindu concerns with purity. *Shuddhi* made Chamars acceptable to caste Hindus.[113] By encouraging them to abstain from consuming meat and alcohol and to adopt Hindu rituals like evening prayers and the singing of *bhajans* (devotional songs), the Arya Samaj sought to cleanse Chamars of their "impure" status. It laid out this strategy at its annual *achhutuddhar* conference in Kanpur in July 1925 and in other places, including Aligarh, Jhansi, and

Agra.[114] Lajpat Rai, as its chief spokesperson, asked Chamars to adopt Hindu rituals, like marriage and funeral rites, in order to become "good" Hindus.[115]

A typical Arya Samaj drive would involve purifying Chamars through a *shuddhi* ceremony, which would be followed by a procession of Chamars to the public well to proclaim their rights to use the well and enter a temple. Such initiatives were undertaken in most districts of western Uttar Pradesh, from Pilibhit and Dehradun in the north to Jhansi in the south, Meerut in the east, and Mainpuri in the west.[116] The right to enter temples and bathe in the river Yamuna during the Garhmukteshwar fair was first demanded in March 1923, in Meerut city.[117] In Benares, Chamars demanded access to the Vishwanath temple and to the Dashavmegha ghat for bathing.[118] In Allahabad, Purshottam Das Tandon and Malaviya led Chamars to the temples of Alopi Devi in Prayag and of Mahabir. Both were later purified by priests.[119] The Arya Samaj also used the Hindu festivals of Holi and Dussehra to incorporate Chamars into an imagined Hindu community of equals. Such functions were organized in Meerut city, Bulandshahr, Agra, Moradabad, Pilibhit, Bijnor, and Muthra, where Hindus were urged to embrace Chamars in the festivals.[120]

Conversion was one way of freeing oneself from the stigma of "untouchability." The possibility that Chamars might convert to Islam or Christianity in an effort to obtain equal treatment frightened Hindu organizations, which responded with alacrity to Chamar demands. In Bulandshahr in 1923 the threat to convert won Chamars access to a public well in a Hindu neighborhood of the city which had previously been restricted.[121] In Agra, Kanpur, and Meerut, the threat was used to demand the right to participate in Hindu festivals, like Dussehra and Holi, from which Chamars had been excluded.[122] In Agra city in 1924 Hindus allowed some two thousand Chamars to enter and perform *puja* at the Mankameshwar temple, the most important temple in the city.[123] In September 1926 in Bareilly, Chamars put up posters "demanding end to all caste distinctions within Hindu religion," failing which they vowed to convert to Islam.[124] A similar threat was repeated in the last week of September 1926, a week of *achhutuddhar* activities organized by the Arya Samaj in Agra, Kheri, Allahabad, and Benares. Once again Chamars threatened that unless Hindus gave them equal status they would convert to Islam or Christianity.[125] In Padrauna *tahsil* of Gorakhpur some 750 Chamars converted to Christianity, as did others in Meerut, Bulandshahr, Etawah, and Moradabad.[126] Hazari, a Chamar from eastern Uttar Pradesh, experimented with multiple alternatives, becoming a Hindu purist, becoming a

Congressman by wearing "a Gandhi cap," becoming a Muslim, and finally converting to Christianity.[127]

As Chamars took the initiative by converting or threatening to convert to Islam, Muslim groups responded by actively seeking Chamar converts. At Deoband in Saharanpur and in Moradabad, Bijnor, Bulandshahr and Dehradun, Muslim organizations mobilized resources to preach Islam in Chamar villages.[128] As part of its larger program for *tabligh* (purity) and *tanzim* (unity), the Jamiat-ul-Ulama-I-Hind of Deoband School in the Saharanpur district sent volunteers to villages in western districts of the province.[129] In Agra and Meerut city the Jamiat distributed leaflets welcoming Chamars into Islam, a religion of equals.[130] The most widely reported mass conversion occurred in Badaun district in May 1925, with five thousand Chamars embracing Islam. Ganesh Shankar Vidyarthi explained that Chamars were incensed at their humiliation at the hands of Hindu society.[131]

Lala Lajpat Rai had predicted that the twin agendas of the Arya Samaj, *shuddhi* and *achhutuddhar,* would be far more difficult to carry out in "the home of Hindu orthodoxy."[132] Indeed, there was scarcely a district in Uttar Pradesh where the Arya Samaj's efforts to gain Chamars access to public wells were not opposed. In some cases where Chamars were allowed access, the wells were later publicly purified. Orthodox Hindus would frequently prevent Chamars from participating in their festivals and ceremonies, using wells, and entering temples. These sections of Hindu society began to protest against the efforts being made by Chamars and the Arya Samaj.[133] In some towns, including Kanpur and Meerut, the temples were guarded by "*lathi* [club]-wielding volunteers" ready to defend the Hindu religion by preventing Chamars from entering. Premchand vividly describes such a defense in his 1924 novel *Karmabhoomi,* which takes place in the city of Benares.[134] The support and participation of the Arya Samaj hardened the attitudes of orthodox Hindus and the dominant peasant communities of western Uttar Pradesh, like the Jats, Gujars, and Chauhans.[135] Purification of Chamars through *shuddhi* did not change *sanatani* Hindus' perceptions of them; they still considered Chamars "untouchables" and therefore refused them access to Hindu spaces.[136] On occasion Hindus and Muslims joined in protesting against Chamars' effort to use public wells. Such joint protests occurred in the towns of Moradabad, Bareilly, Shahjahanpur, and Saharanpur.[137]

Hindu leaders like Lala Lajpat Rai, Malaviya, and Sampurnanand tried to cajole orthodox Hindus by pointing out that "Chamars could leave the

Hindu religion and become Muslims and Christians if caste Hindus did not change their attitudes."[138] The Arya Samaj even organized conciliatory meetings between Chamars and Hindus, such as one held in Meerut city in 1923.[139] It also organized an *achhutuddhar* week, March 22–28, 1928, in the major towns of Uttar Pradesh, appealing to Hindus to treat Chamars as equals by allowing them "to enter temples and draw water from public wells."[140]

Reminding Chamars of their Hindu identity and including them within a larger Hindu community were among the primary objectives of the Arya Samaj and the Hindu Mahasabha.[141] In Najibabad town in the Bijnor district, *shuddhi* meant rejecting Muslim customs and practices, and on another occasion the term was used to prevent them from purchasing at Muslim shops.[142] In Ballashahpur *tahsil* of Jaunpur district Chamars were asked to protect cows, and in Badlapur village they were asked to take up cleaner occupations, weave *khadi* cloth, and become vegetarians.[143] In Hamirpur district the Hindu Mahasabha campaigned in Chamar villages against cooperating with Muslims during the Islamic sacred month of Muharram.[144] *Shuddhi* was aiming at satisfying Hindus by showing, in the words of a Congressman speaking at a Chamar meeting at Mainpuri, "that they had really changed their mode of living."[145] Still, although *mochi* Chamars of Bansgaon *tahsil* of Gorakhpur and of Singramau *tahsil* of Jaunpur decided to use only *murdari* cattle for leather, avoiding the *halali* cattle they got from Muslims, they refused to change their occupation. Similarly, the Chamars of Raidassi village in Premchand's *Karmabhoomi* agreed to abstain from eating beef and drinking alcohol, but not from leatherwork.[146]

The Arya Samaj was the only Hindu organization that, institutionally and actively, addressed some of the concerns raised by the Chamars in the second decade of the twentieth century. The initiatives launched by the Arya Samaj also motivated local members of the Hindu Mahasabha to participate in the programs. By claiming Kshatriya status and adopting clean Hindu practices, Chamars had laid out an agenda of reform and created a "meeting point" where they could join with sections of Hindu society, like the Arya Samaj, who were receptive to some of their concerns.

The Second Phase: Emergence of the Adi-Hindu Movement

The second stage in the evolution of a Chamar agenda represents a radical departure from the first stage, which lasted from 1922 to 1928. Ganesh Shankar Vidyarthi noted this shift in an editorial of April 27, 1925. The second stage, he wrote, was marked by the "birth of a new Adi-Hindu movement in north India" among the *achhuts* of Uttar Pradesh, led by Swami Achhutanand. Vidyarthi underlined the popularity of the Adi-Hindu movement from Delhi to Kanpur, and especially in the Agra-Etawah region of western Uttar Pradesh.[147] In their biographies of Swami Achhutanand the Chamar writers Mangal Jatav and Rajpal Singh put the first meeting of the Adi-Hindu movement in Etawah in December 1923.[148] In 1926 police reports began to mention meetings in Etawah, Allahabad, and Kanpur in which Achhutanand declared that *achhuts* were the original inhabitants and rulers of India.[149] Despite these early signs, the December 1927 All-India Adi-Hindu Conference organized by Swami Achhutanand can be taken as the foundation of the movement, when its program was formally announced. The movement acquired a formidable presence in western and central Uttar Pradesh in 1928.

A decade later, in 1937, Chandrika Prasad Jigyasu published *Bharat ke Adi Nivasiyon ki Sabhyata* (The Civilization of India's Original Inhabitants) in Lucknow. Even though Jigyasu was a close associate of Swami Achhutanand, he was not a Dalit. Mahant Bhodanand Mahasthavir also made a similar claim in his 1930 book *Mool-Bharatvasi aur Arya* (Original Indians and Aryas). We know of it only because Mahasthavir mentioned his own work in his introduction to Jigyasu's book. Jigyasu addressed not just Chamars or Dalits but 80 percent of India's population—peasants, workers, artisans, lower castes, tribal peoples, and "untouchables." His work is the first conception of *bahujan* (oppressed majority) politics by a Chamar intellectual and activist. But despite his inclusive vision, the issues he raised primarily concerned the Dalits. Jigyasu opened his book with an appeal to all Dalits:

> Adi-nivasi friends! Embrace this true glorious history, which the Arya *jati* destroyed through their cunning and deceit. Read this to erase from your mind weakness, confusion, shame; open your heart like a lotus to the light of reawakening.[150]

Jigyasu's call reflects the efforts of Dalit intellectuals of the 1920s to retrieve a history of "untouchables" from Brahmanical sources. They saw the unearthing and recovery of a Dalit history erased by the Aryans and the Hindus as the new agenda of Dalit historiography. But in this second phase, Dalit activists and writers unanimously rejected "what the Brahman-pandits have said with regard to 80 percent of the population, that they are descendants of the natural-unnatural succession of an illegitimate or mixed *varna*." According to Jigyasu, the victorious Aryans had erased "the glorious literature and history of their opponents, the *daityas-danavas-asurs,* by characterizing them as black and irrational people in their epics."[151] Because of this, no historical records remained with which to write a history of Dalit and Shudra *jatis.*

Jigyasu noted that an intelligent reader of the Vedic and Brahmanical poems celebrating the victory of the Aryan rulers over the non-Aryans would naturally wonder about the people mentioned as *asurs, dasas, daityas,* and *danavas.* The Vedic literature also mentions that these people lived in cities and forts. Who were these people who lived in cities and forts? They were known in the three worlds. They worshipped Shiv-mahadev and ruled India during the times of *satyayug.* Under their rule dharma existed in its true form, truth prevailed, and people lived for one hundred thousand years. What, then, happened to the children of these honest, *daitya-danav* ancestors? We do not have their literature which might have told us about their history. The little evidence that we have comes from the Vedic, Puranic, and Brahmanical literature.[152]

Vedic and Brahmanical literature provide many examples of the superiority and greatness of the Adi-Hindu civilization. For instance, Jigyasu quoted from Nehru's *Glimpses of World History* and from the work of Sir John Marshall to claim that the Harappa and Mohenjo-Daro civilizations were pre-Vedic and belonged to the ancestors of the Adi-Hindus. The Rig Vedic hymns praising the victory of the Aryans also tell us about the valor of *dasas* and *asurs* and the destruction of their forts and cities. He also borrowed from contemporary histories being taught in Allahabad and Benares Universities to claim that the Indus civilization predated the Aryans and belonged to the original inhabitants, who were Adi-Hindus.[153] At the same time he cited Puranic sources like *Amarkosha* to claim that the *daityas-danavas* and *asurs* were India's original inhabitants, who had opposed the invasion by the *devatas* or the Aryans. On the basis of this evidence he claimed that the *asurs, daityas,* and *danavas* were the rulers of India during the *satyug,* a period of great prosperity. Among the rulers he named were Raja Vikra, Vidhvatsa, Vairochan, Mutchkand, Bhairav, Nandak, Andhak, Hiranyaksh, Hiranyakashyap, Prahlad, and Bali. King Bali was the greatest of all, and his might is acknowledged in the Aryan literature. The Aryans feared him because he had established a fair and egalitarian rule.

Bali ruled during Vedic times, but was defeated and killed by the Aryans because he refused to accept Vedic values.[154]

Jigyasu borrowed from colonial ethnographic theories of the racial origins of Indian society that were current among Indian scholars to argue that in India the Dravids and non-Aryan social groups were separate ethnic groups, distinct from the Aryans. He quoted Grierson's linguistic survey to argue that his research had proved beyond a doubt that Prakrit and Pali were older languages than Sanskrit and were spoken by the Adi-Hindus. According to him, most of the contemporary regional languages of India, including Hindi, emerged from Prakrit.[155]

What is interesting is the mode of historical reasoning Jigyasu employed. In putting forward his argument, he broke with the *Chanvar Purana* by citing contemporary works by caste Hindu and British historians. He provided references in footnotes to strengthen his claim that his work was well researched. Most striking are the grounds upon which he claimed that *dasas, dasyus,* and *asurs* were his ancestors. Jigyasu made a virtue of the absence of evidence that Dalits are descended from non-Aryans by arguing that the invading Aryans destroyed it all. It is clear that his arguments reflect the politics of the moment. Jigyasu was not simply writing history, he was framing a political project. Dalits in contemporary India felt they had been oppressed, exploited, ruled, and deprived for many centuries. Ultimately, if the Hindus could claim that they were descendants of the Aryans, there was no reason Jigyasu and the Adi-Hindu movement couldn't similarly claim the *dasas, asurs,* and *daityas* as their ancestors. Like all histories, claims to both Aryan and non-Aryan ancestry were constructed in relation to present-day politics.

The history of Adi-Hindus did not appear in a vacuum; instead Jigyasu's narrative reflects a political view widely shared among Chamars and Dalits in Uttar Pradesh in 1937, when his book was published. According to Mangal Jatav, the Adi-Hindu movement was launched by Swami Achhutanand in Etawah in December 1923 at a meeting attended by twenty thousand Dalits and presided over by Ramdayal Jatav, a contractor of quarries who also provided the necessary funds.[156] At this meeting, Achhutanand "declared that the present-day 'untouchables' were the original stock of India, and Hindus and Muslims were the upstarts."[157] He asked the government to employ Dalits in the army and police force and to provide them with facilities to become members of the *panchayats.* He urged Dalits to protest against the continued practice of *begari* in the countryside.[158] In another meeting, at Kanpur, Achhutanand declared that the *shuddhi* movement had been launched to continue the slavery of Dalits.[159] In Allahabad he appealed to all Dalits to unite with the lower castes in their struggle to challenge the dominance of caste Hindus.[160] He asserted that Dalits did not need the Hindus, their Vedas, or their gods, like Ram and Krishna. Dalits had their own tradition, based on saints like Raidas and Kabir.[161] He reminded Dalits that many Hindus ate meat but wanted Dalits to give it up: "Why should we give it up?" He claimed that their oppression was religious and that the Dalit struggle was also directed against the Hindu religion.[162]

Swami Achhutanand demanded separate representation for Dalits within the representative bodies, like that of Sikhs. Indeed, the Sikhs were increasingly taken as a model, since they had successfully separated themselves from the claims of Hindus.[163] In a meeting at Allahabad in April 1926 he proposed that Dalits be properly represented in legislative councils and local bodies, like the boards of municipalities, towns, and districts.[164] Two months later, at a meeting in Kanpur, he went a step further and asserted that British rule meant liberation of the "untouchables" from Hindu hegemony—a point already made by many Chamar groups in their protests. Explaining this position to the audience, he claimed that "we are really indebted to the British government for opening to us the doors of knowledge that have been purposely, with selfish motives, banged shut against us." According to Achhutanand, the Congress *swaraj* meant the continued subordination of the Dalits.[165]

By November 1927 an All-India Adi-Hindu Mahasabha had been established and was organizing annual conferences. The first was organized by Swami Achhutanand in November 1927 at Farrukhabad and was presided over by a Chamar. A month later, on December 27 and 28, a massive All-India Adi-Hindu Conference was held at Mayo Hall in Allahabad.[166] By this time, three features had come to define the second phase in Dalit politics: first, the claim that *achhuts* were the original inhabitants of India; second, the rejection of reforms within the Hindu religion; and third, the demand that the British government recognize Dalits' separate political rights. In an open letter to Gandhi in October 1928 the Adi-Hindu Mahasabha demanded separate representation in the councils and elected bodies. It also criticized as undemocratic the 1927 Nehru Report, which had outlined a constitutional scheme for communities in India, because it did not provide separate constitutional provisions to the minorities.[167] By 1929 the activities of the Adi-Hindu organization had spread to the districts of Fatehpur, Etah, Kanpur, Etawah, Agra, Meerut, Dehradun, Benares, Saharanpur, and Basti.[168] Chamar organizations also continued to raise agrarian concerns, including *begari* and the cesses imposed by the zamindars.

Chamar groups and organizations were becoming disillusioned with and critical of the activities of the Arya Samaj, especially the *shuddhi* program. In May 1924, Sita Ram Pradhan, a member of the Raidass Kureel Sudhar Sabha of Kanpur, asserted that Hindu efforts to gain Dalits access to temples were actually was part of a general effort by them to humiliate Dalits, by convincing Dalits to come to their temples and then closing the doors to them when they arrived.[169] At a massive Chamar meeting in May 1924 in Gorakhpur district, the speakers discussed the differences between themselves and the Hindu community and elaborated on the limitations of reforms within the Hindu religion. Even more importantly, Buddhist literature was distributed in the meeting.[170] In a conference attended by two thousand Chamars in April 1927 in Agra, the Jatav Sabha declared that like Sikhs, Chamars and "untouchables" were a separate community from Hindus.[171] In Etawah in May 1927 a group of twenty-five Chamars, along with Khatiks and Dhanuks, declared that they were Adi-Hindus rather than Hindus and appealed to Dalits to boycott performances of the Ramlila and other Hindu rites and rituals.[172] In March 1928 the Arya Samaj's annual *achhutuddhar* week evoked a very poor response from Chamars.[173] All of these show Chamars becoming increasingly uncomfortable with reform within the confines of Hindu religion.

Ganesh Vidyarthi, who first noted and welcomed the Adi-Hindu movement in 1925, in 1928 criticized the movement's leaders, saying that they were unnecessarily creating divisions within Hindu society by cooperating with the imperialist forces promoted by the British government in India.[174] He proclaimed that "we have faith in our *crores* of *achhut* brothers who will not be deceived by such leaders, neither can they be separated from the body of Hindu society." Once Hindu society has opened its door to Dalits, such leaders, "who are fanning the fire of hatred, will disappear like a bad dream."[175] The Hindi newspaper *Abhyudaya* similarly emphasized the divisive role of the British by pointing out the presence of police constables and government officials at meetings of the Adi-Hindu movement.[176] The May 1928 edition of the Hindi monthly *Chand* stated that leaders of the Adi-Hindu movement had brought disgrace to all Indians by welcoming the Simon Commission and had earned the gratitude of the British government by pleading like beggars for favors and jobs. It concluded that Dalits had sold their independence to the British.[177]

*   *   *

A close analysis of the histories that Chamars and Dalits wrote and the strategies of political organization that they used suggests their politics moved in two stages in the first decades of the twentieth century. The first phase, captured in the Chamar histories and politics of the 1910s and early to mid-1920s, sought a pure Kshatriya status by demanding status equal to that of caste Hindus. The core difficulty confronted by the Chamar activists was the fact that their "impure" origin and "unclean" occupation condemned them to an "untouchable" present, and this fate was recognized and accepted by the British. By writing histories of their caste and by political mobilization of their community, the Chamars challenged British and Hindu representations of both their past and their present. The second phase, beginning in 1927, saw a transition to a more inclusive *achhut* identity, which sought to define all "untouchables" as Adi-Hindus. Writing histories that identified Dalits as the original inhabitants of India and launching political struggles to mobilize all "untouchable" castes in Uttar Pradesh, Chamars were at the forefront of the Adi-Hindu movement. This phase also saw the beginning of a new politics of intervention, in which an *achhut* agenda for social and political transformation through state action was put forward. Chamar politics and struggles were constituted primarily by contesting the dominant Hindu and colonial narratives of their "untouchable" identity, rather than by mobilizing against colonialism. Together, the two phases mark the beginning of struggles for an identity which would liberate Chamars and Dalits from the stigma of "untouchability." I discuss these struggles in the final chapter.

Illustration from the 1937 Adi-Hindu Mahasabha calendar, featuring Swami Achhutanand in the center with Ambedkar on his left. *Photo courtesy of Mangal Singh Jatav (used by permission).*

अम्बेदकर की आवाज़

अर्थात्

अछूतों का फेडरेशन

प्रथम भाग

लेखक

डा० नन्दलाल 'वियोगी'

प्रकाशक :--

श्री एन० एल० जयसवार सेवा सदन

पुस्तक भंडार, नं० ३०८ राजापुर, इलाहाबाद

Title page of Nandlal Viyougi's book *Ambedkar ki Awaz arthat Achhutoin ka Federation* (Allahabad, 1949).

Guru Prasad of Kanpur was a close associate of Swami Achhutanand (undated, c. 1928–32). *Photo courtesy of Mangal Singh Jatav (used by permission).*

Munshi Hari Prasad Tamta of Kumaon district founded the Kumaon Shilpkar (artisan) Sabha. He was a close friend and associate of Swami Achhutanand (undated, c. 1928–32). *Photo courtesy of Mangal Singh Jatav (used by permission).*

Ram Charan Jatav of Mainpuri district was a close associate of Swami Achhutanand (undated, c. 1928–32). *Photo courtesy of Mangal Singh Jatav (used by permission).*

Shivnarayan Das of Kanpur city was a
close associate of Swami Achhutanand
(undated, c. 1928–32). *Photo courtesy of
Mangal Singh Jatav (used by permission).*

Seth Durga Das Ji (Kabirpanthi) of
Shahjahanpur was a major financier and
a close associate of Swami Achhutanand
(undated, c. 1928–32). *Photo courtesy of
Mangal Singh Jatav (used by permission).*

CHAPTER 5

From Chamars to Dalits:
The Making of an Achhut Identity and Politics, 1927–56

In the last week of the past month, a conference by the name of the "All-India Adi-Hindu Conference" was held at Allahabad, in which mostly persons from the Raidass Samaj [Chamars] participated. Doms, Mehtars, Lal-Begis, and other castes were not represented in the conference.

—Pratap, January 8, 1928

The British Government is establishing its claims to be our liberators from this age-long servitude . . . our present wretched conditions cannot be improved unless we have, through our elected representatives, a voice in the various legislatures and local bodies. The only method open to us is [a] separate electorate through which we can [achieve] our political, social and even moral salvation.

—Memorial Address to the Honourable Chairman and Members of the Statutory Commission, November 30, 1928

The emergence of mass nationalism was a distinctive feature of the 1920s anti-colonial movement in India. New social classes and groups were participating, making for a richer and more substantial definition of Indian nationalism.[1] An enormous body of scholarly literature in the last two decades has documented the richly textured history of nationalist mobilization, particularly the peasant and working-class struggles and the many visions that helped shape Indian nationalism. Despite this recent expansion of the understanding of Indian nationalism, there is still little discussion or investigation of Dalit agendas and struggles within the vibrant historiography of Indian nationalism. Indian historiography pertaining to Dalits is summed up by Sumit Sarkar:

> From a more long-term point of view, Harijan welfare work by Gandhians must have indirectly helped to spread the message of nationalism down to the lowest and most oppressed sections of rural society, and Harijans in most parts of the country did come to develop a traditional loyalty towards the Congress which would greatly help the party after independence, too.[2]

Two assumptions form the basis for this statement. First, that there were no specifically Chamar and Dalit struggles in North India in the 1920s and 1930s. Second, that political consciousness was created by the activities of Congress politicians and contributed to their electoral success among Dalits after independence. These assumptions have been fairly persuasive. In his 2003 book on the rise of lower-caste politics, Christophe Jaffrelot has argued that North Indian society comes "closest to the varna model with its four orders (Brahmins, Kshatriyas, Vaishyas and Shudras) and the untouchables," and therefore asserts that "the demographic weight of the upper castes and their role in the local power structure prepared the ground for the development of conservative ideologies and the establishment of the Congress's clientelistic politics." Congress was the sole political force among Dalit groups in North India because, until the 1960s, "Untouchable castes like the Chamars remained not only prisoners of Sanskritisation but also of the *bhakti.*"[3]

Most Dalit histories have focused on Maharashtra, particularly on movements for access to temples and wells in the 1920s and on Dr. Ambedkar's interventions in constitutional politics. These events are generally viewed as marking the beginning of Dalit struggles in India.[4] For instance, Susan Bayly's significant 1999 study of caste sees "constitutional arrangements" as key to understanding the emergence of Dalit movements in India.[5] By highlighting Ambedkar and constitutional history, most histories have represented the Dalit demand for a separate electorate as the sum total of Dalit struggle and mobilization in precolonial India. Mendelsohn and Vicziany's 1998 survey of Dalit struggles and politics in India focuses exclusively on Mahars and

Ambedkar for the period between 1920 and 1960.[6] According to Gail Omvedt, "if it is impossible to conceptualise the Dalit movement in India in the absence of Ambedkar, it is equally difficult to imagine, sociologically, Ambedkar coming out of any other region than the Maratha-speaking areas of Bombay Presidency."[7] Uttar Pradesh saw no Dalit struggles during the colonial period; Mendelsohn and Vicziany assume that "not until Gandhi's campaigns of the 1930s [was] the huge Untouchable population of the Hindi-speaking heartland . . . touched to any extent by the great ferment."[8] Such an assumption has led a political scientist, Sudha Pai, to theorize about the "delayed development of Dalit consciousness" in Uttar Pradesh compared to Maharashtra.[9] Such notions flow from the belief that there were no autonomous Dalit struggles in Uttar Pradesh; instead, Congress politics dominated Dalit activism as part of the Congress's *achhutuddhar* program.

There is not a single monograph that discusses the Adi-Hindu movement or its agenda in colonial Uttar Pradesh. Most of the studies that we do have focus on urban Dalits, like Owen Lynch's study of the Jatavs of Agra and, more recently, Nandini Gooptu's chapter on "untouchable" assertion in the urban centers of Uttar Pradesh.[10] There are few anthropological studies of Chamars, except Briggs's in 1920 and some articles by Bernard Cohn in the 1960s.[11] In fact, the only historical accounts of the Adi-Hindu movement we have are by Dalit activists and writers like Chandrika Prasad Jigyasu, Shankaranand Shastri, Nandlal Viyougi, D. C. Dinkar, Mohandas Nemishray, Mangal Jatav, and Rajpal Singh. These writers have kept the memories of their struggle alive for their community.[12] So far, non-Dalit historians have shown no interest in these accounts and practically no effort has been made to engage with them, leaving the development of Dalit struggles nicely veiled by ignorance. By borrowing from Dalit narratives in Hindi and combining them with archival sources, this chapter recovers a history of Chamar and Dalit struggles in Uttar Pradesh. The epigraphs are intended to draw attention to the role of Chamars in this new movement and to indicate their active role in seeking affirmative action for the *achhuts* of Uttar Pradesh. Ambedkar was not the only one to broach such ideas. They were already circulating amidst a much broader base than is generally acknowledged.

Chapter 4 focused on the Chamar struggle for identity in Uttar Pradesh, which unfolded in two stages, both concerned with constituting a Chamar community. The first, from 1922 to 1928, took the form of histories and protests and sought equality in Hindu society by claiming a pure Kshatriya status. The second was marked by the definition of a more inclusive *achhut* identity and a rejection of Hindu religion. It found an institutional form in the Adi-Hindu Mahasabha, which had been founded in 1923 and which was replaced by the Scheduled Castes Federation (SCF) in the 1940s and became the Republican Party of India (RPI) in 1956. These organizations laid out the *achhut* agenda between 1927 and 1956, aiming to empower *achhuts* by giving their identity new meaning. The leaders of the Adi-Hindu Mahasabha hoped that by emphasizing their *achhut* identity, they could build a new politics that would bring together all the Dalit castes—Doms, Mehtars, Pasis, Lal Begis, Dhanuks, Koris, and Chamars. In an earlier study I argued that "in the 1940s Dalits of Uttar Pradesh articulated an inclusive *achhut* identity to mobilize diverse sections of Dalit society: Jatavs, Chamars, Ad-Dharmis, Pasis," and that this articulation of identity led to the formation of the SCF and was accompanied by the emergence of a new agenda of affirmative action.[13] This proposition needs to be radically modified in the light of the present work, which has put forward evidence indicating that such claims were in fact first made in 1927, and not in 1942.

December 1927 was the foundational moment of the autonomous Dalit movement in Uttar Pradesh. Imbuing the category *achhut* with radical connotations in an effort to rally "untouchables," the Adi-Hindu Mahasabha outlined the core agenda of the Dalit struggle, which included a separate electorate and affirmative action policies in legislative, government, and educational institutions. Swami Achhutanand, Manik Chand, and Chandrika Prasad Jigyasu, leaders of the Adi-Hindu Mahasabha, also led the efforts to mobilize and sustain a Dalit struggle in the 1930s and 1940s that contributed to the crystallization of an *achhut* identity. The second and third sections of this chapter discuss the protests organized by the Adi-Hindu leaders in various parts of Uttar Pradesh to popularize their agenda and challenge the Congress. A commitment to *achhut* identity and to the Adi-Hindu agenda of 1928 has shaped Dalit politics in Uttar Pradesh in the long twentieth century. However, the formation of the RPI has been interpreted as a move away from a politics based on an *achhut* identity to one based on class.

The Formulation of an *Achhut* Agenda by Chamars

Contemporary observers noted the leading role that Chamars played in articulating a new Adi-Hindu identity for "untouchables" by claiming that all Dalits were *achhuts*. Mainstream Hindi newspapers, in particular, emphasized this feature of the Adi-Hindu Mahasabha and argued that it was not a movement of *achhuts* but only of Chamars. In the first epigraph of this chapter, the editor of the Hindi weekly *Pratap*, Ganesh Shankar Vidyarthi, identifies Chamars as prominent in the Adi-Hindu Mahasabha. The Hindi monthly journal *Chand* observed that "members of the Mehtar and Dom *jatis* were almost absent in the proceedings of the meeting," while *Abhyudaya* pointed to the absence of members of the Pasi caste.[14] These journals were drawing attention to an important fact. Chamars constituted almost 60 percent of the total Dalit population, and were the most prosperous and educated of all the Dalit castes in Uttar Pradesh. E. A. H. Blunt, an important contemporary official with wide experience of the province, wrote a memorandum in 1932 to the Uttar Pradesh government in which he opposed any move that would exclude urban Chamars from the percentage of the total voting bloc belonging to the community in the province. In its initial exercise to identify the total Chamar electorate, the Uttar Pradesh government had excluded urban Chamars on the presumption that they had "abandoned their traditional occupation." He argued that such a measure would not only exclude some two million urban Chamars from the voting bloc but also eliminate a class that had provided leadership to the Dalit community in Uttar Pradesh. Such a division never actually materialized, but Blunt's concern is a good indication of the strength of Chamars in shaping the Dalit political movement in Uttar Pradesh.[15]

The Adi-Hindu movement marked a change in the nature of Chamar politics, by fashioning a new *achhut* identity. The first All-India Adi-Hindu Mahasabha conference, held in Allahabad on December 27 and 28, 1927, was an important episode in the history of the movement, and it was reported and discussed extensively in contemporary newspapers. The conference laid out the movement's agenda, but its tone and the temper are also worth paying attention to.[16] It began on December 26 with a procession through Allahabad city by twenty-five thousand Dalits, led by Swami Achhutanand and G. A. Gavai in motorcars, followed by phaetons, buggies, and *tongas* (two-wheeled carriages); protestors carrying banners and flags; and *bhajan-mandlis* (singers) singing songs of the ancient glory of the Adi-Hindus. The conference itself, attended by some 350 delegates from Punjab, Bihar, Delhi, Madhya Pradesh, Poona, Hyderabad, and Bengal began with the slogans *Adi-Hindu vansh ki Jai* and *Angrez Sarkar ki Jai*, thanking the

British for liberating Dalits from Hindu domination. One of the points repeatedly made was "We are no longer afraid" of the Hindus.

This movement had three important ideological strands. The first dealt with history by claiming that *achhuts* are the descendants of the *dasas, asurs,* and *dasyus* mentioned in the Hindu texts and are thus the original inhabitants of India. Members of the movement thanked the British for opening the doors of education to *achhuts* and thus making them aware that they were the "original inhabitants—the 'Aborigines'—who lived and thrived in India before every one else." On these grounds they proclaimed that *achhuts* were the real rulers of India, because they belonged to the *rajavanshis* (royal) lineage. In particular, attendees at the Adi-Hindu conference were grateful to the British for rejecting the Laws of Manu (the *Manusmriti*) and establishing a modern legal system. Access to education was declared the major objective of the movement. The 1928 report of the All-India Adi-Hindu Conference makes the point that the Hindu religion "is the only singular religion in the whole world in which human beings have been regarded as worse than even animals."

Second, the conference declared that all *achhuts* were separate from the Hindu community. Hindus were reminded that if they wanted *achhuts* to be part of their community, they should first regard them as equals, something which they had consistently refused to do. Despite Gandhi's efforts, "there is not a single village in this country where we can use public wells." The movement claimed that unless caste Hindus "treat us equally in religious and social matters, to give Swaraj to India would mean nothing short of tightening the bonds of our slavery." The Adi-Hindu Mahasabha justified its strategy of aligning with the British by arguing that the struggle was one "between the strong and the weak and therefore the weak have to invoke the aid of some one else if they want to successfully fight with the strong." It described itself as a movement of all *achhuts,* the "Chamar, Pasi, Dhor, Mang, Mehtar, Pariah, Pancham, Dom, Dhobi, Dharkar etc.," under "our true leader," Swami Achhutanand. It defined its struggle against social injustice as *achhut* nationalism, social uplift as its religion, and self-respect as its Home Rule, and advised the audience to ignore Hindus who called them traitors.

Third, the conference demanded adequate safeguards for *achhuts* in the legislative institutions through separate electorates, a demand which was to become the cornerstone of the movement's struggle in the coming years. Because *achhuts* were inadequately represented, the Adi-Hindu Mahasabha demanded "proportional representation in the Central and Provincial Legislatures," as well as special provisions for educational facilities and reserved places in government service. It was very clear about the reasons for this inadequate representation, stating that the Hindus who "sit there as our nominal representatives, far from being guardians of our interest, are the very men whose oppressions we can no longer tolerate." *Achhuts* had no faith in the Hindu leadership of the Congress. Acutely aware that the "British Government is contemplating conferring political rights on India," the leaders of the movement welcomed the investigations of the Statutory (Simon) Commission, which toured India in 1928–29 to explore the possibility of extending "the principle of responsible Government." They expressed "full confidence in the European Members of the said Commission, for if Indians [i.e., Hindus] had been appointed, the grievances of the Adi-Hindus would have been totally ignored."[17]

Ten resolutions were passed at the conference. They affirmed loyalty to the British emperor and confidence in the Simon Commission, proposed "Adi-Hindu" as the new common identity of all *achhuts,* and asked for proportionate representation of Adi-Hindus in elected bodies, "fair representation in the Government services" and the reservation of a "sufficient number of scholarships" for *achhuts,* free education for their children, a ban on the *Manusmriti,* and the repeal of the Criminal Tribes Act.[18] The conference also established a committee, comprising Ambedkar and M. C. Rajah (a Dalit leader from the Madras Presidency), to collect evidence of popular support for its resolutions. The committee submitted this evidence to the Simon Commission in a memorandum in May 1928.[19]

The leaders of the Adi-Hindu Mahasabha were keen to define the objectives of their struggle as "confined to those depressed classes known as untouchables." This is the first evidence we have of efforts to distinguish the Adi-Hindu movement from movements of the lower castes. In their representation to the Simon Commission, the Adi-Hindu leaders clearly distanced themselves from Babu Rama Charana and his politics.[20] Babu Rama Charana, who belonged to the lower Mallah (boatman) caste, was a leader of a separate political organization, the Audi-Hindu Sabha, and advocated a joint struggle by Shudras and *achhuts.*[21] He argued that the Audi-Hindus consisted of the "Sudras and Panchamas, touchables and untouchables," and urged the British government to adopt the term "Hindu Backward Classes" instead of the undefined "depressed classes."[22] He was invited by the British to the Round Table Conferences in London in 1932.

Yet it has been assumed that the Adi-Hindu movement was a joint political struggle by Dalits and Shudras.[23] Although Rama Charana desired a unified struggle and agenda in the late 1920s, it is clear that *achhut* leaders from late 1927 onward did not. Dalit leaders rejected his argument that Shudras and *achhuts* faced similar discrimination. The leaders of the Adi-Hindu movement claimed that the Shudras were dominant landed communities, economically and politically powerful, with access to Hindu temples and public wells. They pointed out that the "attitude of the Sudras towards the untouchables is even worse than that of the other three Varnas."[24] In their opinion Babu Rama Charana's politics would be detrimental to the *achhut* struggle, and for this reason he was not invited to the Allahabad conference of December 1927. The schism between Rama Charana and the leaders of the Adi-Hindu Mahasabha was an important factor in the evolution of *achhut* politics. Even the leaders of the Jatav Mahasabha of Agra, in their resolution of 1928, distanced their politics from "backward class" politics.[25]

Shudra or lower-caste activists were opposed to any kind of affirmative action for the Dalits. Jiwa Ram, a lawyer in Moradabad, claimed in his petition to the Simon Commission that Dalits were part of the Hindu community and needed no special privileges from the British, which might ruin their integration with the Hindus.

> The undersigned [Jiwa Ram] eagerly suggests that no fuss should be made about the depressed classes. They are the part and parcel of the Indian nation or at least of the Hindus. No special provision regarding them should be made in any law or rules. They will, if they can, seek their own way. A seat in the Assembly or Local Councils, or Local Self-Governing bodies, with all the other doors shut, is not likely to improve their status, but is sure to take away the feelings of sympathy and brotherhood from the minds of the higher classes.[26]

Similarly, Ram Prasad Ahir, a Shudra from Sultanpur, in his own petition contended that the British, by employing the Chamars as syces and by providing new opportunities for them in the leather industries, had improved their conditions, and therefore they did not need special privileges. On the other hand, he said, the conditions of the lower castes, like Ahirs and Kurmis, had not changed, because they were "touchables," and they therefore ended up providing more *begari* than the Chamars.[27]

What we have here is evidence that backward-class politics and Dalit politics were moving on two different trajectories. Although the backward classes considered themselves an integral part of the Hindu community, the Dalits increasingly did not.

The Adi-Hindu Mahasabha's memorandum was just one among many that were sent by Dalit organizations to the Simon Commission. These memoranda and petitions illuminate the various elements of the Dalit agenda that were being assembled around this time.[28] What is most striking is that almost all of the Dalit organizations that submitted petitions to the Simon Commission claimed a separate *achhut* identity; the claim is a notable feature of Dalit politics of this time.

Many of the other principles of the Adi-Hindu movement were also shared by other Dalit groups across Uttar Pradesh. The Ad Dharmis of Dehradun argued that the historical wrongs done to their community for the last five thousand years could now be righted, thanks to the British. Pointing out that they were agriculturalists, they demanded the right to own land and houses, which had been denied to them both by Hindus and by the British. They demanded that Dalits be recognized as a separate community from Hindus.[29]

The Kumaon Shilpakar Sabha of Almora (led by Munshi Hari Prasad Tamta, a key player in contemporary Dalit politics), claimed to represent the Doms of Kumaon. It reminded the British of their loyalty, compared their conditions to "that of Pasi, Chamars," and argued that the dominant caste Hindus had reduced their status to that of slaves. It asked for the twelve-year rule in Agra province, preventing eviction, to be extended to Kumaon.[30] In its own petition to the Simon Commission, the Jatav Mahasabha of Agra (led by Babu Khem Chand, a member of the Legislative Council) reiterated some of the same points made by the Adi-Hindu Mahasabha, but differed in others. First, Khem Chand claimed that the Jatav Mahasabha represented "the community of Jatavs, more generally known as Chamars," who were "numerically the most important among the depressed classes," rather than making a claim on behalf of all *achhuts*.[31] Second, although Khem Chand emphasized the separateness of the "depressed classes" from the Hindus because of the discrimination practiced by the latter, he nevertheless did not demand separate electorates, as the Adi-Hindu Mahasabha did. Rather, he demanded that the government reserve jobs and special educational opportunities for Jatavs. According to Yadvendu, Khem Chand's major achievement was forcing the Uttar Pradesh government to provide for the nomination of Dalits to the municipal and district boards.[32]

Another Dalit organization, the Dom Sudhar Sabha of Garhwal, in its representation to the Simon Commission argued that if Muslims, with a population of three thousand, were entitled to separate representation in the Garhwal district board, why were the Doms, who number half a million, denied separate representation?[33] The *sabha* sought representation in district, municipal, and legislative bodies, the reservation of government jobs for them, and funds for education. The *mochis* of Kanpur described their protest as a *barabari ki ladai,* or struggle for equal status with the Hindus. Because "we manufacture every kind of article of leather," they said, the municipalities had passed resolutions "turning us out of city limits." They reminded the government of the tyranny of the Hindus who had usurped their seats in the local bodies and demanded that those seats be protected, because "we have been truly loyal to the British Government." The *mochis* argued that their "caste should not be called and recorded as Chamar" in the census. They insisted that their caste name, which was their true identity, "should be recorded as Aharwar, Kurli, Dhusia, Jatia etc, and not Chamar."[34]

Almost all the mainstream political parties, including the Congress, unanimously boycotted the Simon Commission, leading to its failure. The viceroy of India, Lord Irwin, candidly observed that the Simon Commission failed to advance Indian participation "towards responsibility in the central Government" and that it maintained a "total silence on Dominion Status." He concluded that the commission was out of touch with the political realities of India.[35] Yet the Dalit organizations participated seriously and conscientiously in its investigations. According to Eleanor Zelliot, the "untouchable" organizations "came out in full force to express their grievances" and demand a constitutionally defined affirmative action program from the British, founded on separate electorates for *achhut* castes in all the provinces.[36] At the same time the Muslim League, led by Muhammad Ali Jinnah, was working for some kind of accommodation with the Congress on the basis of joint electorates with "reservation of seats on a population basis in each province."[37] It is ironic that at this time the leaders of Dalit groups were far more convinced of the necessity of parting ways with the Congress and the Hindus than were Jinnah and the Muslim League. It was not until 1929 that Jinnah was ready to accept the "parting of the ways," as he came to call the failure of the Congress and the Hindu right to accept his minimum requirements.[38]

As a significant leader, Swami Achhutanand played a prominent role in building the Adi-Hindu movement (see chapter 4), by visiting towns and villages, usually with a group of five prominent members of the movement, giving speeches and distributing pamphlets in the Chamar *mohallas*.[39] As a founding editor of the *Adi-Hindu* newspaper, he propagated his ideas in print.[40] In fact, there was a general awareness among *achhuts* that since caste Hindus owned most of the presses, publishing their own paper and managing their own printing press were important means of forwarding their own agendas. For this purpose the Chamars collected donations to start such a paper in Kanpur.[41]

Achhutanand began to mobilize *achhuts* before the Simon Commission had even arrived in India, arguing that *achhuts* should not join the Congress boycott, but rather use the commission's visit as an opportunity to make the British aware of their demands. The decision to set up the Statutory (Simon) Commission was made on November 8, 1927, and Achhutanand immediately began organizing meetings in Farrukhabad, Allahabad, Etawah, Mainpuri, and Fatehgarh. He even traveled to Basti in eastern Uttar Pradesh to speak in favor of the Simon Commission, and spoke at a well-attended public meeting in the Jatav stronghold of Agra as well.[42]

In Allahabad the Adi-Hindu Sabha issued an appeal for donations to meet the expenses of organizing their representation before the Simon Commission.[43] In Agra the Jatav and Adi-Hindu Mahasabhas welcomed the special train carrying the Statutory Commission on March 9, 1928.[44] In Lucknow as well, the Adi-Hindus welcomed the Simon Commission by staging a famous demonstration, with the support of the Muslim League, on November 27 and 28, 1928: the same days on which the Congress, led by Nehru, demonstrated against it.[45] The Congress and several Hindu organizations took countermeasures against the Adi-Hindu campaign by organizing meetings at Meerut, Allahabad, Benares, and Lucknow at which they urged Dalits to oppose the Simon Commission and Achhutanand's politics.[46]

Articulating an *Achhut* Identity and Polity

Following the failure of the Simon Commission, the British government initiated constitutional negotiations in London and invited Indian leaders of various parties and communities to what were called the Round Table Conferences. By this time it was not just Ambedkar and most of the Dalit organizations but also Jinnah who had "parted ways" with the Congress. The Nehru report of 1928 played a crucial role in alienating both of these minorities by making a "number of concessions to the [Hindu] Mahasabha," accepting joint electorates and reserved seats only for Muslims in Punjab and Bengal, where they were in the majority, and offering no such safeguards to Dalits.[47] Zelliot has argued that as late as 1928 neither Ambedkar nor M. C. Rajah "stood for separate electorates," but that they changed their position after the Nehru report, which they viewed as undemocratic.[48] The leaders of the Adi-Hindu movement also criticized the Nehru report at a two-day conference in Etawah in September 1929 in which they demanded status and rights equal "to those of the Mohammedans."[49]

The discussions at the two Round Table Conferences between September 1931 and January 1932 brought to the fore the question of who truly represented the Dalits, Gandhi or Ambedkar. The British received scores of representations from Dalit organizations demanding proportional representation and affirmative action in government jobs and education, issues that were raised again by Ambedkar at the Round Table Conferences. Achhutanand organized a demonstration of five thousand people at Kanpur in support of Ambedkar during the Round Table Conference to show that a sizeable proportion of the people were against Gandhi.[50] The Adi-Hindu leaders, led by Chandrika Prasad Jigyasu, addressed a meeting of two thousand *achhuts* in Lucknow in 1931 to demand affirmative action in representative bodies and services.[51] Similar meetings were organized in the districts of Bareilly, Benares, Allahabad, Farrukhabad, Kanpur, and Etawah. Leaflets were distributed in these districts laying out the agenda of the Adi-Hindu movement, demanding separate rights for *achhuts,* and criticizing Gandhi.[52] The Kumaon Shilpakar Sabha of Almora and the Jatav Mahasabha sent telegrams to the British government in London, which had organized the Round Table Conference, expressing their support for Ambedkar's leadership and criticizing Gandhi's.[53] There was a sustained campaign in Etawah against the Round Table Conference, in which Achhutanand played an important part. This campaign included meetings, processions, and the distribution of leaflets.[54] Prominent Dalit organizations in other parts of India also extended support to Ambedkar. The leaders of the powerful Ad Dharma movement in Punjab and of the Namasudra movement in Bengal sent telegrams to the Round Table Conference stating that Ambedkar was the sole representative of all Dalits.[55]

A notable feature of this period was the substantial Chamar support for the Adi-Hindu Mahasabha. The Chamars stood in sharp contrast to certain other Dalit castes, including Balmikis (Bhangis), who supported the Congress. In Allahabad and Kanpur the Chamar participants in Congress meetings opposed the resolution that criticized Ambedkar and registered their protest by walking out of the meetings.[56] In Beharigarh village in Saharanpur district, the Chamar *panchayat* of the surrounding villages organized a two-day conference in which resolutions were passed advocating a separate electorate and boycotting the Congress.[57] Indicating the new mood of the times, a meeting of Chamars in Etah refused to accept any assistance from the Congress. Even police reports were commenting on the confidence Chamars were gaining in their ongoing political struggle.[58] In Farrukhabad, Jaunpur, and Etawah, Chamars took the lead in organizing meetings of their caste to support the demand for affirmative action at the Round Table Conference and emphasize Dalits' separate identity from Hindu society.[59] In Meerut and Muthra the Congress had to cancel *harijan* conferences because it couldn't get Dalits to attend them. It became increasingly clear that, as a police report noted in January 1932, the Congress had "obtained very little support from the depressed classes" despite its best efforts at the popular level.[60]

The constitutional negotiations at the Round Table Conference ended in a deadlock over the nature of representation for minorities in the legislative assemblies.[61] Prime Minister Ramsay MacDonald announced the Communal Award on August 16, 1932, to break the impasse over the rights of minorities in India. The award extended separate electorates to the "untouchables" of India, allowing them to elect their own representatives in areas where they made up a large proportion of the population. Gandhi decided to protest against the award by beginning a "fast unto death" on September 20, 1932.[62] Gandhi's "epic fast" was successful in forcing a compromise between the representatives of the Hindus and the representative of the Dalits. Although Ambedkar eventually gave in to Gandhi's pressure, it is significant that he was accepted and acknowledged as a representative of Dalits. The representatives of the caste Hindus, led by Gandhi, and of the Dalits, led by Ambedkar, signed the Poona Pact on September 24, 1932. Under the pact, Ambedkar gave up his demand for separate electorates in favor of a system of primary and secondary elections, which allowed separate electorates for Dalits in primary elections, but maintained a joint electorate without separate constituencies in the general elections.[63] Prominent Congress leaders like Jawaharlal Nehru were critical of Gandhi for "choosing a side-issue for his final sacrifice—just a question of electorate."[64] There is no doubt about Gandhi's personal commitment to ending the practice of untouchability. This is what Gandhi had to say:

> I would not sell the vital interests of the Untouchables even for the sake of winning the freedom of India. I claim myself in my own person to represent the vast mass of the Untouchables . . . to let the whole world know that to-day there is a body of Hindu reformers who are pledged to remove this blot of untouchability.[65]

Yet Gandhi's statements, including this one, rarely acknowledged the agenda of reform proposed by the Dalit organizations.

Gandhi's fast drew an immediate response from a cross section of Indians. The Congress and various Hindu organizations, including the Arya Samaj and the Hindu Mahasabha, worked together to restart the *achhutuddhar* program, now renamed *harijanuddhar* following Gandhi's coinage of the term *harijan* (children of God) for the *achhuts*. The *achhutuddhar* programs of the Hindu organizations were limited to western parts of the province, but Congress's participation broadened the *harijan*-uplift efforts.[66] The Congress latched onto the familiar patterns of *achhutuddhar* by emphasizing temple entry, access to public wells, and communal dining as means of giving Dalits an equal status in Hindu society and integrating them within Indian nationalism.[67] Yet *sanatani* Hindus from all the major cities and towns of Uttar Pradesh opposed any concessions to the Dalits. A leading Congress leader, Pandit Malaviya, convened a session of the All-India Sanatan Dharma Mahasabha in January 1933 to resolve the religious aspect of untouchability. The session agreed to allow Dalits to enter temples, but restricted them from entering the inner sanctum of the temple.[68] Gandhi's work against untouchability at least made one fact clear to Dalits: that the orthodox sections of Hindu society would never accept their demand to be treated as equals. These developments must have convinced many Dalits, including Ambedkar, to pronounce that they had been born as Hindu untouchables but would not die as Hindus.[69]

One contemporary Hindi monthly magazine, *Chand*, commented on a significant shift in the Congress's *harijanuddhar* program. The editors of *Chand* observed that leaders of the *harijanuddhar*, including Jamunalal Bajaj and Madan Mohan Malaviya, had initiated a policy of opening separate temples and building separate wells for *achhuts*, and Rameshwar Das Birla had donated Rs 10,000 for these projects. The editorial commented that such measures would only further divide *achhuts* from Hindus and prevent them from becoming a part of Hindu society.[70] By noting that the *harijanuddhar* program was a political stunt, guided by concern to maintain the numbers of Hindus, *Chand*'s editorial also captured another dominant, but critical, perception of such initiatives. The editors of *Chand* blamed the Congress for failing to deal with the issue of Hindu religious reform. But the program's leaders were responding to the harsh impossibility of reconciling the religious and cultural barriers between Hindu society and Dalits. By providing Dalits with their own wells and temples, they were offering a political solution to a cultural problem—a solution that they believed would be more acceptable to the Hindu majority.

Lack of popular support within Hindu society for Gandhi's *harijanuddhar* tour was increasingly noted in contemporary journals. By the time the tour ended, the *harijanuddhar* program and activities had also petered out over much of Uttar Pradesh. One indication of this, frequently cited, was the meager donations Gandhi was able to collect: having toured the entire country, he collected only eight hundred thousand rupees. By comparison, the appeals of the Tilak Swaraj fund brought in more than one million rupees, without any tour.[71] One Dalit writer, Shankaranand Shastri, noted in 1946 that millions of rupees were collected in the name of Kasturba Gandhi, whereas only a few lakhs were collected in the name of the Dalits, because in their hearts the Brahman *banius* were not committed to their cause. Shastri took Gandhi to task for "begging in the name of Dalits," which he said insulted "the work culture of their community by ridiculing their poverty and vulnerability." He asserted that begging was not a part of Dalit culture, and that Dalits would prefer to work to earn their day's meal, unlike the Brahman, who begs and steals from the gods but would never work.[72]

The Adi-Hindu Mahasabha coordinated a series of protests against the Poona Pact in 1933–34.[73] Adi-Hindu leaders, including Shyam Lal, Manik Chand, and Chandrika Prasad Jigyasu, held a series of meetings in Azamgarh, Jalaun, Hardoi, Kanpur, Lucknow, Etah, Muzaffarnagar, Agra, Mainpuri, and Jaunpur to criticize it.[74] They also focused the annual conference of the Adi-Hindu Mahasabha, held in Jaunpur in May 1933, on protest against the Poona Pact; the conference was attended by more than a thousand *achhuts* and presided over by the Namasudra leader B. C. Mandal.[75] Stray protests in 1933–34 were followed by more organized agitation in 1937–38, led by the Adi-Hindu leaders, against the Congress Ministry. The protests by the

Scheduled Castes Federation in 1946 and 1947 were probably the most popular agitation launched by the Dalits in Uttar Pradesh, indicating that Viyougi and Shastri's anger at the pact was shared at the popular level.

Dalit groups worked out a new strategy of counterpolitical protests in response to Congress's meetings. In the last week of September 1932, a Congress meeting in Agra was marked by the absence of Chamars. The Jatav Mahasabha had organized a meeting at the same time in support of separate electorates and against the Poona Pact.[76] This strategy appeared in many of the areas where the Adi-Hindu movement was active.[77] Similar parallel demonstrations were noted in Aligarh, Etah, Farrukhabad, Fatehpur, Ghazipur, Benares, Gorakhpur, Hardoi, Kheri, Kumaon, Lucknow, Allahabad, Jalaun, Meerut, and Muzaffarnagar. Karori Mal Khatik, an Adi-Hindu leader and a member of the Kanpur municipal board, organized a meeting of five hundred Dalits to protest against the Poona Pact.[78] In Sitapur the Chamars of one village decided to fine other Chamars who had joined the Congress, and threatened to expel from the community those who maintained their membership.[79] In Jaunpur the Chamars leaders were advising members of their community against joining the Congress party, which had started a campaign to recruit Dalits.[80]

Dissatisfaction with the Poona Pact galvanized the activists of the Adi-Hindu Mahasabha to launch a popular struggle against the formation of Congress Ministries in 1937. On April 3 Manik Chand, an important leader of the Jatav Mahasabha of Agra, led an Adi-Hindu demonstration of some 2500 *achhuts* to submit eleven demands to the Congress premier of Uttar Pradesh. This was followed by another demonstration the next day in which four thousand *achhuts* participated.[81] Their demands included proportionate representation in legislative bodies, the reservation of government jobs for Dalits, adequate representation in the Congress Ministry, changes in the Tenancy Acts to give them permanent rights over land, fixed wages for their agricultural labor (including the removal and skinning of dead animals), the right to use public wells, the abolition of *begari,* the right to convert to any religion, and an end to use of the term *harijan.*[82] Shastri claimed that the Congress Ministry, which ruled from 1937 to 1939, did not take up a single initiative for the benefit of the *achhuts.*[83] The Adi-Hindu activists in the Sidhari police circle of Azamgarh organized a demonstration of five thousand Chamars to protest against the failure of the Congress government to undertake any measures for the benefit of their community. Similar demonstrations were held in Basti, Azamgarh, Allahabad, Jaunpur, Dehradun, Etah, Bijnor, Aligarh, Kanpur, Shahjahanpur, Meerut, Muthra, Fatehpur, Jalaun, Farrukhabad, Muzaffarnagar, Mainpuri, Kanpur, and Bareilly, attended by one to five thousand *achhuts*. Manik Chand of Agra played a particularly important role by participating in and helping organize demonstrations in Bijnor, Aligarh, Allahabad, Lucknow, Etah, and Meerut.[84] In Bijnor demands for the right to use the public well that Jats used led to an eight-month-long agitation in the district, which was also led by Manik Chand.[85]

It is interesting that the Adi-Hindu movement, in its 1937–38 protest against the Congress Ministry, allied with the Muslim League. After the formation of the Congress Ministry in Uttar Pradesh in 1937, relations between the Congress and the League collapsed. In 1938 the League published the Pirpur Report, detailing the misrule of the Congress Ministries, and began a mass recruitment campaign in Uttar Pradesh.[86] Manik Chand first mentioned the necessity of an alliance between the League and the Adi-Hindu movement in a protest at Aligarh in the summer of 1938, and he urged Chamars to accept food from Muslims.[87] In Lucknow, Adi-Hindu leaders decided to accept the help of the Muslim League in their proposed two-day demonstration against the Congress Ministry.[88] Dharam Prakash, a Dalit leader from Bareilly, advocated a similar alliance in Aligarh.[89] The leaders of the Adi-Hindu Mahasabha emphasized the similarity of the two organizations' struggles against the Congress in meetings at Bijnor, Pilibhit, Mainpuri, Etawah, and Etah.[90] In 1940 the Muslim League announced its demand for the creation of an independent Muslim state (Pakistan); in August 1941 Dalits at a meeting at Badaun demanded a separate "Achhutistan" "in a portion of India" and sought the help of the Muslim League in gaining it.[91]

This popular protest by Chamar organizations and the Adi-Hindu Mahasabha against the Congress Ministry in Uttar Pradesh has been ignored both in the contemporary accounts and in subsequent histories.[92] Gopinath Srivatava's *When Congress Ruled,* published in the 1940s, does not mention the Adi-Hindu Mahasabha's protest against the Congress Ministry, but does mention the Muslim League. The 1999 *Towards Freedom* volume for the year 1938, published by the Indian government in three parts amounting to nearly 3,600 pages, mentions only two newspaper reports about the protest and describes it as a communal agitation, without discussing the agenda or actions of the Adi-Hindu Mahasabha or the Dalit protests against the Congress Ministry, although it does provide considerable information on the Muslim

League's agitation. Because of Dalits' alliance with the Muslim League, their struggle is categorized as communal in the official history of the Indian nation.[93] This absence highlights the important role of police reports in providing information on marginalized and dominated groups like Chamars and Dalits. Police officials, employees of the state, were keen to report the fissures in the Congress-led national movement.

Chamar individuals and organizations played an important role in mobilizing on behalf of *achhut* identity and spreading the agenda of the Adi-Hindu Mahasabha. From the outset they were equally keen to distance their political goals from those of the Congress. In the next two sections I elaborate further on the continued support of the Chamar caste organizations for the idea of an *achhut* identity.

Institutionalizing *Achhut* Identity: The Rise of the Scheduled Castes Federation

In 1949, Nandlal Viyougi published a book in Allahabad entitled *Ambedkar ki Awaz Arthat Achhutoin ka Federation* (The Voice of Ambedkar, or, The Federation of Untouchables). The Scheduled Castes Federation had emerged in the 1940s as a party that offered a political platform for all *achhuts,* and Viyougi's title proclaimed the significance of Ambedkar and the Federation in reshaping *achhut* identity and politics by giving them a new voice or *awaz.* The title also underscored the role of the Federation in bringing together diverse *achhut* social organizations of Jatavs, Raidassis, Pasis, Dhanuks, and Chamars in a single political formation. Viyougi's book and Shankaranand Shastri's *Poona Pact banam Gandhi* were among a new wave of Dalit books and pamphlets that were published in the 1940s on the Adi-Hindu movement and on Dalit cultural heritage, appearing from such presses as Bahujan Kalyan Prakashan in Lucknow and the Jagriti Press in Allahabad. These works captured the rebellious mood of the times. Besides the appeal of the Scheduled Castes Federation, the core issue that brought together the Dalits of Uttar Pradesh was the popular anger against the Poona Pact, as indicated by the title of Shastri's book, *Poona Pact banam Gandhi* (Poona Pact versus Gandhi).

Viyougi and Shastri told *achhuts* that it was their duty to know about the Poona Pact.[94] The pact became a metaphor for the Brahman-*bania* conspiracy and was characterized as "criminal" and "destructive," "Gandhi's poisonous gift to the Dalits," a new marker of their slavery.[95] Commenting on the politics of the Congress and Gandhi's leadership, Viyougi observed that "every conservative Hindu by entering politics claims to be a revolutionary" and asserted that Gandhi was no exception to the rule.[96] Their lack of faith in the Congress and its Swaraj was matched by an appreciation of the benefits of British rule. According to Shastri, the *achhut* struggle for freedom had to start by demanding the pact's abrogation.[97]

The anger and opposition which surrounded discussions of the Poona Pact was magnified by the Dalits' experience of the 1937 and 1945–46 elections, in which the electoral provisions enshrined in the Poona Pact made it impossible for non-Congress candidates to be elected. Moreover, the 1946 Cabinet Mission to India, which was sent to discuss the transfer of political power to Indians, refused to accept the Federation's claim to represent the Dalits because of its poor showing in the 1946 elections, and rejected its demand for proportional representation and constitutional safeguards. The Federation had been formed in part to outline the Dalit agenda to the British, who had inaugurated a new round of constitutional negotiations on transferring power to Indians, beginning with the Cripps Proposals in 1942 and the Cabinet Mission in 1946.[98] These negotiations foregrounded the core issues of the Adi-Hindu movement: proportional representation and the claim to a separate identity.

Achhuts identified the Poona Pact as a major obstacle to electing genuine Dalit representatives to the legislative bodies. Viyougi argued that if the Congress wanted to claim that only Indians could represent Indians in framing the constitution, then similarly only *achhuts* could represent *achhuts*. Viyougi stressed that only through separate electorates could *achhuts* successfully challenge the candidates belonging to the Congress and elect their own representatives. Separate electorates would keep Hindus from usurping the seats reserved for *achhuts*. The Poona Pact was supposed to enable the Dalits to send their representatives to the Legislative Assembly; instead, he said, it had allowed the Congress and the Hindus to nominate and elect Dalit candidates of their choice. Both Viyougi and Shastri questioned the moral right of the Congress and Gandhi to contest the elections of Dalit representatives after the Poona Pact.[99]

By the 1940s, all sections of *achhuts* and even the Dalit Congressmen were demanding proportional representation and feeling a sense of separate identity. In June 1946 the District Harijan Conference at the Kumar Ashram in Meerut passed a resolution demanding proportional representation in the Legislative and Constituent Assemblies. Kumar Ashram was the center of *harijanuddhar* in the district. The *harijanuddhar sabha* of Saharanpur district passed a similar resolution later that month. Both resolutions were addressed to the Congress's president and criticized the Congress for failing to protect the rights of Dalits.[100] Jaipal Singh and Girdhari Lal, leading Dalit leaders of the Congress, also attended these two conferences. Jaipal Singh was elected to the reserved seat of Fyzabad (east) in the 1946 elections, while Girdhari Lal was elected from the Saharanpur (east) constituency.[101] Even the most famous Dalit leader in the Congress, Jagjivan Ram, for once agreed more with the Federation than with Gandhi. At a press conference in July 1946 at Lucknow, Ram said that the "scheduled castes should be given representation in the Constituent Assembly in proportion to their population in a province."[102]

The Scheduled Castes Federation provided an institutional platform to Dalits by launching a concerted campaign against the Poona Pact. The Federation was founded in July 1942 in Nagpur, and Adi-Hindu leaders from Uttar Pradesh were present to offer their support, along with leaders from other parts of India. In Uttar Pradesh the Federation was considered a worthy successor to the Adi-Hindu Mahasabha and rapidly replaced the earlier organization. According to Viyougi, the Federation also replaced *achhut* organizations like the Ad-Dharm Mandal in Punjab, the Depressed Classes League of Namasudras in Bengal, and the Depressed Classes Association in the Central Provinces.[103] The Federation attracted Dalit organizations, and it is worth underlining here that, although the Kumaon Shilpakar Mahasabha is a notable exception, most of these organizations were of Chamars: the Jatav Mahasabha, the Raidass Mahasabha of Allahabad, the Kureel Mahasabha, and the Chamar Mahasabha of Kanpur.[104] District branches of the Federation were established in Agra, Aligarh, Allahabad, Etah, Etawah, Lucknow, Kanpur, Meerut, and Kumaon, and these branches attest to its growing popularity.[105]

The Scheduled Castes Federation rapidly entered elections. For instance, Karan Singh Kane was a Congress candidate in the 1936 primaries but entered the 1945 primaries as a candidate of the Federation. Similarly, R. S. Shyamlal of Allahabad, a Federation candidate in 1945, had stood as an independent in the 1936 primaries.[106] Such was the support for the Federation that in 1945 all nine of its candidates won in the primary elections, compared to only four candidates of the Congress from the four urban seats of Agra, Allahabad, Kanpur, and Lucknow in Uttar Pradesh. In the primaries, only Dalits voted for Dalit candidates. But in the general elections held in 1946, all the Federation candidates lost to the Congress's Dalit candidates, because in this stage the votes of caste Hindus and Dalits were pooled. The Hindus voted for Congress's Dalit candidates to ensure that the Federation's candidates would be defeated.[107]

In Uttar Pradesh the Federation decided to launch a satyagraha (struggle) in 1946 and 1947 to protest against the Poona Pact, the Congress, and the Cabinet Mission Award for rejecting their demands for proportional representation and a separate electorate, and to demand the abolition of *begari,* the distribution of land to Dalits, free education and scholarships, and reservation of government jobs.[108] The first phase of this struggle affected twenty-three districts of Uttar Pradesh, out of which Meerut, Bareilly, Muzaffarnagar, Aligarh, Etah, Etawah, Kheri, Kanpur, Azamgarh, and Gorakhpur witnessed prolonged agitation from June through November 1946.[109] The Federation also organized two satyagrahas in Lucknow, in July–August 1946 and March–May 1947. The first was timed to coincide with the working days of the Legislative Assembly, from July 16 to August 16. *Satyagrahis* demonstrated daily in front of the Assembly to question its democratic credentials, because Dalits were not proportionally represented in it. They carried placards and chanted slogans like *Poona Pact ko wapas lo* ("Scrap the Poona Pact").[110] This series of protests culminated in the arrest of nearly four hundred Dalits, including prominent leaders of the Federation such as Behari Lal Jaiswar, Piyare Lal Talib, and Shankaranand Shastri, as well as Tilak Chand Kureel, president of the Uttar Pradesh Scheduled Castes Federation. Similar demonstrations were held in other parts of the state, including Etah, Etawah, Kanpur, Farrukhabad, Fyzabad, Aligarh, Agra, Fatehgarh, Gorakhpur, and Azamgarh.[111]

By creating for the first time a broadly based *achhut* unity, the Poona Pact became the focal point of agitation. The Pact was cited as an example of the undemocratic character of the Congress. In many places the Federation activists staged mock funerals for it, in which they burned copies of the Pact along with other congressional symbols, like *khadi* and Gandhian caps.[112] Attendance at these demonstrations and meetings ranged between one and five thousand, with the highest numbers in Azamgarh and Gorakhpur, where

Tilak Chand Kureel addressed a series of meetings.[113] Manik Chand and his brother Fakir, leaders of the Jatav Mahasabha and the Federation in Agra, organized similar protests in Agra, Ferozabad, and Saharanpur.[114]

The second phase of the Federation's agitation against the Congress government and the undemocratic character of the Legislative Assembly was held from March to April 1947. The decision to launch satyagraha was made during its annual conference on March 1–2, 1947, in Ferozabad town near Agra, which was attended by twenty-five thousand Dalits.[115] Once again the agitation was planned to coincide with the days when the Legislative Assembly was in session, beginning on March 25 and continuing until March 29.[116] Almost all the prominent leaders of the Federation in Uttar Pradesh courted arrest as a part of the satyagraha in Lucknow, including Manik Chand, Gopi Chand Pipal, Tilak Chand Kureel, and Swami Chhamanand, who were the key organizers of this protest.[117] More Dalits participated in the second phase than had in the first.[118] According to one report nearly 1,407 activists of the Federation were arrested, including twelve women. Volunteers for the satyagraha came from all parts of the province.[119]

The Federation's ongoing agitation also provided an opportunity for *achhuts* to protest collectively against *begari*. A new and notable feature of these protests was that Dalits for the first time began to file complaints with the police and with the Congress government in Lucknow. By lodging police complaints, Chamars challenged the authority of the zamindars to determine their wages. In a letter to the police dated January 10, 1946, the Chamars of Amika village in Bulandshahr forwarded a complaint against local landlords who forced them to provide *begari*.[120] From Gorkha village in Ghazipur district, Chamars lodged complaints against the atrocities of the zamindars and the local police.[121] In Kealowara village in Azamgarh district, a woman named Jhunia Chamarin went to the police station to a file a complaint against the zamindars of the village. She accused them of forcibly demanding *begari,* and when she and others asked for wages they were brutally beaten by the zamindars' henchman.[122]

Dalit representatives in the Legislative Assembly, including Gajadhar Prasad and Jagpal Singh, were actively involved in anti-*begari* agitation and repeatedly brought such complaints to the attention of the government in the first quarter of 1946. The proceedings of the Uttar Pradesh Legislative Assembly tell us of complaints lodged by Chamars in the districts of Barabanki, Banda, and Sitapur, where a protracted protest against *begari* had been launched.[123] More than a hundred Chamars were killed in *begari*-related violence in Uttar Pradesh between April 1 and September 30, 1946.[124] However, the Congress government refused to launch an official inquiry into these deaths, claiming that it would be a waste of precious resources. Still, the tone and temper of the movement forced the Congress government in Uttar Pradesh to set up an inquiry on June 5, 1947, into *begari* and its abuses.[125] On the basis of this inquiry we can say that at least fifteen districts in Awadh and the eastern region of Uttar Pradesh reported more than four complaints having been lodged against *begari:* Azamgarh, Gorakhpur, Deoria, Mirzapur, Allahabad, Fatehpur, Banda, Rae Bareli, Sitapur, Kanpur, Barabanki, Partabgarh, Kheri, Etawah, and Etah.[126]

Har Prasad, a Congress member of the Legislative Assembly, asked the Congress government in 1947 whether it had "specially authorized the Muslim Leaguers and the Ambedkarites for organizational work in meetings of the Harijan Chamars?"[127] His question indicates that an aspect of the movement that was mentioned earlier was continuing: the joint demonstrations by the Adi-Hindu movement and the Muslim League against the Congress Ministry in 1937 were again noted in 1946–47. By entering into an alliance with the League, the Federation was sharing its concern for social justice with members of another deprived section of Indian society, the Muslims, and strengthening its relationships with potential allies. The Federation activists in Agra, Allahabad, and Gorakhpur began to participate in the meetings of the League to emphasize the similarities of their struggles.[128] The leaders of the Muslim League similarly participated in the Federation's demonstrations in Kanpur and Farrukhabad.[129] In the meetings of the Federation at Kanpur, Farrukhabad, Kheri, Lucknow, and Mainpuri, Jinnah was congratulated for supporting the Dalit struggle by getting Ambedkar elected to the Constituent Assembly despite opposition from the Congress.[130] The relationship between the two minority groups would continue to play an important role in shaping Uttar Pradesh politics.

The Emergence of the Republican Party of India: Caste or Class?

Ambedkar announced the formation of the Republican Party of India on October 13, 1956, and a day later he and 300,000 Mahars converted to

Buddhism in a mass ceremony at Nagpur in Maharashtra. According to Jigyasu, Ambedkar dissolved the Scheduled Castes Federation, of which he was president, in its final meeting in Delhi on November 30, 1956.[131] He did not live to formally establish the Republican Party, which his fellow activists founded on October 3, 1957. Most scholars assume that the leaders of the Federation decided to abandon their earlier strategy of emphasizing a separate *achhut* identity in favor of the Republican Party's stress on class mobilization with the goal of a more inclusive alliance of classes and communities in Indian society. In recent years scholars and observers have pointed to the ways that such a move contradicted the objectives of the Dalit movement. Mendelsohn and Vicziany's 1998 study sums up the dominant view by arguing that the Republican Party represented "a party along class rather than caste lines."[132] Ambedkar's unofficial biographer Dhananjay Keer has convincingly argued that Ambedkar was keen to erase the barriers the Federation had created "between them and the other classes" by establishing a new party.[133] A fellow socialist politician, Rammanohar Lohia, welcomed Ambedkar's desire to move from caste-based to class-based mobilization by incorporating workers, peasants, members of the lower castes, Muslims, and Dalits into a single party.[134]

But an alternative interpretation of this change is closer to the Dalit perspective. By becoming involved in the Republican Party, Chamars in Uttar Pradesh were trying to intervene in the political process by creating alliances with other social classes and groups, but without diluting their commitment to an *achhut* identity. Their recent struggles had underlined the absolute necessity of fighting for their own rights, and they were confident in their ability to achieve a wider political influence.

From a Dalit point of view, Indian independence arrived with a series of contradictions. The Constituent Assembly unanimously passed a bill abolishing untouchability and making its practice a criminal offense. It also created a plan of affirmative action. In doing so, the leaders of independent India were fulfilling demands that the Adi-Hindu movement had first made in January 1928. Ambedkar was an elected member of the Assembly, as a Muslim League candidate from Bengal, but had to vacate his seat after the creation of Pakistan. The Congress nominated Ambedkar to the Constituent Assembly from the Bombay Legislative Council in July 1947, paving the way for his appointment as law minister in Nehru's new cabinet.[135] Ambedkar's decision to join the Congress government prompted some leaders of the Federation in Uttar Pradesh, including Manik Chand, Piyare Lal Talib, R. S. Shyamlal, and Nandlal Jaiswar, to follow suit and join the Congress.[136] Manik Chand and Piyare Lal Talib were elected to the Indian Parliament from the states of Uttar Pradesh and Rajasthan in the 1952 elections.[137]

The Federation held its annual conference in Lucknow on April 24 and 25, 1948. It reaffirmed its commitment to the Dalit struggle and demanded adequate representation in government services and legislative assemblies, access to public places, and the abolition of *begari*.[138] It was at this conference that Ambedkar gave one of the most important speeches of his political career, a speech which has gone entirely unnoticed in much of the scholarly writing on him. The speech is significant because he explained his decision to join the Congress ministry, after decades of opposition to the Congress. Reminding his audience that they had negotiated with the British when they were in power, he emphasized that after independence the Dalits had to do the same with the Hindus and the Congress. By joining the Congress Ministry, Ambedkar explained, he was sharing in the Congress's power for the benefit of *achhuts*.[139] He made it clear that he has not joined the Congress Party. At the heart of the speech was his proposition that

> now is the time for the Scheduled Castes to unite under one banner, one slogan, one leader, one party and one programme . [The Scheduled Castes] must maintain their separate entity and attempt to make themselves a potential political force so that they may be in a position to do political bargaining.[140]

He underlined the singular role played by Dalits in Uttar Pradesh in their successful struggles of the last few decades. In this speech, Ambedkar was underscoring his enduring commitment to an *achhut* perspective, through which Dalits in Uttar Pradesh had been able to formulate effective social and political agendas.

The most enduring legacy of the Adi-Hindu movement in Uttar Pradesh was the conceptualization of a separate *achhut* identity, one that was not merely political but also social and cultural, a way of thinking not just about Dalit society but also about Hindu society. The Dalits of Uttar Pradesh had crafted a well-defined agenda and a way of thinking. Because of their struggles since the 1920s, by the 1950s Dalits had become aware of the strength of their movement. Indeed, Shastri insisted that the Congress was forced to include Ambedkar in its government because of their satyagraha and agitation in 1946–47.[141]

He disagreed with those who claimed, as some continue to claim even today, that Ambedkar's inclusion was a "gift" from the Congress to the Dalits.[142] It was only by recognizing the history of their movement and the way of thinking which accompanied it that Chandrika Prasad Jigyasu and millions of other Dalits were able to describe the Congress as a Hindu party.

The 1940s saw the bringing together of disparate Dalit organizations in the Scheduled Castes Federation, giving them a shared vision of *achhut* politics and a commitment to their rights that continues to define the lives of Dalits today. The idea that Dalits shared an interest and an identity as *achhuts* gained acceptability among diverse groups in the 1940s, groups which in the 1920s would not have recognized themselves as sharing this identity. For instance, the Independent Labour Party, founded by Ambedkar in 1937, failed to capture the imagination of the Dalits in Uttar Pradesh, despite the fact that its aim was to "advance the welfare of the labouring classes."[143] A few years later Ambedkar established the Scheduled Castes Federation, which became hugely popular among Dalit groups of many castes and regions. Almost all the Chamar-caste *mahasabhas* (like the Jatav Mahasabha of Agra, the Kureel and Chamar Mahasabhas of Kanpur, and the Adi-Hindu Raidass Mahasabha of Allahabad), and Dalit organizations like the Kumaon Shilpakars Sabha of Almora helped to establish the Federation in their regions. This gave an institutional shape to the idea of *achhut* identity.

Even those outside the Federation affirmed their commitment to *achhut* identity. At a press conference in 1945 Jagjivan Ram, the most influential Dalit leader in the Congress, defended Lord Wavell's characterization of the Congress as a caste Hindu party the year before. Ram expressed surprise at Gandhi's criticism of Wavell, describing it as self-contradictory because the Poona Pact acknowledged that Dalits and Hindus were two separate groups. He claimed that although he was a member of the Congress, his first commitment was to the interests of the Dalits.[144] Never before had he represented himself in quite this way. Likewise, two identical petitions submitted in 1946 by the Congress *harijan* organizations in Meerut and Saharanpur urged the Congress to recognize the rights of Dalits as separate from the Hindus. A prominent Dalit Congress politician, Jaipal Singh, was involved in the activities of *harijans* in western Uttar Pradesh.[145]

The agenda laid out by the Adi-Hindu Mahasabha in 1928, including a program for defining a set of rights, seemed to have reached fruition in the 1940s. It was no longer the agenda of the Adi-Hindu Mahasabha alone, but was shared by various Dalit organizations, including individuals and organizations belonging to the Congress like Jagjivan Ram. This agenda had been worked out through their movements and struggles from 1928 to 1947 in Uttar Pradesh, and it was his clear perception of it that convinced Ambedkar to join the Congress Ministry in 1947. The formation of the Republican Party did not represent abandonment of *achhut* identity and politics, nor did it represent a move to class politics, as suggested by a host of scholars like Mendelsohn and Vicziany. By framing the formation of Republican Party as a shift in emphasis "from caste to class" we miss the Dalit point of view, which concentrated on building up political alliances without losing the focus and power of a united *achhut* identity.

The formation of the Republican Party was an effort by Dalits to come to terms with the new realities of independent India: citizenship, adult suffrage, affirmative action, and elections. After initial uncertainties, the principles behind the foundation of the Federation were found to now be inadequate. It had been formed as a party of *achhuts* allied with other interests, in order to strengthen what Ambedkar called the *achhuts'* "bargaining power." Tilak Chand Kureel, its president in Uttar Pradesh, advised *achhuts* in June 1948 that they should vote for socialist candidates in order to defeat the Congress in the coming elections.[146] We can take Kureel's statement as an indication of wider thinking among the leaders of the Federation, who were taking up even more sophisticated strategies for achieving their goals. Others, like Swami Chhamanand and Asharfi Lal Pasi, were advocating an alliance with the socialists in Uttar Pradesh.[147]

Explaining the objectives behind the formation of the Republican Party in 1957, Jigyasu claimed that its principles were based on the constitution that Ambedkar framed: "justice, equality, liberty, and fraternity." It wanted every Indian to be able to enjoy these opportunities and benefits. Through these principles, Ambedkar wanted to attract Hindus, Muslims, Sikhs, Jains, Buddhists, Christians, and Dalits to the party. According to Jigyasu, "if 80 percent of India's population, consisting of the oppressed, backward, exploited, and deprived, comes together," then they could capture political power.[148] The Republican Party and the conversion to Buddhism were Ambedkar's lasting legacies to the Dalits and have continued to shape and inspire their struggle throughout India.

A careful reader of Owen Lynch's anthropological study of Jatav politics in the early 1960s may note that a Jatav politician, irrespective of his political affiliation—Congress or the Jan Sangh—was involved in politics to secure benefits for *achhuts*. The Jatav leaders in the Congress party explained their motives for joining the party in terms familiar from Ambedkar's work, saying, "We intend to get [the backing of the Jatav masses] so that we can present our demands forcefully to Congress, who alone can help us now. If we have the people [the Jatavs and Dalits] behind us, Congress will meet our demands."[149] The Jatavs were members of the Congress because they believed it was the best way to get their voice heard and their agenda implemented by the state. R. S. Khare's study of Lucknow Chamars in the 1970s elucidates their distinctive ideological world. Khare demonstrates that the Dalit agenda has enabled Chamars to maintain their separate, radical Dalit identity, which equips them to deal with the dominant sections of society.[150]

Mobilization by Republican Party activists and politicians in Uttar Pradesh was rooted in the cultural and political premise of *achhut* politics which hoped to attract support from other sections of society. The Charter of Demands issued by the Republican Party in 1964 addressed Dalit concerns, demanding that reservations of government jobs and of places in state-run schools and universities for the Dalits and Tribals be better implemented, that the reservations be extended to Buddhist converts from these communities, and that the legislative provisions against the practice of untouchability be tightened. It also addressed concerns of the rural poor by demanding that land go to its actual tiller, that *panchayat* and waste land be distributed to landless Dalit laborers, and that the Minimum Wage Act of 1948 be enforced.[151] The Republican Party launched a popular struggle to achieve its goals by organizing a massive protest rally in front of the Indian Parliament in Delhi on October 1, 1964. Two demands were made in the demonstration: land for the landless and the extension of affirmative action policies to Dalits who had converted to Buddhism.[152] On December 6, 1964, to honor the anniversary of Ambedkar's death, the popular struggle was extended into the states of Maharashtra, Punjab, and Uttar Pradesh.[153]

In Uttar Pradesh the issue of land redistribution took center stage in this struggle. Activists attempted to take over and cultivate fallow and waste land, especially in the western part of the state. It was widely reported that the demonstrators in western Uttar Pradesh were primarily landless Chamar laborers, and that they had little support from non-Dalit laborers and poor peasant proprietors.[154] In his substantive 1979 study of the Republican Party in Aligarh, Ian Duncan has argued that "however much the leaders of the

RPI in Aligarh claimed to seek support from all sections of the scheduled castes, its propaganda was mainly directed at the Jatavs."[155] The issues raised in its campaigns were the economic inequities perpetuated by the dominant Hindu castes, and the Republican Party was fighting exploitation along caste lines, not class. A pamphlet it issued makes this clear:

> Listen, Jatav and Muslim are friends. Down trodden and backward brothers. It is clear that during the ten years the Congress has done only for the advancement of the Brahmans and it has done nothing for the Jatav community. They have after winning spread black marketing, bribery, dacoity, controls and excessive taxes in broad day-light and brought about ruin in the country and Jatava in particular.[156]

Political necessity induced the Republican Party to enter into a coalition with the Muslims in western Uttar Pradesh, especially in the Aligarh and Agra regions. In both areas, as described earlier, Dalits had a history of political alliances with Muslims, first in 1937–38 and then in 1946–47. It was therefore easier for them to enter into an alliance with other minorities who had repeatedly borne the brunt of communal riots after independence. The alliance between Dalits and Muslims was transformed into an electoral triumph for the Republican Party. It is ironic that this triumph occurred in Uttar Pradesh, where the party elected three candidates to Parliament and eight to the state assembly in the 1962 general elections. Out of these, one member of Parliament and three members of the assembly were Muslims. In Maharashtra the Republican Party could only get three candidates elected to the state assembly.[157]

The most important leader of the Republican Party in Uttar Pradesh, B. P. Maurya, had participated in the 1946–47 Dalit movement in Agra and played an important role in building the alliance with the Muslims. A Chamar from Khair *tahsil* in Aligarh district who came from a well-off peasant family, he led some hundred thousand Chamars to renounce Hinduism in favor of Buddhism.[158] The alliance between the Muslim leaders formerly associated with the Congress and the Republican Party emerged following the communal riot of October 1961 in Aligarh. The Republican Party's slogans summed up the mood of the times and revealed the party's ideological moorings: *Jatav-Muslim bhai bhai: Hindu kaum kahan se ayee?* (Jatavs and Muslims are brothers: Where did the Hindus come from?) and *Thakur, Brahman, aur Lala: Kar do inka munha kala* (Thakurs, Brahmans, and Banias: Blacken their faces). These slogans indicate that the Dalits' struggles against Hindu domination were fought along caste lines, by emphasizing their separate *achhut* identity. Over time, the idea of a shared Dalit identity has become more attractive rather than less.

*   *   *

The idea of a united *achhut* identity and politics acquired dramatic popular support among various Dalit caste groups beginning with the Adi-Hindu movement in the 1920s and 1930s, and it continued to gain popularity as the Scheduled Caste Federation emerged in the 1940s and the Republican Party of India in the 1950s. This idea formed the platform upon which a successful political mobilization was made possible, and it has been that struggle's enduring legacy. The *achhut* identity has refused to bow to the more powerful and dominant identities of nation and nationalism, or to the politics of Hindutva, or to class-based formulations. In the 1920s, when the idea of an *achhut* identity was first laid out, it faced competition from other, equally vibrant, notions of Dalit identity: the Jatavs, Raidassis, Kureels, and Adi-Hindus claimed Kshatriya status, and the Ad-Dharmis saw themselves as a small community outside of Hinduism. In Uttar Pradesh, the Scheduled Castes Federation was the first organization of its kind that was able to mobilize disparate Chamar and Dalit organizations around the notion of a united *achhut* identity with a common agenda. The Republican Party of India was formed in order to negotiate the new opportunities that independence had brought and help redefine Dalit political objectives, without abandoning the commitment to an *achhut* identity and politics. The agenda for affirmative action and constitutional provisions to protect Dalit rights were worked out in Uttar Pradesh between 1927 and 1956 on the foundation of this *achhut* identity. It did not disappear with the formation of the Republican Party; rather, the construction of alliances with non-*achhuts* enabled political mobilization for a Dalit agenda to be even more successful.

Overcoming Domination:
The Emergence of a New Achhut Identity

By the 1960s a fundamental transition had occurred in the nature and character of Dalit politics, as well as in the lives and identities of Dalits in Uttar Pradesh. One indication of this dramatic transformation can be seen in the success of a Dalit political party, the Bahujan Samaj Party, which captured political power in the state in the 1990s. In May 2007, the party won a historic electoral victory in Uttar Pradesh without allying with any other political party; it is the only Dalit party ever to achieve such an electoral victory in India. This development has reaffirmed the role of *achhut* identity in the lives of both Chamars and Dalits in general. Chamars, along with other Dalit groups, are today staunch supporters of the party. By the 1960s a commitment to the liberation of Dalit communities, a concern with the social and economic progress of Dalits, and a firm resolve to resist the domination perpetuated by Hindu society had all become securely ingrained in the minds and actions of Chamar and Dalit activists and ideologues, and they continue today. That these concerns were first raised as early as 1927 in Uttar Pradesh has never before been acknowledged by mainstream Indian historiography. This book has underscored the crucial role of identity in shaping and transforming the lives of Chamar and Dalit communities and in constituting an *achhut* movement in Uttar Pradesh from 1927 onward. It has also sought to demonstrate the important role played by Chamar organizations in launching these struggles.

Through a range of organizations and caste *mahasabhas*, Chamars struggled to transform their lives in Uttar Pradesh. They initially contested the dominant colonial and Hindu narratives of their "untouchable" identity by emphasizing the "purity" of their lives and by demanding a status equal to that claimed by caste Hindus. By composing new histories of their caste, U. B. S. Raghuvanshi, Pandit Sunderlal Sagar, and Ramnarayan Yadvendu supported their claim to a pure status dating from ancient times. They insisted that they had become "impure" because of historical wrongs, but that they were now ready to reclaim their original "pure" Kshatriya identity. These histories were a means of enlightening their own caste fellows. Not just in urban centers but also in rural areas, Chamar organizations held meetings and demonstrations to mobilize their members and spread and sustain these ideas. In the rural areas of the western districts of Uttar Pradesh the movement appealed to well-off Chamar agricultural peasants, and even the poorer Chamar peasants with smaller landholdings in eastern Uttar Pradesh began to adopt a vegetarian lifestyle to stress their "pure" status. It was this drive to claim a Kshatriya status that compelled Chamars to enter into a relationship with Hindu organizations like the Arya Samaj and the Hindu Mahasabha that offered a "meeting point" for articulating their concerns in a language understandable to both parties. To sustain the movement, Chamar organizations promoted and adopted practices already embraced by caste Hindus such as abstaining from meat and alcohol and engaging in specific Hindu religious and ritual practices. In addition, Chamar groups also demanded access to education and protested against the practices of untouchability, cesses, and *begari* imposed on Chamar peasants by caste Hindus. Together these issues constituted the core agenda of their reform program.

In December 1927 the leaders of the Adi-Hindu Mahasabha offered the alternative of an *achhut* identity that would include all Dalits. Those Chamar organizations and individuals who promoted an inclusive *achhut* identity were also the most vocal supporters of the claim that untouchables were the original inhabitants of the subcontinent, and they continue to be so today. The core issue of refashioning a pure, "untouched" identity remained, but the most significant contribution of this new politics was its creation of *achhut* identity as a foundational category for political organization. This category constituted a new way of thinking and helped to outline a new agenda. This new agenda in turn led to the composition of new Dalit histories and defined a set of core issues that have continued to shape Dalit politics over the past eight decades. A clear conception of *achhut* identity and politics has enabled Dalits to maintain a separate but radical identity that has been effective in confronting the structures of dominance established and perpetuated by Hindu society. This identity remains the most enduring legacy of *achhut* politics from 1927 to the present, shaping the political and cultural lives of Dalits in profound ways that make them dramatically different from what they were in the pre-1927 period. Despite challenges from the more inclusive politics of nationalism, socialism, and Hindutva, *achhut* politics have steadfastly maintained their relevance in the lives of both Chamars and Dalits.

The significance of these struggles, especially the role of identity in constituting a new politics, is of central importance in understanding Chamar history and society over the last 150 years. More specifically, awareness of them enables us to question the understanding of Chamar society and history which has been formulated and perpetuated by the dominant colonial and Hindu narratives premised on the occupational identity of Chamars. The overarching goal of this book is to suggest ways of writing a new Dalit history that refuses to fit within the colonialism-nationalism dichotomy of Indian historiography. It does so by investigating the assumption that leatherwork was the traditional occupation, identity, and history of Chamars, all rolled into one; by examining the role of colonial and nationalist discursive practices, rooted in Hindu religion, in establishing a "fit" between colonial policies and the actual conditions of Chamars; and by focusing on Chamars as active subjects of that history, highlighting their agendas, experiences, and actions in ways that help us question the dominant narratives.

The most common assumption concerning Chamars in colonial and postcolonial writings is that they were traditionally leatherworkers and landless laborers. A major objective of the present study has been to point to the persistence of this limited and inaccurate stereotype in virtually all studies of Chamar society and history. This stereotype was based almost exclusively on abstract descriptions found in Hindu Brahmanical texts, which were cited repeatedly by colonial accounts that paid little attention to actual occupational patterns among nineteenth-century Chamars. Twentieth-century anthropological and historical interpretations reified and reproduced these colonial stereotypes.

From the point of view of Chamars, both the colonial and nationalist practices lay out a hegemonic agenda by conceptualizing their lives in particular ways to reinforce the occupational stereotype. Colonial practices not only drew from existing Brahmanical frameworks but also played an important role in reifying and perpetuating them, altering them from abstract textual categories to foundational categories according to which social and economic practices and identities were reorganized. Colonial investigations into cattle mortality and the codification of the crime of cattle poisoning to account for it defined the activities of Chamars as criminal for the first time. Colonial accusations of criminality, which held the entire Chamar community responsible for "organized and professional crime," relied exclusively on Chamars' occupational identity. Sections of Hindu society readily shared and perpetuated such accusations against Chamars, as is evident in social and cultural movements like the 1890s cow protection movement. In the absence of any evidence, large-scale arrest and persecution of Chamars was only possible because at the popular level sections of Hindu society fully backed such colonial "witch-hunts." Chamars' involvement in the leather trade and the export of raw hides and skins was depicted as a criminal conspiracy. The colonial state also redefined Chamars' relationship with agriculture on the basis of their caste. It refused to accept Chamars' claims that they had cultivated their lands for generations, even though they paid regular rents and had rights over land. By classifying Chamars as non-proprietary tenants and depriving them of rights over land, and by passing laws to prevent them from buying and selling land, the colonial state not only denied Chamars rights over their existing land but also accelerated their eviction.

Colonial monographs on the leather industry published in the first two decades of the twentieth century were concerned with the social origins of workers available for the industry. Convinced that Chamars were naturally connected to leather by their occupational identity, their authors assumed that Chamars would play a significant role in the future of the leather industry as laborers. Indian nationalists in the colonial and postcolonial periods embraced these ideas because of their own location in caste Hindu society. The Congress and the postcolonial state deliberately adopted policies intended to create a fit between Chamars and their occupation. Both nationalist and colonial practices, discursive and non-discursive ones, reinforced and expanded the association of Chamars with leatherwork.

A New Dalit History: Chamars as Active Subjects

Rethinking Dalit histories must start by investigating the dominant stereotype of Chamar and other Dalit castes that has equated their identity with an occupation mentioned in Hindu texts. This study has fundamentally questioned such an assumption about the Chamars by arguing that in the nineteenth and twentieth centuries they were involved in a wide range of occupations, with the most common being agriculture. Far from "traditionally" being leatherworkers, Chamars were primarily a peasant-agricultural caste.

Colonial officers were surprised when they first discovered a massive Chamar population in Uttar Pradesh, making them the largest "Hindu" caste. This discovery stood in sharp contrast to the early nineteenth-century colonial assumptions that the Chamars were a small artisan caste. In an effort to account for the large population of Chamars, colonial sociologists and administrators offered a series of often awkward explanations intended to fit the community to the stereotypes. But a handful of marginalized and largely ignored settlement reports and inquiries offer us evidence that there continued to be a decisive "lack of fit" between the colonial framework and actual Chamar occupations, and they attest to the importance of agriculture in Chamars' lives.

Instead of accepting colonial descriptions of Chamars as criminals, I have argued that those Chamars who were involved in the leather trade were genuine entrepreneurs and contractors who took advantage of the growing export trade in raw hides and skins during the nineteenth and early twentieth centuries. Despite this expansion, Chamars who were connected to the leather trade, as either part-time or full-time leatherworkers, were based in *qasbas* or market towns and not in the villages. A few colonial officials and judges raised a series of objections to the claim that there existed an "organised and professional crime of cattle poisoning." They declared that such an accusation was based on the caste and social position of Chamars and not on actual evidence. These objections force us to question the existing dominant frameworks for understanding Chamars and help us see them instead as historical actors. Evidence from other industries further substantiates the argument.

Chamars worked in the leather factories, as they did in jute and textile factories, not because of any natural or traditional caste affinity for leatherwork, but because these were among the few employment opportunities available to them, given the prejudices of Hindu society, which viewed them as untouchable. Rather than Chamars, it was members of the Muslim community who were centrally involved in the leather trade, and who ultimately controlled it. Nevertheless, no one has ever suggested that Muslims be characterized as "traditionally" leatherworkers. Indeed, the Chamar elite that emerged in Agra, unlike the common stereotype, emerged from agriculture, stone quarries, and labor contracting. The Chamar and Dalit social and cultural movement began by engaging with groups advocating social and cultural reform of Hindu religion. Because of their substantial presence as occupancy peasants and non-occupancy tenants in agriculture, Chamars, like other lower-caste groups, sought Kshatriya status. But they would eventually move on from this claim.

The persistence of the stereotype of Chamars' untouchability has resulted in the absence of Dalit histories in India. Modern Indian historiography's central dichotomy of colonialism and nationalism has contributed to the failure to acknowledge the role of Chamars and Dalits as historical subjects. The subjects of the received narrative are nationalist, revolutionary, and anti-communal organizations, from the elite Congress party to the subaltern groups, both belonging to caste Hindu society, but not Chamars or Dalits. Assumptions and stereotypes about Chamars have persisted despite the changes in the disciplines in the last forty years.

We must recognize that Chamars are historical actors who have themselves questioned the dominant mainstream assumptions concerning their society and history. The evidence of vibrant Dalit struggle and movement is overwhelming, but it has remained buried in the colonial records, although Dalit and Chamar histories in Hindi have managed to keep it alive.

Chamar organizations and activists launched their struggle in the first two decades of the twentieth century by writing new histories of their community to claim Kshatriya status within Hindu society. They drew from the existing literature not just evidence for this claim but also a methodology, the same one that had produced the dominant narratives. By using a dominant idiom and language they attempted to bring their own claims into conversation with existing histories and to counter and resist the narratives being produced about them. At the same time, by organizing and mobilizing members of their caste, Chamar organizations defied the existing structures of dominance in Hindu society. Chamar activists and *mahasabhas* formulated a new agenda to claim a broader *achhut* identity, and constituted an *achhut* or Dalit political community capable of intervening within the existing political and social processes in order to overcome domination.

APPENDIX: STATISTICAL TABLES

A: Principal castes of Uttar Pradesh in 1881

Caste	Number of people	Percentage of the total Hindu population
Chamar	5,360,548	14.09
Brahman	4,655,204	12.23
Ahir	3,584,185	9.42
Rajput	3,027,400	7.96
Kurmi	2,075,026	5.45
Kachhi	1,941,663	5.10
Kahar	1,209,350	3.18
Bania	1,204,130	3.16
Pasi	1,033,184	2.72
Lodha	1,000,599	2.63
Gadaria	860,220	2.26

Source: Census of India, 1881, vol. 17, pt. 1, Report, pp. 136–38.

B: Cattle censuses from 1890–91 to 1899–1900. The term "cattle" includes cows and bulls, buffaloes, and young stock.

Years	Gorakhpur	Azamgarh	Ghazipur	Jaunpur	Allahabad	Ballia
1890–91	1,243,304	815,636	400,550	482,649	713,994	294,207
1891–92	841,962	799,208	437,530	509,220	730,244	295,770
1892–93	NA	800,743	421,935	513,379	747,657	304,765
1893–94	1,446,755	832,902	423,104	529,313	749,259	309,726
1894–95	1,372,841	780,394	383,919	526,728	722,765	308,876
1895–96	1,414,642	798,183	391,311	510,238	697,416	304,922
1896–97	1,377,798	723,284	373,501	501329	662,941	295,254
1897–98	1,439,345	754,853	374,397	497,701	737,128	305,805
1898–99	1,645,137	827,553	446,295	650,532	873,948	402,373
1899–1900	1,645,137	827,553	446,295	650,532	873,948	402,373

Source: Annual volumes of Agricultural Statistics of British India for the years cited.

C: The occupations of Chamars in 1911 and 1961.
The terms used in the two censuses varied, but are broadly similar.

Year	Total Chamar population	Workers (male and female)	Cultivators of all kinds	Field or agricultural laborers	Herders, raisers of livestock, milk sellers	Unspecified laborers	Industrial workers, artisans, and others	Leatherworkers	Contractors
1911	6,068,382	3,467,317 (57%)	1,373,184 (40%)	1,355,387 (40%)	107,922 (3%)	331,244 (9.5%)	142,786 (4.1%)	130,233 (4%)	1,800 (0.05%)
1961	8,194,154	3,577,216 (44%)	1,788,134 (50%)	1,224,263 (34.2%)	11,638 (0.32%)	311,275 (8.7%)	190,356 (5.3%)	21,441 (0.6%)	22,193 (0.6%)

Sources: *Census of India, 1911,* vol. 15, pt. 2, Tables, pp. 757–62; *Census of India,* 1961, vol. 15, pt. 5A(i), *Special Tables for Scheduled Castes,* pp. 4–7.

D: The position of Chamar cultivators in relation to those of other castes in the district of Moradabad in 1909

Caste of cultivators	Area (acres)	Total annual rent(Rs.)	Grain-rented land (acres)	Sir and khudkasht land (acres)	Rent-free land (acres)	Total area cultivated (acres)
Jat	69,046	281,268	56,036	12,528	178	137,788
Sheikh	68,955	313,733	27,571	17,895	365	114,786
Chamar	67,695	324,571	39,246	131	453	107,525
Ahar	54,554	188,024	9,522	5,097	83	70,066
Chauhan	34,875	147,288	27,233	6,304	293	68,705
Bhagwan	36,006	194,041	26,157	416	1,039	63,618
Thakur	37,848	164,419	3,307	20,122	231	61,508
Brahman	34,473	142,597	10,314	3,888	457	49,132
Ahir	9,196	39,099	10,845	1,107	50	21,198

Source: Final Report on the Eleventh Settlement of the Moradabad, 1909, H. J. Boas, pp. 10–11.

E: The position of Chamar cultivators in relation to those of other castes in the district of Agra in 1880 and 1930

Caste of cultivators	1880: Total area cultivated (acres)	1880: Percentage of total cultivated area	1880: Total annual rent (Rs)*	1930: Total area cultivated (acres)
Brahman	165,118	19.6	495,354	152,495
Thakur	182,403	21.6	547,209	158,370
Jat	120,485	14.2	361,455	92,940
Chamar	60,286	7.1	241,144	65,020
Ahir	37,945	4.4	144,191	40,312
Kachhi	32,398	3.9	129,592	39,273
Gujar	24,432	3.0	73,296	21,367
Lodha	23,486	2.8	93,944	16,325

*Annual rents were calculated from the average rent—which varied by caste and locality—and the total land held by each caste.

Sources: Report on the Settlement of the Agra District, 1880, H. F. Evans, p. 29; Final Report on the Settlement and Record Operations in District Agra, 1930, R. F. Mudie, p. 40.

F: The position of Chamar cultivators in relation to those of other castes in the district of Bulandshahr in 1891 and 1919

Caste of cultivators	1891: Total area cultivated (acres)	1891: Number of plows	1919: Total cultivated area (acres)
Thakur	137,611	12,922	100,000+
Brahman	118,375	11,159	100,000+
Jat	113,050	10,779	100,000+
Gujar	87,375	8,442	54,000
Chamar	81,179	7,722	65,000
Lodha	70,352	6,857	71,000
Ahir	15,875	1,527	NA
Kachi	1,325	127	NA

Sources: *Final Report on the Settlement of Land Revenue in the Bulandshahr District,* 1891, B. T. Stoker, pp. 20–21; *Final Report on the Settlement of Bulandshahr,* 1919, E. A. Phelps, p. 10.

G: The position of Chamar cultivators in relation to those of other castes in the district of Jhansi in 1893 and 1947

Caste of cultivators	1893: Area cultivated (acres)			1893: Khatas	1893: Number of plows	1893: Acres per plow	1947: Area cultivated (acres)	1947: Percentage of total area under cultivation
	Total	By proprietors	By tenants					
Brahman	69,960	20,801	40,159	15,080	5,563	12.6	160,164	14.8
Lodh	56,150	22,283	33,867	11,897	4,921	11.4	176,556	16.8
Thakur	45,357	28,871	16,486	6,232	3,287	13.8	138,716	12.8
Ahir	52,925	25,653	27,272	8,935	4,888	10.8	132,769	12.2
Kachhi	30,738	1,280	29,453	11,181	4,637	6.6	106,168	9.8
Kurmi	35,764	20,166	15,598	4,750	2,501	14.3	75,695	7.0
Chamar	17,314	23	17,291	5,952	2,177	8.0	67,206	6.2

Sources: Final Report on the Settlement of the Jhansi District, 1893, W. H. L. Impey, p. 61; Final Settlement Report of Jhansi District, 1947, H. T. Lane, p. 9.

H: The position of Chamar cultivators in relation to those of
other castes in the district of Bareilly in 1903 and 1942

Caste of cultivators	1903: Total area of holdings (acres)*	1903: Number of holdings	1903: Average area of holdings (acres)	1903: Holdings as percentage of total acreage under cultivation	1942: Total area cultivated (acres)	1942: Percentage of total cultivated area
Kurmi	169,835	57,377	2.96	23.51	174,461	21.2
Kisan	61,498	27,578	2.23	8.49	61,656	7.5
Ahir	58,350	19,450	3.0	8.03	54,152	6.5
Brahman	53,580	24,921	2.15	7.39	53,974	6.6
Thakur	40,942	17,879	2.29	5.64	59,796	7.2
Chamar	49,506	24,753	2.0	6.81	49,553	6.0
Murao	43,734	27,680	1.58	6.01	45,707	5.5

*Calculated from the percentage of total acreage and the number of holdings.

Sources: Final Settlement Report of the District Bareilly, 1903, S. H. Freemantle, p. 4; Final Settlement Report of District Bareilly, 1942, I. W. Lewys-Loyd, p. 5.

I: The position of Chamar cultivators in relation to those of
other castes in the district of Gorakhpur in 1891

Caste of cultivators	Acres cultivated	Number of tenants
Brahman	350,028.58	146,530
Kurmi	221,614.45	80,490
Ahir	203,806.31	101,157
Chhatri (Rajput)	179,331.12	56,536
Koeri	119,250.70	53,453
Chamar	117,501.31	72,857
Kahar	64,471.92	38,809
Bania	42,949.69	56,536
Kayasth	42,770.92	14,199

Source: Final Report on the Settlement of Gorakhpur District, 1891, A. W. Cruickshank, pp. 42A–45A (appendix 8).

J: THE POSITION OF CHAMAR CULTIVATORS IN RELATION TO THOSE OF OTHER CASTES IN THE DISTRICT OF SAHARANPUR IN 1921

Caste of cultivators	Area cultivated by proprietors at previous settlement (acres)	1921 settlement: Proprietors		% change in % of total area cultivated between settlements	1921: Land rented for cash by cultivators		1921: Total area cultivated under cash, *sir*, khudkasht, and other tenure (acres)
		Area cultivated (acres)	Area cultivated as % of total area under cultivation		Area (acres)	Rent (Rs.)	
Gujar	232,852	205,387	17.0	-11.1	74,517	491,813	155,896
Rajput	190,920	189,188	16.2	0	34,546	216,657	96,295
Mali (Siana)	10,064	8,101	0.7	-22.2	60,728	435,515	80,222
Gara	33,247	34,877	3.0	+7.1	52,517	386,775	79,988
Chamar	13,332	15,209	1.3	+18.2	31,457	263,260	41,465
Jat	34,652	31,508	2.7	-10.0	14,824	107,585	32,481
Brahman	34,185	37,076	3.2	+10.3	13,942	93,882	26,848
Ahir	7,157	7,752	0.7	+16.7	4,792	32,176	9,638

Source: Final Report on the Settlement Operations of the Saharanpur District, 1921, D. L. Drake-Brockman, pp. 47–48. Data are presented here exactly as given in the report, although the acreages do not match the percentage increases indicated.

K: Export of hides and skins from Uttar Pradesh to the Port of Calcutta and elsewhere, and from the Port of Calcutta, 1880–81 to 1900–1901.

Year	Total exports from Uttar Pradesh (maunds)	Value of exports (Rs)	Exports from Uttar Pradesh to Calcutta (maunds)	Value of exports from Uttar Pradesh to Calcutta (Rs)	Exports from Calcutta (maunds)*	Value of exports from Calcutta (Rs)	Exports from Uttar Pradesh to Calcutta as % of exports from Calcutta
1880–81	145,404	2,035,656	124,644	1,737,699	755,708	19,413,921	16.49
1881–82	136,883	2,053,240	101,640	1,524,600	686,347	18,306,747	14.81
1882–83	211,099	3,197,003	106,266	1,569,251	726,969	19,724,476	14.62
1883–84	193,676	2,855,618	96,729	1,378,388	816,492	22,663,002	11.85
1884–85	297,669	6,837,918	212,864	5,454,035	965,586	25,315,379	22.05
1885–86	290,713	6,971,336	196,221	5,442,035	965,586	26,841,721	20.33
1886–87	279,713	7,399,672	175,396	5,606,372	873,813	25,293,965	20.08
1887–88	268,285	7,349,335	156,890	5,687,339	700,192	20,768,574	22.42
1888–89	284,288	8,353,313	150,938	5,956,060	640,788	19,082,457	23.55
1889–90	225,794	6,000,606	98,927	3,592,744	606,854	18,421,934	16.31
1890–91	246,445	6,915,299	121,410	4,352,744	692,494	20,704,763	17.54
1891–92	270,818	8,195,995	152,072	5,701,604	725,313	22,572,638	20.97
1892–93	NA	NA	NA	NA	NA	NA	NA
1893–94	248,819	6,045,109	112,893	3,399,718	730,522	24,360,735	15.45
1894–95	462,509	13,423,071	246,375	9,206,513	812,900	27,206,868	30.31

Year	Total exports from Uttar Pradesh (*maunds*)	Value of exports (Rs)	Exports from Uttar Pradesh to Calcutta (*maunds*)	Value of exports from Uttar Pradesh to Calcutta (Rs)	Exports from Calcutta (*maunds*)*	Value of exports from Calcutta (Rs)	Exports from Uttar Pradesh to Calcutta as % of exports from Calcutta
1895–96	407,264	12,099,150	256,524	8,917,619	823,144	31,275,285	31.17
1896–97	326,326	9,962,254	198,406	7,206,354	734,827	28,560,259	27.01
1897–98	424,597	12,507,002	291,011	9,772,179	11,700,083	41,717,531	26.46
1898–99	312,416	7,968,982	199,077	5,659,299	986,846	38,258,162	20.19
1899–1900	735,804	15,242,661	635,250	13,182,720	11,522,578	57,698,821	41.73
1900–1901	511,001	9,763,225	364,503	6,784,059	1,471,808	55,561,596	24.77

*converted from cwt. to *maunds*.

Sources: Annual volumes of *Annual Report of the Inland Trade of North-Western Provinces and Oudh*; for exports from Calcutta, annual volumes of *Annual Statement of the Sea-Borne Trade and Navigation of the Bengal Presidency*.

GLOSSARY

For simplicity, I use the English "s" to form noun plurals throughout the text.

achhut Literally "untouched"; an alternative and less negative term for "untouchable."

achhutuddhar A program for the social and moral uplift of "untouchables" devised by caste Hindu organizations.

aika Unity.

arhar Split lentils.

Arzal A category of low or "untouchable" castes, whose members are often non-proprietary tenants.

Ashraf A category of dominant peasant castes, whose members possess hereditary and transferable rights over land.

bania A small shopkeeper or trader in provisions and agricultural products, who may also lend money.

bedekhli Eviction from land.

begari Forced unpaid labor.

bhaiyachara A system of coparcenary tenure in which land is held in severalty by a group of dominant peasants belonging to a common lineage, who also cultivate their land. In this it differs from *zamindari* tenure, where the zamindar is not involved with actual cultivation.

bigha A measure of land, varying from locality to locality but generally equivalent to five-eighths of an acre or 3,025 square yards.

biswa A measure of land, one-twentieth of a bigha.

chamrai Agricultural cesses imposed by zamindars on Chamars, who were expected to pay by performing agricultural work.

chaukidar A village watchman.

crore Ten million.

dai An "untouchable" woman who cuts the umbilical cord of a newborn baby and nurses the baby and mother for the first three to six days.

deva lok The abode of gods, heaven.

devata A Hindu god.

dihuyar	A village divinity worshipped at a consecrated place, usually an elevated mound or a location under a large tree.
dwija	A pure or caste Hindu.
gaurakshini sabha	A cow protection (*go-raksha*) society or organization.
ghair-maurusi	A non-resident cultivator, from 1859 defined by the colonial state as a tenant-at-will.
gramdevata	A *dihuyar*.
gur	Unrefined brown sugar; cane juice boiled until solid.
halali	Hides of slaughtered cattle.
halwaha	Literally a plowman; more generally, a low-caste or untouchable *ghair-maurusi* tenant who cultivates a zamindar's land as *begari*.
hari	Unpaid labor in the form of plowing, imposed on tenants by zamindars.
harijan	Literally "child of God": an alternative and less negative term for "untouchable."
hat	A regularly held (weekly or fortnightly) village market.
jajmani	A system of mutual obligations among castes in a village.
jati	A subcaste.
juar	A species of millet.
kalayuga	The fourth and final age according to Hindu mythology, typically referring to the present dark or corrupt age, as opposed to *satyug*.
karkhana	A factory.
kharif	The autumn harvest season.
khata	An undivided unit of land in a village; a form of proprietary tenure specific to the Bundelkhand region.
khudkasht	A kind of land tenure, under which land is cultivated under the supervision of proprietors.
kodon	A species of millet.
lakh	One hundred thousand.
mahasabha	An association or organization, usually formed on caste or community lines.
maurusi	A resident tenant, from 1859 defined as an occupancy tenant or statutory tenant.
maund	A unit of weight, roughly equal to 82 lb.
mauza	A village.

mochi	A shoemaker.
mohalla	A neighborhood, generally defined on caste, community, or class lines.
murdari	Hides of cattle that died naturally rather then being slaughtered.
nazrana	Literally tribute, but in practice a form of land rent imposed on and extracted from low-caste and "untouchable" tenants.
panchayat	A council.
puja	Worship or prayer.
qasba	A market town, often with an important industry, that holds an important place in the economy and trade of a district.
rabi	The spring harvest season.
rasad	Literally provisions, demanded by zamindars from tenants.
sabha	A society or association.
sanatani	Fundamentalist.
sangathan	Literally an organization, more generally a politics to unite all Hindus.
satayuga	An earlier age of truth and piety, as opposed to *kalayuga*.
seer	A unit of weight, roughly equal to 2 lb.
shuddhi	Literally to purify, generally to purify "untouchables" and others through a Hindu ceremony.
sir land	Land held by a zamindar under title of personal cultivation.
suryavanshi	Royal.
swaraj	Independence.
tahsil	A subdivision within a district.
thanedar	A native Indian officer in charge of a local police station.
theka	A contract.
thekadar	A contractor.
urad	Black lentils.

NOTES

Abbreviations

AICC	All India Congress Committee
GAD	General Administration Department
IESHR	*Indian Economic and Social History Review*
NAI	National Archives of India, New Delhi
NMML	Nehru Memorial Museum and Library
PAI	Weekly Police Abstracts of Intelligence
OIOC	Oriental and India Office Collection, British Library
Progs.	Proceedings
SVN	*Selections from Vernacular Newspapers* (variously titled *Native Newspaper Reports* and *Note on Press*)
UPSA	Uttar Pradesh State Archives, Lucknow
UPSRA	Uttar Pradesh State Regional Archives, Allahabad

Introduction

The epigraph is from Viyougi, *Ambedkar ki Awaz*, p. 33. All translations from Hindi are mine.

1. *Frontline* 19, no. 23 (November 9–22, 2002).

2. The term "Dalit" or *achhut* ("untouched" or "pure") was used as early as the 1920s by those labeled "untouchables" in order to claim a radical new sociopolitical identity.

3. Human Rights Watch, *Broken People*, pp. 8–9.

4. Scheduled Castes and Scheduled Tribes Population, from the 2001 census, available at http://www.censusindia.gov.in/Census_Data_2001/Census_data_finder/A_Series/SC_ST.htm (accessed May 28, 2009).

5. http://www.censusindia.gov.in/Census_Data_2001/Census_Data_Online/Population/SC_Population.htm (accessed May 28, 2009).

6. The province of Uttar Pradesh (established in 1950) was formerly known as the United Provinces (1921), the United Provinces of Agra and Oudh (1902), the North-Western Provinces and Oudh (1877), and the North-Western Provinces (1836). In order to avoid confusion and ensure consistency I have used the current name, Uttar Pradesh, throughout the book.

7. In 1999, more than fifty years after India's independence, Chandra Bhan Prasad became India's first Dalit to publish a regular column in an English-language newspaper

in Delhi. His weekly columns, which appear in *The Pioneer,* are also translated into Telugu, Tamil, Malayalam, Marathi, Bengali, and Hindi.

8. The Bahujan Samaj Party was founded in 1984 by Kanshi Ram to represent the oppressed majority of Dalits, lower castes, and Muslims in India, but it is viewed by all as a Dalit political party. Since its foundation, the party has made remarkable progress in the political and electoral arena of Uttar Pradesh.

9. Deliege, *The Untouchables of India,* pp. 27–28; Dube, *Untouchable Pasts,* p. 1.

10. Briggs, *The Chamars,* p. 15.

11. Letter from George Campbell, Magistrate, Azamgarh district, to H. C. Tucker, Superintendent of Police, Benares Division, October 21, 1854, "Papers Relating to the Crime of Cattle Poisoning," *Selections from the Records of the Government of India, 1881,* no. 180, p. 27.

12. Wiser and Wiser, *Behind Mud Walls,* pp. 53–54.

13. Lynch, *The Politics of Untouchability,* p. 28.

14. Bernard Cohn, "Changing Traditions of a Low Caste," in *An Anthropologist among the Historians,* p. 284. This essay was first published in the *Journal of American Folklore* 71, no. 280 (April–June 1958), pp. 413–21.

15. K. Singh, *The Scheduled Castes,* p. 301; Deliege, *The Untouchables of India,* pp. 27–50.

16. Cohn, "Notes on the History of the Study of Indian Society and Culture," in *An Anthropologist among the Historians,* pp. 136–71.

17. Deliege, *The Untouchables of India,* p. 27.

18. Briggs, *The Chamars,* p. 45.

19. Deliege, *The Untouchables of India,* pp. 28–29.

20. Cohn, "The Changing Traditions of a Low Caste," in *An Anthropologist among the Historians,* p. 285.

21. Deliege, *The Untouchables of India,* pp. 29–30.

22. Moffatt, *An Untouchable Community.*

23. Deliege, *The Untouchables of India,* p. 63.

24. Briggs, *The Chamars;* Wiser and Wiser, *Behind Mud Walls;* Lynch, *The Politics of Untouchability;* Juergensmeyer, *Religion as Social Vision;* Roy, *Traditional Industry.*

25. "Cow-Killing Agitation in the Azamgarh District," file no. 461, box no. 57, GAD Block Files, UPSA.

26. Chakrabarty, *Habitations of Modernity,* p. 5. Chakrabarty discusses the centrality of this framework in Indian historiography.

27. Nehru, *An Autobiography,* pp. 59–64; Pandey, "Peasant Revolt and Indian Nationalism."

28. Pandey, "Peasant Revolt and Indian Nationalism," pp. 167–68, 178–79.

29. "Report on the Awadh Peasant Movement," file no. 50, 1921, box nos. 133–34, GAD, UPSA, pp. 687–93.

30. "Papers Relating to Peasant Movement of 1921," file no. 1, Baba Ramchandra Papers, NMML, p. 21.

31. "Papers Relating to Praja Sangh, 1929–1934," file no. 6, and "Tour Reports and Programmes, 1929–1940," file no. 7, Baba Ramchandra Papers, NMML.

32. *Report on the Second Settlement of the Rae Bareli District, 1898,* S. H. Fremantle, p. 19.

33. Prashad, "Untouchable Freedom," especially pp. 184–91.

34. Ilaiah, "Productive Labour, Consciousness and History," pp. 165–67. The terms "scheduled classes," "scheduled tribes," and "other backward classes" were coined in the 1930s and identify classification schemes of the colonial and postcolonial governments.

35. O'Hanlon, "Maratha History as Polemic," p. 3.

36. S. Bayly, *Caste, Society and Politics in India*, pp. 158, 239–42.

37. Police Progs., vol. 101, July–December 1894, Police Dept., UPSA, p. 75–76.

38. Babu Ram Charana belonged to a Shudra (Mali) caste, but not to a Dalit caste as most historians assume. Gooptu, *The Politics of the Urban Poor*, p. 155.

39. Gooptu, *The Politics of the Urban Poor*, p. 144. See also her chapter "Untouchable Assertion," pp. 141–84.

40. S. Bayly, *Caste, Society and Politics in India*, pp. 229–32.

41. Prashad, *Untouchable Freedom*, p. 82.

42. Raghuvanshi, *Shree Chanvar Purana* (A Puranic History of Chamars). The book is not dated, but its British Library acquisition date is August 1917.

43. Dirks, *Castes of Mind*, p. 199. Dirks does not develop this point, because he is concerned with the census. See his chapter 6 on the archives and chapter 10 on the enumeration of caste.

44. Ibid., p. 123.

45. Shahid Amin, "Introduction," in Crooke, *A Glossary of North Indian Peasant Life*, pp. xxxix, xiv, xix.

46. Dirks, *Castes of Mind*, p. 109.

1. Making Chamars Criminal

The first epigraph is from a letter from W. Hoey, Commissioner, Gorakhpur Division, to Director of Land Records and Agriculture, North-Western Provinces and Oudh, August 26, 1899, file no. 154(C), box no. 27, February 1900, Judicial (Criminal) Dept., UPSA.

1. *Times of India* (Lucknow), April 1, 2000.

2. Letter from George Campbell, Magistrate of Azamgarh, to H. C. Tucker, Superintendent of Police, Benares Division, October 21, 1854, pp. 24–28; letter from R. D. Spedding, Joint Magistrate of Gorakhpur, to Officiating Magistrate, Gorakhpur, October 2, 1873, pp. 34–49; in "Papers Relating to the Crime of Cattle Poisoning," *Selections from the Records of the Government of India, 1881*, no. 180.

3. Yang, "Dangerous Castes and Tribes."

4. *Census of India, 1881*, vol. 17, pt. 1, *Report*, pp. 136–38.

5. Yang, "Dangerous Castes and Tribes," pp. 111–12.

6. Freitag, "Crime in the Social Order of Colonial North India," pp. 241, 248.

7. Nigam, "Disciplining and Policing the 'Criminals by Birth,'" part 1, p. 141.

8. Mayaram, "Criminality or Community?" pp. 81, 73.

9. "Note on Cattle Poisoning by Captain Dodd," no. 34, August 27, 1870, Judicial Progs. (Home Dept.), NAI. Captain Dodd was Personal Secretary to the Inspector General of Police, Uttar Pradesh.

10. Major, "State and Criminal Tribes in Colonial Punjab," p. 661.

11. Kotani, "Conflict and Controversy over the Mahar Vatan," pp. 105–30.

12. Singha, *A Despotism of Law*, pp. 37–46.

13. Chevers, *A Manual of Medical Jurisprudence,* pp. 127–35.

14. Cattle Plague Commission, *Report of the Commissioners,* appendix 4, "Report on Cattle Poisoning," p. 646.

15. Ibid., p. 645.

16. Letter from Campbell to Tucker, October 21, 1854, "Papers Relating to the Crime of Cattle Poisoning," *Selections from the Records of the Government of India, 1881,* no. 180, pp. 24–28. See also Campbell's memo on cattle poisoning, October 19, 1854, Basta no. 7, vol. 84, Pre-Mutiny Records in the Gorakhpur Collectorate, UPSRA.

17. Letter from Campbell to Tucker, October 21, 1854, "Papers Relating to the Crime of Cattle Poisoning," *Selections from the Records of the Government of India, 1881,* no. 180, p. 27.

18. Ibid., p. 25.

19. Ibid., p. 26.

20. Ibid., p. 27.

21. Letter from Campbell to Tucker, October 7, 1854, Miscellaneous Judicial Files, Basta no. 109, vol. 4, Benares Commissioner's Office, UPSRA.

22. Sleeman's "Notes on Crime and Caste," Benares Judicial Files, Basta no. 131, vol. 1, Pre-Mutiny Records, Benares Commissioner's Office, UPSRA.

23. Singha, *A Despotism of Law,* p. 170.

24. Letter from W. Hoey to Director of Land Records and Agriculture, August 26, 1899, file no. 154(C), box no. 27, February 1900, Judicial (Criminal) Dept., UPSA.

25. "Report on Cattle Diseases," Public Progs. (Home Dept.), nos. 93–94, 1869, NAI, pp. 71–73, 78.

26. Letter from H. Farell, Veterinary Surgeon, to J. Westland, Collector, Jessore, October 20, 1869, "Report on Cattle Diseases," Public Progs. (Home Dept.), nos. 93–94, 1869, NAI, pp. 4–5.

27. Ibid., p. 4.

28. Cattle Plague Commission, *Report of the Commissioners,* appendix 4, "Report on Cattle Poisoning," p. 651.

29. Letter from R. D. Spedding, Joint Magistrate of Gorakhpur, to Officiating Magistrate, Gorakhpur, October 2, 1873, pp. 34–49; letter from R. D. Spedding, Magistrate of Gorakhpur, to the Commissioner of Benares Division, October 11, 1879, pp. 60–65; in "Papers Relating to the Crime of Cattle Poisoning," *Selections from the Records of the Government of India, 1881,* no. 180.

30. Letter from R. D. Spedding, Joint Magistrate of Gorakhpur, to Officiating Magistrate, Gorakhpur, October 2, 1873, in "Papers Relating to the Crime of Cattle Poisoning," *Selections from the Records of the Government of India, 1881,* no. 180, p. 35.

31. Ibid., p. 37.

32. Police Progs., vol. 78, January–June 1883, UPSA, p. 5.

33. Ibid., vol. 79, July–December 1883, pp. 121–23; vol. 101, July–December 1894, pp. 53–54.

34. Ibid., vol. 101, July–December 1894, p. 54.

35. Ibid., vol. 102, January–June 1895, p. 17.

36. Letter from William Hoey to Director of Land Records and Agriculture, August 26, 1899, file no. 154(C), box no. 27, February 1900, Judicial (Criminal) Dept., UPSA.

37. Letter from Capt. L. Rogers, M.D., Imperial Bacteriologist, to Secretary to Government, September 18, 1899, file no. 154(C), box no. 27, February 1900, Judicial (Criminal) Dept., UPSA.

38. Letter from W. H. Moreland, Director of Land Records and Agriculture, to Secretary, North-Western Provinces Govt., October 21, 1899, UPSA.

39. Letter from L. M. Thornton, Secretary, North-Western Provinces Govt., to All Commissioners of Division, December 7, 1899, file no. 154(C), box no. 27, February 1900, Judicial (Criminal) Dept., UPSA.

40. George Campbell, "Importation of Arsenic into the Benares Division for Unlawful Purposes," in *Selections from the North-West Provinces*, vol. 3, second series, no. 14, p. 268.

41. Letter from the Medical Board (Fort William, Calcutta), to J. R. Colvin, Lieutenant-Governor, NWP, January 24, 1855, in *Selections from the North-West Provinces*, vol. 3, second series, no. 14, p. 273.

42. Letter from S. Wauchope, Commissioner of Police, Calcutta, to Secretary, Govt. of Bengal, June 4, 1872, "Papers Relating to the Crime of Cattle Poisoning," *Selections from the Records of the Government of India, 1881*, no. 180, p. 14.

43. Letter from A. C. Mangles, Collector, Patna, to Commissioner, Patna Division, June 13, 1872, "Papers Relating to the Crime of Cattle Poisoning," *Selections from the Records of the Government of India, 1881*, no. 180, pp. 17–18.

44. Memorandum from Dr. J. C. Brown, Surgeon General, Indian Medical Department, to Secretary, Govt. of Bengal, November 5, 1873, "Papers Relating to the Crime of Cattle Poisoning," *Selections from the Records of the Government of India, 1881*, no. 180, p. 22.

45. Dr. H. B. Buckle, Surgeon General, Indian Medical Department, to Secretary, Govt. of Bengal, October 16, 1873, "Papers Relating to the Crime of Cattle Poisoning," *Selections from the Records of the Government of India, 1881*, no. 180, p. 21.

46. Letter from Apothecary, Hon'ble East Indian Company, to the Officiating Secretary, Medical Board, October 31, 1855, "Importation of Arsenic into the Benares Division for Unlawful Purposes," in *Selections from the North-West Provinces*, vol. 3, second series, no. 14, pp. 278–79.

47. Letter from Babu Kanny Lall Dey, Teacher of Chemistry and Medical Jurisprudence to the Vernacular Classes, Medical College, to Secretary, Surgeon General, Indian Medical Department, "Importation of Arsenic into the Benares Division for Unlawful Purposes," in *Selections from the North-West Provinces*, vol. 3, second series, no. 14, October 16, 1873, p. 23.

48. Holmes, "A Note on Some Interesting Results," p. 1.

49. *Encyclopaedia Britannica* (Chicago: Encyclopaedia Britannica, 1965), s.v. "Poison."

50. *The New Encyclopaedia Britannica* (Chicago: Encyclopaedia Britannica, 1997), s.v. "Arsenic."

51. Cattle Plague Commission, *Report of the Commissioners*, appendix 4, "Report on Cattle Poisoning," p. 651.

52. Ibid., pp. 647–48.

53. Ibid., pp. 650–51.

54. Letter from R. D. Spedding to Commissioner of Benares Division, October 11, 1879, "Papers Relating to the Crime of Cattle Poisoning," *Selections from the Records of the Government of India, 1881*, no. 180, pp. 63–64.

55. Cattle Plague Commission, *Report of the Commissioners*, appendix 4, "Report on Cattle Poisoning," pp. 647–48.

56. Judicial (Criminal) Progs., vol. 60, January–June 1874, UPSA, p. 5.

57. Chaudhuri, "Foreign Trade and Balance of Payments," p. 806.

58. Letter from Horace Cockerell, Secretary to Government of Bengal, Judicial, Political and Appointment Dept., to the Secretary to the Govt. of India, Home, Revenue and Agricultural Dept., Calcutta, June 28, 1880, "Papers Relating to the Crime of Cattle Poisoning," *Selections from the Records of the Government of India, 1881,* no. 180, p. 109.

59. Police Progs., vol. 95, July–December 1892, p. 11.

60. Home, Revenue and Agricultural Dept. Resolution dated February 20, 1880, Govt. of India, "Papers Relating to the Crime of Cattle Poisoning," *Selections from the Records of the Government of India, 1881,* no. 180, pp. 2–11.

61. Cattle Plague Commission, *Report of the Commissioners,* appendix 4, "Report on Cattle Poisoning," pp. 690–702.

62. Ibid., "Memorandum by M. Smith," p. 694. The case was tried at the Sessions court of Nizamut Adawlut in Azamgarh by a three-member bench consisting of Judges M. Smith, N. W. Begbie, and C. C. Jackson.

63. Ibid.

64. Ibid., S. J. Becher, Sessions Judge, Azamgarh, February 16, 1855, p. 696.

65. Ibid., Campbell's reply to the Sessions Judge of Azamgarh, February 26, 1855, pp. 698, 696.

66. Ibid., remarks by the Sessions Judge in the case of Jakhooa and forty-four Chamars, p. 697.

67. Ibid., p. 697.

68. Misra, *The Central Administration of the East India Company,* pp. 299–301.

69. Letter from Campbell to Tucker, October 21, 1854, "Papers Relating to the Crime of Cattle Poisoning," *Selections from the Records of the Government of India, 1881,* no. 180, p. 25; Campbell's memo on cattle poisoning, October 19, 1854, Basta no. 7, vol. 84, Pre-Mutiny Records in the Gorakhpur Collectorate, UPSRA.

70. Misra, *Central Administration of the East India Company,* pp. 339–46.

71. Ibid., p. 338.

72. Letter from W. Muir, Secretary to the Government of the North-Western Provinces, to Superintendent of Police, Benares Division, November 6, 1854, "Papers Relating to the Crime of Cattle Poisoning," *Selections from the Records of the Government of India, 1881,* no. 180, pp. 28–29.

73. Letter from H. C. Tucker, Commissioner of Benares Division, to W. Muir, Secy. to Govt., North-Western Provinces, December 11, 1854, North-Western Provinces Judicial (Criminal) Progs., P/233/71, OIOC.

74. Letter from Campbell to Tucker, December, 9, 1854, North-Western Provinces Judicial (Criminal) Progs., P/233/71, OIOC.

75. Cattle Plague Commission, *Report of the Commissioners,* appendix 4, "Report on Cattle Poisoning," p. 697.

76. Miscellaneous Judicial Files, Basta no. 109(A), vols. 2, 5, Benares Commissioner's Office, UPSRA.

77. "Note on Cattle Poisoning by Dodd," Judicial Progs. (Home Dept.) no. 34, August 27, 1870, NAI, pp. 3–5.

78. Ibid., p. 1.

79. Extract from the Report of W. Walker, M.D., Chemical Examiner to Govt., North-Western Provinces, 1869, in Cattle Plague Commission, *Report of the Commissioners,* appendix 4, "Report on Cattle Poisoning," pp. 726–27.

80. Ibid., p. 727.

81. Ibid., p. 726.

82. "Note on Cattle Poisoning by Captain Dodd," no. 34, August 27, 1870, Judicial Progs. (Home Dept.), NAI, p. 5.

83. Extract from the Report of W. Walker, M.D., Chemical Examiner to Govt., North-Western Provinces, 1869, in Cattle Plague Commission, *Report of the Commissioners*, appendix 4, "Report on Cattle Poisoning," p. 726.

84. Annual Report of Murray Thomson, M.D., Chemical Examiner, Judicial (Criminal) Dept., Progs., vol. 63, January–June 1876, UPSA, pp. 5–7.

85. Police Progs., vol. 93, July–December 1890, p. 53.

86. Ibid., vol. 106, July–December 1895, p. 14.

87. The average is based on the sum of awards given to *chaukidars* and policemen according to the annual reports, Police Progs.

88. Police Progs., vol. 79, July–December 1883, p. 4.

89. Ibid., vol. 97, July–December 1892, pp. 5, 35.

90. Ibid., vol. 103, July–December 1895, p. 50.

91. Ibid., vol. 91, July–December 1889, p. 30.

92. Ibid., vol. 101, July–December 1894, pp. 76–77.

93. Ibid., vol. 97, July–December 1892, p. 33.

94. "Note on Cattle Poisoning by Captain Dodd," no. 34, August 27, 1870, Judicial Progs. (Home Dept.), NAI, pp. 3–4.

95. Police Progs., vol. 105, July–December 1896, pp. 13–14.

96. *Annual Report of the Inland Trade of North-Western Provinces and Oudh,* 1898, p. 7.

97. Letter from W. Hoey, August 26, 1899, file no. 154(C), box no. 27, February 1900, Judicial (Criminal) Dept., UPSA.

98. "Report on Cattle Diseases, 1869," pp. 74–75.

99. Ibid.

100. Ibid., pp. 81–82.

101. Police Progs., vol. 97, July–December 1892, p. 4.

102. For a similar discussion of criminal communities see "Criminal Communities: The Thuggee Act XXX of 1836," in Singha, *A Despotism of Law*, pp. 168–228.

103. Crooke, *Popular Religion and Folklore of North India*, pp. 80–81, 103–104, 125–26, 139.

104. "Report on Cattle Diseases," Public Progs. (Home Dept.), no. 93–94, 1869, NAI, pp. 81–82.

105. Letter from W. Hoey, August 26, 1899, file no. 154(C), box no. 27, February 1900, Judicial (Criminal) Dept., UPSA.

106. Evidence of Gobra Thakoor, inhabitant of the village of Rameree, Station Hamirpur district, in Cattle Plague Commission, *Report of the Commissioners,* p. 381.

107. "Cow-Killing Agitation in the Azamgarh District," file no. 461, box no. 57, GAD Block Files, UPSA. For a detailed discussion of the history and historiography of the movement, see "Mobilizing the Hindu Community" in Pandey, *The Construction of Communalism,* pp. 155–200.

108. Police Progs., vol. 101, pt. 2, July–December 1894, pp. 2–5, 58.

109. "Cow-Killing Agitation in the Azamgarh District," file no. 461, box no. 57, GAD Block Files, UPSA, p. 2.

110. Police Progs., vol. 101, July–December 1894, pp. 75–76.

111. *SVN* for Uttar Pradesh, various issues from 1894 to 1900.

112. *Hindustan, SVN,* vol. 28, November 28, 1894.

113. *Hindustan, SVN,* vol. 33, February, 6, 1900; see also *Almora Akhbar, SVN,* vol. 28, January 17, 1894, June 7, 1899; *Hindustan, SVN,* vol. 31, September 31, 1898, vol. 34, July 20, 1901; *Bharat Jiwan* (Hindi weekly, Benares), *SVN,* vol. 32, June 14, 1899.

114. "Cow-Killing Agitation in the Azamgarh District," file no. 461, box no. 57, GAD Block Files, UPSA, p. 2.

115. *Abhyudaya,* July 20, 1929.

116. Crooke, *The Tribes and Castes of the North-Western Provinces and Oudh,* vol. 1, p. 194.

117. *Marwar Gazette* (Hindi-Urdu weekly, Jodhpur), *SVN,* vol. 14, May 22, 1881; *Al-Bashir* (Urdu weekly, Etawah), *SVN,* vol. 32, February 21, 1899; *The Rohilkhand Ukbar* (Urdu weekly), *SVN,* vol. 3, February 22, 1870.

118. *Pradeep* (Hindi monthly, Allahabad), *SVN,* vol. 21, May 1888.

119. *The Oordoo Delhi Gazette* (Urdu weekly, Delhi), *SVN,* vol. 2, July 5, 1869.

120. *Nasim-I-Agra* (Urdu weekly, Agra) *SVN,* vol. 31, February 9, 1898.

121. Pandey, *The Construction of Communalism,* p. 179.

122. Police Progs., vol. 98, July–December 1892, p. 9.

123. Ibid., vol. 93, July–December 1890, pp. 66–68. Also see vol. 100, July–December 1893.

124. Ibid., vol. 93, July–December 1890, p. 67.

125. Ibid., vol. 91, July–December 1889, p. 30.

126. Ibid., vol. 93, July–December 1890, p. 68.

127. Ibid. pp. 69–70.

128. Cattle Plague Commission, *Report of the Commissioners,* appendix 4, "Report on Cattle Poisoning," p. 649.

129. Police Progs., vol. 97, July–December 1892. p. 10; vol. 98, January–June 1893, pp. 41–42.

130. Ibid., vol. 93, July–December 1890, p. 68.

131. Ibid., vol. 91, July–December 1889, p. 30.

132. Ibid., vol. 97, July–December 1892, p. 11; vol. 99, January–June 1893, p. 41.

133. D. M. Stewart, "Cesses in Oudh, 1922," Revenue (A) Progs., May 1925, UPSA, pp. 38–39.

134. Police Progs., vol. 103, July–December 1895, p. 53.

135. Letter from R. D. Spedding, October 11, 1879, "Papers Relating to the Crime of Cattle Poisoning," *Selections from the Records of the Government of India, 1881,* no. 180, p. 63.

136. Police Progs., vol. 105, January–June 1896, p. 50.

137. This feature of the leather trade was regularly noted in police reports from 1889 onward.

138. Police Progs., vol. 97, July–December 1892, pp. 10–11; vol. 99, July–December 1893, pp. 41–42.

139. *Abhyudaya,* July 20, 1929.

140. *Annual Report of the Inland Trade of North-Western Provinces and Oudh,* 1906, p. 3.

141. Letter from L. M. Thornton, Secretary, Govt. of North-Western Provinces, to All Commissioners of Division, December 7, 1899, box no. 27, February 1900, Judicial (Criminal) Dept., UPSA, p. 7.

2. Investigating the Stereotype

The first epigraph is from "Memorandum, C. Currie, Settlement Commissioner, Oude," in *Further Papers Relating to Under-Proprietary Rights and Rights of Cultivators in Oude*, p. 157. The second epigraph is from file no. 498 (1930), box no. 315, Industries Dept., UPSA.

1. *Census of India, 1911*, vol. 15, pt. 2, *Tables*, pp. 756–62. The total Chamar population was 6,068,382. The categories are defined in part 1, *Report*, e.g., the term "cultivator" includes zamindars and both occupancy and non-occupancy tenants.

2. *Census of India, 1961*, vol. 15, pt. 5A(i), *Special Tables for Scheduled Castes*, pp. 4–7.

3. Crooke, *The Tribes and Castes of the North-Western Provinces and Oudh*, vol. 1, p. 190.

4. K. Singh, *The Scheduled Castes*, p. 303.

5. The British government defined non-proprietors as those who neither owned land nor had transferable rights over it. They were therefore not responsible for collecting or paying land revenue.

6. *Census of India, 1881*, vol. 17, pt. 1, *Report*, p. 136.

7. Briggs, *The Chamars*, p. 21.

8. Tennant, *Indian Recreations*, vol. 1, p. 195.

9. *Report on the Settlement of the District of Goruckpoor*, 1837, E. A. Reade, p. 445.

10. *Report on the Settlement of the Ceded Portion of the District of Azimgurh*, 1837, J. Thomason, pp. 35–36.

11. *Report on the Settlement of the District of Seharunpore*, 1837, Edward Thornton, pp. 112–13.

12. *Report on the Settlement of the Zillah of Humeerpoor*, 1842, C. Allen, p. 781.

13. Russell, *Report on the Census of the Central Provinces, 1866*, p. 13.

14. *Final Report on the Settlement of Gorakhpur District*, 1891, A. W. Cruickshank, pp. 30, 42A–45A.

15. Nesfield, *Brief View of the Caste System*, p. 22. Nesfield wrote the first authoritative account of the caste system, a task assigned by the government of Uttar Pradesh.

16. Briggs, *The Chamars*, pp. 17–19.

17. Ibid., pp. 17–18.

18. "William Crooke's Report on Etah District," in *A Collection of Papers Connected with an Inquiry into the Conditions of the Lower Classes*, vol. 2, p. 41, file no. 2/1887–88, box no. 129, UPSA.

19. Chenevix-Trench, *Monograph on Tanning and Working in Leather*, p. 4.

20. Briggs, *The Chamars*, pp. 58–59.

21. *Census of India, 1931*, vol. 18, *United Provinces, General Report* (Allahabad: Superintendent of Government Press United Provinces, 1931), part 1, pp. 538, 611.

22. K. Singh, *The Scheduled Castes*, p. 303.

23. *Census of India, 1911*, vol. 15, pt. 1, *Report*, pp. 412–14. See also Blunt, *The Caste System of Northern India*, pp. 50–57. For a similar argument see M. Singh, *The Depressed Classes*, p. 22.

24. *Census of North-Western Provinces, 1865*, vol. 1, p. 15.

25. *Report of the Settlement of the Etawah District*, 1875, C. H. T. Crosthwaite and W. Neale, p. 20.

26. *Final Report of the Settlement of the Basti District*, 1891, J. Hooper, p. 28. For the other districts, see *Final Report on the Revision of Settlement in the District of Aligarh*, 1882,

T. E. Smith, p. 130; *Report on the Settlement of the Shahjehanpore District,* 1874, Robert G. Currie, p. 61; *Final Report of the Settlement of the Cawnpore District,* 1878, F. N. Wright, p. 46; *Report on the Revision of Settlement of the Bahraich District, Oudh,* 1873, E. G. Clark and H. Scotty Boys, p. 66; *Report on the Settlement Operations in the District of Azamgarh,* 1881, J. R. Reid, p. 31.

27. *A Collection of Papers Connected with an Inquiry into the Conditions of the Lower Classes,* p. 8.

28. *Final Report on the Eleventh Settlement of the Moradabad,* 1909, H. J. Boas, p. 10.

29. This legislation also affected political mobilization. The well-known peasant movement in the Awadh region of Uttar Pradesh demanded protection from arbitrary eviction.

30. *Report on the Settlement of the Ceded Portion of the District of Azimgurh,* 1837, J. Thomason, pp. 33–36. See Asiya Siddiqi's discussion of Thomason's report in *Agrarian Change in a Northern Indian State,* pp. 15–25, 33, 35–36.

31. *Report on the Settlement of the Ceded Portion of the District of Azimgurh,* 1837, J. Thomason, p. 36.

32. Cohn, "Structural Change in Indian Rural Society, 1596–1885," in *An Anthropologist among the Historians,* p. 402.

33. *Report on the Settlement of the Ceded Portion of the District of Azimgurh,* 1837, J. Thomason, p. 37.

34. Elliot, *Memoirs on the History, Folk-Lore, and Distribution of the Races of the North Western Provinces of India,* p. 88.

35. *Notes on Tenant-Right,* pp. 77–78.

36. Grover, "Nature of Land Rights in Mughal India."

37. A. Siddiqi, *Agrarian Change in a Northern Indian State,* chapters 1 and 2; Whitcombe, *Agrarian Conditions in Northern India,* chapter 3.

38. Moreland, *The Revenue Administration of the United Provinces,* pp. 56–59.

39. M. Singh, *The Depressed Classes,* p. 24.

40. M. Siddiqi, *Agrarian Unrest in Northern India,* chapter 1.

41. "Memorandum, C. Currie, Settlement Commissioner, Oude," in *Papers Relating to Under-Proprietary Rights and Rights of Cultivators in Oude,* pp. 163, 166.

42. M. Siddiqi, *Agrarian Unrest in Northern India,* pp. 10–15.

43. V. N. Mehta, "Report on the Peasant Movement in Partabgarh," file no. 753, box no. 6, 1920, Revenue Dept., UPSA, pp. 5–7.

44. *Further Papers Relating to Under-Proprietary Rights and Rights of Cultivators in Oude.*

45. Ibid., Memorandum by G. B. Maconochie, Settlement Officer, Oonao (Unnao), March 16, 1865, pp. 386, 407.

46. Ibid., H. B. Harrington, Assistant Settlement Officer, Durriabad (Lucknow District), Commissioner, April 4, 1865, p. 518.

47. Ibid., From Settlement Officer, Hurdui [Hardoi] to Commissioner, Khyrabad Division, April 30, 1865, p. 154.

48. Dutta, *The Bundelkhand Alienation of Land Act,* p. 13.

49. Prashad, *Untouchable Freedom,* p. 38.

50. A. Siddiqi, *Agrarian Change in a Northern Indian State,* especially chapter 2.

51. Stokes, *The Peasant and the Raj,* p. 58.

52. *Final Report on the Settlement of the Jhansi District,* 1893, W. H. L. Impey, p. 91.

53. *The Final Report on the Settlement Operations of the Saharanpur District,* 1921, D. L. Drake-Brockman, p. 12.

54. *Report on the Settlement of the Agra District*, 1880, H. F. Evans, p. 57.

55. *Statistical, Descriptive and Historical Account of the North-Western Provinces of India*, Edwin T. Atkinson, vol. 3, pp. 560–61.

56. A. Siddiqi, *Agrarian Change in a Northern Indian State*, p. 31.

57. Stokes, *The Peasant and the Raj*, p. 58.

58. *Statistical, Descriptive and Historical Account of the North-Western Provinces of India*, Edwin T. Atkinson, vol. 7, pp. 109–10; *Final Report on the Revision of Settlement in the District of Aligarh*, 1882, T. E. Smith, pp. 128–32.

59. M. Singh, *The Depressed Classes*, p. 29.

60. *Final Report on the Seventh Settlement of the Azamgarh District*, 1908, C. E. Crawford, p. 15.

61. M. Singh, *The Depressed Classes*, pp. 25–26.

62. *Final Report on the Settlement of the Jhansi District*, 1893, W. H. L. Impey, p. 91.

63. *Final Report on the Revision of Settlement in the Lalitpur Subdivision, District Jhansi*, 1899, H. J. Hoare, pp. 7–8.

64. *Final Report of the Settlement of the Jhansi District*, 1893, W. H. L. Impey, pp. 91, 61A.

65. *Statistical, Descriptive and Historical Account of the North-Western Provinces of India*, Edwin T. Atkinson, vol. 1, p. 312.

66. *Assessment Report of Tahsil Mau, District Jhansi*, 1943, H. T. Lane, p. 5; *Assessment Report of Tahsil Garotha, District Jhansi*, 1945, H. T. Lane, p. 5.

67. *Final Settlement Report of Jhansi District*, 1947, H. T. Lane, p. 7.

68. *Report on the Settlement of the Agra District*, 1880, H. F. Evans, pp. 28–29.

69. *Final Report on the Settlement and Record Operations in District Agra*, 1930, R. F. Mudie, p. 20.

70. *Rent-Rate Report of Pargana Etamadpur and Firozabad, District Agra*, 1928, R. F. Mudie, p. 24.

71. *Rent-Rate Report of Pargana and Tahsil Bah, District Agra*, 1928, R. F. Mudie, p. 9.

72. *Report on the Settlement of the Bareilly District*, 1874, S. M. Moens, pp. 51–53.

73. *Final Settlement Report of the District Bareilly*, 1903, S. H. Freemantle, p. 4.

74. *Final Settlement Report of the District Bareilly*, 1942, I. W. Lewys-Loyd, p. 5.

75. *The Final Report on the Settlement Operations of the Saharanpur District*, 1921, D. L. Drake-Brockman, pp. 26, 47–48.

76. *Statistical, Descriptive and Historical Accounts of the North-Western Provinces of India*, Edwin T. Atkinson, vol. 2, p. 225.

77. *The Final Report on the Settlement Operations of the Saharanpur District*, 1921, D. L. Drake-Brockman, p. 26.

78. *Final Report on the Settlement of Land Revenue in the Bulandshahr District*, 1891, B. T. Stoker, pp. 16–17, 20–21.

79. *Final Report on the Settlement of Bulandshahr*, 1919, E. A. Phelps, pp. 10–11.

80. *Statistical, Descriptive and Historical Account of the North-Western Provinces of India*, Edwin T. Atkinson, vol. 6, p. 386.

81. *Final Report on the Settlement of Gorakhpur District*, 1891, A. W. Cruickshank, pp. 42–45.

82. *Statistical, Descriptive and Historical Account of the North-Western Provinces of India*, Edwin T. Atkinson, vol. 6, p. 408.

83. *Report on the Settlement of the Agra District*, 1880, H. F. Evans, p. 28.

84. Bhattacharya, "Agricultural Labour and Production," pp. 123–24.

85. E. Rose, District Magistrate, Ghazipur, "Note on Ghazipur District," in *A Collection of Papers Connected with an Inquiry into the Conditions of the Lower Classes,* pp. 170, 176. See also M. Singh, *The Depressed Classes,* pp. 28, 32.

86. *Report on the Settlement of the Guruckpore-Bustee District,* 1871, vol. 1, p. 46.

87. Saksena, "An Agricultural Survey of Bakhshi-ka-Talab, District Lucknow," p. 136.

88. Dayal, "Agricultural Labourers," pp. 246, 235–38.

89. Saksena, "An Agricultural Survey of Bakhshi-ka-Talab, District Lucknow," in RadhaKamal Mukerjee ed., *Fields and Farmers in Oudh,* p. 119.

90. Dayal, "Agricultural Labourers," 273.

91. Premchand, "Poos ki Raat," pp. 154–60. First published in May 1930 in the Lucknow journal *Madhuri.*

92. "William Crooke's Report on Etah District," in *A Collection of Papers Connected with an Inquiry into the Conditions of the Lower Classes,* pp. 62–63.

93. "A. Cadell's Report on Mathura," in ibid., pp. 52–54.

94. For a discussion of these issues see V. N. Mehta, "Report on the Peasant Movement in Partabgarh," file no. 753, box no. 6, 1920, Revenue Dept., UPSA, p. 9.

95. Ibid. See also M. Singh, *The Depressed Classes,* p. 34.

96. D. M. Stewart, "Cesses in Oudh, 1922," Revenue (A) Progs., May 1925, UPSA, pp. 22–24.

97. V. N. Mehta, "Report on the Peasant Movement in Partabgarh," file no. 753, box no. 6, 1920, Revenue Dept., UPSA, p. 68. Both Mehta and Stewart report many examples of such complaints by Chamar peasants.

98. *Assessment Report of Tahsil Khurja of the Bulandshahr District,* 1889, B. T. Stoker, p. 27.

99. V. N. Mehta, "Report on the Peasant Movement in Partabgarh," file no. 753, box no. 6, 1920, Revenue Dept., UPSA, p. 63.

100. "Rasad and Begari Agitation in UP, 1920," file no. 694, box no. 153/1920, GAD, UPSA, p. 1, 3.

101. Mehta, "Report on the Peasant Movement in Partabgarh," file no. 753, box no. 6, 1920, Revenue Dept., UPSA, pp. 7–8, 68, 48.

102. D. M. Stewart, "Cesses in Oudh, 1922," Revenue (A) Progs., May 1925, UPSA, p. 125.

103. "Book 2: An Account of the District of Shahabad," Buchanan-Hamilton, MSS Eur. D.88, OIOC, pp. 117–18.

104. "Crooke's Report on Etah District," in *A Collection of Papers Connected with an Inquiry into the Conditions of the Lower Classes,* pp. 53, 60–61, 137.

105. Ibid., pp. 65, 79.

106. Crooke, Dampier, and Conybeare, *A Note on the Tract of Country South of the River Son,* p. 21.

107. "Crooke's Report on Etah District," in *A Collection of Papers Connected with an Inquiry into the Conditions of the Lower Classes,* pp. 46, 109.

108. Amin, *Event, Metaphor, Memory,* p. 28.

109. Srinivas, *Caste in Modern India,* p. 17. So common is this belief that Srinivas does not cite a source.

110. Yadvendu, *Yaduvansh ka Aitihas,* pp. 206–31. Yadvendu was a member of the Jatav Mahasabha and founder of the All India Jatav Youth League.

111. Interview with Mr. Puttulal Jatav (born 1927), September 12, 2002. Since mid-1940s he has been involved with Jatav politics in Agra, where he now lives as a retired district judge.

112. *Statistical, Descriptive and Historical Account of the North-Western Provinces of India,* Edwin T. Atkinson, vol. 2, p. 225.

113. Lal, *Chalo Jhaji,* pp. 100, 106–107.

114. File no. 478, box no. 191/1914, Industry Dept., UPSA, p. 53.

115. Lal, *Chalo Jhaji,* pp. 111–112, 114–16, 229.

116. File no. 478, Industry Dept., UPSA, pp. 62–65.

117. "Secretary to the Government of India to Secretary to Government, N-W Provinces and Oudh, August 17, 1887," in *A Collection of Papers Connected with an Inquiry into the Conditions of the Lower Classes,* p. 1. See also Elizabeth Whitcombe's discussion of the inquiry in *Agrarian Conditions in Northern India,* pp. 266–70.

118. "A. Cadell's Report on Mathura," in *A Collection of Papers Connected with an Inquiry into the Conditions of the Lower Classes,* pp. 52–54.

119. "Crooke's Report on Etah District," in ibid., pp. 114–15. Crooke's reports from Etah give us the first glimpse of his sharp ethnographic skills.

120. "Crooke's Report on Etah District" and "T. W. Holderness's Report on Pilibhit," in ibid., pp. 135–38, 154–55.

121. F. Wright, *Memorandum on Agriculture in the District of Cawnpore,* pp. 76–78, 88, 92–94.

122. "T. W. Holderness's Report on Pilibhit," in *A Collection of Papers Connected with an Inquiry into the Conditions of the Lower Classes,* pp. 154–55.

123. "H. C. Irwin's Report on Rae Bareli," in ibid., p. 220.

124. "Crooke's Report on Etah District," in ibid., pp. 109, 117.

125. "H. C. Irwin's Report on Rae Bareli," in ibid., pp. 99–100, 225.

126. "A. Cadell's Report on Mathura," in ibid., p. 46.

127. "Crooke's Report on Etah District," in ibid., pp. 74, 76, 78–79.

128. "Speeches and Writings," file no. 2, Baba Ramchandra Papers, NMML. The petition by a group of Raidassis is also separately kept in the collection and is dated January 1931.

129. "Papers Relating to Praja Sangh, 1929–1934," file no. 6, and "Tour Reports and Programmes, 1929–1940," file no. 7, Baba Ramchandra Papers, NMML.

130. "Report on Kisan Sabha Movement," file no. 50, boxes nos. 133–34/1921, GAD, UPSA, pp. 687–93, 985–1001.

131. "Papers Relating to Peasant Movement of 1921," file no. 1, Baba Ramchandra Papers, NMML, p. 20.

132. K. Kumar, *Peasants in Revolt,* pp. 189–212. The chief demand of the movement was security of tenure.

133. Asthana, "A Social and Economic Survey of Village Malhera," pp. 18–21.

134. "Papers Relating to Peasant Movement of 1921," file no. 1, Baba Ramchandra Papers, NMML, p. 18.

135. Pandey, "Peasant Revolt and Indian Nationalism," p. 168; M. Siddiqi, *Agrarian Unrest in Northern India,* pp. 213–16.

136. "Papers Relating to Praja Sangh, 1929–1934," file no. 6, and "Tour Reports and Programmes, 1929–1940," file no. 7, Baba Ramchandra Papers, NMML.

137. Ibid., "Notebook containing autobiographical notes," file no. 2, Speeches & Writings, 1933–42.

138. Deliege, *The Untouchables of India,* pp. 89–94.

139. Briggs, *The Chamars*, p. 45; Cohn, "The Changing Traditions of a Low Caste," in *An Anthropologist among the Historians*, p. 285. I discuss this aspect in the introduction to this book.

140. *Report on the Settlement of the Bareilly District*, 1874, S. M. Moens, p. 69. Moens does not mention any specific caste, but generally refers to the non-proprietary "cultivators" who were primarily from the lower and "untouchable" castes. According to Moens, "the best cultivators in Bareilly are Coormis [Kurmis], Lodhas, Kisans, Moraos, Chamars, Rains and Jats" (p. 51).

141. "Book 1, Part 2: Section on Hindus and Religion, Gorakhpur," Buchanan-Hamilton, D.91–92, OIOC. The survey provides a rare glimpse into the cultural world of the Chamars of eastern Uttar Pradesh.

142. Briggs, *The Chamars*, p. 172.

143. "Book 1, Part 2: Section on Hindus and Religion, Gorakhpur," Buchanan-Hamilton, D.91–92, OIOC.

144. Ibid. Buchanan-Hamilton observes that in South India and Bengal similar gods were considered illegal by Brahmans, whereas in the north their worship was accepted.

145. "Book 2: An Account of the District of Shahabad," Buchanan-Hamilton, D.88, OIOC.

146. *North Indian Notes and Queries* 3, no. 1 (April 1893), p. 40.

147. This paragraph and the next are based on Briggs, *The Chamars*, pp. 171–77.

148. Amin, *Event, Metaphor, Memory*, p. 34.

3. Is the Leather Industry a Chamar Enterprise?

The first epigraph is from Chandra, *Monograph on Tanning and Working in Leather in the Province of Bengal*, p. 17. The second epigraph is from Industrial Committee on Tanneries and Leather Goods Manufactories, *Summary of Proceedings*, p. 15. It is interesting to note that Jitulal, a member of the Indian parliament, intervened in the discussion on setting the wages of workers in the tanneries and leather industries.

1. Joshi, *Lost Worlds*, pp. 78, 239–40.

2. Mukhtar, *Report on Labour Conditions*, p. 29.

3. Niehoff, *Factory Workers in India*, pp. 54–55.

4. Lynch, *The Politics of Untouchability*, p. 33; Knorringa, "Artisan Labour in the Agra Footwear Industry," p. 304. Knorringa describes leatherworking and shoemaking as Chamars' "hereditary skills."

5. Roy, *Traditional Industry*, p. 197.

6. "Oral Evidence of A. C. Inskip, Cooper Allen & Co., Kanpur," November 6, 1929, in Hides Cess Enquiry Committee, *Report*, vol. 2, p. 12.

7. S. Sharma, *The Chamar Artisans*, p. 35.

8. Roy, *Traditional Industry*, p. 156. Roy's quotation from George Watt's *A Dictionary of the Economic Products of India*, vol. 4, indicates that he is referring to the *jajmani* system.

9. Mukhtar, *Report on Labour Conditions*, p. 29.

10. *Census of India, 1931*, vol. 18, pt. 1, *Report*, p. 422.

11. Chakrabarty, *Rethinking Working-Class History*, chapters 2 and 3; Chandavarkar, *The Origins of Industrial Capitalism in India*.

12. Chakrabarty, *Rethinking Working-Class History,* pp. 14, 93–96.

13. Das Gupta, "Factory Labour in Eastern India," pp. 326, 316–17.

14. Lal, *Chalo Jhaji,* pp. 106–107.

15. Freemantle, *Report on the Supply of Labour in the United Provinces and Bengal,* appendix A.

16. Roy, *Traditional Industry,* p. 176; Joshi, *Lost Worlds,* p. 35.

17. File no. 434, December 7, 1866, L/MIL/7/13506, Harness and Saddlery Factories, Cawnpore, Military Dept., OIOC.

18. Ibid.

19. Letter from F. L. Petre, Commissioner, Allahabad Division, to Secretary, Government, North-Western Provinces and Oudh, August 29, 1899, file no. 71B, box no. 547/1900, Misc. (Genl.), Municipal Dept., UPSA, pp. 29–32.

20. Yalland, *Boxwallahs,* pp. 129–30, 272. Yalland's account is based on the Stewart family papers.

21. Chenevix-Trench, *Monograph on Tanning and Working in Leather,* pp. 1–3. The six provinces are Bengal, Bombay, Madras, the United Provinces, and Punjab.

22. Chenevix-Trench, *Monograph on Tanning and Working in Leather,* p. 13.

23. *Report on the Industrial Survey of the Jalaun District,* 1924, G. N. Bhargava, p. 28.

24. Briggs, *The Chamars,* pp. 225–28.

25. Walton, *Monograph on Tanning and Working in Leather,* p. 27.

26. Indian Industrial Commission, *Report,* p. 36.

27. Briggs, *The Chamars,* p. 228.

28. Ibid.

29. Walton, *Monograph on Tanning and Working in Leather,* p. 27.

30. "Oral Evidence of R. B. Ewbank," November 30, 1917, in Indian Industrial Commission, *Minutes of Evidence,* vol. 4, p. 552.

31. "Oral Evidence of A. C. Inskip, Cooper Allen & Co., Kanpur," November 6, 1929, Hides Cess Enquiry Committee, *Report,* vol. 2, p. 12.

32. Roy, *Traditional Industry,* p. 157.

33. Briggs, *The Chamars,* p. 226.

34. Ibid., p. 230.

35. Chandra, *Monograph on Tanning and Working in Leather,* p. 25.

36. Ibid., p. 25.

37. Ibid., p. 2.

38. *Report on the Industrial Survey of the Muzaffarnagar District,* 1923. M. Zia-Ur-Rub, pp. 14–15, 19; *Report on the Industrial Survey of the Sultanpur District,* 1923, H. N. Sapru, p. 14; *Report on the Industrial Survey of the Rae Bareli District,* 1923, B. K. Ghoshal, p. 27.

39. *Report on the Industrial Survey of the Fyzabad District,* 1923, H. N. Sapru, p. 34; see also *Report on the Industrial Survey of the Fatehpur District,* Jaghish Sahai Vatal, p. 23; *Report on the Industrial Survey of the Sultanpur District,* 1923, H. N. Sapru, p. 14.

40. *Report on the Industrial Survey of the Muzaffarnagar District,* 1923. M. Zia-Ur-Rub, p. 14.

41. Walton, *Monograph on Tanning and Working in Leather,* pp. 1–2.

42. Ibid.; Briggs, *The Chamars,* pp. 1–2.

43. Cattle Plague Commission, *Report of the Commissioners,* appendix 4, "Report on Cattle Poisoning," p. 649.

44. Crooke, *The Tribes and Castes of the North-Western Provinces and Oudh*, vol. 1, pp. 171–72.

45. Directorate of Marketing and Inspection, *Report on the Marketing of Hides*, pp. 131–32, 253–54.

46. Nesfield, *Brief View of the Caste System*, p. 22.

47. Walton, *Monograph on Tanning and Working in Leather*, p. 12.

48. Roy, *Traditional Industry*, pp. 156, 25, 164–67, 33–34.

49. Colebrooke, *Remark on the Husbandry and Internal Commerce of Bengal*, pp. 181–84. His optimism was based on the growing trade in hides from Brazil to Portugal, which was worth 80,000 pounds annually.

50. Tennant, *Indian Recreations*, vol. 1, p. 103.

51. Prinsep, *Remarks on the External Commerce and Exchanges of Bengal*, pp. 30, 7–8. Prinsep's report deals with India's foreign trade between 1813–14 and 1820–21.

52. Colebrooke, *Remark on the Husbandry and Internal Commerce of Bengal*, p. 183.

53. H. Wright, *East-Indian Economic Problems*, pp. 200–201.

54. Chaudhuri, "Foreign Trade and Balance of Payments."

55. Crawfurd, *A Sketch of the Commercial Resources*, pp. 277–78.

56. Hides Cess Enquiry Committee, *Report*, p. 10. According to G. N. Bhargava, one *maund* is the weight of roughly seven and a half hides. *Report on the Industrial Survey of the Jhansi District*, 1923, G. N. Bhargava, pp. 15–17.

57. File no. 5/1830, box no. 232; file no. 5/1818, box no. 84; file no. 6/1808, box no. 26, Commissioner's Office, Allahabad, Custom House Series, 1801–57, UPSRA. The pre-Mutiny Custom House records from the collector's and commissioner's offices give us detailed information about the trade that passed through Uttar Pradesh between 1800 and 1861.

58. File no. 5/1818, box no. 84, Commissioner's Office, Allahabad (Pre-Mutiny), Custom House Series, 1801–57, UPSRA.

59. George Campbell, "Importation of Arsenic into the Benares Division for Unlawful Purposes," in *Selections from the North-West Provinces*, vol. 3, second series, no. 14, pp. 260–66.

60. File no. 19, 1829–53, Commissioner's Office, Agra Division (Pre-Mutiny), Custom House Series, UPSRA. Also see Trevelyan, *Report upon the Inland Customs and Town Duties of the Bengal Presidency*, p. 229.

61. A. Siddiqi, *Agrarian Change in a Northern Indian State*, p. 143; C. A. Bayly, *Rulers, Townsmen and Bazaars*, pp. 250–51.

62. C. A. Bayly, *Rulers, Townsmen and Bazaars*, p. 462; see also chapters 3, 4, and 6.

63. Naqvi, *Urban Centres and Industries in Upper India*, p. 114.

64. Buchanan, *An Account of the Districts of Bihar and Patna*, vol. 1, pp. 627–28, 678.

65. Hoey, *A Monograph on Trade and Manufacturers in Northern India*, pp. 124–26.

66. Naqvi, *Urban Centres and Industries in Upper India*, p. 119.

67. Roy, *Traditional Industry*, p. 158.

68. Montgomery, *Statistical Report of the District of Cawnpore*, appendix 7.

69. "Cawnpore Custom House, May 8, 1829," file no. 14/B, box no. 82, Pre-Mutiny Records, Commissioner's Office, Allahabad, 1801–57; "Proposed Rates for 1816," Commissioner's Office, Agra, Custom Series, vol. 1, 1808–17, UPSRA.

70. Prinsep, *Remarks on the External Commerce and Exchanges of Bengal*, p. 3.

71. Buchanan, *An Account of the Districts of Bihar and Patna*, vol. 1, pp. 765–73.

72. Crawfurd, *A Sketch of the Commercial Resources,* pp. 231–33.

73. Tapan Raychaudhuri, "Non-agricultural Production: Mughal India," in *The Cambridge Economic History of India,* ed. Raychaudhuri and Habib, vol. 1, pp. 276–77.

74. Naqvi, *Urban Centres and Industries in Upper India,* pp. 30–38, 51. See also Grover, "An Integrated Pattern of Commercial Life," p. 235.

75. Naqvi, *Urban Centres and Industries in Upper India,* pp. 66, 71.

76. Fazl, *Ain I Akbari,* vol. 2, p. 67.

77. Raychaudhuri, "Non-agricultural Production: Mughal India," in *The Cambridge Economic History of India,* ed. Raychaudhuri and Habib, vol. 1, p. 281.

78. Grover, "An Integrated Pattern of Commercial Life," pp. 224–27.

79. *Report on the Industrial Survey of the Rae Bareli District,* 1923, B. K. Ghoshal, p. 29.

80. *Annual Report of the Rail-Borne Traffic of the North-Western Provinces and Oudh, 1890.*

81. *Report on the Industrial Survey of the Saharanpur District,* 1923. M. Zia-Ur-Rub, p. 16.

82. *Report on the Industrial Survey of the Hardoi District,* 1923, B. K. Ghoshal, pp. 32, 51.

83. *Report on the Industrial Survey of the Jhansi District,* 1923, G. N. Bhargava, pp. 15–17.

84. *Report on the Industrial Survey of the Aligarh District of the United Provinces,* 1923, Maulvi H. R. Jaffrey, pp. 25-27.

85. *Report on the Industrial Survey of the Rae Bareli District,* 1923, B. K. Ghoshal, pp. 27–29.

86. *Report on the Industrial Survey of the Lucknow District,* 1923, B. K. Ghoshal, pp. 38–39.

87. *Report on the Industrial Survey of the Rae Bareli District,* 1923, B. K. Ghoshal, pp. 66–67.

88. *Report on the Industrial Survey of the Fatehpur District,* 1923, J. S. Vatal, pp. 14–17.

89. *Report on the Industrial Survey of the Gorakhpur District,* 1923, M. Mushtaq, p. 17.

90. *Report on the Industrial Survey of the Azamgarh District,* 1923, M. Mushtaq, p. 10.

91. *Report on the Industrial Survey of the Hamirpur District,* 1923, G. N. Bhargava, p. 10.

92. *Report on the Industrial Survey of the Pilibhit District,* 1924, B. R. Bhatta, p. 18.

93. *Report on the Industrial Survey of the Kheri District,* 1923, B. K. Ghoshal, p. 28.

94. *Report on the Industrial Survey of the Hamirpur District,* 1923, G. N. Bhargava, p. 9; *Report on the Industrial Survey of the Shahjahanpur District,* 1923, M. Mushtaq, p. 23.

95. *Report on the Industrial Survey of the Jhansi District,* 1923, G. N. Bhargava, p. 16.

96. *Report on the Industrial Survey of the Moradabad District,* 1923, R. Saran, p. 22. Khatiks exported skins to Amritsar.

97. D. M. Stewart, "Cesses in Oudh, 1922," Revenue (A) Progs., May 1925, UPSA, p. 38.

98. Amin, *Event, Metaphor, Memory,* p. 25.

99. *Report on the Industrial Survey of the Fatehpur District,* 1923, J. S. Vatal, p. 15.

100. *Report on the Industrial Survey of the Moradabad District,* 1923, R. Saran, p. 24.

101. *Report on the Industrial Survey of the Kheri District,* 1923, B. K. Ghoshal, p. 27; *Report on the Industrial Survey of the Rae Bareli District,* 1923, B. K. Ghoshal, p. 27.

102. *Report on the Industrial Survey of the Cawnpore District,* 1923, J. S. Vatal, p. 30.

103. Amin, *Event, Metaphor, Memory,* pp. 24–25.

104. "Book 5. Of the state of arts and commerce," Gorakhpur, "Book 1, Topography and Antiquities: An account of the northern part of the district of Gorakhpur," Buchanan-Hamilton, MSS Eur. D.91–92, OIOC.

105. Hoey, *A Monograph on Trade and Manufacturers in Northern India,* pp. 90–91.

106. Amin, *Event, Metaphor, Memory,* p. 25. Their dominance was underlined by a mosque in the bazaar.

107. *Report on the Industrial Survey of the Benares District,* 1923, B. R. Bhatta, p. 26; *Report on the Industrial Survey of the Allahabad District,* 1923, J. S. Vatal, p. 34.

108. *Report on the Industrial Survey of the Agra District,* 1924, M. Zia-Ur-Rub, pp. 61–65.

109. *Report on the Industrial Survey of the Cawnpore District,* 1923, J. S. Vatal, pp. 87–92.

110. *Report on the Industrial Survey of the Pilibhit District,* 1924, B. R. Bhatta, pp. 59–61. It is striking that all the surveys list shoemakers at the end.

111. Hoey, *A Monograph on Trade and Manufactures in Northern India,* p. 90.

112. Roy, *Traditional Industry,* pp. 164–65.

113. *Report on the Industrial Survey of the Banda District,* 1923, G. N. Bhargava, pp. 13–14.

114. Hides Cess Enquiry Committee, *Report,* vol. 1, p. 136.

115. E. L. Price, "Minute of Dissent," in ibid., vol. 2, p. 132.

116. Letter from J. C. Donaldson, Director of Industries, February 18, 1931, Industries Dept., UPSA.

117. "Notes and Orders," Donaldson, January 21, 1931, Industries Dept., UPSA.

118. Letter from Campbell to Tucker, October 21, 1854, "Papers Relating to the Crime of Cattle Poisoning," *Selections from the Records of the Government of India, 1881,* no. 180, pp. 27–28.

119. Cattle Plague Commission, *Report of the Commissioners,* appendix 4, "Report on Cattle Poisoning," pp. 648–49.

120. Crooke, *Tribes and Castes of the North-Western Provinces and Oudh,* vol. 1, p. 190.

121. Hoey, *A Monograph on Trade and Manufactures in Northern India,* p. 91.

122. Mayer, "Inventing Village Tradition," p. 387.

123. Smith, *Rule by Records,* pp. 61, 74.

124. D. M. Stewart, "Cesses in Oudh, 1922," Revenue (A) Progs., May 1925, UPSA, pp. 2–4.

125. Police Progs., vol. 91, July–December 1889, p. 30; vol. 93, July–December, 1890, p. 67, Police UPSA. See last section of chapter 1.

126. Police Progs., vol. 97, pt. 2, July–December 1892, p. 10; vol. 98, pt. 1, January–June 1893, pp. 41–42.

127. D. M. Stewart, "Cesses in Oudh, 1922," Revenue (A) Progs., May 1925, UPSA, pp. 38–39.

128. Jones, "The Rise and Progress of Cawnpore," p. 495. Jones's family was associated with various trading activities, including the trade in indigo, in Kanpur from the 1820s, and Jones, along with Maxwells and Coopers, moved from trading to industrial entrepreneurship after the Mutiny.

129. Yalland, *Traders and Nabobs,* pp. 223–32.

130. Jones, "The Rise and Progress of Cawnpore," p. 495; Yalland, *Boxwallahs,* p. 127.

131. Yalland, *Boxwallahs,* p. 163.

132. Montgomery, *Statistical Report of the District of Cawnpore*, p. 114.

133. Freemantle, *Report on the Supply of Labour in the United Provinces and Bengal*, p. 2.

134. Royal Commission on Labour in India, *Evidence*, vol. 3, pt. 1, p. 136.

135. Hides Cess Enquiry Committee, *Report*, vol. 1, p. 10.

136. Chaudhuri, "Foreign Trade and Balance of Payments," p. 844.

137. Cattle Plague Commission, *Report of the Commissioners*, appendix 4, "Report on Cattle Poisoning," p. 705.

138. Royal Commission on Labour in India, *Evidence*, vol. 3, pt. 1, p. 10.

139. Tozier, *British India and Its Trade*, p. 2.

140. A. Chatterjee, *Notes on the Industries of the United Provinces*, preface, pp. 103–104.

141. *Report on the Industrial Survey of the Fatehpur District*, 1923, J. S. Vatal, p. 23; *Report on the Industrial Survey of the Rae Bareli District*, 1923, B. K. Ghoshal, p. 27; *Report on the Industrial Survey of the Sultanpur District*, 1923, H. N. Sapru, p. 14; *Report on the Industrial Survey of the Kheri District*, 1923, B. K. Ghoshal, p. 34; *Report on the Industrial Survey of the Muzaffarnagar District*, 1923, M. Zia-Ur-Rub, pp. 14–15.

142. *Papers Relating to the Industrial Conference*, pp. 2, 4, 52.

143. "Chrome Leather Factory in the United Provinces," file no. 518, box no. 105/1908, Industries Dept., UPSA, p. 4.

144. "Boot and shoe-making school," Industries Progs., vol. 3, January–June, 1909, UPSA, pp. 44–45.

145. "Opening of a leather-working school at Meerut," file no. 149, box no. 214/1919, Industries Dept., UPSA, p. 2.

146. Industries Reorganization Committee, *Report*, p. 99.

147. "Establishment of a leather working school at Agra," file no. 175, box no. 260/1925, Industries Dept., UPSA, pp. 4–5.

148. Industries Progs., vol. 42, July–December 1928, Industries Dept., p. 43.

149. A. Chatterjee, *Notes on the Industries of the United Provinces*, p. 104.

150. Industries Reorganization Committee, *Report*, p. 98. Also see "Establishment of a leather working school at Agra," file no. 175, box no. 268/1925, Industries Dept., UPSA, pp. 5–6.

151. "Establishment of a leather working school at Agra," pp. 4–5.

152. Ibid., p. 6.

153. *Report on the Industrial Survey of the Fatehpur District*, 1923, J. S. Vatal, p. 23; *Report on the Industrial Survey of the Rae Bareli District*, 1923, B. K. Ghoshal, p. 27; *Report on the Industrial Survey of the Sultanpur District*, 1923, H. N. Sapru, p. 14.

154. L. Srivastava, *Leather Industry*, p. 4.

155. Industries Progs., vol. 25, January–June 1920, UPSA, p. 43.

156. Industries Progs., vol. 28, July–December 1921, UPSA, p. 8.

157. "Proposal for replacing by a cess the custom duty on export of hides," file no. 588, box no. 292/1928, Industries Dept., UPSA, p. 26.

158. "Report on the working of the Noor-Ul-Uloom, Leather Working School, Bahraich," file no. 731, box No. 412/1937, Industries Dept., UPSA.

159. "Letter from A. N. Sapru, Director of Industries and Commerce," May 1, 1940, file no. 731, box No. 412/1937, Industries Dept., UPSA.

160. Mukhtar, *Report on Labour Conditions*, p. 6.

161. Royal Commission on Labour in India, *Evidence*, vol. 3, pt. 1, pp. 241–49.

162. Mukhtar, *Report on Labour Conditions*, p. 10.

163. "Harijan Udyougshala, Delhi: A Year's Progress," file no. G-35/1937, AICC Papers, NMML, p. 36.

164. "Report on Congress Ministries," file no. 9 (Misc)/1938, AICC Papers, NMML, pp. 48–49.

165. G. Srivastava, *When Congress Ruled,* pp. 13–14.

166. Industrial Committee on Tanneries and Leather Goods Manufactories, *Summary of Proceedings,* p. 21.

167. "Written Evidence by A. Carnegie, Leather Manufacturer, Kanpur," in Indian Industrial Commission, *Minutes of Evidence,* vol. 1, p. 121.

168. Viyougi, *Ambedkar ki Awaz,* p. iii.

4. Struggle for Identities

The first epigraph is from Raghuvanshi, *Shree Chanvar Purana,* p. i. The second epigraph is from Jigyasu, *Bharat ke Adi Nivasiyon ki Sabhyata,* pp. 10–11.

1. Orsini, *The Hindi Public Sphere,* pp. 175–242; Dalmia, "Vernacular Histories in Late Nineteenth-Century Banaras."

2. P. Chatterjee, *The Nation and Its Fragments,* pp. 95–115.

3. Yadvendu, *Yaduvansh ka Aitihas,* p. 157.

4. My most challenging interactions, besides those with my Dalit friends in Delhi, were with Dalit activists in Allahabad. Some of these questions were part of our discussions, especially those concerning the past and present of the Dalits and Hindu academia.

5. Gooptu, *The Politics of the Urban Poor,* pp. 97–100.

6. Briggs, *The Chamars,* p. 20.

7. Guha, *Dominance without Hegemony,* p. 155.

8. Raghuvanshi, *Shree Chanvar Purana,* p. i.

9. Ibid., pp. ii–iii.

10. Ibid., p. 1; Jaiswar Mahasabha, *Suryavansh Kshatriya Jaiswar Sabha,* p. 9.

11. Raghuvanshi, *Shree Chanvar Purana,* pp. 2–4; Jaiswar Mahasabha, *Suryavansh Kshatriya Jaiswar Sabha,* p. 1.

12. Raghuvanshi, *Shree Chanvar Purana,* p. 5.

13. Ibid., pp. 6–12; Jaiswar Mahasabha, *Suryavansh Kshatriya Jaiswar Sabha,* p. 1.

14. Raghuvanshi, *Shree Chanvar Purana,* pp. 14–22; Jaiswar Mahasabha, *Suryavansh Kshatriya Jaiswar Sabha,* pp. 2–6.

15. Raghuvanshi, *Shree Chanvar Purana,* pp. 23–40; Jaiswar Mahasabha, *Suryavansh Kshatriya Jaiswar Sabha,* pp. 6–9.

16. Raghuvanshi, *Shree Chanvar Purana,* pp. 41–42.

17. Ibid., pp. 40–47; Jaiswar Mahasabha, *Suryavansh Kshatriya Jaiswar Sabha,* p. 9.

18. Jaiswar Mahasabha, *Suryavansh Kshatriya Jaiswar Sabha,* pp. 9–10.

19. Sagar, *Yadav Jivan,* pp. 11, 20–40.

20. Ibid., p. 22. Clarke's statement is quoted in English in the Hindi text.

21. Ibid., pp. 21, 31.

22. Ibid., pp. 34–38.

23. Ibid., pp. 22–33.

24. Thapar, "Society and Historical Consciousness," pp. 134–38.

25. Dalmia, "Vernacular Histories in Late Nineteenth-Century Banaras," p. 60.

26. Ibid., p. 78.

27. Harischandra, "Khatriyon ki Utpatti," pp. 251–53, 247–50.

28. Sagar, *Yadav Jivan,* pp. 34–35.

29. *Census of the North-Western Provinces, 1865,* appendix B, pp. 43, 64, 71.

30. Elliot, *Memoirs on the History, Folk-Lore, and Distribution of the Races,* vol. 1, p. 69. See also Crooke, *The Tribes and Castes of the North-Western Provinces and Oudh,* vol. 1, p. 169.

31. Briggs, *The Chamars,* p. 15. See also K. Singh, *The Scheduled Castes,* p. 301.

32. K. Singh, *The Scheduled Castes,* p. 301. See also Lynch, *The Politics of Untouchability,* pp. 28–29.

33. I have made a detailed study of the weekly police reports (officially known as Police Abstracts of Weekly Intelligence, Criminal Investigation Department, Lucknow, Uttar Pradesh) from 1922 to 1928.

34. Sagar, *Yadav Jivan,* pp. 40–41.

35. PAI, March 24, March 31, October 6, 1923; February 23, May 3, May 17, May 24, June 14, September 6, 1924.

36. PAI, March 18, April 22, April 8, 1922.

37. PAI, February 4, November 4, 1922; June 9, January 12, 1923.

38. PAI, January 14, January 28, May 6, May 13, June 17, November 4, 1922; February 23, May 24, June 7, June 14, August 30, October 4, 1924.

39. PAI, February 4, 1922; June 9, 1923.

40. PAI, February 4, July 22, November 4, 1922; June 9, June 28, May 5, 1923; November 20, 1926; August 6, December 24, 1927.

41. Yadvendu, *Yaduvansh ka Aitihas,* p. 140.

42. PAI, January 14, January 28, 1922. These are the first of the weekly Criminal Investigation Department reports in 1922.

43. PAI, February 4, 1922.

44. PAI, May 6, 1922.

45. PAI, June 17, 1922.

46. PAI, June 17, July 22, November 11, 1922; March 24, 1923; August 29, October 10, 1925.

47. PAI, April 22, 1922.

48. Amin, "Agrarian Bases of Nationalist Agitations in India," pp. 106–107.

49. Premchand, *Karmabhoomi,* pp. 168–71.

50. Amin, "Agrarian Bases of Nationalist Agitations in India," pp. 106–107.

51. PAI, February 4, March 25, April 1, April 8, April 22, April 29, May 6, May 13, May 20, June 17, July 22, July 29, August 5, 1922.

52. PAI, January 28, April 1, November 4, 1922, January 20, 1923.

53. PAI, November 4, 1922.

54. PAI, May 24, 1924.

55. PAI, November 4, 1922.

56. PAI, December 24, 1927; January 7, 1928.

57. PAI, December 19, 1923; May 3, May 10, 1924; November 7, 1925; March 27, 1926.

58. PAI, August 7, 1926.

59. PAI, May 6, May 20, June 17, 1922; June 9, 1923.

60. Premchand, *Karmabhoomi,* pp. 152–53.

61. PAI, January 28, May 20, 1921, February 4, March 25, April 1, April 22, April 29, May 6, May 13, June 17, July 22, July 29, August 5, November 4, 1922; January 22, 1923.

62. PAI, October 27, 1923.

63. PAI, May 2, 1924.

64. PAI, March 6, 1926; October 13, 1928.

65. Sagar, *Yadav Jivan*, p. 54; Yadvendu, *Yaduvansh ka Aitihas*, p. 126.

66. *Chand* (Hindi monthly, Allahabad), September 1933.

67. D. M. Stewart, "Cesses in Oudh, 1922," Revenue (A) Progs., May 1925, UPSA, pp. 23–147; V. N. Mehta, "Oudh Kisa Sabha," file no. 753, box no. 6/1920, Revenue Dept., UPSA.

68. "Rasad and Begari Report Agitation in UP, 1920," file no. 694, box no. 153/1920, GAD, UPSA.

69. Premchand, *Premashram*, pp. 155–65.

70. PAI, March 18, 1922.

71. *Pratap*, April 27, 1928.

72. PAI, February 4, 1922; July 12, August 30, 1924; June 17, July 22, 1922; April 19, 1924; May 16, May 23, June 6, 1925; April 7, 1928.

73. PAI, February 11, February 23, May 3, May 10, May 24, 1924; June 4, November 7, December 5, December 19, 1925; March 27, June 19, October 1, December 24, 1927; January 7, 1928.

74. PAI, April 1, May 13, September 30, November 4, 1922; March 24, April 14, June 9, September 29, 1923; May 15, 1926.

75. PAI, September 30, 1922.

76. PAI, May 20, 1922.

77. PAI, April 1, April 22, May 13, September 30, November 4, 1922; March 24, August 18, 1923; October 18, 1924; October 9, 1926.

78. PAI, June 9, 1923.

79. PAI, October 6, 1923.

80. PAI, June 9, 1923.

81. Pinch, *Peasants and Monks in British India*, pp. 82, 93.

82. Gopal Baba Walangkar's 1890 petition cited and discussed in Zelliot, "Dr. Ambedkar and the Mahar Movement," pp. 57–59, 71–72.

83. PAI, November 3, November 10, 1923.

84. Jordens, *Swami Shraddhananda*, pp. 142–43, 154. See also Thursby, *Hindu-Muslim Relations in British India*, p. 167.

85. *Pratap*, March 3, 1924; *Abhyudaya*, May 17, 1924; PAI, March 1, 1924.

86. Jordens, *Swami Shraddhananda*, pp. 142–51; Thursby, *Hindu-Muslim Relations in British India*, pp. 166–69.

87. Baldev Chaube, "The Work of *Achhutuddhar* in the United Provinces," *Pratap*, March 25, 1928.

88. *Abhyudaya*, May 17, June 21, 1924.

89. Gooptu, *The Politics of the Urban Poor*, pp. 151, 144. See also Lynch, *The Politics of Untouchability*, pp. 67–85.

90. Hardiman, *The Coming of the Devi*, pp. 156–65, especially 163–64.

91. Orsini, *The Hindi Public Sphere*, pp. 224–39, 267–74, 351–53. In May 1930, *Chand* acknowledged the historical role of the Arya Samaj in *achhutuddhar*.

92. *Pratap*, April 20, 1925. This is the earliest evidence of the term "Dalit." Vidyarthi's point about *sanatani* religion was reiterated by *Chand* in March 1927.

93. *Chand,* May 1927.

94. *Chand,* May 1930.

95. *Pratap,* June 1, 1925.

96. *Chand,* February 1930.

97. *Pratap,* March 21, 1926.

98. Gooptu, *The Politics of the Urban Poor,* pp. 155–57; Prashad, *Untouchable Freedom,* pp. 66–75; Orsini, *The Hindi Public Sphere,* pp. 203–205; Charu Gupta, "Hindu Women, Muslim Men," pp. 133–34.

99. Prashad, *Untouchable Freedom,* pp. 66–67.

100. Gooptu, *The Politics of the Urban Poor,* pp. 155–56.

101. Lynch, *The Politics of Untouchability,* pp. 67–70.

102. Sagar, *Yadav Jivan,* pp. 2–3; Yadvendu, *Yaduvansh ka Aitihas,* p. 6.

103. Yadvendu, *Yaduvansh ka Aitihas,* p. 140.

104. Duncan, "Levels, the Communication of Programmes, and Sectional Strategies," pp. 265–66.

105. Jatav, *Shri 108 Swami Achhutanand Ji ka Jeevan Parichay,* pp. 11–15; Singh "Raj," *Swami Achhutanand Harihar,* pp. 13–16.

106. Rai, *The Arya Samaj,* p. 232.

107. *Pratap,* March 25, 1928. See also *Abhyudaya,* February 1, 1930.

108. Lynch, *The Politics of Untouchability,* p. 68.

109. Juergensmeyer, *Religion as Social Vision,* p. 38, 67.

110. Ibid., p. 64.

111. Ibid., pp. 37–39; Gooptu, *The Politics of the Urban Poor,* p. 155.

112. Zelliot, "Dr. Ambedkar and the Mahar Movement," pp. 102–17.

113. *Pratap,* April 10, 1927.

114. *Pratap,* July 27, 1925; February 8, 1926; *Abhyudaya,* June 21, 1924.

115. *Abhyudaya,* February 13, May 8, June 19, 1926.

116. PAI, January 20, April 14, May 5, May 26, June 2, June 9, June 16, June 26, June 30, October 20, October 27, 1923; February 9, March 1, April 5, April 19, May 3, May 10, May 17, August 26, September 9, September 13, 1924; May 23, August 1, August 15, October 17, December 19, 1925; February 13, May 15, May 29, June 26, July 24, October 9, November 16, 1926; April 23, October 1, 1927; July 21, August 18, October 13, 1928. The records indicate the peak of Arya Samaj activities and a decline from 1926 onward.

117. PAI, April 14, May 5, 1923; *Pratap,* March 3, 1924.

118. *Chand,* March 1927.

119. *Pratap,* March 24, August 11, 1924; *Abhyudaya,* August 16, 1924; March 31, 1928.

120. PAI, March 10, November 3, 1923; April 5, October 18, October 25, 1924; April 2, October 8, 1927.

121. PAI, June 7, 1923.

122. PAI, November 3, 1923; February 23, 1924.

123. PAI, February 23, 1924.

124. PAI, October 9, 1926.

125. PAI, April 21, 1928.

126. PAI, March 17, 1923; February 2, 1924; January 10, 1925; September 26, March 27, 1926.

127. Hazari, *I Was an Outcaste.* According to its preface, the book was written in 1935.

128. PAI, April 14, May 5, May 26, November 24, 1923; June 7, 1924.

129. Thursby, *Hindu-Muslim Relations in British India,* p. 154.

130. PAI, March 1, October 10, 1925.

131. *Pratap*, May 18, June 1, 1925; PAI, May 16, May 23, June 6, 1925.

132. Rai, *The Arya Samaj*, p. 231.

133. PAI, March 10, November 3, 1923; April 5, October 18, October 25, 1924; April 2, October 8, 1927.

134. PAI, October 4, 1924; Premchand, *Karmabhoomi*, pp. 193–206.

135. PAI, April 21, 1923; *Pratap*, January 9, 1927.

136. PAI, May 5, 1923.

137. PAI, May 5, October 20, 1923; August 15, 1925.

138. PAI, September 20, 1924; *Pratap*, July 27, 1925; February 8, 1926; *Abhyudaya*, March 3, 1928.

139. PAI, March 10, 1923.

140. PAI, March 31, April 7, 1928.

141. PAI, October 17, December 19, 1925; February 13, June 26, 1926. These include reports from Meerut, Saharanpur, Muzaffarnagar, Moradabad, and Gorakhpur.

142. PAI, June 16, 1923.

143. PAI, June 4, October 1, 1927; September 13, 1924.

144. PAI, August 1, 1925.

145. PAI, March 31, 1923.

146. *Abhyudaya*, August 2, 1924; February 4, 1926; Premchand, *Karmabhoomi*, pp. 169–72.

147. *Pratap*, April 27, 1925.

148. Jatav, *Shri 108 Swami Achhutanand Ji ka Jeevan Parichay*, p. 14; Singh "Raj," *Achhutanand Harihar*, p. 41.

149. PAI, April 23, July 10, 1926.

150. Jigyasu, *Bharat ke Adi Nivasiyon ki Sabhyata*, p. 9.

151. Ibid., pp. 11, 10.

152. Ibid., p. 9.

153. Ibid., pp. 45–46, 74–75, 65–69.

154. Ibid., pp. 11–13.

155. Ibid., pp. 26–35.

156. Jatav, *Shri 108 Swami Achhutanand Ji ka Jeevan Parichay*, p. 14. See also Singh "Raj," *Swami Achhutanand Harihar*, p. 41.

157. Jatav, *Shri 108 Swami Achhutanand Ji ka Jeevan Parichay*, p. 14.

158. PAI, April 23, 1926.

159. *Abhyudaya*, April 24, 1926.

160. PAI, April 23, 1926.

161. *Abhyudaya*, April 24, 1926.

162. *Abhyudaya*, April 14, 1928.

163. *Abhyudaya*, April 24, 1926.

164. PAI, July 10, 1926.

165. *The Leader*, April 14, 1926.

166. *Pratap*, January 8, 1928; *Aaj*, January 1, 1928; *Chand*, February 1928; *Abhyudaya*, April 14, 1928.

167. *Pratap*, October 13, 1928.

168. PAI, April 7, April 28, May 5, June 23, October 13, December 8, 1928; January 19, June 8, June 22, August 31, October 5, October 26, 1929.

169. *Pratap*, November 24, 1924.

170. PAI, May 17, 1924.

171. PAI, April 23, 1927; April 21, 1928.

172. PAI, June 4, 1927.

173. PAI, March 31, April 7, 1928.

174. Lala Lajpat Rai, *"Achhut* bhaiyon! Sarkari Jaal Mein Mat Fason" (*Achhut* brothers! Don't get trapped in the government's web), *Pratap*, April 1, 1928.

175. *Pratap*, January 8, 1928.

176. *Abhyudaya*, April 14, 1928.

177. *Chand*, February 1928.

5. From Chamars to Dalits

The first epigraph is from Ganesh Shankar Vidyarthi, "Adi-Hindu Andoolan," *Pratap*, January 8, 1928. The second epigraph is from "Memorial Address to the Honourable Chairman and Members of the Statutory Commission" by the members of the Uttar Pradesh Adi-Hindu Sabha, November 30, 1928, emphasis in the original, file no. 566/1928, box no. 503, GAD (1901–47), UPSA.

1. Sarkar, *Modern India,* chapter 5. Sarkar's work remains the best survey, but see also Pandey, *The Construction of Communalism,* chapter 7.

2. Sarkar, *Modern India,* p. 329.

3. Jaffrelot, *India's Silent Revolution,* 8, 185.

4. Some representative works are Mendelsohn and Vicziany, *The Untouchables;* Omvedt, *Cultural Revolt in a Colonial Society;* Keer, *Dr. Ambedkar.*

5. S. Bayly, *Caste, Society and Politics in India,* p. 233. See Bayly's discussion in chapter 6.

6. Mendelsohn and Vicziany, *The Untouchables,* pp. 88–92, 96–117.

7. Omvedt, *Dalits and the Democratic Revolution,* p. 139. There are two references to Achhutanand.

8. Mendelsohn and Vicziany, *The Untouchables,* p. 81.

9. Pai, *Dalit Assertion and the Unfinished Democratic Revolution,* pp. 27–41.

10. Lynch, *The Politics of Untouchability;* Gooptu, *The Politics of the Urban Poor.*

11. Briggs, *The Chamars;* Cohn, *An Anthropologist among the Historians.*

12. Shastri, *Poona Pact banam Gandhi;* Viyougi, *Ambedkar ki Awaz;* Jigyasu, *Bharat ke Adi Nivasiyon ki Sabhyata;* Jigyasu, *Shri 108 Swami Achhutanandji "Harihar";* Jatav, *Achhutanand Ji ka Jeevan Parichay;* Singh "Raj," *Swami Achhutanand Harihar.*

13. Rawat, "Making Claims for Power," p. 586.

14. *Chand,* February 1928; *Abhyudaya,* March 3, 1928. See also *Pratap,* April 8, 1928; October 13, 1929; *Chand,* February 1928; *Abhyudaya,* March 3, 1928; April 14, 1928; *Aaj,* January 1, 1928.

15. Blunt's report is quoted in the letter of J. M. Clay, Secretary to Uttar Pradesh Government, to the Secretary of Indian Franchise Commission, April 8, 1932, series Q, Indian Delimitation Committee, vol. 14, OIOC. A widely respected officer of the civil service, Blunt was commissioner of the 1911 census of the United Provinces, published a monograph on the subject of the caste system of North India, authored parts of the Basti settlement report in 1916–17, and went on to become the secretary of Uttar Pradesh.

16. The following account of the conference is based on "Report of the All-India Adi-Hindu Conference," January 7, 1928, submitted to the Simon Commission, Appendix: List of Memoranda, Evidence, UP/427, Report on United Provinces, 3 vols., Indian Statutory (Simon) Commission, OIOC. Quotations are taken from this report unless otherwise cited.

17. " Report of the All-India Adi-Hindu Conference," January 7, 1928, Resolution No. 2, Evidence, UP/427, OIOC.

18. "Report of the All-India Adi-Hindu Conference," January 7, 1928, Evidence, UP/427, OIOC; *Chand,* February 1928.

19. "Memorandum from All-India Adi-Hindu Mahasabha," Kanpur, May 25, 1928, Evidence, UP/427, OIOC.

20. "Memorial Address to the Statutory Commission," UP Adi-Hindu Mahasabha, November 30, 1928 file no. 566, box no. 503/1928, UPSA.

21. "Presidential Address by Rama Charana Mallah delivered at the Special Session of the 'Audi Hindu' Aborigines Conference," Lucknow, January 29, 1928; Memorandum from Rama Charana, B.A., LL.B., Advocate to the Chief Court of Oudh and M.L.C. (Uttar Pradesh), Evidence, UP/118, OIOC.

22. "Supplementary Memorandum submitted by Rama Charana," Evidence, UP/118, OIOC.

23. For a recent example see Gooptu, *The Politics of the Urban Poor,* pp. 161–66.

24. "Memorial Address," Uttar Pradesh Adi-Hindu Mahasabha, November 30, 1928, UPSA.

25. "Memorandum of All India Shri Jatav Mahasabha," 1928, submitted by Babu Khem Chand, President of the Mahasabha, Evidence, UP/425, OIOC.

26. Ibid.

27. "Memorandum from Ram Prasad Ahir, Pleader, Sultanpur," January 29, 1928, Evidence, UP/455, OIOC.

28. Moore, *Escape From Empire,* p. 2. Almost all these memoranda and petitions are part of John Simon's private papers in MSS Eur. F.77, Simon Collection, OIOC. The representations from the United Provinces are catalogued in MSS Eur. F.77/138 and 77/141.

29. "Memorial from the UP Addharm (Aborigines) Sabha," Dehra Dun (1928), Evidence, UP/334, OIOC.

30. "Memorandum submitted by Munshi Hari Tamta, Chairman of the Kumaon Shilpkar Sabha," Almora, UP, Evidence, UP/429, OIOC.

31. "Memorandum of All India Shri Jatav Mahasabha," (1928) submitted by Babu Khem Chand, Almora, UP, Evidence, UP/429, OIOC.

32. Yadvendu, *Yaduvansh ka Aitihas,* p. 138.

33. "Memorandum," Arjun Deo, President, Dom Sudhar Sabha, Garhwal, UP, July 18, 1928, Evidence, UP/652, OIOC.

34. "Memorandum from the Chamars (Cobblers) of Cawnpore," 1928, Evidence, UP/659, OIOC.

35. Moore, *Crisis of Indian Unity,* p. 108.

36. Zelliot, "Dr. Ambedkar and the Mahar Movement," p. 168.

37. Moore, *Crisis of Indian Unity,* p. 34.

38. For a discussion of these issues see Sarkar, *Modern India,* pp. 261–66.

39. File no. 380, box no. 119/1932, GAD, UPSA.

40. PAI, October 30, 1926. Despite my best efforts, I have not been able to find copies of this newspaper.

41. PAI, December 17, 1927.

42. PAI, November 19, November 26, December 10, 1927; February 25, February 21, April 28, May 23, June 23, August 25, 1928.

43. PAI, February 18, 1927.

44. PAI, March 24, 1928.

45. "Simon Commission's Visit to Agra, Kanpur and Lucknow in UP," file no. 566, box no. 503/1928, GAD, UPSA.

46. PAI, March 3, April 21, 1928; January 19, 1929.

47. Sarkar, *Modern India,* pp. 263–64.

48. Zelliot, "Dr. Ambedkar and the Mahar Movement," pp. 174–75.

49. PAI, October 5, 1929; May 23, 1931.

50. PAI, October 3, 1931.

51. Ibid. Jigyasu was also the author of many books on the Adi-Hindu movement.

52. PAI, December 12, June 20, 1931; January 30, March 19, June 18, October 8, 1932.

53. PAI, December 19, 1931. According to Zelliot, Ambedkar read this cable, among others, at the Round Table Conference to argue that Dalits did not support Gandhi. Zelliot, "Dr. Ambedkar and the Mahar Movement," p. 179.

54. PAI, January 9, March 26, 1932.

55. Juergensmeyer, *Religion as Social Vision,* chapter 12 on Ad Dharma's opposition to the Congress and Gandhi, p. 127; Bandyopadhyay, *Caste, Protest and Identity in Colonial India,* pp. 153–57.

56. PAI, November 7, November 21, 1931.

57. PAI, July 2, 1932.

58. PAI, July 25, 1931; March 12, 1932.

59. PAI, September 24, October 22, 1932.

60. PAI, January 9, 1932.

61. For discussions of the Round Table Conferences from the British point of view see, Moore, *Crisis of Indian Unity,* chapters 2, 3, and 4; for the Congress point of view see Sarkar, *Modern India,* pp. 261–66, 308–11, 318–20; and for the Dalit point view see Zelliot, "Dr. Ambedkar and the Mahar Movement," pp. 167–82.

62. Moore, *Crisis of Indian Unity,* p. 265.

63. On implications of the Poona Pact, see Rawat, "Making Claims for Power," pp. 604–12.

64. Nehru, *An Autobiography,* pp. 370–71.

65. Pyarelal, *The Epic Fast,* p. 99.

66. PAI, October 1, October 8, October 15, 1932; these three rather long weekly reports on Gandhi's fast give details of activities in all parts of Uttar Pradesh.

67. PAI, September 24, October 1, October 8, October 15, 1932.

68. PAI, February 11, 1933.

69. Zelliot, "Dr. Ambedkar and the Mahar Movement," p. 202.

70. *Chand,* January 1930.

71. *Chand,* August 1934.

72. Shastri, *Poona Pact banam Gandhi,* pp. 35–36.

73. Ibid., pp. 24–26.

74. PAI, June 3, June 10, July 1, October 7, November 11, 1933; January 20, January 27, February 3, 1934; January 19, January 26, February 9, February 16, February 23, March 2, March 9, July 6, August 3, September 7, September 28, October 12, 1935; June 6, 1936.

75. PAI, May 20, 1933.

76. PAI, October 1, 1932.

77. PAI, October 1, October 8, October 15, 1932.

78. PAI, October 8, 1932.

79. Ibid.

80. PAI, October 22, 1932.

81. PAI, April 16, April 23, 1938.

82. PAI, April 23, May 21, June 4, June 18, June 25, July 9, July 23, August 6, August 13, August 20, September 3, September 10, September 17, October 1, October 15, October 22, October 29, November 19, November 26, December 3, December 10, December 24, 1938; February 4, February 11, April 29, May 13, May 27, June 3, June 10, June 17, July 22, 1939.

83. Shastri, *Poona Pact banam Gandhi,* p. 25.

84. PAI, April 16, August 6, October 1, October 8, 1938.

85. PAI, July 23, July 6, July 13, July 20, August 27, September 3, September 10, September 17, September 24, October 1, October 15, October 22, October 29, November 19, November 26, December 3, December 10, December 24, 1938.

86. Sarkar, *Modern India,* pp. 353–56.

87. PAI, August 6, 1938.

88. PAI, April 9, 1938.

89. PAI, October 27, 1934.

90. PAI, September 24, October 22, 1938; February 4, 1939.

91. PAI, August 29, 1941.

92. See, for example, G. Srivastava, *When Congress Ruled;* Nehru, *An Autobiography;* Kesavan, *Congress and the Muslims of UP and Bihar.*

93. Chatterji, *Towards Freedom,* pp. 174–75.

94. Shastri, *Poona Pact banam Gandhi,* p. 9; Viyougi, *Ambedkar ki Awaz,* pp. 11–12.

95. Shastri, *Poona Pact banam Gandhi,* pp. 83–86, 99.

96. Viyougi, *Ambedkar ki Awaz,* p. 33.

97. Shastri, *Poona Pact banam Gandhi,* p. 76.

98. Ibid., pp. 91–93.

99. Viyougi, *Ambedkar ki Awaz,* pp. 50, 62–65; Shastri, *Poona Pact banam Gandhi,* p. 15.

100. "Request from the Scheduled Castes of UP," file no. 41/4/47-R, Reforms Office, NAI.

101. File no. ED/1/KW-II/1946, AICC papers, NMML.

102. *The Pioneer,* July 25, 1946; Shastri, *Poona Pact banam Gandhi,* p. 50.

103. Viyougi, *Ambedkar ki Awaz,* p. 11. See also Juergensmeyer, *Religion as Social Vision,* pp. 161–63; Dube, *Untouchable Pasts,* pp. 177–81; Bandyopadhyay, *Caste, Protest and Identity in Colonial India,* pp. 202–208.

104. File no. 164, box no. 370/1946, Harijan Sahayak Dept., UPSA.

105. PAI for years of 1945 and 1946.

106. Reeves et al., *A Handbook to Elections,* pp. 318–19.

107. On the electoral system in Dalit constituencies see Rawat, "Making Claims for Power," pp. 604–12.

108. Nandlal Viyougi, *Ambedkar ki Awaz*, p. 12.

109. Based on PAI reports for 1946.

110. The account is based on reports from *The Pioneer*, July 16, August 16–30, 1946; PAI, July 5, July 26, August 2, August 9, August 16, August 23, September 6, 1946.

111. PAI, February 8, June 21, June 27, July 5, July 26, August 2, August 9, August 16, August 23, September 6, 1946.

112. PAI, February 8, July 26, November 8, 1946.

113. PAI, April 26, June 26, July 26, August 30, September 6, September 20, September 27, November 1, 1946.

114. PAI, February 8, March 29, June 26, July 5, July 26, August 9, August 16, August 23, September 13, September 20, September 27, 1947.

115. *The Dawn*, March 6, 1947; *The Pioneer*, March 9, 1947.

116. *The Pioneer*, March 26, March 30, 1947.

117. *The Dawn*, April 28, 1947.

118. *The Pioneer*, April 25, 1947; Fortnightly Reports of United Provinces, file no. 18/4/1947, Home Dept. (Political), NAI.

119. *The Dawn*, April 28, 1947.

120. File no. P-19/1945–46, Uttar Pradesh Provincial Congress Committee, AICC Papers, NMML.

121. *Proceedings of the Uttar Pradesh Legislative Assembly*, vol. 26 (January 11, 1947), pp. 629–31.

122. Ibid., vol. 38 (April 25, 1947), pp. 27–29.

123. Ibid., vol. 33 (March 24, 1947), pp. 344–47, 558, 572–93; vol. 27 (February 10, 1947), pp. 2117–30.

124. Ibid., vol. 35 (April 8, 1947), pp. 538–41.

125. File no. F-175/1946, box no. 20, Harijan Sahayak Dept., UPSA.

126. File no. F-175/1947, box no. 20, Harijan Sahayak Dept., UPSA.

127. *Proceedings of the Uttar Pradesh Legislative Assembly*, vol. 31 (March 14, 1947), pp. 42–45.

128. PAI, March 29, April 19, April 26, 1946.

129. PAI, September 20, August 30, 1946.

130. PAI, October 18, October 25, November 8, 1946.

131. Jigyasu, *Bhartiya Republican Party*, p. 3.

132. Mendelsohn and Vicziany, *The Untouchables*, p. 212.

133. Keer, *Dr. Ambedkar*, pp. 499–500.

134. Lohia, *The Caste System*, pp. 33–36.

135. *The Pioneer*, July 2, 1947.

136. *The Pioneer*, May 10, 1947.

137. Kshirsagar, *Dalit Movement and Its Leaders*, pp. 230–32, 253–58.

138. *National Herald*, April 26, 1948.

139. *The Leader*, April 26, 1948. See also Shastri, *Poona Pact banam Gandhi*, pp. 147–48.

140. *National Herald*, April 26, 1948.

141. Shastri, *Poona Pact banam Gandhi*, p. 147.

142. Pai, *Dalit Assertion and the Unfinished Democratic Revolution*, p. 74; Zelliot, "Congress and the Untouchables," p. 193.

143. Zelliot, "Dr. Ambedkar and the Mahar Movement," p. 246.

144. N. Sharma, *Jagjivan Ram*, pp. 127, 132; *Hindustan Times*, June 18, 1945.

145. "Request from the Scheduled Castes of UP," file no. 41/4/4/47-R, Reforms Office, NAI.

146. PAI, September 28, 1948.

147. PAI, June 18, 1948.

148. Jigyasu, *Bharatiya Republican Party,* pp. 2–3, 7; Shastri, *Poona Pact banam Gandhi,* pp. 187–88.

149. Lynch, *The Politics of Untouchability,* p. 113; see generally pp. 93–120.

150. Khare, *The Untouchable as Himself,* introduction.

151. Republican Party of India, *Charter of Demands.*

152. Shastri, *Poona Pact banam Gandhi,* pp. 187–89.

153. Khobragade, *Report of the General Secretary,* p. 2. For Punjab see Juergensmeyer, *Religion as Social Vision,* p. 165.

154. *Hindustan Times,* January 13, January 17, 1965.

155. Duncan, "Levels, The Communication of Programmes, and Sectional Strategies," p. 287.

156. Quoted in ibid.

157. Election Commission, *Report on the Third General Elections,* vol. 2, pp. 6–7, 12–13, 80–81, 84–85.

158. Duncan, "Levels, The Communication of Programmes, and Sectional Strategies," pp. 271–73. As *maurusi* tenants the Chamars held 10 percent of the rented land in Aligarh. *Final Settlement Report of the Aligarh District,* 1903, W. J. D. Burkitt, p. 8.

BIBLIOGRAPHY

Archival Material
Official Manuscript Sources

UTTAR PRADESH STATE ARCHIVES, LUCKNOW

Files and Proceedings of the Government of the North-Western Provinces of Agra and Oudh, United Provinces of Agra and Oudh, United Provinces: General Administration (GAD) (1860–1900 and 1900–1947), Police (1860–1910), Political (1860–1910), Judicial Civil (1860–1910), Judicial Criminal (1860–1910), Industries (1908–1932), Finance (A) (1860–1936), Revenue Department (1902–1939), Finance Departments (1860–1936), Industries (1907–1936), Mutiny and Pre-Mutiny Records of Revenue Proceedings, Revenue Block Series (various years), Board of Revenue Different Districts Series and Oudh General series, GAD Block, Financial and Commerce Department (Separate Revenue-A series) (1895–1905), Various Departments, Revenue and Scarcity Department (1860–1933), Agriculture Department, Irrigation Department, Municipal Department, Harijan Sahayak Department, Reforms Department (1932–1939), Legislative Department, Register of Intending Emigrants, Board of Revenue: Files of Oudh General and Districts, Files of NWP Different Districts, Revenue Department, Village statements.

CRIMINAL INVESTIGATION DEPARTMENT, LUCKNOW

Weekly Police Abstracts of Intelligence of the Government of the Uttar Pradesh (1921–1948).

UTTAR PRADESH STATE REGIONAL ARCHIVES, ALLAHABAD

Pre-Mutiny Records in the Collectorate of Gorakhpur: Letters issued and received (1833–1858).

Pre-Mutiny Records in the Collectorate of Benares: Letters issued and received (1831–1858), Educational correspondence (1843–1850), Letters issued and received (series 1–3, 1799–1855), miscellaneous files.

Pre-Mutiny Records in the Commissioner's Office of Benares (Duncan Records) (1788–1858): Residents Proceedings (May 1788–October 1793), Letters issued and received (1853–1856), Village statements, Judicial Despatch Register (1850–1857), Benares revenue files, Jaunpur judicial files (1830–1857).

Pre-Mutiny Records in the Commissioner's Office of Gorakhpur: Azamgarh judicial files, Gorakhpur district files, miscellaneous files (1823–1856).

Pre-Mutiny Records in the Commissioner's Office of Agra: Customs correspondence of letters issued and received (1817–1848), Agra judicial files (1848–1868), Miscellaneous files (1814–1841), Agra revenue files (1840–1853).

Pre-Mutiny Records in the Commissioner's Office Allahabad: Custom and revenue correspondence of various districts in 1801–1857 and 1803–1840.

NATIONAL ARCHIVES OF INDIA, DELHI

Files and Proceedings of the Government of India: Home Department, Home Judicial, Home Political, Home Public, Home Legislative, Commerce and Industry Department (1905–1920), Labour, Military, Fortnightly Reports on political situation in India (1917–1924 and 1944–1945).

ORIENTAL AND INDIA OFFICE COLLECTION, BRITISH LIBRARY, LONDON

Proceedings and Consultations of Uttar Pradesh (1834–1943): Agra judicial proceedings, NWP judicial proceedings, Agra Sudder Board of Revenue (Custom) proceedings, NWP Sudder Board of Revenue (Custom) proceedings, NWP judicial proceedings, Public and Judicial Papers series, Constitutional Reforms; Indian Statutory Commission proceedings (1927–1930), Q series of Committees and Commissions, Acts and Codes, Military Department Records (1830–1880 and 1910–1922), Official Publications: Law Reports (annual volumes), Selection from the Records, Indian Departmental Series, Uttar Pradesh Department of Agricultural Bulletin, Bengal Industries Department Bulletin, Committees and Commissions.

BOARD OF REVENUE LIBRARY, LUCKNOW

Settlement Reports of the districts of Uttar Pradesh (1830–1945—complete series), Assessment Reports and Rent-Rate Reports of Parganas and *tahsils* of the districts of Uttar Pradesh, Annual Volumes of trade reports of Uttar Pradesh for various years, Annual Volumes of foreign trade of Uttar Pradesh for various years, Volumes of District Industrial Surveys of Uttar Pradesh, Annual Volumes of foreign trade of India for various years, Inquiries and reports relating to land and agriculture.

Uttar Pradesh State Secretariat Records Library, Lucknow: Proceedings and volumes of Gazetteers, Criminal Justice of Agra and Oudh, Land Records, Agriculture, Royal Commissions, Tribe and Caste, Customs, Revenue List, Annual Revenue administration reports.

Non-official Manuscript Sources

NEHRU MEMORIAL MUSEUM AND LIBRARY, NEW DELHI

All India Congress Committee Papers (AICC).
Peasant Movement (1929–1949).
Rajbhoj, P. N. Papers (1956–1962).
Ramchandra, Baba. Papers (1914–1950).
Uttar Pradesh Congress Committee Papers (Uttar Pradesh CC).
Vidyarthi, Ganesh Shankar. Papers (1919–1930).

ORIENTAL AND INDIA OFFICE COLLECTION, BRITISH LIBRARY, LONDON

Buchanan-Hamilton, Francis. MS Eur. D.91–92, 93, 88–90.
Campbell Collection. MSS Eur. E.349.
Dufferin Collection. MSS Eur. F.130.
Elliot, Henry. Collection. MSS Eur. J.671–83.
Hartog Collection. MSS Eur. E.221.
Lawrence, Henry. Collection. MSS Eur. F.85.

Risley Collection. MSS Eur. E.295, K.532–36, J.734–35.
Simon Collection. MSS Eur. F.77/138–45.

Printed Sources
Official

GENERAL

Agricultural Labour Enquiry: Report on Intensive Survey of Agricultural Labour, Vol. II—
North India. Delhi: Manager of Publications Government of India, 1955.

Agricultural Statistics of British India. (1884–1900, title varies.) Allahabad: North-Western
Provinces and Oudh Government Press, 1884–1900.

Annual Report of the Foreign Trade of North-Western Provinces and Oudh. (1876–1921; title
varies.) Allahabad: North-Western Provinces and Oudh Government Press, 1876–
1900; Superintendent of Government Press, United Provinces, 1901–1921.

Annual Report of the Inland Trade of North-Western Provinces and Oudh. (1877–1921; title
varies.) Allahabad: North-Western Provinces and Oudh Government Press, 1876–
1900; Superintendent of Government Press, United Provinces, 1901–1921.

Annual Report of the Rail-Borne Traffic of the North-Western Provinces and Oudh, 1890. Allahabad: North-Western Provinces and Oudh Government Press, 1890.

Annual Statement of the Sea-Borne Trade and Navigation of the Bengal Presidency. (1880–
1900; title varies.) Calcutta: Superintendent of Government Printing, 1880–1900.

Blunt, E. A. H. *The Caste System of Northern India: With Special Reference to the United
Provinces of Agra and Oudh.* Allahabad: Superintendent of Government Press,
United Provinces, 1931.

Cattle Plague Commission. *Report of the Commissioners Appointed to Inquire into the Origin, Nature, etc. of Indian Cattle Plagues.* Calcutta: Superintendent of Printing, Government of India, 1871.

Census of India, 1881, vol. 17, pt. 1, *Report, North West Provinces and Oudh.* Allahabad:
North-Western Provinces and Oudh Government Press, 1882.

Census of India, 1891, vol. 9, pt. 16, *Report, North-West Provinces and Oudh.* Allahabad:
North-Western Provinces and Oudh Government Press, 1891.

Census of India, 1901, vol. 16, pt. 1, *Report, North West Provinces and Oudh.* Allahabad: Superintendent of Government Press United Provinces, 1902.

Census of India, 1911, vol. 15, pt. 1, *Report,* and pt. 2, *Tables, United Provinces of Agra and
Oudh.* Allahabad: Superintendent of Government Press United Provinces, 1912.

Census of India, 1921, vol. 16, pt. 1, *Report,* and pt. 2, *Tables, United Provinces of Agra and
Oudh.* Allahabad: Superintendent of Government Press, 1923.

Census of India, 1931, vol. 18, pt. 1, *Report,* and pt. 2, *Tables, United Provinces of Agra and
Oudh.* Allahabad: Superintendent of Government Press, United Provinces, 1931.

Census of India, 1941, vol. 5, *United Provinces of Agra and Oudh.* Simla: Manager of Publications, Government of India, 1942.

Census of India, 1961, vol. 15, pt. 5A(i), *Special Tables for Scheduled Castes.* 2 vols. Delhi:
Manager of Publications Government of India, 1965.

Census of India, 2001, Series 1: India. Delhi: Controller of Publications, 2003. http://www
.censusindia.gov.in/Census_Data_2001/index.html (accessed May 28, 2009).

Census of the North-Western Provinces, 1865, vol. 1, *General Report and Appendices A, B, C, D.* Allahabad: Superintendent of Government Press, North-Western Provinces, 1867.

Census of the North-Western Provinces, 1872, vol. 1, *General Report.* Allahabad: Superintendent of Government Press North-Western Provinces, 1873.

Chandra, Rowland N. L. *Monograph on Tanning and Working in Leather in the Province of Bengal.* Calcutta: Secretariat Press, 1904.

Chatterjee, A. C. *Notes on the Industries of the United Provinces.* Allahabad: Superintendent of Government Press, 1908.

Chatterton, A. C. *A Monograph on Tanning and Working in Leather in the Madras Presidency.* Madras: Government Central Press, 1904.

Chenevix-Trench, C. G. *A Monograph on Tanning and Working in Leather in the Central Provinces.* Nagpur: Secretariat Press, 1904.

A Collection of Papers Connected with an Inquiry into the Conditions of the Lower Classes of the Population, Especially in Agricultural Tracts, in the North-Western Provinces and Oudh, Instituted in 1887–88. Allahabad: North-Western Provinces and Oudh Government Press, 1888.

Collection of Papers Relating to the Conditions of the Tenantry and the Working of Present Rent Law in Oudh. Allahabad: North-Western Provinces and Oudh Government Press, 1883.

Congress Labour Enquiry Committee. *Report of the Congress Labour Enquiry Committee.* In *Dr. Rajendra Prasad: Correspondence and Select Documents,* vol. 2, ed. Valmiki Choudhary. Delhi: Allied Publishers, 1984.

Crooke, William. *A Glossary of North Indian Peasant Life.* Edited by Shahid Amin. Delhi: Oxford University Press, 1989.

———. *An Introduction to the Popular Religion and Folklore of North India.* Allahabad: North-Western Provinces and Oudh Government Press, 1893.

———. *A Rural and Agricultural Glossary for the North-Western Provinces and Oudh.* Calcutta: Superintendent of Government Printing, 1888.

———. *The Tribes and Castes of the North-Western Provinces and Oudh.* 4 vols. Calcutta: Superintendent of Government Printing, 1896.

Crooke, W., G. R. Dampier, and H. C. A. Conybeare. *A Note on the Tract of Country South of the River Son in the Mirzapur District, N.W. Provinces.* Allahabad: North-Western Provinces and Oudh Government Press, 1894.

Deewar, D. *A Handbook to the English Pre-Mutiny Records in the Government Record Rooms of the United Provinces of Agra and Oudh.* Allahabad: Superintendent of Government Press, United Provinces, 1919.

Directorate of Marketing and Inspection. *Report on the Marketing of Hides in India and Burma: Agricultural Marketing in India.* Delhi: Manager of Publications, Government of India, 1943.

Dutta, J. N. *The Bundelkhand Alienation of Land Act (No. 2 of 1903).* Allahabad: Superintendent of Government Press, United Provinces, 1929.

Election Commission. *Report on the Third General Elections in India, 1962.* Vol. 2. Delhi: Manager of Publications, Government of India, 1963.

Freemantle, S. H. *Report on the Supply of Labour in the United Provinces and Bengal.* Nanital: Superintendent of Government Press, United Provinces, 1906.

Further Papers Relating to Under-Proprietary Rights and Rights of Cultivators in Oude. Calcutta: Foreign Department Press, 1867.

Hadi, Saiyid Muhammad. "A Note on Breeds of Cattle in the District of Bahraich (Oudh)." *Department of Land Records and Agriculture Bulletins.* Allahabad: North-Western Provinces and Oudh Government Press, 1895.

Hides Cess Enquiry Committee. *Report of the Hides Cess Enquiry Committee, 21st October 1929–18th February 1930.* 2 vols. Calcutta: Superintendent of Printing, Government of India, 1930.

Holmes, J. D. E. "A Note on Some Interesting Results following the Internal Administration of Arsenic in Canker and Other Diseases of the Foot in Horses." Agricultural Research Institute Bulletins, Pusa. Calcutta: Superintendent of Printing, Government of India, 1912.

Indian Industrial Commission. *Minutes of Evidence.* Vol. 4, *Bombay.* Calcutta: Superintendent of Printing, Government of India, 1919.

———. *Report.* Calcutta: Superintendent of Printing, Government of India, 1918.

Industrial Committee on Tanneries and Leather Goods Manufactories, Ministry of Labour. *Summary of Proceedings of the Industrial Committee on Tanneries and Leather Goods Manufactories.* Delhi: Manager of Publications, Government of India, 1949.

Industries Reorganization Committee. *Report of the Industries Reorganization Committee, 1934.* Allahabad: Superintendent of Government Press, United Provinces, 1934.

Martin, J. R. *Monograph on Tanning and Working in Leather in the Bombay Presidency.* Bombay: Government Central Press, 1903.

Mathur, Jai Krishna. "The Pressure of Population: Its Effects on Rural Economy in Gorakhpur District." Department of Agriculture Bulletins. Allahabad: Superintendent of Government Press, United Provinces, 1931.

Mehta, V. N. *Agricultural Sayings of the United Provinces.* Allahabad: Superintendent of Government Press, United Provinces, 1926.

———. *Report on the Cesses in Partabgarh District.* Allahabad: Superintendent of Government Press, United Provinces, 1922.

Misra, Babu Ram. "Economic Survey of a Village in Cawnpore District." Department of Agriculture Bulletins. Allahabad: Superintendent of Government Press, United Provinces, 1932.

Misra, Bholanath. "Over-Population in Jaunpur." Department of Agriculture Bulletins. Allahabad: Superintendent of Government Press, United Provinces, 1932.

Montgomery, Robert. *Statistical Report of the District of Cawnpore.* Calcutta: Bengal Military Orphan Press, 1849.

Moreland, William H. *The Revenue Administration of the United Provinces.* Allahabad: Superintendent of Government Press, United Provinces, 1911.

Mudie, R. F. *Cultivators' Debt in the Agra District.* Allahabad: Superintendent of Government Press, United Provinces, 1931.

Mukhtar, Ahmad. *Report on Labour Conditions in Tanneries and Leather Goods Factories.* Simla: Manager of Publications, Government of India, 1946.

Nesfield, J. S. *Brief View of the Caste System of the North-Western Provinces and Oudh.* Allahabad: North-Western Provinces and Oudh Government Press, 1882.

Notes on Tenant-Right, On Rights to Sub-settlement, and on Rights of Jagheerdars. Allahabad: Superintendent of Government Press, North-Western Provinces, 1869.

Papers Relating to the Industrial Conference. Nainital: Superintendent of Government Press, United Provinces, 1907.

Papers Relating to Under-Proprietary Rights and Rights of Cultivators in Oude. Calcutta: Bengal Military Orphan Press, 1865.

Proceedings of the Uttar Pradesh Legislative Assembly. Vols. 26–38 (January 11–April 25, 1947). Allahabad, 1948.

Review of the Trade of India. (1880–1921, title varies.) Simla: Manager of Publications Government of India, 1880–1921.

Royal Commission on Labour in India. *Evidence.* Vol. 3, *Central Provinces and United Provinces.* London: Her Majesty's Stationary Office, 1931.

———. *Evidence.* Vol. 11, *Supplementary.* London: Her Majesty's Stationary Office, 1934.

———. *Report.* London: Her Majesty's Stationary Office, 1931.

Russell, A. M. *Report on the Census of the Central Provinces, 1866.* Calcutta: Superintendent, Government Printing, 1867.

Selections from the North-West Provinces. Vol. 3, second series, no. 14. Allahabad: North-Western Provinces Government Press, 1861–67.

Selections from the Records of the Government of India, 1881. Home Department nos. 1–196. Calcutta: Superintendent of Government Printing, 1853–84.

Selections from Vernacular Newspapers, Uttar Pradesh, 1894–1929. Allahabad: North-Western Provinces and Oudh Government Press, and Superintendent of Government Press, United Provinces, 1901–29.

Srivastava, L. N. *Leather Industry.* Department of Industries Bulletin, n.s. 19. Allahabad: Superintendent of Government Press, United Provinces, n.d. [after 1934].

Statistical Abstracts for British India. Annual volumes. Allahabad: North-Western Provinces and Oudh Government Press, 1880–1900.

Sudder Board of Revenue. *Reports on the Revenue Settlement of the North Western Provinces of the Bengal Presidency, under Regulation 9, 1833.* 2 vols. Benares: The Medical Hall Press, 1862–63.

Walton, H. G. *A Monograph on Tanning and Working in Leather in the United Provinces of Agra and Oudh.* Allahabad: Superintendent of Government Press, United Provinces, 1903.

Watt, George. *A Dictionary of the Economic Products of India.* Calcutta: Superintendent of Government Printing, 1896.

Wright, F. N. *Memorandum on Agriculture in the District of Cawnpore.* Allahabad: North-Western Provinces and Oudh Government Press, 1877.

SETTLEMENT, RENT-RATE, AND ASSESSMENT REPORTS OF UTTAR PRADESH

Agra

Rent-Rate Report for Pargana Farah, Zila Agra. Allahabad: North-Western Provinces and Oudh Government Press, 1877. W. H. Smith.

Report on the Settlement of the Agra District. Allahabad: North-Western Provinces and Oudh Government Press, 1880. H. F. Evans.

Rent-Rate Report of Pargana and Tahsil Bah, District Agra. Allahabad: Superintendent of Government Press, United Provinces, 1928. R. F. Mudie.

Rent-Rate Report of Pargana Kiraoli, Tahsil Kiraoli, District Agra. Allahabad: Superintendent of Government Press, United Provinces, 1929. Nand Lal.

Rent-Rate Report of Pargana Agra, District Agra. Allahabad: Superintendent of Government Press, United Provinces, 1928. R. F. Mudie.

Rent-Rate Report of Pargana and Tahsil Bah, District Agra. Allahabad: Superintendent of Government Press, United Provinces, 1928. R. F. Mudie.

Rent-Rate Report of Pargana Fatehabad, Tahsil Fatehabad, District Agra. Allahabad: Superintendent of Government Press, United Provinces, 1928. H. J. Frampton.

Rent-Rate Report of Pargana Etamadpur and Firozabad, District Agra. Allahabad: Super-intendent of Government Press, United Provinces, 1928. R. F. Mudie.

Rent-Rate Report of Pargana Kheragarh, District Agra. Allahabad: Superintendent of Government Press, United Provinces, 1929. R. F. Mudie.

Final Report on the Settlement and Record Operations in District Agra. Allahabad: Superin-tendent of Government Press, United Provinces, 1930. R. F. Mudie.

Aligarh

Final Report on the Revision of Settlement in the District of Aligarh. Allahabad: North-Western Provinces and Oudh Government Press, 1882. T. E. Smith.

Final Settlement Report of the Aligarh District. Allahabad: Superintendent of Government Press, United Provinces, 1903. W. J. D. Burkitt.

Final Settlement Report of the Aligarh District. Allahabad: Superintendent of Government Press, United Provinces, 1943. S. Ahmad Ali.

Allahabad

Final Settlement Report of the Allahabad District. Allahabad: North-Western Provinces and Oudh Government Press, 1878. F. W. Porter.

Final Settlement Report of the Farrukhabad District. Allahabad: Superintendent of Government Press, United Provinces, 1902. H. J. Hoare.

Rent-Report of Pargana Kiwai, Tahsil Handia, District Allahabad. Allahabad: Superinten-dent of Government Press, United Provinces, 1915. D. L. Drake-Brockman.

Azamgarh

Report on the Settlement of the Ceded Portion of the District of Azimgurh. Agra: Secundra Orphan Press 1837. J. Thomason. In *Reports on the Revenue Settlement of the North Western Provinces of the Bengal Presidency, under Regulation IX, 1833,* vol. 1. Benares: The Medical Hall Press, 1862.

Report on the Settlement Operations in the District of Azamgarh. Allahabad: North-West-ern Provinces and Oudh Government Press, 1881. J. R. Reid.

Final Report on the Seventh Settlement of the Azamgarh District. Allahabad: Superinten-dent of Government Press, United Provinces, 1908. C. E. Crawford.

Bahraich

Report on the Revision of Settlement of the Bahraich District, Oudh. Lucknow: North-Western Provinces and Oudh Government Press, 1873. E. G. Clark and H. Scotty Boys.

Final Report on the Settlement of the Bahraich District. Allahabad: Superintendent of Gov-ernment Press, United Provinces, 1901. P. Harrison.

Rent-Rate Report of Pargana Fakharpur, Tahsil Qaisarganj, District Bahraich. Allahabad: Superintendent of Government Press, United Provinces, 1938. Y. D. Gundevia.

Ballia

Report on the Revision of Records in Ballia District. Allahabad: North-Western Provinces and Oudh Government Press, 1886. D. T. Roberts.

Banda

Final Settlement Report for Banda District Exclusive of the Karwi Sub-division. Allahabad: North-Western Provinces and Oudh Government Press, 1881. Alan Cadell.

Rent-Rate Report on Pargana Tarauhan, District Banda. Allahabad: North-Western Provinces and Oudh Government Press, 1881. A. B. Patterson.

Bareilly
Report on the Settlement of the Bareilly District. Allahabad: North-Western Provinces and Oudh Government Press, 1874. S. M. Moens.
Final Settlement Report of the District Bareilly. Allahabad: Superintendent of Government Press, United Provinces, 1903. S. H. Freemantle.
Final Settlement Report of the District Bareilly. Allahabad: Superintendent of Government Press, United Provinces, 1942. I. W. Lewys-Loyd.

Basti
Final Report of the Settlement of the Basti District. Allahabad: North-Western Provinces and Oudh Government Press, 1891. J. Hooper.
Rent-Rate Report of Tahsil Harraiya, District Basti. Allahabad: Superintendent of Government Press, United Provinces, 1918. G. M. Harper.
Rent-Rate Report of the Alluvial Mahals of Tahsil Harraiya, District Basti. Allahabad: Superintendent of Government Press, United Provinces, 1918. E. A. H. Blunt.
Rent-Rate Report of Pargana Naghar East, Mahuli West, Basti East, Tahsil and District Basti. Allahabad: Superintendent of Government Press, United Provinces, 1918. E. A. H. Blunt.
Rent-Rate Report of the Pargana Maghar East, Tahsil Khalilabad, District Basti. Allahabad, 1918: Superintendent of Government Press, United Provinces. E. A. H. Blunt.
Rent-Rate Reports, Alluvial Mahals, Pargana, Maghar West, Tahsil and District Basti. Allahabad: Superintendent of Government Press, United Provinces, 1918. E. A. H. Blunt.
Rent-Rate Report on Tahsil Bansi, District Basti. Allahabad: Superintendent of Government Press, United Provinces, 1918. A. G. Clow.
Rent-Rate Report on the Alluvial Mahals of Mahauli East, District Basti. Allahabad: Superintendent of Government Press, United Provinces, 1918. E. A. H. Blunt.
Rent-Rate Report Pargana of Mahuli East Tahsil Khalilabad, District Basti. Allahabad: Superintendent of Government Press, United Provinces, 1918. G. L. Vivian.
Rent-Rate Report of Pargana Nagar West, District Basti. Allahabad: Superintendent of Government Press, United Provinces, 1918. G. L. Vivian.
Final Settlement Report of the Basti District. Allahabad: Superintendent of Government Press, United Provinces, 1919. A. G. Clow.

Badaun
Final Settlement Report of the Budaun District. Allahabad: Superintendent of Government Press, United Provinces, 1930. A. W. Waugh.

Bulandshahr
Report of the Settlement of the Bulandshahr District. Allahabad: North-Western Provinces and Oudh Government Press, 1877. Robert G. Currie.
Assessment Report of Tahsil Khurja of the Bulandshahr District. Allahabad: North-Western Provinces and Oudh Government Press, 1889. B. T. Stoker.

Final Report on the Settlement of Land Revenue in the Bulandshahr District, North-Western Provinces. Allahabad: North-Western Provinces and Oudh Government Press, 1891. B. T. Stoker.

Rent-Rate Report of Tahsil and District Bulandshahr. Allahabad: Superintendent of Government Press, United Provinces, 1918. H. T. Lane.

Rent-Rate Report of Tahsil Anupshahr, District Bulandshahr. Allahabad: Superintendent of Government Press, United Provinces, 1918. E. A. Phelps.

Rent-Rate Report of Tahsil Bulandshahr, and District Bulandshahr. Allahabad: Superintendent of Government Press, United Provinces, 1918. H. T. Lane.

Rent-Rate Report of Tahsil Sikandarabad, District Bulandshahr. Allahabad: Superintendent of Government Press, United Provinces, 1918. E. A. Phelps.

Final Report on the Settlement of Bulandshahr. Allahabad: Superintendent of Government Press, United Provinces, 1919. E. A. Phelps.

Etah

Final Settlement Report of the Eta District. Allahabad: North-Western Provinces and Oudh Government Press, 1874. S. O. B. Ridsale.

Final Settlement Report of the Etah district. Allahabad: Superintendent of Government Press, United Provinces, 1906. H. O. W. Robarts.

Final Settlement Report of Etah District. Allahabad: Superintendent of Government Press, United Provinces, 1944. M. M. Siddiqui.

Etawah

Report of the Settlement of the Etawah District. Allahabad: North-Western Provinces and Oudh Government Press, 1875. C. H. T Crosthwaite and W. Neale.

Final Settlement Report of the Etawah District. Allahabad: Superintendent of Government Press, United Provinces, 1915. E. S. Liddard.

Farrukhabad

Final Report of the Settlement of Farrukhabad District. Allahabad: North-Western Provinces and Oudh Government Press, 1875. H. F. Evans.

Assessment Report of Tahsil Kanauj, District Farrukhabad. Allahabad: Superintendent of Government Press, United Provinces, 1943. S. M. Srivastava.

Assessment Report of Tahsil Kumgunj, District Farrukhabad. Allahabad: Superintendent of Government Press, United Provinces, 1944. S. M. Srivastava.

Fatehpur

Report on the Final Settlement of Fatehpur District. Allahabad: North-Western Provinces and Oudh Government Press, 1878. A. B. Patterson.

Final Settlement Report of the Fatehpur District in the Uttar Pradesh. Allahabad: Superintendent of Government Press, United Provinces, 1915. C. L. Alexander.

Fyzabad

Report on the Settlement of the Land Revenue of Fyzabad District. Allahabad: North-Western Provinces and Oudh Government Press, 1880. A. F. Millett.

Final Settlement Report of Fyzabad District. Allahabad: Superintendent of Government Press, United Provinces 1942. S. M. A. Zaidi.

Ghazipur

Report on the Revision of Records and Settlement, Ghazipur District. Allahabad: North-Western Provinces and Oudh Government Press, 1886. W. Irvine.

Rent-Rate Report of Tahsil Saidpur, District Ghazipur. Allahabad: Superintendent of Government Press, United Provinces, 1931. Jai Krit Singh.

Gonda

Report on the Settlement of Gonda District. Allahabad: North-Western Provinces and Oudh Government Press, 1878. W. C. Benett.

Final Settlement Report of the Gonda District. Allahabad: Superintendent of Government Press, United Provinces, 1903. H. C. R. Hailey.

Final Settlement of the Gonda District. Allahabad: Superintendent of Government Press, United Provinces, 1943. J. L. Sathe.

Gorakhpur

Report on the Settlement of the District of Goruckpoor. Agra: Secundra Orphan Press, 1837. E. A. Reade. In *Reports on the Revenue Settlement of the North Western Provinces of the Bengal Presidency, under Regulation IX, 1833,* vol. 1. Benares: The Medical Hall Press, 1862.

Report on the Settlement of the Guruckpore-Bustee District. 2 vols. Allahabad: North-Western Provinces and Oudh Government Press, 1871.

Assessment Report of Pargana Binayakpur and Tilpur, Tahsil Maharajganj, District Gorakhpur. Allahabad: North-Western Provinces and Oudh Government Press, 1888. A. W. Cruickshank.

Final Report on the Settlement of Gorakhpur District. Allahabad: North-Western Provinces and Oudh Government Press, 1891. A. W. Cruickshank.

Rent-Rate Report of the Northern Portion of Padrauna, District Gorakhpur. Allahabad: Superintendent of Government Press, United Provinces, 1917. K. N. Knox.

Final Report on the Revision of Settlement in the Gorakhpur District (Tahsil Padrauna, Hata and Deoria). Allahabad: Superintendent of Government Press, United Provinces, 1919. K. N. Knox.

Rent-Rate Report on the Southern Portion of Padrauna, Pargana Sidhua Jobna, Tahsil Padrauna, District Gorakhpur. Allahabad: Superintendent of Government Press, United Provinces, 1917. G. J. E. O'Byrne.

Final Settlement Report of the Western Portion of the Gorakhpur District. Allahabad: Superintendent of Government Press, United Provinces, 1919. D. M. Stewart.

Hamirpur

Report on the Settlement of the Zillah of Humeerpoor. Agra: Secundra Orphan Press, 1842. C. Allen. In *Reports on the Revenue Settlement of the North Western Provinces of the Bengal Presidency, under Regulation IX, 1833,* vol. 1. Benares: The Medical Hall Press, 1863.

Report on the Settlement of the Hamirpur District. Allahabad: North-Western Provinces and Oudh Government Press, 1880. W. E. Neale.

Rent-Rate Report of Pargana Maudha of the Hamirpur District. Allahabad: North-Western Provinces and Oudh Government Press, 1876. Alan Cadell.

Final Report on the Revision of Settlement of the Hamirpur District. Allahabad: Superintendent of Government Press, United Provinces, 1908. W. Raw.

Hardoi

Report of the Regular Settlement of the Hardoi District. Allahabad: North-Western Provinces and Oudh Government Press, 1880. E. O. Bradford, A. H. Harrington, and W. Blennerhassett.

Rent-Rate Report of Tahsil Sandila, District Hardoi. Allahabad: Superintendent of Government Press, United Provinces, 1929. A. Hasan.

Rent-Rate Report of Pargana Barwan, Tahsil Hardoi, District Hardoi. Allahabad: Superintendent of Government Press, United Provinces, 1930. Brij Chand Sharma.

Jalaun

Final Settlement Report of the Jalaun District. Allahabad: Superintendent of Government Press, United Provinces, 1906. H. C. R. Hailey.

Jaunpur

Report on the Revision of Records and Settlement of Jaunpur. Allahabad: North-Western Provinces and Oudh Government Press, 1886. P. C. Wheeler.

Jhansi

Final Report on the Settlement of the Jhansi District. Allahabad: North-Western Provinces and Oudh Government Press, 1893. W. H. L. Impey.

Final Report on the Revision of Settlement in the Lalitpur Subdivision, District Jhansi. Allahabad: North-Western Provinces and Oudh Government Press, 1899. H. J. Hoare.

Final Settlement Report on the Revision of the Jhansi District including Lalitpur Subdivision. Allahabad: Superintendent of Government Press, United Provinces, 1907. A. W. Pim.

Assessment Report of Tahsil Jhansi, District Jhansi. Allahabad: Superintendent of Government Press, United Provinces, 1942. J. B. Langford.

Assessment Report of Tahsil Moth, District Jhansi. Allahabad: Superintendent of Government Press, United Provinces, 1942. J. B. Langford.

Assessment Report of Tahsil Lalitpur, District Jhansi. Allahabad: Superintendent of Government Press, United Provinces, 1943. J. B. Langford.

Assessment Report of Tahsil Mahroni, District Jhansi. Allahabad: Superintendent of Government Press, United Provinces, 1943. H. T. Lane.

Assessment Report of Tahsil Mau, District Jhansi. Allahabad: Superintendent of Government Press, United Provinces, 1943. H. T. Lane.

Assessment Report of Tahsil Garotha, District Jhansi. Allahabad: Superintendent of Government Press, United Provinces, 1945. H. T. Lane.

Final Settlement Report of Jhansi District. Allahabad: Superintendent of Government Press, United Provinces, 1947. H. T. Lane.

Kanpur

Final Report of the Settlement of the Cawnpore District. Allahabad: Superintendent of Government Press, United Provinces, 1878. F. N. Wright.

Kheri

Report of the Regular Settlement of Kheri District. Allahabad: North-Western Provinces and Oudh Government Press, 1879. T. R. Redfern.

Lucknow
Report of the Land Revenue Settlement, Lucknow District. Allahabad: North-Western
Provinces and Oudh Government Press, 1873. H. H. Butts.

Mainpuri
Report on the Settlement of the Mainpuri District. Allahabad: North-Western Provinces
and Oudh Government Press, 1875. D. M. Smeaton and M. A. McConaghey.
Final Settlement Report of Mainpuri District. Allahabad: Superintendent of Government
Press, 1906. M. A. McConaghey.
Final Settlement Report of Mainpuri District. Allahabad: Superintendent of Government
Press, United Provinces, 1944. Sheikh Zahurul Hasan.

Meerut
Report on the Settlement of Meerut District. Allahabad: North-Western Provinces and
Oudh Government Press, 1874. W. A. Forbes and J. S. Porter.
Final Settlement Report of the Meerut District. Allahabad: Superintendent of Government
Press, United Provinces, 1901. R. W. Gillan.

Moradabad
Rent-Rate Report of Pargana Thakurdwara, District Moradabad. Allahabad: North-West-
ern Provinces and Oudh Government Press, 1878. D. M. Smeaton.
Rent-Rate Report of Pargana Kashipur, Tarai, District Moradabad. Allahabad: North-
Western Provinces and Oudh Government Press, 1878. D. M. Smeaton.
Final Report on the Settlement of the Moradabad District. Allahabad: North-Western Prov-
inces and Oudh Government Press, 1881. E. Alexander.
Final Report on the Eleventh Settlement of the Moradabad. Allahabad: Superintendent of
Government Press United Provinces, 1909. H. J. Boas.

Muttra
Report on the Settlement of the Muttra District. Allahabad: North-Western Provinces and
Oudh Government Press, 1879. R. S. Whiteway.
Final Settlement Report of the Muttra District. Allahabad: Superintendent of Government
Press, United Provinces, 1926. H. A. Lane.

Muzaffarnagar
Final Report of the Settlement of the Muzaffarnagar District. Allahabad: North-Western
Provinces and Oudh Government Press, 1892. J. O. Miller.

Partabgarh
Report on the Revenue Settlement of Partabgarh District. Allahabad: North-Western Provinces and Oudh Government Press, 1877. W. A. Forbes.
Final Settlement Report of the Partabgarh District. Allahabad: North-Western Provinces
and Oudh Government Press, 1896. J. Sanders.

Rae Bareli
Report on the Settlement Operations of Rae Bareli District. Allahabad: North-Western
Provinces and Oudh Government Press, 1872. J. M. Macandrew.

Report on the Second Settlement of the Rae Bareli District, Oudh, 1897. Allahabad: North-Western Provinces and Oudh Government Press, 1898. S. H. Fremantle.

Rent-Rate Report Pargana Dalmau and Tahsil Dalmau, District Rae Bareli. Allahabad: Superintendent of Government Press, United Provinces 1928. L. Owen.

Rent-Rate Report of Pargana Khiron and Sareni, Tahsil Dalmau, Rae Bareli District. Allahabad: Superintendent of Government Press, United Provinces, 1928. A. C. Turner.

Rent-Rate Report of Pargana and Tahsil Rae Bareli, District Rae Bareli. Allahabad: Superintendent of Government Press, United Provinces, 1928. A. C. Turner.

Final Report on the Third Regular Settlement of the Rae Bareli District. Allahabad: Superintendent of Government Press, United Provinces, 1929. A. C. Turner.

Saharanpur

Report on the Settlement of the District of Seharunpore. Agra: Secundra Orphan Press, 1837. Edward Thornton. In *Reports on the Revenue Settlement of the North Western Provinces of the Bengal Presidency, under Regulation IX, 1833,* vol. 1. Benares: The Medical Hall Press, 1862.

Final Report of the Settlement of the Saharanpur District. Allahabad: North-Western Provinces and Oudh Government Press, 1891. L. A. S. Porter.

Assessment Report of the Saharanpur Tahsil, District Saharanpur. Allahabad: North-Western Provinces and Oudh Government Press, 1890. L. A. S. Porter.

Assessment Report of the Roorkee Tahsil, District Saharanpur. Allahabad: North-Western Provinces and Oudh Government Press, 1890. L. A. S. Porter.

Rent-Rate Report of Pargana Faizabad, Tahsil and District Saharanpur. Allahabad: Superintendent of Government Press, United Provinces, 1919. D. L. Drake-Brockman.

Rent-Rate Report of Pargana Saharanpur, Tahsil and District Saharanpur. Allahabad: Superintendent of Government Press, United Provinces, 1919. D. L. Drake-Brockman.

The Final Report on the Settlement Operations of the Saharanpur District. Allahabad: Superintendent of Government Press, United Provinces, 1921. D. L. Drake-Brockman.

Rent-Rate Report on Pargana Bhagwanpur and Rurki, Tahsil Rurki, District Saharanpur. Allahabad: Superintendent of Government Press, United Provinces, 1919. Brij Chand Sharma.

Rent-Rate Report on Pargana Haraura, Tahsil and District Saharanpur. Allahabad: Superintendent of Government Press, United Provinces, 1919. Brij Chand Sharma.

Shahjahanpur

Report on the Settlement of the Shahjehanpore District. Allahabad: North-Western Provinces and Oudh Government Press, 1874. Robert G. Currie.

Rent-Rate Report for Tahsil Shahjahanpur, District Shahjahanpur. Allahabad: Superintendent of Government Press, United Provinces, 1939. G. A. Haig.

Rent-Rate Report for Tahsil Jalalabad, District Shahjahanpur. Allahabad: Superintendent of Government Press, United Provinces, 1939. Sheikh Zahurul Hasan.

Sitapur

Final Report on the Settlement of District Sitapur. Allahabad: North-Western Provinces and Oudh Government Press, 1875. M. L. Farrar.

Sultanpur

Report on the Settlement of the Land Revenue of Sultanpur District. Allahabad: North-Western Provinces and Oudh Government Press, 1873. A. F. Millett.

Final Report of the Settlement of the Sultanpur District. Allahabad: North-Western Provinces and Oudh Government Press, 1898. F. W. Browrigg.

Unnao
Report on the Revised Settlement of the Oonao District. Allahabad: North-Western Provinces and Oudh Government Press, 1867. W. Maconochie.
Final Report on the Settlement of Land Revenue in the Unao District. Allahabad: North-Western Provinces and Oudh Government Press, 1896. W. H. Moreland.
Rent-Rate Report of Pargana Safipur, Tahsil Safipur, District Unao. Allahabad: Superintendent of Government Press, United Provinces, 1928. S. M. A. Zaidi.
Rent-Rate Report of Pargana Mohan Auras, Tahsil Mohan, District Unao. Allahabad: Superintendent of Government Press, United Provinces, 1928. H. S. K. Maheshwari.
Rent-Rate Report of Parganas Bangarman and Fatehpur-Chaurasi, Tahsil Safipur, District Unnao. Allahabad: Superintendent of Government Press, United Provinces, 1929. S. M. A. Zaidi.

GAZETTEERS OF UTTAR PRADESH
Statistical, Descriptive and Historical Account of the North-Western Provinces of India. Vols. 1–9, 13. Allahabad: North-Western Provinces and Oudh Government Press, 1874–83. Edwin T. Atkinson.

United Provinces District Gazetteers
Agra. Allahabad, 1905. H. R. Nevill.
Allahabad. Allahabad: Superintendent of Government Press, United Provinces, 1911. H. R. Nevill.
Azamgarh. Allahabad: Superintendent of Government Press, United Provinces, 1911. D. L. Drake-Brockman.
Banda. Allahabad: Superintendent of Government Press, United Provinces, 1909. D. L. Drake-Brockman.
Basti. Allahabad: Superintendent of Government Press, United Provinces, 1907. H. R. Nevill.
Benares. Allahabad: Superintendent of Government Press, United Provinces, 1909. H. R. Nevill.
Cawnpore. Allahabad: Superintendent of Government Press, United Provinces, 1909. H. R. Nevill.
Etah. Allahabad: Superintendent of Government Press, United Provinces, 1911. E. R. Neave.
Etawah. Allahabad: Superintendent of Government Press, United Provinces, 1911. D. L. Drake-Brockman.
Farrukhabad. Allahabad: Superintendent of Government Press, United Provinces, 1911. E. R. Neave.
Fatehpur. Allahabad: Superintendent of Government Press, United Provinces, 1906. H. R. Nevill.
Fyzabad. Allahabad: Superintendent of Government Press, United Provinces, 1905. H. R. Nevill.
Ghazipur. Allahabad: Superintendent of Government Press, United Provinces, 1909. H. R. Nevill.

Gonda. Allahabad: Superintendent of Government Press, United Provinces, 1909. H. R. Nevill.

Hamirpur. Allahabad: Superintendent of Government Press, United Provinces, 1909. D. L. Drake-Brockman.

Hardoi. Nanital: Superintendent of Government Press, United Provinces, 1904. H. R. Nevill.

Jalaun. Allahabad: Superintendent of Government Press, United Provinces, 1909. D. L. Drake-Brockman.

Jaunpur. Allahabad: Superintendent of Government Press, United Provinces, 1908. H. R. Nevill.

Jhansi. Allahabad: Superintendent of Government Press, United Provinces, 1911. D. L. Drake-Brockman.

Kheri. Allahabad: Superintendent of Government Press, United Provinces, 1905. H. R. Nevill.

Lucknow. Allahabad: Superintendent of Government Press, United Provinces, 1904. H. R. Nevill.

Mainpuri. Allahabad: Superintendent of Government Press, United Provinces, 1910. E. R. Neave.

Meerut. Allahabad: Superintendent of Government Press, United Provinces, 1904. H. R. Nevill.

Mirzapur. Allahabad: Superintendent of Government Press, United Provinces, 1911. D. L. Brockman.

Moradabad. Allahabad: Superintendent of Government Press, United Provinces, 1911. H. R. Nevill.

Muttra. Allahabad: Superintendent of Government Press, United Provinces, 1911. D. L. Drake-Brockman.

Muzaffarnagar. Allahabad: Superintendent of Government Press, United Provinces, 1903. H. R. Nevill.

Partabgarh. Allahabad: Superintendent of Government Press, United Provinces, 1904. H. R. Nevill.

Pilibhit. Allahabad: Superintendent of Government Press, United Provinces, 1911. H. R. Nevill.

Rae Bareli. Allahabad: Superintendent of Government Press, United Provinces, 1905. H. R. Nevill.

Saharanpur. Allahabad: Superintendent of Government Press, United Provinces, 1909. H. R. Nevill.

Shahjahanpur. Allahabad: Superintendent of Government Press, United Provinces, 1910. H. R. Nevill.

Sitapur. Allahabad: Superintendent of Government Press, United Provinces, 1905. H. R. Nevill.

DISTRICT INDUSTRIAL SURVEYS OF UTTAR PRADESH

Report on the Industrial Survey of the Agra District of the United Provinces. Allahabad: Superintendent of Government Press, United Provinces, 1924. Mohammed Zia-Ur-Rub.

Report on the Industrial Survey of the Aligarh District of the United Provinces. Allahabad: Superintendent of Government Press, United Provinces, 1923. Maulvi Hamid Raza Jaffrey.

Report on the Industrial Survey of the Allahabad District of the United Provinces. Allahabad: Superintendent of Government Press, United Provinces, 1923. Jaghish Sahai Vatal.

Report on the Industrial Survey of the Azamgarh District of the United Provinces. Allahabad: Superintendent of Government Press, United Provinces, 1923. Mohammad Mushtaq.

Report on the Industrial Survey of the Bahraich District of the United Provinces. Allahabad: Superintendent of Government Press, United Provinces, 1923. H. N. Sapru.

Report on the Industrial Survey of the Ballia District of the United Provinces. Allahabad: Superintendent of Government Press, United Provinces, 1923. B. R. Bhatta.

Report on the Industrial Survey of the Banda District of the United Provinces. Allahabad: Superintendent of Government Press, United Provinces, 1923. G. N. Bhargava.

Report on the Industrial Survey of the Bara Banki District of the United Provinces. Allahabad: Superintendent of Government Press, United Provinces, 1923. H. N. Sapru.

Report on the Industrial Survey of the Bareilly District of the United Provinces. Allahabad: Superintendent of Government Press, United Provinces, 1923. Raghunandan Saran.

Report on the Industrial Survey of the Basti District of the United Provinces. Allahabad: Superintendent of Government Press, United Provinces, 1923. Mohammad Mushtaq.

Report on the Industrial Survey of the Benares District of the United Provinces. Allahabad: Superintendent of Government Press, United Provinces, 1923. B. R. Bhatta.

Report on the Industrial Survey of the Bijnor District of the United Provinces. Allahabad: Superintendent of Government Press, United Provinces, 1923. Raghunandan Saran.

Report on the Industrial Survey of the Bulandshahr District of the United Provinces. Allahabad: Superintendent of Government Press, United Provinces, 1923. H. N. Sapru.

Report on the Industrial Survey of the Cawnpore District of the United Provinces. Allahabad: Superintendent of Government Press, United Provinces, 1923. Jaghish Sahai Vatal.

Report on the Industrial Survey of the Dehradun District of the United Provinces. Allahabad: Superintendent of Government Press, United Provinces, 1923. Mohammed Zia-Ur-Rub.

Report on the Industrial Survey of the Etawah District of the United Provinces. Allahabad: Superintendent of Government Press, United Provinces, 1923. Jaghish Sahai Vatal.

Report on the Industrial Survey of the Farrukhabad District of the United Provinces. Allahabad: Superintendent of Government Press, United Provinces, 1923. Jaghish Sahai Vatal.

Report on the Industrial Survey of the Fatehpur District of the United Provinces. Allahabad: Superintendent of Government Press, United Provinces, 1923. Jaghish Sahai Vatal.

Report on the Industrial Survey of the Fyzabad District of the United Provinces. Allahabad: Superintendent of Government Press, United Provinces, 1923. H. N. Sapru.

Report on the Industrial Survey of the Ghazipur District of the United Provinces. Allahabad: Superintendent of Government Press, United Provinces, 1923. B. R. Bhatta.

Report on the Industrial Survey of the Gorakhpur District of the United Provinces. Allahabad: Superintendent of Government Press, United Provinces, 1923. Mohammad Mushtaq.

Report on the Industrial Survey of the Hamirpur District of the United Provinces. Allahabad: Superintendent of Government Press, United Provinces, 1923. G. N. Bhargava.

Report on the Industrial Survey of the Hardoi District of the United Provinces. Allahabad: Superintendent of Government Press, United Provinces, 1923. B. K. Ghoshal.

Report on the Industrial Survey of the Jalaun District of the United Provinces. Allahabad: Superintendent of Government Press, United Provinces, 1924. G. N. Bhargava.

Report on the Industrial Survey of the Jaunpur District of the United Provinces. Allahabad: Superintendent of Government Press, United Provinces, 1923. B. R. Bhatta.

Report on the Industrial Survey of the Jhansi District of the United Provinces. Allahabad: Superintendent of Government Press, United Provinces, 1923. G. N. Bhargava.

Report on the Industrial Survey of the Kheri District of the United Provinces. Allahabad: Superintendent of Government Press, United Provinces, 1923. B. K. Ghoshal.

Report on the Industrial Survey of the Lucknow District of the United Provinces. Allahabad: Superintendent of Government Press, United Provinces, 1923. B. K. Ghoshal.

Report on the Industrial Survey of the Mainpuri District of the United Provinces. Allahabad: Superintendent of Government Press, United Provinces, 1923. Maulvi Hamid Raza Jaffrey.

Report on the Industrial Survey of the Meerut District of the United Provinces. Allahabad: Superintendent of Government Press, United Provinces, 1922. Mohammed Zia-Ur-Rub.

Report on the Industrial Survey of the Mirzapur District of the United Provinces. Allahabad: Superintendent of Government Press, United Provinces, 1923. B. R. Bhatta.

Report on the Industrial Survey of the Moradabad District of the United Provinces. Allahabad: Superintendent of Government Press, United Provinces, 1923. Raghunandan Saran.

Report on the Industrial Survey of the Muzaffarnagar District of the United Provinces. Allahabad: Superintendent of Government Press, United Provinces, 1923. Mohammed Zia-Ur-Rub.

Report on the Industrial Survey of the Partabgarh District of the United Provinces. Allahabad: Superintendent of Government Press, United Provinces, 1923. H. N. Sapru.

Report on the Industrial Survey of the Pilibhit District of the United Provinces. Allahabad: Superintendent of Government Press, United Provinces, 1924. B. R. Bhatta.

Report on the Industrial Survey of the Rae Bareli District of the United Provinces. Allahabad: Superintendent of Government Press, United Provinces, 1923. B. K. Ghoshal.

Report on the Industrial Survey of the Saharanpur District of the United Provinces. Allahabad: Superintendent of Government Press, United Provinces, 1923. Mohammed Zia-Ur-Rub.

Report on the Industrial Survey of the Shahjahanpur District of the United Provinces. Allahabad: Superintendent of Government Press, United Provinces, 1923. Mohammad Mushtaq.

Report on the Industrial Survey of the Sultanpur District of the United Provinces. Allahabad: Superintendent of Government Press, United Provinces, 1923. H. N. Sapru.

Report on the Industrial Survey of the Unnao District of the United Provinces. Allahabad: Superintendent of Government Press, United Provinces, 1923. B. K. Ghoshal.

Non-official

PERIODICALS

Aaj (Hindi daily, Benares)
Abhyudaya (Hindi daily, Allahabad)
Calcutta Review (English, monthly, Calcutta)

Chand (Hindi Monthly, Allahabad)
Dawn (English daily, Lahore)
Frontline (English fortnightly, Madras)
Hindustan Times (English daily, Delhi)
Indian Notes and Queries (English monthly)
Leader (English daily, Allahabad)
National Herald (English daily, Lucknow)
North Indian Notes and Queries (English monthly, edited by William Crooke)
Pioneer (English daily, Lucknow)
Pratap (Hindi weekly, Kanpur)
Punjab Notes and Queries (English monthly)
Times of India (English daily, Lucknow)
Vartman (Hindi weekly, Kanpur)

HINDI SOURCES

Aharwar, Gauri Shankar. *Chamar Jati ki Utpatti avam Uski Pragati* (The Origins of the Chamar Caste and Its Progress). Kanpur: Chandra Kant Publisher, 1990.
All-India Koli-Rajput Mahasabha. *Koli Rajput Jati ka Sankshipt Parichay Arthat Koli Rajput Jati ki Aitihasik Jhalak* (A Short Introduction to the Koli Rajput *Jati*, or, A Historical Glimpse of the Koli Rajput *Jati*). Ajmer: All-India Koli-Rajput Mahasabha, 1936.
Dayal, Harmohan. *Varna Vayavastha aur Kureel Vansha* (The Caste System and the Kureel Lineage). Lucknow: Rajmohan Publishers, n.d.
Harischandra, Bharatendu. "Aggarwalon ki Utpatti" (Origin of the Aggarwal Caste). 1871. In *Bharatendu Granthavali: Tisra Bhag* (The Collected Works of Bharatendu [Harishchandra]: Part 3), ed. Brajratnadas, pp. 5–12. Benares: Nagari Pracharini Sabha, 1954.
———. "Khatriyon ki Utpatti" (Origin of the Khatris). 1873. In *Bharatendu Granthavali: Tisra Bhag* (The Collected Works of Bharatendu [Harishchandra]: Part 3), ed. Brajratnadas, pp. 247–60. Benares: Nagari Pracharini Sabha, 1954.
Jaiswar Mahasabha. *Suryavansh Kshatriya Jaiswar Sabha.* Lahore: Bombay Machine Press, 1926.
Jatav, Mangal Singh. *Shri 108 Swami Achhutanand Ji ka Jeevan Parichay* (An Introduction to the Life of Shri 108 Swami Achhutanand). Gwalior: Saraswati Press, 1997.
Jigyasu, Chandrika Prasad. *Bharat ke Adi Nivasiyon ki Sabhyata* (The Civilization of India's Original Inhabitants). Lucknow: Bahujan Kalyan Prakashan, 1965 [1937].
———. *Bhartiya Republican Party hi Kyon Avashyak Hai?* (Why Is the Republican Party of India Necessary?). Lucknow: Bahujan Kalyan Prakashan, 1965; 7th ed., 1984.
———. *Shri 108 Swami Achhutanandji "Harihar."* Lucknow: Bahujan Kalyan Prakashan, 1968.
Kaushalyanandan, *Kadhere Kaun Hai? Hamari Khoj* (Who Are Kadheres? Our Search). Jabbalpur: Babu Amritlal Bijoraha Publikhser, 1933.
Nauvatrai. *Kahar Jati aur Varnavayastha: Uski Poorva aur Vartaman Dasha* (The Kahar Caste and the Caste System: Its Past and Present Condition). Agra: Fakirchand, 1920.
Premchand. *Godaan* (Gift of a Cow). 1936. Allahabad: Hans Prakashan, 1993.
———. *Karmabhoomi* (An Arena of Action). 1932. Delhi: Rajkamal Paperbacks, 2002.

————. "Poos ki Raat" (A Cold Night in January). In *Mansarovar,* vol. 1, pp. 154–60. Allahabad: Saraswati Press, 1975.

————. *Premashram* (Romanticist's Refuge). 1922. Delhi: Vani Prakashan, 2002.

Raghuvanshi, U. B. S. *Shree Chanvar Purana* (A Puranic History of Chamars). Kanpur: Commercial Press, n.d. [the British Library's acquisition date is August 1917].

Sagar, Pandit Sunderlal. *Yadav Jivan* (The Life of the Yadavs). Agra: Shree Jatav Mahasabha, 1929.

Shastri, Shankaranand. *Poona Pact banam Gandhi* (Poona Pact versus Gandhi). Lucknow: Bahujan Kalyan Prakashan, 1994 [1946]. A revised edition appeared in 1965, with additional chapters covering events to 1956.

Singh "Raj," Rajpal. *Swami Achhutanand Harihar.* Delhi: RajLaxmi Prakashan, 2003.

Veer Janamshatabdi Samaroh, 1997: Smarika (The Birth Centenary Celebration of Our Hero, 1997: A Commemorative Volume). Agra: Manikchand Veer Sansthan, 1998.

Viyougi, Nandlal. *Ambedkar ki Awaz Arthat Achhutoin ka Federation* (The Voice of Ambedkar, or, The Federation of Untouchables). Allahabad: Jagriti Press, 1949.

Yadvendu, Ramnarayan. *Yaduvansh ka Aitihas* (A History of the Yadavs). Agra: Navyug Sahitya Niketan, 1942.

English Sources

Amin, Shahid. "Agrarian Bases of Nationalist Agitations in India: An Historiographical Survey." In *The Indian National Congress: Centenary Hindsights,* ed. D. A. Low, pp. 98–128. Delhi: Oxford University Press, 1988.

————. *Event, Metaphor, Memory: Chauri Chaura, 1922–1992.* Delhi: Oxford University Press, 1996.

————. *Sugarcane and Sugar in Gorakhpur: An Inquiry into Peasant Production for Capitalist Enterprise in Colonial India.* Delhi: Oxford University Press, 1984.

Asthana, Krishna Sahai. "A Social and Economic Survey of Village Malhera, District Hardoi." In *Fields and Farmers in Oudh,* ed. RadhaKamal Mukerjee, pp. 1–132. Madras: Longmans, 1929.

Bandyopadhyay, Sekhar. *Caste, Protest and Identity in Colonial India: The Namasudras of Bengal, 1872–1947.* London: Curzon, 1997.

Bayly, C. A. *Indian Society and the Making of the British Empire.* New Cambridge History of India 2.1. Cambridge: Cambridge University Press, 1987.

————. *Rulers, Townsmen and Bazaars: North Indian Society in the Age of British Expansion, 1770–1870.* Cambridge: Cambridge University Press, 1983.

Bayly, Susan. *Caste, Society and Politics in India from the Eighteenth Century to the Modern Age.* New Cambridge History of India 4.3. Cambridge: Cambridge University Press, 1999.

Bhargava, Meena. "Perception and Classification of the Rights of the Social Classes: Gorakhpur and the East India Company in the Late Eighteenth and Early Nineteenth Centuries." *Indian Economic and Social History Review* 30, no. 2 (1993): 214–37.

Bhattacharya, Neeladri. "Agricultural Labour and Production: Central and South-East Punjab, 1870–1940." In *Essays on the Commercialization of Indian Agriculture,* ed. K. N. Raj et al., 105–62. Delhi: Oxford University Press, 1985.

Briggs, George W. *The Chamars.* Oxford University Press, 1920.

Buchanan, Francis. *An Account of the Districts of Bihar and Patna in 1811–1812.* 2 vols. Patna: The Bihar and Orissa Research Society, 1934.

Chakrabarty, Dipesh. *Habitations of Modernity: Essays in the Wake of Subaltern Studies.* Delhi: Permanent Black, 2002.

———. *Rethinking Working-Class History: Bengal, 1890–1940.* Delhi: Oxford University Press, 1996.

Chandavarkar, Rajnarayan. *The Origins of Industrial Capitalism in India: Business Strategies and the Working Classes in Bombay, 1900–1940.* Cambridge: Cambridge University Press, 1994.

Chatterjee, Partha. *The Nation and Its Fragments: Colonial and Post-colonial Histories.* Princeton, N.J.: Princeton University Press, 1993.

Chatterji, Basudev. *Towards Freedom: Documents on the Movement for Independence in India, 1938.* 3 parts. Delhi: Oxford University Press, 1999.

Chaudhuri, K. N., ed. *The Economic Development of India under the East India Company, 1914–58: A Selection of Contemporary Writings.* Cambridge: Cambridge University Press, 1971.

———. "Foreign Trade and Balance of Payments (1754–1947)." In *The Cambridge Economic History of India, Volume 2: c. 1757–1970,* ed. Dharma Kumar, pp. 804–77. Cambridge: Cambridge University Press, 1983.

Chevers, Norman. *A Manual of Medical Jurisprudence for India, including the Outline of a History of the Crime against the Person in India.* Calcutta: Thacker, Spink, 1870.

Cohn, Bernard S. *An Anthropologist among the Historians and Other Essays.* Delhi: Oxford University Press, 1987.

———. *Colonialism and Its Forms of Knowledge: The British in India.* Princeton, N.J.: Princeton University Press, 1996.

Colebrooke, H. T. *Remarks on the Husbandry and Internal Commerce of Bengal.* Calcutta: printed by the author, 1804.

Commonwealth Institute. Committee for India. *Report on Hides and Skins.* London: J. Murray, 1920.

Crawfurd, John. *A Sketch of the Commercial Resources and Monetary and Mercantile System of British India, with Suggestions for Their Improvement, by Means of Banking Establishment.* London: Smith, Elder and Co., 1837. Reprinted in *The Economic Development of India under the East India Company, 1914–58: A Selection of Contemporary Writings,* ed. K. N. Chaudhuri, pp. 217–316. Cambridge: Cambridge University Press, 1971.

Dalmia, Vasudha. *The Nationalisation of Hindu Traditions: Bharatendu Harishchandra and Nineteenth-Century Banaras.* Delhi: Oxford University Press, 1997.

———. "Vernacular Histories in Late Nineteenth-Century Banaras: Folklore, Puranas and the New Antiquarianism." *Indian Economic and Social History Review* 38, no. 1 (2001): 59–79.

Das Gupta, Ranjit. "Factory Labour in Eastern India: Sources of Supply, 1855–1946: Some Preliminary Findings." *Indian Economic and Social History Review* 13, no. 3 (1976): 277–329.

Dayal, Hari Har. "Agricultural Labourers: An Inquiry Into Their Condition in the Unao District." In *Fields and Farmers in Oudh,* ed. RadhaKamal Mukerjee, pp. 225–298. Madras: Longmans, 1929.

Deliege, Robert. *The Untouchables of India.* New York: Berg, 1999.

Dirks, Nicholas. *Castes of Mind: Colonialism and the Making of Modern India.* Princeton, N.J.: Princeton University Press, 2001.

Dube, Saurabh. *Untouchable Pasts: Religion, Identity, and Power among a Central Indian Community, 1780–1950.* Albany: State University of New York Press, 1998.

Duncan, R. Ian. "Levels, the Communication of Programmes, and Sectional Strategies in Indian Politics, with Reference to the Bharatiya Kranti Dal and the Republican Party of India in U.P. State and Aligarh District (U.P.)." Ph.D. diss., University of Sussex, 1979.

Eden, Emily. *Up the Country: Letters Written to her Sister from Upper Provinces of India.* Oxford University Press, 1993.

Elliot, Henry Meirs. *Memoirs on the History, Folk-Lore, and Distribution of the Races of the North Western Provinces of India.* 2 vols. Ed. John Beames. London: Trubner, 1869.

Fallon, S. W. *A Dictionary of Hindustani Proverbs.* Banaras: The Medical Hall Press, 1886.

Fazl, Abul. *Ain I Akbari.* 2 vols. Trans. H. Blochmann. Calcutta: The Asiatic Society, 1873.

Freitag, Sandria B. "Crime in the Social Order of Colonial North India." *Modern Asian Studies* 25, no. 2 (1991): 227–61.

Gilmartin, David. "Cattle, Crime and Colonialism: Property as Negotiation in North India." *Indian Economic and Social History Review* 40, no. 1 (2003): 33–56.

Gooptu, Nandini. *The Politics of the Urban Poor in Early Twentieth-Century India.* Cambridge: Cambridge University Press, 2001.

Grover, B. R. "An Integrated Pattern of Commercial Life in the Rural Society of North India during the Seventeenth and Eighteenth Centuries." In *Money and the Market in India, 1100–1700,* ed. Sanjya Subrahmanyam, pp. 219–55. Delhi: Oxford University Press, 1994.

———. "Nature of Land Rights in Mughal India." *Indian Economic and Social History Review* 1, no. 1 (1963): 1–23.

Guha, Ranajit. *Dominance without Hegemony: History and Power in Colonial India.* Cambridge, Mass.: Harvard University Press, 1997.

———. *Elementary Aspects of Peasant Insurgency in Colonial India.* Delhi: Oxford University Press, 1983.

———. "The Small Voice of History." In *Subaltern Studies,* vol. 9, ed. Shahid Amin and Dipesh Chakrabarty, pp. 1–12. Delhi: Oxford University Press, 1996.

———, ed. *Subaltern Studies: Writings on South Asian History and Society.* Vols. 1–6. Delhi: Oxford University Press, 1982–89.

Gupta, Charu. "Hindu Women, Muslim Men: Cleavages in Shared Spaces of Everyday Life, United Provinces, c. 1890–1930." *Indian Economic and Social History Review* 37, no. 2 (2000): 121–49.

Hardiman, David. *The Coming of the Devi: Adivasi Assertion in Western India.* Delhi: Oxford University Press, 1987.

Hazari. *I Was an Outcaste: The Autobiography of an Unknown Indian.* Delhi: Hindustan Times, 1951.

Hoey, William. *A Monograph on Trade and Manufactures in Northern India.* Lucknow: The American Methodist Mission Press, 1880.

Human Rights Watch. *Broken People: Caste Violence against India's "Untouchables."* New York: Human Rights Watch, 1999.

Ilaiah, Kancha. "Productive Labour, Consciousness and History: The Dalitbahujan Alternative." In *Subaltern Studies,* vol. 9, ed. Shahid Amin and Dipesh Chakrabarty, 165–200. Delhi: Oxford University Press, 1996.

Jaffrelot, Christophe. *India's Silent Revolution: The Rise of the Lower Castes in North India.* New York: Columbia University Press, 2003.

Jones, Gavin. "The Rise and Progress of Cawnpore." In *The Bombay Presidency, the United Provinces, the Punjab, Etc: Their History, People, Commerce, and Natural Resources,* by Somerset Playne, pp. 495–99. London: The Foreign and Colonial Compiling and Pub. Co., 1920.

Jones, K. W. *Socio-religious Reform Movements in British India.* New Cambridge History of India 3.1. Cambridge: Cambridge University Press, 1989.

Jordens, J. T. F. *Swami Shraddhananda: His Life and Causes.* Delhi: Oxford University Press, 1981.

Joshi, Chitra. *Lost Worlds: Indian Labour and Its Forgotten Histories.* Delhi: Permanent Black, 2003.

Juergensmeyer, Mark. *Religion as Social Vision: The Movement against Untouchability in Twentieth-Century Punjab.* Berkeley: University of California Press, 1982.

Keer, Dhananjay. *Dr. Ambedkar: Life and Mission.* Bombay: Popular Prakashan, 1954.

Kesavan, Mukul. *Congress and the Muslims of UP and Bihar, 1937 to 1939.* Occasional Papers on History and Society, 2nd series, no. 27. New Delhi: Nehru Memorial Museum and Library, 1990.

Khare, R. S. *The Untouchable as Himself: Ideology, Identity and Pragmatism among the Lucknow Chamars.* Cambridge: Cambridge University Press, 1984.

Khobragade, B. D. *Report of the General Secretary of the Republican Party of India.* Delhi, 1966.

Knorringa, Peter. "Artisan Labour in the Agra Footwear Industry: Continued Informality and Changing Threats." *Contributions to Indian Sociology* 33, nos. 1–2 (1999): 303–28.

Kotani, Hiroyuki, ed. *Caste System, Untouchability and the Depressed.* Delhi: Manohar Publishers, 1999.

———. "Conflict and Controversy over the Mahar Vatan in the Nineteenth–Twentieth Century Bombay Presidency." In *Caste System, Untouchability and the Depressed,* ed. Hiroyuki Kotani, pp. 103–135. Delhi: Manohar Publishers, 1999.

Kshirsagar, R. K. *Dalit Movement and Its Leaders (1857–1956).* Delhi: M.D. Publications, 1994.

Kumar, Dharma, ed. *The Cambridge Economic History of India, Volume 2: c. 1757–1970.* Cambridge: Cambridge University Press, 1983.

Kumar, Kapil. *Peasants in Revolt: Tenants, Landlords, Congress and the Raj in Oudh, 1886–1922.* Delhi: Manohar Publishers, 1984.

Lal, Brij V. *Chalo Jhaji: A Journey through Indenture in Fiji.* Canberra: The Australian National University, 2001.

Lohia, Rammanohar. *The Caste System.* Hyderabad: Navahind, 1964.

Lynch, Owen. *The Politics of Untouchability: Social Mobility and Social Change in a City of India.* New York: Columbia University Press, 1969.

Martin, Robert Montgomery. *The History, Antiquities, Topography, and Statistics of Eastern India: Comprising the Districts of Behar, Shahabad, Bhagalpoor, Goruckpoor, Dinajpoor, Purniya, Rungpoor, and Assam, in Relation to Their Geology, Mineralogy, Botany, Agriculture, Commerce, Manufactures, Fine Arts, Population, Religion, Education, Statistics, Etc.* 3 vols. London: W. H. Allen, 1838.

Major, Andrew J. "State and Criminal Tribes in Colonial Punjab: Surveillance, Control and Reclamation of the 'Dangerous Classes.'" *Modern Asian Studies* 33, no. 3 (1999): 657–88.

Mayaram, Shail. "Criminality or Community? Alternative Constructions of the Mev Narrative of Darya Khan." *Contributions to Indian Sociology* 25, no. 1 (1991): 57–84.

Mayer, Peter. "Inventing Village Tradition: The Late Nineteenth Century Origins of the North Indian 'Jajmani System.'" *Modern Asian Studies* 27, no. 2 (1993): 357–95.

Mendelsohn, Oliver, and Marika Vicziany. *The Untouchables: Subordination, Poverty and the State in Modern India.* Cambridge: Cambridge University Press, 1998.

Misra, B. B. *The Central Administration of the East India Company, 1773–1834.* Manchester: Manchester University Press, 1959.

Moffatt, Michael. *An Untouchable Community in South India: Structure and Consensus.* Princeton, N.J.: Princeton University Press, 1979.

Moon, Vasant, ed. *Dr. Babasaheb Ambedkar: Writings and Speeches.* Vols. 1, 2, 7, 8, and 9. Bombay: Education Dept., Govt. of Maharashtra, 1979–91.

Moore, R. J. *Escape from Empire: The Attlee Government and the Indian Problem.* Oxford: Oxford University Press, 1983.

Moore, R. J. *The Crisis of Indian Unity, 1917–1940.* Delhi: Oxford University Press, 1974.

Molund, Stefan. *First We Are People: The Koris of Kanpur between Caste and Class.* Stockholm: University of Stockholm, 1988.

Naqvi, Hameeda Khatoon. *Urban Centres and Industries in Upper India, 1556–1803.* New York: Asia Publishing House, 1968.

Narayan, Badri, and A. R. Misra, eds. *Multiple Marginalities: An Anthology of Identified Dalit Writing.* Delhi: Manohar Publishers, 2004.

Nehru, Jawaharlal. *An Autobiography.* London: John Lane, 1936.

Niehoff, Arthur. *Factory Workers in India.* Milwaukee: Milwaukee Public Museum, 1959.

Nigam, Sanjay. "Disciplining and Policing the 'Criminals by Birth': The Making of a Colonial Stereotype; The Criminal Tribes and Castes of North India." Parts 1 and 2. *Indian Economic and Social History Review* 27, no. 2 (1990): 131–64; 3 (1990): 257–87.

O'Hanlon, Rosalind. *Caste, Conflict and Ideology: Mahatama Jotirao Phule and Low Caste Protest in Nineteenth-Century Western India.* Cambridge: Cambridge University Press, 1985.

———. "Maratha History as Polemic: Low Caste Ideology and Political Debate in Late Nineteenth Century Western India." *Modern Asian Studies* 17, no. 1 (1983): 1–33.

Omvedt, Gail. *Cultural Revolt in a Colonial Society: The Non-Brahman Movement in Western India, 1873 to 1930.* Bombay: Scientific Socialist Education Trust, 1973.

———. *Dalits and the Democratic Revolution: Dr Ambedkar and the Dalit Movement in Colonial India.* Delhi: Sage, 1994.

Orsini, Francesca. *The Hindi Public Sphere, 1920–1940: Language and Literature in the Age of Nationalism.* Delhi: Oxford University Press, 2002.

Pai, Sudha. *Dalit Assertion and the Unfinished Democratic Revolution: The Bahujan Samaj Party in Uttar Pradesh.* Delhi: Sage, 2002.

Pandey, Gyanendra. *The Ascendancy of the Congress in Uttar Pradesh, 1926–34: A Study in Imperfect Mobilization.* Delhi: Oxford University Press, 1978.

———. *The Construction of Communalism in Colonial North India.* Delhi: Oxford University Press, 1990.

———. "Peasant Revolt and Indian Nationalism: The Peasant Movement in Awadh, 1919–1921." In *Subaltern Studies,* vol. 1, ed. Ranajit Guha, 143–97. Delhi: Oxford University Press, 1982.

Pinch, William R. *Peasants and Monks in British India.* Delhi: Oxford University Press, 1996.

Playne, Somerset. *The Bombay Presidency, the United Provinces, the Punjab, Etc: Their History, People, Commerce, and Natural Resources.* London: The Foreign and Colonial Compiling and Pub. Co., 1920.

Prakash, Gyan. "Reproducing Inequality: Spirit Cults and Labour Relations in Colonial Eastern India." *Modern Asian Studies* 20, no. 2 (1986): 209–30.

Prasad, Chandra Bhan. *Dalit Diary, 1999–2003: Reflections on Apartheid in India.* Pondicherry: Navayana, 2004.

Prashad, Vijay. "Untouchable Freedom: A Critique of the Bourgeois-Landlord Indian State." In *Subaltern Studies,* vol. 10, ed. Gautam Bhadra, Gyan Prakash, and Susie Tharu, 170–200. Delhi: Oxford University Press, 1999.

———. *Untouchable Freedom: A Social History of a Dalit Community.* Delhi: Oxford University Press, 2000.

Prinsep, George A. *Remarks on the External Commerce and Exchanges of Bengal, with Appendix of Accounts and Estimates.* London: Kingsbury, Parbury and Allen, 1823.

Pyarelal. *The Epic Fast.* Ahmadabad: Mohanlal Maganlal Bhatt, 1932.

Rai, Lajpat. *The Arya Samaj: An Account of Its Origin, Doctrines and Activities, with a Biographical Sketch of the Founder.* New York: Longmans, Green, 1915.

Raikes, Charles. *Notes on the North-Western Provinces of India.* London: W. H. Allen, 1852.

Rawat, Ramnarayan S. "Making Claims for Power: A New Agenda in Dalit Politics of Uttar Pradesh, 1946–48." *Modern Asian Studies* 37, no. 3 (2003): 585–612.

———. "Partition Politics and *Achhut* Identity: A Study of Scheduled Castes Federation and Dalit Politics in U.P. 1946–1948." In *The Partitions of Memory: The Afterlife of the Division of India,* ed. Suvir Kaul, pp. 111–39. Delhi: Permanent Black, 2001.

Raychaudhuri, Tapan, and Irfan Habib, eds. *The Cambridge Economic History of India, volume I, c. 1200–1750.* Cambridge: Cambridge University Press, 1982.

Reeves, P. D., B. D. Graham, and J. M. Goodman, eds. *A Handbook to Elections in Uttar Pradesh, 1920–1951.* Delhi: Manohar Book Service, 1975.

Republican Party of India. *Charter of Demands.* Delhi, 1964.

Roy, Tirthankar. *Traditional Industry in the Economy of Colonial India.* Cambridge: Cambridge University Press, 1999.

Saksena, Girwar Sahai. "An Agricultural Survey of Bakhshi-ka-Talab, District Lucknow." In *Fields and Farmers in Oudh,* ed. Madras RadhaKamal Mukerjee, pp. 133–227. Madras: Longmans, 1929.

Sarkar, Sumit. *Modern India, 1885–1947.* Delhi: Macmillan, 1983.

Sharan, Awadhendra. "Culture and Dignity: The Question of Untouchability in Colonial Bihar (1860s to 1950s)." Ph.D. diss., University of Chicago, 1998.

Sharma, Nalin Vilochan *Jagjivan Ram: A Biography.* Patna: Sanjivan Press, n.d. [1953].

Sharma, S. K. *The Chamar Artisans: Industrialisation, Skills and Social Mobility.* Delhi: B. R. Publishers, 1986.

Siddiqi, Asiya. *Agrarian Change in a Northern Indian State: Uttar Pradesh, 1819–1833.* Oxford: Oxford University Press, 1973.

Siddiqi, Majid H. *Agrarian Unrest in Northern India: The United Provinces, 1918–1922.* Delhi: Vikas Publishers, 1978.

Singh, K. Suresh. *The Scheduled Castes.* National Series 2: People of India. Delhi: Oxford University Press, 1993.

Singh, Mohinder. *The Depressed Classes: Their Economic and Social Condition.* Bombay: Hind Kitabs, Ltd., 1947.

Singha, Radhika. *A Despotism of Law: Crime and Justice in Early Colonial India.* Delhi: Oxford University Press, 1998.

Sleeman, W. A. *A Journey through the Kingdom of Oude in 1849–1850.* 2 vols. London: Richard Bentley, 1858.

———. *Rambles and Recollections of an Indian Official.* London: Oxford University Press, 1915.

Smith, Richard S. *Rule by Records: Land Registration and Village Custom in Early British Panjab.* Delhi: Oxford University Press, 1996.

Srinivas, M. N. *Caste in Modern India and Other Essays.* Bombay: Asia Publishing House, 1962.

Srivastava, Gopinath. *When Congress Ruled: A Close-Range Survey of the Congress Administration during the Twenty-Eight Months (1937–39) in the United Provinces.* Lucknow: Upper India Pub. House, n.d. [1940s].

Stokes, Eric. *The Peasant and the Raj: Studies in Agrarian Society and Peasant Rebellion in Colonial India.* Cambridge: Cambridge University Press, 1978.

Tennant, William. *Indian Recreations: Consisting Chiefly of Strictures on the Domestic and Rural Economy of the Mahomedans and Hindoos.* 2 vols. London: Longman, Hurst, Rees, and Orme, 1804.

Thapar, Romila. "Genealogical Patterns as Perceptions of the Past." In *Cultural Pasts: Essays in Early Indian History,* pp. 709–53. Delhi: Oxford University Press, 2000.

———. "Society and Historical Consciousness. The *Itihasa-purana* Tradition." In *Cultural Pasts: Essays in Early Indian History,* pp. 123–54. Delhi: Oxford University Press, 2000.

Thursby, G. R. *Hindu-Muslim Relations in British India: A study of Controversy, Conflict, and Communal Movements in Northern India, 1923–1928.* Leiden: Brill, 1975.

Tozier, H. J. *British India and Its Trade.* London: Harper, 1902.

Trevelyan, Charles E. *Report upon the Inland Customs and Town Duties of the Bengal Presidency.* Ed. Tarasankar Banerjee. Calcutta: Academic Publishers, 1976 [1835].

Whalley, Paul. *Handbook of the Elements of Place Names in the North-Western Provinces of India.* London, 1899.

Whitcombe, Elizabeth. *Agrarian Conditions in Northern India: The United Provinces under British Rule.* Berkeley: University of California Press, 1972.

Wiser, William, and Charlotte Wiser. *Behind Mud Walls.* New York: R. R. Smith, 1930.

Wright, H. R. C. *East-Indian Economic Problems of the Age of Cornwallis and Raffles.* London: Luzac, 1961.

Yalland, Zoe. *Boxwallahs: The British in Cawnpore, 1857–1901.* Wilby: M. Russell, 1994.

———. *Traders and Nabobs: The British in Cawnpore, 1765–1857.* Salisbury: M. Russell, 1987.

Yang, Anand A., ed. *Crime and Criminality in British India.* Tucson: University of Arizona Press, 1985.

———. "Dangerous Castes and Tribes: The Criminal Tribes Act and the Magahiya Doms of Northeast India." In *Crime and Criminality in British India,* ed. Anand A. Yang, pp. 108–27. Tucson: University of Arizona Press, 1985.

Zelliot, Eleanor. "Congress and the Untouchables, 1917–1950." In *Congress and Indian Nationalism: The Pre-Independence Phase,* ed. Richard Sisson and Stanley Wolpert, pp. 182–97. Delhi: Oxford University Press, 1988.
———. "Dr. Ambedkar and the Mahar Movement." Ph.D. diss., University of Pennsylvania, 1969.

Interviews

BAMCEF (Backward and Minorities Central Government Employees Federation) Dalit discussion group. December 20, 2000–January 22, 2001.
Darapuri, S. R. Dalit writer and activist, retired police officer (Indian Police Service). Lucknow and Kanpur, March–April 2000.
Dosadh, H. L. Dalit Hindi writer and activist. Delhi, August–September 1998; February, July, September, and October 1999; June, September, and November 2000; March 2001.
Jatav, Hira Lal. Dalit, retired government officer and activist. Agra, September 2002.
Jatav, Puttu Lal. Dalit, retired district judge and activist. Agra, September 2002.
Prasad, Chanderbhan. Dalit columnist, writer, and activist. Delhi and Lucknow, August–September 1998; February, July, September, and October 1999; June, September, and November 2000; March 2001.
Ram, Gama. Dalit social activist and writer, retired police inspector. Lucknow, March, 2000.
Sathi, Dr. Cheddi Lal. Dalit, lawyer, politician, and social activist. March–April, 2000.
Shankar, Daya. Dalit, retired government officer, lawyer, and activist. September 2002.
Singh "Bechhain," Sheoraj. Dalit Hindi writer, teacher, and activist. Delhi, December 1998; September–October 1999.

INDEX

CONTEMPORARY INDIAN STUDIES
Published in association with the American Institute of Indian Studies

The Edward Cameron Dimock, Jr. Prize in the Indian Humanities

Temple to Love: Architecture and Devotion
in Seventeenth-Century Bengal
PIKA GHOSH

Art of the Court of Bijapur
DEBORAH HUTTON

India's Immortal Comic Books: Gods, Kings, and Other Heroes
KARLINE MCLAIN

The Joseph W. Elder Prize in the Indian Social Sciences

The Regional Roots of Developmental Politics in India:
A Divided Leviathan
ASEEMA SINHA

Wandering with Sadhus: Ascetics in the Hindu Himalayas
SONDRA L. HAUSNER

Wives, Widows, and Concubines:
The Conjugal Family Ideal in Colonial India
MYTHELI SREENIVAS

Language, Emotion, and Politics in South India:
The Making of a Mother Tongue
LISA MITCHELL

Reconsidering Untouchability:
Chamars and Dalit History in North India
RAMNARAYAN S. RAWAT

RAMNARAYAN S. RAWAT is Assistant Professor of History at the University of Delaware.